The third volume of Joy Packer's
autobiography, *Apes and Ivory* tells of
her African travels during the
period when her husband the late
Admiral Sir Herbert Packer was
Commander-in-Chief of the South
Atlantic (Africa) Station. She went
to the three British Protectorates –
beautiful Basutoland and Swaziland,
and lonely Bechuanaland; the
Rhodesias, in the the throes of
growing-pains; the Congo 'emerging
into a tropical welfare state'; and
the island of Madagascar, where
she witnessed the Sacrifice to the
Crocodiles. And much, much more.

Lady Packer finds people even
more fascinating than places, and,
whether she is writing of Helen
Keller or Sobhuza II, Paramount
Chief of the Swazis, we find the
same warm human touch which has
endeared her to so many.

Also by Joy Packer

Fiction
THE HIGH ROOF
NOR THE MOON BY NIGHT
THE GLASS BARRIER

Non-Fiction
PACK AND FOLLOW
THE GREY MISTRESS

and published by Corgi Books

Joy Packer

Apes and Ivory

CORGI BOOKS
A DIVISION OF TRANSWORLD PUBLISHERS LTD

APES AND IVORY

A CORGI BOOK 0 552 09450 1

Originally published in Great Britain by
Eyre & Spottiswoode (Publishers) Ltd.

PRINTING HISTORY
Eyre & Spottiswoode edition published 1953
Eyre & Spottiswoode edition reprinted six times
Corgi edition published 1974

This Book is set in 10 on 11 Times

Corgi Books are published by
Transworld Publishers Ltd.,
Cavendish House, 57–59 Uxbridge Road,
Ealing, London W.5.
Made and printed in Great Britain by
Cox & Wyman Ltd., London, Reading and Fakenham

For
PIET and GLEN

Contents

PART ONE

Our First Year, August 1950–September 1951:
South and East

PART TWO

Our Second Year, October 1951–September 1952:
North and West

APES AND IVORY

'For the King had at sea a navy of Tharshish with the navy of Hiram: once in three years came the navy of Tharshish, bringing gold, and silver, ivory, and apes, and peacocks.'

THE BIBLE. *First Book of Kings*. Chapter 10. Verse 22.

'Gold, and silver, ivory, and apes, and peacocks' –
These were the symbols of Africa when King Solomon's navies sailed south down the Indian Ocean in search of treasure for his Temple. They were the symbols of Africa when the galleons of the first Elizabeth sailed down the west coast seeking cargoes of gold and silver, ivory and precious stones, and black slaves for the New World across the Atlantic. And they are still her symbols today when the grey warships of our own Elizabeth's Royal Navy keep the wide sea-routes open for her Merchant Fleets to carry the wealth of Africa, now more valuable than ever before.

JOY PACKER, 1953.

AUTHOR'S FOREWORD

ONCE a book of mine is published, I seldom re-read it. But when it was decided to publish my travel autobiographies in paperback, it was obvious that the tremendous world changes of the past three decades required certain footnotes to assist the new reader.

This has been particularly the case with APES AND IVORY, which was written between 1950 and 1953 when the whole African continent was poised on the launching-pad of 'emergence'. It was a turbulent period electric with the excitement inevitably preceding the bloody birth of young angry Black nations not yet unified. Since 1960, the key year of the European scurry out of Black Africa, the alien ideal of democratic government has gone rapidly overboard in favour of dictatorships, the natural evolution of tribal history combined with the profoundly disturbed and insecure mood of adolescent nations rocketed into premature responsibility.

APES AND IVORY is, I suppose, a period piece in its way, written with the immediacy of reportage. I recorded my impressions of people, places, events and snatches of dialogue that struck me as significant or amusing while they were still fresh in my mind. Africa, with its multi-racial populations and its many conflicts, stimulates a sense of theatre, of tragi-comedy and imminent drama in any writer, particularly in one with deep roots in this continent. (My own go back for over three centuries.)

The personalities mentioned in this book are many and various. Some have changed their names and status, like the countries of Africa, and others have passed out of my life altogether. I have not attempted to follow their fortunes with even the briefest footnotes.

I have, in writing of South Africa, referred to the African sometimes as Native or as Bantu. The original and objectionable term Kaffir meant Heathen; Native simply means indigenous and Bantu is the overall word for 'the people'. 'African' is now the most acceptable term, except to the Afrikaners (who comprise 60 per cent of the white population of the Republic of South Africa) because, in Afrikaans, the translation of 'African' is 'Afrikaner' – the term applied to their own white nationals.

Where the obnoxious expression 'boy' of or towards an African man appears it must be remembered that at the time of writing the proper dignity of the African had not yet been fully appreciated by the Europeans of many nations who employed African labour throughout the continent.

That period was the twilight of the colonial gods.

JOY PACKER

Cape Peninsula, 1973

PART ONE

Our first year,
August 1950–September 1951

SOUTH AND EAST

CHAPTER ONE

FULL CIRCLE

IN 1950 my husband was a member of the Board of Admiralty as Fourth Sea Lord in charge of Transport and Supplies. We had a small flat in Chelsea. When the sun shone it flowed into our three rooms and kitchen and reminded me of my homeland, South Africa. But when snow was thick on the blitzed church outside our windows, the gulls came wheeling and crying from the river to set me longing for the sea again – for warships passing upon their lawful occasions, for the Royal Navy at sea.

One day my husband came home, and his face was full of gladness.

'I have been offered Commander-in-Chief South Atlantic,' he said. 'That's South Africa, of course – and Simon's Town . . .'

My heart made a great gay leap and turned over three times in my chest. Could it be true? Was Fate really going to tie up the loose ends of a story that had begun in Simon's Town over a quarter of a century ago? Was she really spinning the wheel full circle for us in this lovely way? The fitness, the timing and the setting – surely it was all too perfect!

Bertie took the old school atlas out of its place on the bookshelf and opened it at the map of Africa. He took a pencil and drew a line round the great continent – down the west coast from the bulge of French Senegal, past the equator and south to Cape Town; then up the east coast, past the equator once more, to Portuguese East Africa.

'It's a wide parish,' he said thoughtfully.

'Yes,' I said. 'Tremendous!'

But I saw only the map and the names on it – the Gulf of Guinea, the Tropic of Capricorn, the Mozambique Channel, the Congo and the Cape of Good Hope – for I could not then begin to guess how rich and varied a harvest this two year appointment would yield. Even now, in retrospect, much of it is dream-like and fantastic.

In our first year there was the Indian Ocean seaboard, and a voyage in the flag-ship to the strange pre-history island of Madagascar; there was Equatorial Africa emerging from the dark travail of her past into a tropical Welfare State; and the young Rhodesias with their herds of living ivory and their hosts of new settlers. We toured the British Protectorates of Basutoland, Swaziland and Bechuanaland – two of them opening up a primitive world of rare beauty and ancient terror, and the third caught in the web of Seretse Khama's love for a young white woman, Ruth, the eternal alien. We saw gold and diamonds at their source, but, above all, we knew once more the personal joy of reunion with those dearest to us. In the second year Fate kept up her high and lavish standard. She gave us a glimpse of Northern Nigeria, the home of desert caravans, of weird plagues and dark-skinned Emirs. And she showed us the whole long Slave Coast, rich in past and present history, in steamy physical glamour and boiling political emotionalism. She took us to South West Africa, the lonely territory of baby lambs and seals doomed to a swift death, of precious stones, proud Hereros and the *Baster's* 'land of the lost'. And in the Union she made us laugh and cry at the racial tragicomedy of Boer and Briton – Montague and Capulet fighting down the ages when the vendetta is already dead and the need of friendship as vital to their lovely land as breath is vital to life itself.

Now, when the map of Africa lies open before me, the printed names swell into living pictures. The shadow show of the past two years moves before my eyes, a caravanserai peopled by human beings well-loved and familiar, or strange and exotic, and by all those who were part of our daily lives

16

in the lovely old house and garden at Simon's Town. I see them again – Tony, the Flag Lieutenant, hurrying in from a hockey match in shorts, and a terrible red jersey clashing with his rumpled red hair, looking more like nine years old than twenty-nine; Veronica, the tall girl-gardener, in slacks and a buttercup yellow shirt, swinging across the wide green lawn with Sammy, the harlequin Great Dane, always at her heels; Veronica's Bantu garden boys chasing marauding baboons out of the kloof garden; our two young seamen digging the little bathing-box out of the piled white sand after a south-easter; or Piet running into the sea with baby Ronnie on his shoulder and Glendyr at his heels, her brown hair flying in the wind. And there is a tender memory of my mother's silver head bent patiently over the files in my sun-trap study helping to sift the material gathered on our African travels.

Fate, you gave us a great deal in those two wonderful years! You even threw in apes and peacocks for good measure; a lion too, and giraffes; elephants by the score; and rhinos, white and black – to say nothing of one very precious stone. So, if at the end, you exacted your price, and cut your pound of flesh, I have no cause for complaint. Happiness and experience are not bought for nothing.

That spring day in Chelsea, in the year 1950, as we pored over the 'wide parish' of the Commander-in-Chief South Atlantic, the old excitement of a new door opening, a new world ahead, went tingling through my veins. For that is the wonder and thrill of life in the Navy – the blessed spice of variety, of the unexpected and the unknown. And this time it was greater than ever before, this time the threshold of the new world was my own old home – the Cape Peninsula.

As Bertie put the atlas back in its place and lit his pipe, he smiled and said:

'Tim Sherwin will come with me, of course. And Corney. And I must get cracking about a flag lieutenant—'

Commander (S) Sherwin had been my husband's secretary throughout most of World War Two, and Chief Petty Officer Corney, his coxswain, had served with him even

longer. He 'got cracking' about his flag lieutenant in rather
an unusual way. He went to see the General who was the
Head of all the Royal Marines, and he said, 'I want a Royal
Marine for my Flags. Will you find me one?' So, quite soon,
I was introduced to Lieutenant A. S. Harris, a lean young
man with an eight handicap at golf and a fine record of
service in the Royal Marine Commandos. Tony Harris, then
still a stranger to us, was, to the best of our knowledge, the
first Royal Marine ever to be appointed as a flag lieutenant.

Tim Sherwin's wife, Kathie, was delighted at the prospect
of going to South Africa. We were to sail in August, which
would just give her time to produce her third baby before we
left. Her little sons, Philip and Martin, aged seven and four,
would be all the better for two years of sunshine. Coxswain
Corney decided to uproot his wife and seven-year-old boy
from the Isle of Wight and give them a look at the world. It
would probably be his last commission in the Royal Navy,
and, from what little he had seen of South Africa during the
War, it should be a happy one.

When the time came to say good-bye to the Chelsea flat
we felt that we were leaving an important slice of our lives
behind – a satisfying slice in many ways.

Naval people lead a piecemeal existence, and, whenever
they move on, they close a door upon something of themselves.

Piet had lived with us in this little flat. For almost the first
time in our lives I had had both my husband and son with
me under the same roof for more than a few months. Piet
had been a medical student at Guy's, and many strange
things had dwelt with him in his tiny room. A golden-jackal
karos from South Africa covered his bed and breathed a
pungent odour reminiscent of all the carnivora at the Zoo;
often as not a preserved frog or dog-fish, partly dissected,
lay upon a board on the shelf over his writing table; and
under his bed lived 'Bones', half a skeleton. 'Bones' had a
tendency to get about the flat in sections. Like naval fam-

ilies, he was seldom neatly assembled in one box. Fate, in the shape of Piet, took 'Bones' apart. Sometimes we came into the flat and found a skeleton hand reposing upon the arm of a chair, or a cold fleshless foot warming itself in vain at the fireside, or a skull grinning at us from the mantel-piece.

Even my housekeeper, Mrs. Elton, who had a family of four enterprising sons and two daughters, and who under-stood young people and all their weird ways and pos-sessions, had been shaken by 'Bones'. He had given her quite a turn. The dog-fish she regarded as a necessary evil.

'First him – then us,' she had remarked, as Piet operated delicately upon the creature. 'And the more of *him* the better for *us*!'

A girl friend of Piet's school days arrived in London. Her name was Glendyr Orr, and she was thin and pretty with the casual carefree look of modern youth. She wrinkled up her nose at Piet's possessions and then became interested to see how they worked. Like he did, she always wanted to know what made things tick – except the *karos*, which brought savage Africa ever nearer as the summer advanced.

There was a good deal of running around in Piet's little second-hand sports car that summer, with Glen's hair blow-ing out behind her, wild and shiny brown as seaweed in a gale, and her eyes bright between their thick lashes.

'He's walking out with her,' was Mrs. Elton's description of this rapid progress round the countryside.

'At his age? Twenty-one.'

'What's wrong with twenty-one?' she asked.

What indeed.

Piet and Glen were married in London in the following spring of 1949, and soon afterwards they went back to South Africa to live, and Piet continued his medical studies at the University of Cape Town.

It was just a year after that, on a soft mellow August day, when deserted London was basking and yawning in the drowsy half dream of its 'silly season', that we closed the black polished door of our flat on the Chelsea interlude.

New fingers would crumble the stale bread for the doves and sparrows who had made their home in the blitzed church, new hands would fling crusts to the rowdy gulls from the River Thames, and no longer would their planing white forms and raucous clamour evoke memories of ships and far off ports, and days with the Royal Navy in peace and war, and all the glory of a great Service – for the next tenants were not sea-gipsies with grey warships forever tugging at their heart-strings.

On the fourteen day sea passage to Cape Town we began to know Bertie's Flag Lieutenant. At the fancy dress dance he appeared dressed in a *burnous* and a headgear which concealed his red hair. It was clear that his desert service had not been wasted, for Tony was quite the most convincing Arab merchant I have seen in or out of the Middle East.

'He's so nice,' giggled Kathie Sherwin, 'though you wouldn't think it to see him now! But I can't help wondering if he's *ruthless* enough for a flag lieutenant. They are always having to disappoint people – about parties and all that sort of thing.'

'He might get ruthless,' I suggested. 'It grows on people. But do you think he's girl-proof? Because that would be a useful asset.'

'There's no test like a voyage,' said Kathie wisely.

And, as the sunny days and moonstruck nights went by, we came to the conclusion that Tony was as reasonably girl-proof as any young man could expect to be.

Among our fellow-passengers were the Governor-General and Mrs. Brand van Zyl, who were returning to South Africa after a brief visit to Europe. Immediately on their arrival they would set out on a farewell tour of the Union. They had married fifty years ago as University students, and together they had gone a long way. Now, on holiday, the fine looking old Governor-General enjoyed a game of quoits and captained the passengers against the officers in a deck-cricket match.

His wife was white-haired and frail looking and always

carefully dressed. She said to me one evening. 'You are going to get the best out of the next two years. I feel it. You and your husband will find them very interesting, but strenuous. However, you are both young, so you will enjoy yourselves.'

I had to smile, thinking that age is, after all, relative. In the year of their Golden Wedding they no doubt found us – in the year of our Silver Anniversary – quite junior. It was a pleasant thought.

Mrs. Van Zyl often sat on the children's deck, and when, on the second day out, someone asked Kathie to play deck tennis, the little old lady turned to her and said, 'You go, my dear, I will watch your baby.' So Kathie left sleeping baby Judy in her care. Afterwards Kathie said to me: 'It was awful! I should never have let her keep an eye on Judy, but then I hadn't the faintest idea that my good angel was Mrs. H.E.!'

Our last night at sea sleep was elusive and I woke early and ran across the cabin to the porthole, hungry for the first sight of Table Mountain in the dawn. The old precious thrill of home-coming shook me from top to toe, and I called to Bertie, 'It's so beautiful! It's never been so beautiful before!' The setting moon trailed her sequined net across Table Bay, and the lights of Cape Town and her long coastline winked and glimmered in a fringe of incandescent glory. The stern square-cut old mountain, winged by its attendant peaks, was indigo against the fading stars. It challenged me with its ancient majesty, defying me to take it for granted, although I had been cradled in its lap.

Somewhere up there, in the Gardens, were the lights of Trees Lodge, my childhood home. Surely Mother would be awake by now, for old people sleep lightly, especially when they are excited. But Piet and Glen, in their cottage among the oaks of Newlands, would rub their eyes and groan when the Native maid brought their early tea. Over there, at Sea Point, was Nannie's little house. Sometime today she would go into town to Tees Lodge to welcome us. How good to see them all again! And then I remembered that this home-coming would be different from any other. Personal greetings would have to stand aside and bide their time. For today the new Commander-in-Chief would arrive officially to take up his post.

We heard the tug come alongside our great liner and presently the engines were throbbing slowly once more.

Farther down the corridor Tim Sherwin was organizing his family and a tower of baggage, and presently there was a brisk double knock on our door as the Flag Lieutenant came in with a sheaf of signals. I came to know that knock very well in the next two years – that and the executive tread of Tony's Royal Marine boots. It was a knock that stood no nonsense, always exactly on time. We grew to rely upon it.

In the second class Chief Petty Officer Corney was trying to persuade his wife and son, Melvin, that they were going to enjoy South Africa. Mrs. Corney, who had seldom been out of the Isle of Wight and never out of the United Kingdom, was far from sure that she held with the barbarous scenery that stared her in the face.

'That's Table Mountain, see,' said Corney. 'And on either side is Devil's Peak and Lion's Head.'

He had passed through Cape Town seven years ago when he and his present Admiral had been on the way to Durban to join that grand old lady of the sea, H.M.S. *Warspite*. In fact, Melvin had been born the night they sailed from England and it was two years before Corney saw his son.

'Devil's Peak and Lion's Head,' echoed Mrs. Corney. They were savage names to fling at a woman who had never seen a full-grown mountain in her life. It is not easy for the Mrs. Corneys to pull up their roots; their dependence on their own background goes deep.

Corney's smile was disarming. He said, 'Eastwards, round the other side, is the Twelve Apostles.' As if that serrated row of peaks could safely be relied upon to counteract the influence of the Devil to the southward.

It was half past seven when we heard familiar voices outside our cabin, and the next moment we were caught in a whirl of happy astonished greeting.

'Piet and Glen! How did you get here? We thought only official people were allowed on board.'

'We got a special permit. Isn't this the greatest thing!'

Reporters and camera-men slipped through the open door.

'Hold it, please! Just one more with your son, Lady Packer. And now the four of you. . . . Thanks. And we'd like a picture of you and the Admiral, there by the porthole. That's fine.'

'Now, sir, can we have your views on . . .' Pencil poised attentively, or busily in action as the *Cape Times* representative asked questions or recorded answers.

'Are you glad to be home, mevrou?' asked the young lady from *Die Burger*, the Afrikaans newspaper. 'Oh, but you needn't answer, anyone can see that for themselves. Is it true that you are the first South African ever to preside at Admiralty House?'

'I believe so, yes.'

In the expressions of our son and his pretty young wife pleasure and amusement did battle with an urgent desire for breakfast. At last the Press evaporated with the *Argus* photographer in the lead. He must be sure to get photographs of the Governor-General going ashore. The movie cameras were already set up on the quay in readiness.

Piet and Glen guided us firmly towards the dining saloon.

'We've been up for hours and we're famished. We want everything on the menu.'

Between mouthfuls of egg and bacon we heard the family news. And then the Flag Lieutenant found us to say that Admiral and Lady McCarthy were on board.

'Come, Glen,' said Piet. 'This is where we disappear. Tot siens, Mom and Dad, see you later.'

Queer, I thought, one moment we are entirely ourselves, the next we are the Commander-in-Chief and his Lady. This is how it will be for the next two years, the double of life of anyone in an official position. We saw the two young figures melt into the crowd milling round the foot of the gangway, the tall broad shouldered young man with his head well back and the girl with her tossed brown hair and her childish trick of skipping a step or two at his side.

We turned to greet Admiral and Lady McCarthy.

My mother's house was exactly as it had always been. Somehow it had kept its character and integrity in a changing scene. On every side new buildings pressed about it as if determined to elbow this old place out of existence, but Tees Lodge remained, as dignified and old-fashioned as its white-haired mistress who had lived there for over half a century.

Curiously my mother had no objection to the invasion of what had once been a quiet residential street by more and more of the noise and bustle of the ever-encroaching city.

'I like it,' she would say. 'I like the noise of traffic, even at night. It makes me feel safe.'

The sounds of her street were as companionable to her as the purring of a cat or the crackle of a fire in the hearth.

From the road it was impossible to see across the green lawns into the rather Edwardian drawing-room beneath the tall gable. The width of the front stoep and her net curtains took care of that. But from behind those discreet curtains my mother had her special lookout post – a stiff little easy chair from which you could rise in a hurry, even if you were nearly eighty and not quite so nimble as you had been.

So it happened that when the official car drew up outside the gate and we came up the flagged path she was on the stoep to meet us, and behind her was faithful Teena of the dark complexion and wide white smile. It was noon, and down the passage, broadly beaming, walked Josephine with the sherry tray, and, even on this day of days, deaf David, the garden boy, tapped on the french windows of the drawing-room to ask if there were letters for him to post.

'Oh, Mum, does nothing ever change here?'

24

We laughed and kissed each other, knowing that here habit reigned supreme. Only our little old Cookie was absent. Two years ago Mother had stood at her graveside, the one white mourner among those who were there to bid a good and gentle soul farewell.

Outside, the carnations bloomed in their tins and the stocky figure of Arend, grizzled now, worked among them. Driver, head gardener, house-painter and general factotum, he was, as he put it, 'my ole Madam's handy man'. Once Arend, hearing that Miss Joy, in her book, 'Pack and Follow', had referred to him as a factotum, had been disturbed. The word was new to him. But Mother explained, with her usual punctilious care. 'A factotum is a good kind man who does everything in his power to help his employer – I could not manage without a factotum.' Arend was moved and impressed. 'Den Madam, I am glad Miss Yoy called me a factotum.'

We went out to see him and ask after his considerable family.

'Dey is all well, Sir Atmiral and Miss Yoy. But dere is less now. Some is married, and de wife and me is finished wit' de babies.' When a child married Arend ceased to count it among his brood. His arithmetic embraced only those still in the nest.

We heard a singing Norwegian voice as Gudrun Digre, Mother's neighbour, came on to the stoep bearing an armful of mountain flowers. She was in her white working overall, for she had 'run in, between patients'. She often 'ran in' to fetch my mother or Teena for a treatment. They both suffered from rheumatism and Gudrun's strong small hands worked wonders. The vibrant Norwegian voice calling to our old Coloured maid, 'You come now Teena! I fit you in with a massage', was to the humble sufferer a clarion call of herald angels.

She held out the magnificent proteas to me, pink and amber velvet with silken sugary stamens.

'We picking these for you at the week-end, knowing you love your own wild flowers best.'

She seldom used any tense other than the present participle. It was characteristic and immediate, not yesterday or tomorrow, but *now*.

Bertie left us reluctantly to drive the twenty-five miles to Simon's Town and Admiralty House.

'There'll be a good deal of turning over to be done,' he said to Mother. 'But Flags and I will manage. He's down there already. I haven't the heart to take Joy from you at once. You bring her down this evening, that will be time enough.'

My surgeon brothers, Fred and Norman, came up from their consulting rooms in Church Square to lunch at Tees Lodge.

'Oh, dear, you've both been operating!' I wrinkled my nose at their embrace, and they laughed, remembering my aversion to the odour of anaesthetic. I drew Fred on one side.

'Mum's got rather deaf. Is it always as bad as this?'

'No, she's had a cold. Next week I'll give her ears a blow through. You'll be surprised at the improvement.'

'I can't bear to see her trying to listen with her eyes.'

'I know,' he said gently. 'It's the concentration of the deaf. In old people and children it's distressing. One feels it isn't fair.'

When Fred spoke of his work his jester's attitude to life fell from him and his true quality came to the surface – compassion for all who came to him prisoned in silence. If he could make the birds sing again for one of these he knew no greater joy.

Norman's wife, Molly, looked in for a few moments after lunch.

'I just had to pop in and welcome you – and here are Lucian and Andrea!' She bloomed with pride and contentment in their post-war family – the little ones I had not yet seen. Richard, the eldest son was at boarding school. 'But he sent his best love,' she said.

And presently there was old Nannie's brisk step on the flagged path. Lame she might be, and cursing inwardly at

26

'my blessed legs', adding a few German expletives of her own, but she never lost her energetic air or her natural warmth and gusto. As we hugged each other, all the happy shared memories of my own childhood and Piet's, and Nan's part in them, flooded over both of us.

'Nan, it's so good to be home!'

She laughed, and held me away from her. 'My girlie – well, darling, it's *my lady* these days!'

We threw our heads back and enjoyed the joke. The absurdity of it – '*milady!*'

On the way down to Simon's Town, Arend drove Mother and Nan and me to Langi Banool, where we had tea with Piet and Glen.

Langi Banool, in some primitive dialect, means 'Happy Home', and the cottage among the oaks was living up to its name. The garden was not very big and a good deal of it was occupied by a battered old ship's lifeboat Piet was reconditioning with Glen's able assistance.

'That's the *Nausea*,' he said. 'We are putting a second-hand engine into her, and we'll soon have her seaworthy.'

'You have a work-shop?'

'Come and see.'

I looked round at the lathe, the carpenter's bench and well-kept engineering tools, and recalled the small boy who had always managed to find some corner where he could make things. Fundamentally people did not change – only developed one way or another.

It was late afternoon when Mother and I took our leave. Nan stayed to give the young couple good advice on various matters in which she had reason to consider herself expert, and they listened attentively enough and went their own sweet way as they usually did.

The level evening light gilded the road to the sea. Wild arums starred the low-lying meadows, and the hillsides were white with daisies. The vineyards still had a month to go before they would lay their emerald carpet over the Constantia valleys. The mountains, woods and shining beaches had never seemed more lovely in my eyes. Across False Bay

27

the Hottentots Hollands were topaz in the reflected glow of sunset.

'There's nowhere in the whole world to beat the Cape,' I said.

'No,' said Mother. 'There's no place like home.'

As we turned into the great teak gates of Admiralty House Mother said to Arend, 'Wait a few minutes for me, I won't be long.'

He grinned.

'A few minutes is not'ing, Madam. When I used to bring Miss Yoy here to dance in de ole days, den I really had to *wait*! And dere was no wireless in de car.'

It was strange to come back to this house where, as a young girl, I had first met my husband.

For a moment we paused in the small outer hall, and I glanced up at the polished mahogany boards on the wall above the handsome new visitors' book. The names of Commanders-in-Chief from 1795 to 1950 were inscribed upon them in gold lettering. One day Bertie's name would be recorded there.

'Good evening, Milady,' said the Chief Steward. 'I will inform the Commander-in-Chief that you have arrived.'

I felt my mother's eyes upon me – affectionate, indulgent, half amused. But the present had not yet caught up with me, and, as we went into the big inner hall, with its portraits of kings and queens and its fine wide polished floor where I had once danced the hours away – those nights when Arend 'really had to *wait*' – the past still had me in its spell, and a young ghost went with me.

Strange how the wheel of Fate had spun full circle!

Bertie came down the narrow Georgian staircase between the photographs and photographed portraits of his predecessors, all reduced to a standard size and severely framed in black. Even under the regard of this stair-gallery he looked casual and unconcerned.

'Those Admirals!' I gasped.

He smiled. 'I am the eighty-first incumbent of this parish, and – I'd better confess it – as I came downstairs just now I heard those old salts mutter, "You're not the fellow I was, young Packer!" Shall we have a gin and tonic? The sun is well over the yard arm.'

We went into the gracious drawing-room with its French windows opening on to the terrace above the sunk garden and looking out to sea.

Bertie said to Mother: 'You are sitting where Lady Bentinck did the day Joy and I first met – the day I rescued her from Riki, Renira Bentinck's meer-kat – and she disgraced herself by throwing tea all over the carpet.'

'I was terrified of Lady Bentinck then,' I said.

My husband's eyes twinkled. 'Perhaps that'll help you to realize that *all* C.-in-C.'s wives are terrifying!' He relented. 'But not as terrifying as meer-kats perhaps.'

Suddenly I wondered if Lady Bentinck had really been terrifying. She had been tall and very English, but kind and full of fun, and she had been able to sit on the floor and scratch her right ear with her left toe – a remarkable accomplishment in one who should have been stiff with age and honour.

Mum stood up presently, disregarding a helping hand.

'Good-bye darlings. It's wonderful to have you both here. I am so very happy. It's been a glorious and exciting day, but tiring for all of us.'

We saw her to her car and called good-bye to the old lady sitting so straight in the back seat smiling at us. But somehow I felt that when Simon's Town was behind her the smile might die and the shadow of the years deepen round her fine features – for, although this had been 'a glorious and exciting day', it was not as other home-comings. Her daughter had indeed come back – though not to Tees Lodge and to her, but to Admiralty House and the obligations that went with it.

Bertie linked his arm in mine and we strolled out into the

29

garden and across the main lawn. Looking back, we could see the white Georgian house among its trees, with the Simon's Berg behind it.

We paused to lean against the stone balustrade separating the broad expanse of turf from a wild aloe shrubbery and a wattle windbreak. Beyond the windbreak was the sea washing softly on to our own little beach. Birds twittered drowsily, the first stars pricked the sky, and Flora, the noble white figurehead of a long ago frigate, gleamed between two ancient bronze cannons cast in Goa in the seventeenth century. She leaned seawards, and it seemed to me that she sought vanished sails filled by the wild winds of other years.

Along the curving waterfront, in the folds of the mountains, the lights of the coast villages quickened – Sunny Cove, Fish Hoek, Kalk Bay, St. James, Muizenbeg. The electric train snaked round the beaches, a chain of gold, and in Simon's Bay there was the regular flash of Roman Rock lighthouse, and the red glow that marked the end of the Bullnose Jetty. In the harbour lay warships. Once again the past was closer than the present. This sea-garden held memories for us.

> 'Ah, Moon of my Delight who
> know'st no Wane,
> The Moon of Heaven is
> rising once again:
> How oft hereafter rising
> shall she look
> Through this same Garden
> after me – in vain!'

'It's getting chilly,' said my husband. 'We'll go in.'

Behind us a girl phantom stole away into the shadows – but she did not go alone – and I knew then that my companion too had felt the wings of yesterday brush past us.

CHAPTER TWO

SIMON'S TOWN

SIMON'S TOWN, the British naval base in the Union of
South Africa, is one of those distinctive pockets in the Cape
Peninsula which has so many odd corners. It is sandwiched
between the Simon's Berg and Simon's Bay in the north-
western angle of the wide fine sweep of False Bay, and its
whole existence revolves round the naval base.

All the varied human ingredients of our complex South
African background are packed into this little port with the
one winding main street curving along the high dockyard
wall to Jubilee Square. Off that street are many lanes. In
some dwell the Indian owners of fruit and vegetable shops
with their teeming families; in others the Malay Quarter
clusters round the little mosque which is also the school for
the long-eyed Moslem children and tailors and laundresses.
The Coloured dockyard employees live mostly up in the
modern tenements round the waterfall that cascades down
the kloof in a peaty torrent – 'like beer', said the Flag Lieutenant the first time he saw it – and the European houses
straggle up and down the slopes of the Simon's Berg. In the
surrounding valleys are the Bantu locations.

In winter Simon's Town is lashed by gales, and, as far as
Cape Point where the Indian and Atlantic Oceans meet,
there are landslides, and every now and again some cottage
is engulfed by an avalanche of mountain soil and boulders.
In summer the south-easter blows the stinging white sand
inland on to the dunes of Fish Hoek and Clovelly and lorry-
loads of natives sweep it from road and rail as if it were
snow. But for weeks together the weather is pure perfection

31

and the beaches swarm with naval and dockyard children having the time of their lives.

Since the war naval families are moved to foreign stations at Admiralty expense, and in consequence the housing situation in the port is acute. But where in the world is it not acute?

Philip Sherwin and Melvin Corney, the small sons of the secretary and the coxswain, were immediately absorbed into the convent school where the good nuns dealt valiantly with far more little pupils than they could reasonably be expected to manage. The older English children attended the Simon's Town secondary school where they were exempted from learning Afrikaans, the compulsory second language of the country.

Up at the Palace Barracks the Union Defence Force attended to matters of land defence in amiable co-operation with the Royal Navy, and often ships of the South African Naval Forces came into the harbour to share the amenities of Simon's Town or to exercise with the South Atlantic Squadron in the best of good comradeship.

Occasionally some stranger to the port would say gravely to my husband:

'Aren't you people afraid of being thrown out of Simon's Town any minute?'

And he would answer equably that undoubtedly some day the Union would take over the Dockyard, but that, in doing so, it would only be following the example of Australia, Canada and New Zealand.*

On Sundays we did not go to St. Francis's, the lovely historic little church adjoining Admiralty House property and set in a rose garden instead of a graveyard, because we

* In 1957 Simonstown was officially taken over from the Royal Navy by the South African Naval Forces. The goodwill between the two Navies is still maintained. The Royal Navy is officially represented in the Republic by a high ranking Naval Officer.

went instead to the old Sail Loft in the Dockyard where Edgar Rea, the Dockyard Padre, preached simple sincere good sense and didn't mind making little jokes in the pulpit. No one fidgeted or stole glances at their watch when Edgar preached.

The Loft made a bright seamanlike church, always polished and shining, with flowers arranged on the altar by one or another of the dockyard ladies. The lesson was read by the Captain-in-Charge of the Dockyard, stalwart Joe Selby, or, in his absence, by Thomas Donkin, the King's Harbour Master. The choir girls in purple and the boys in scarlet cassocks under their white surplices sang their heads off and off and then scampered out of doors filled with short-lived virtue.

On our first Sunday at Simon's Town, as we stood in the breezy spring sunshine outside the open gothic door, Captain and Mrs. Selby introduced us to many of those who made up our naval and dockyard community.

I wondered if they found me more terrifying than a meerkat? Probably. For the advent of a new Commander-in-Chief is usually a period of sheer nightmare for unfortunate dockyard officials. Everything at Admiralty House that can conceivably be altered must be turned upside down so that the new lady may stamp her particular taste and personality upon the old house. Under their helpful and patient exteriors the heads of dockyard departments must regard successive Commanders-in-Chiefs' wives in much the same light as a biennial dose of 'flu – an inescapable affliction which occurs every two years and is bound to run its course before it can be eradicated from the system.

As we strolled home we passed the Residency where Mr. Stewart, the Magistrate, had his combined house and court over the Slave Quarters of the bad old days. He and his wife, Magda, who cooked and sewed for her family and worked indefatigably for the good of the port, were as much a part of our lives as our own naval people.

Almost opposite the Residency were the offices of the

33

Commander-in-Chief and the guarded Admiralty Compound in which stood the timber cottages of his personal staff. Right on the little private beach that ran parallel with the sea-garden of Admiralty House was the Secretary's Cottage. We stopped for a word with the Sherwins before turning into our grounds.

'How are you all shaking down?' asked Bertie.

'Well, on the whole,' said Kathie. 'But poor Martin is frightened to death of the Bantus who work in the Compound. And we've just discovered that Philip has been telling him that Black men eat boys!'

I said, 'It's nice to know that Philip's information is out of date. South Africa was done with cannibalism years ago. Black men here eat almost anything in the meat line – but not boys.'

My husband complains that I am inclined to give incorrect information with great conviction, and this was one of the times.

I had much to see and to learn about my own country.

In the garden we found Piet and Glen and their three dogs – Pop, the big beige collie, and Priscilla and Chips, the smooth-haired terriers. From the start it was understood that Sundays should, if possible, be our 'family day'.

'Priscilla, put that tortoise down!'

Glen was off like a streak across the lawn to rescue the tortoise who had been rudely awakened from his winter sleep by the shrill yapping and eager scrabbling claws of Priscilla. Priscilla, newly emerged from puppyhood, was always the ringleader when trouble or adventure called.

'See here, Mom, we've brought "Bones" with us,' said Piet. 'Could you put him up for us while you're here?'

'Bones – your old skeleton?'

'Yes,' said Piet. 'Victoria, our Native maid, was springcleaning yesterday, and she came across "Bones's" box. Of course she had to lift the lid and look inside. The next thing Glen knew, Victoria was running like a scalded cat, yelling her head off. Luckily Glen is a good sprinter and she got Victoria back and quietened her down. But nothing will convince her that Bones doesn't mean to *come after her*, and unless we get rid of him she'll leave. She slept out last night rather than take any risks.'

We laughed, and I said, 'They really are the most superstitious folk in the world! But even Mrs. E. didn't go much on "Bones". Certainly we'll put him up. He can go in the big white cupboard on the back landing.'

So Admiralty House acquired a skeleton in the cupboard just like any other self-respecting human home.

Across the main road from the house was our kloof-garden, which meandered up the mountainside towards the waterfall in a tangle of woodbine, briar roses and morning glory. The upper part had been turned into a playground for the Coloured children of the Waterfall Flats, and the stream which was their delight was also ours.

The way of this stream took it through the palms and pomegranates, the quinces, loquats and oleanders of our wild garden, into a culvert under the road, and down through the Admiralty Compound to the sea. Beside it, in the quiet of the kloof – a wide ravine – my husband had a bamboo shelter constructed from the tall bamboo plants that fringed its banks, and there he grew carnations in the tradition of my old home. In fact his first plants came from Tees Lodge.

'You have too many, Mum,' he had said one day, looking covetously at her hundreds of tins of blooms. 'You're positively cluttered up with them!'

She smiled. 'You can't be thinking of growing them at Simon's Town?'

'Why not? They'd do very well by the sea.'

She took the hint, and, after that, when the world was too much with him, Bertie went to his carnations and worked peacefully among them, pruning, budding, stirring up the soil, and listening to the chuckle of running water and the evening whistling of the red-wing starlings. A grapevine made a green ceiling over the bamboo shelter in summer, but we seldom ate any fruit from it, the birds always got there first.

35

Veronica, our girl-gardener, grew vegetables near the carnations. She must have walked miles a day between the sea-garden and the kloof-garden but she never appeared tired. This tall young Rhodesian carried herself with Olympian grace and wore a rope of sun-bleached hair twisted round her head like the gold laurel crown of Flora our figurehead. Her face was the more engaging for one platinum eyebrow and one brown. She had her own way of accounting for herself.

'When I was born my parents happened to be breeding harlequin Great Danes.'

Her parents had not changed their habits, and wherever Veronica went, she was shadowed by Sammy, the black and white Great Dane who had one silver eye and one gold, and by two or three Pekes. Collectively her dogs were known as 'the pets', and sometimes they went to shows and won prizes.

Her real responsibility lay in keeping the five Bantu garden-boys at their job. They knew little English and spoke among themselves in Xosa. Milton, the head boy, was a mild fellow who lived next door to a horse, and Veronica made a convenient arrangement whereby the horse took grass and carrot-tops from Milton and Milton took the consequences from the horse, to the advantage of both animal and vegetables.

With the brothers Good and Bad Kapusa she occasionally had trouble. Good Kapusa suffered from his stomach and had to be dosed with Sammy's Great Dane powders from time to time, while Bad Kapusa drank his wages. Old Mamputa was the most original. He was a herbalist with a sensitive sinus, and we frequently met him going about his work with twigs and leaves protruding from his ears and nostrils for all the world like a Salvidor Dali portrait.

There were some small graves among the rioting nasturtiums near the Carnation shelter. 'BECKY – CECILIA GOODENOUGH'S DEAR DOG', 'SIMON' and 'JOCKEY' all had their tablets. And higher up the stream near a solitary pine was a sadder tombstone recalling the gallant days of sail.

In memory of
Mr. Percival George Duddy
Midshipman
of His Majesty's Ship Maidstone
who died at the Cape of Good Hope
on the 20th April 1828
after a lingering illness borne with
extreme fortitude and resignation
occasioned by a fall from the mizen top
on the 27th day of February previous
Aet 16 years.
This stone
is erected by his messmates
as a small token of esteem
to
departed juvenile worth.

We wondered how this poor lad had come to find his final
resting place in the friendly solitude of our garden. We were
glad that he was there and Veronica grew flowers in the dust
of courage and 'departed juvenile worth'.

But we shared the kloof with the living as well as the dead,
and some of these had little charm for us.

A report about changes at Admiralty House between
1946 and 1948 remarks laconically: 'The paddock and wood
were dejungled and all Port Jackson trees and bushes cut
down but not dug out ... twenty-two puff-adders were
found, of which nineteen were killed.'

Since three known puff-adders had survived it seemed
likely that by 1950 there might be many more in the wood.
And one day when the Flag Lieutenant was tinkering with
his newly acquired car in the yard by the garden he saw a
snake and killed it, only to find a large baboon watching him
with an approving eye. The snake is the mortal enemy of the
baboon. Behind the 'sentinel' was a troop of about twenty
more. The red-haired young man, supported by Veronica,
the pets and the Bantus, chased the hairy marauders up the
kloof.

'They've had all my potato crop,' moaned Veronica. 'And now they're after the carrots!'

The Simon's Town baboons were a perpetual headache to the town council. With every winter, stimulated by hunger, they grew bolder. They entered houses and stole from the kitchens, they opened refrigerators and helped themselves, they went into gardens and collected eggs from under sitting hens, and on one occasion they invaded the Convent School to the hysterical delight of the children and the confusion of the nuns who fluttered about like frantic white birds as the dog-faced brigade tore up exercise books, hurled ink-pots about and paraded with waste-paper baskets on their heads. The people had instructions to call the police when they were troubled by thieving apes and it was even suggested that the entire troop be condemned to death, but somehow sentence was never carried out.

Simon's Town was soft-hearted. It condemned but did not execute. Take, for instance, the matter of our pepper-tree.

Adjoining the kloof-garden and the garages was a row of disreputable hovels condemned as long ago as 1909 when the Commander-in-Chief complained that every time he had guests for dinner offensive remarks were shouted at them by the denizens of these dubious dwellings. But the tempo of life was leisurely and it was not till our time that the order to demolish was put into effect. Then one morning Veronica came to me with a troubled face.

'That beautiful old pepper-tree in the corner of the kloof-garden nearest the pavement – they are going to cut it down.'

We knew that a strip of the garden must go to widen the road but the great umbrella-shaped tree with its long green tresses was dear to us.

'They say,' said Veronica, 'that the line of the new wall goes bang through the middle of the tree and you can't go through the middle of a tree without sawing it in half.'

'The wall mustn't go through the tree, the tree must go through the wall.'

38

'It seems that its roots interfere with the drains, they want the new culvert where its roots are. What will the Admiral do?'

'He'll fight for the tree.'

So the Battle of the Pepper-Tree began. It swayed this way and that for many weeks, and then at a local function I sat beside Mr. Preston, the Mayor. Inevitably the tree, which had assumed the melancholy importance of the doomed, cast its shadow upon us. At last I said:

'Mr. Preston, you are the man who can reprieve our tree. If you do so you will go down to fame as the Man Who Saved the Pepper-Tree.'

He gave me a long solemn look and squared his shoulders.

'I will go down to fame as the Man Who Saved the Pepper-Tree,' he said.

So in time the ancient tree rose unharmed through a gap in the new wall, culverts by-passed its sturdy roots, and its opaque pink berries, scattered by the wind, created their own small untidiness on the sidewalk. But the heat of the day was the cooler for that delicate spreading foliage, squalid houses on the hill were screened from view, and a passerby, loving a thing of beauty, might murmur 'Poems are made by fools like me, but only God can make a tree.'

Next spring Mr. Preston was re-elected Mayor of Simon's Town.

Soon after my husband's appointment to the South Atlantic had been announced, a certain good lady had been heard to say that Joy Packer would be the first South African 'charlatan' of Admiralty House. And, indeed, that was how I felt, for I had everything to learn about my new situation.

Even managing my household presented its peculiar difficulties. An official establishment cannot be run like a private home, and I was quite inexperienced. Our staff of naval stewards and two cooks could not give us notice if they were displeased, nor could I send them packing if they did not suit me. Stewards came and went as their time on the station began and ended, so that those accustomed to our ways were constantly exchanged for new ones.

Most of our stewards were in their early twenties, and, naturally enough, in love, so they forgot what they were told as soon as they had been told it. The Chief Steward, who was conscientious and painstaking, complained more in sorrow than in anger that none of them had their heart in their work, which – as their hearts were floating round the suburbs of Observatory and Salt River – was hardly surprising. Since there was no Wren to maid me, I employed a gentle-voiced tactful Coloured girl, called Gladys, who came in the mornings to do my washing and pressing and anything else I required. She moved softly and had a ready smile that revealed well-kept white teeth, and she was always good-tempered. I often longed to know what really went on behind her nice wide forehead, because she had maided four of my predecessors and must by now have quite a line on the Ladies of Admiralty House.

'You should write a book,' I said. 'Wives of Commanders-in-Chief off guard!'

She laughed, and the large short-sighted eyes she raised to heaven behind her spectacles were expressive.

'I wish I could, Milady!'

Three or four times a week I went into the big old-fashioned kitchen to consult with our Chief Petty Officer Cook and the Chief Steward.

At first the Chief Steward was inclined to think nothing of South African fish. But he soon allowed himself to take a more tolerant view.

'It's not like English fish,' I agreed. 'That would be too much to hope for. But king klip and Cape salmon are very good – and there's that fish we call seventy-four, and quite a lot of others.'

'But not an abundance, Milady. The best goes up the line.'

But somehow he soon managed to intercept 'the best' before it got to the little station at the bottom of the hill.

The Chief Cook had studied South African dishes, and

40

the Cape version of the traditional Mrs. Beeton was on a shelf in the kitchen. From this volume of 650 recipes collected by Hildagonda Duckitt – Mrs. Beeton's South African contemporary – he soon learned to make 'bredies' and 'bobooties', and when in doubt we rang up Magda Stewart, the Magistrate's wife, who had been brought up on a farm near Van Rynsdorp, and knew everything in the world about Afrikaner cookery.

But there was an even more interesting book than Hildagonda Duckitt's in our kitchen, and that was the Xosa translation of the Bible. It belonged to the kitchen-Bantu and was the joy of his life. I often found him poring over it at the deal table, and he would rise to his feet sheepishly, slip it into the pocket of his white overall and begin washing potatoes – slowly and rather shyly, for the Bantu is not quick in his movements and it is his habit to keep his eyes downcast.

'He's mad on his Old Testament,' I said to Bertie. 'He reads it whenever he gets half a chance.'

'It's right up his street,' said my husband. 'Plenty of polygamy, tribal warfare and magic.'

Off the large inner hall, where I had danced so light-heartedly as a young girl, was the hub of our small universe, the Flag Lieutenant's office.

Tony Harris was an excellent organizer who knew his own mind. His mornings were the absolute negation of the saying that it is impossible to do two things at once. To find him with a telephone in either hand, a third muttering on the blotter, and several people waiting outside to see him on a variety of matters, was completely in character. On his desk were four trays, marked respectively, IN, OUT, PENDING and TOO DIFFICULT.

TOO DIFFICULT intrigued me. It was seldom empty.

'What happens to these in the end?' I asked, picking up one or two messages and letters from this defeatist basket.

'They solve themselves if you give them time,' said Tony.

41

He was more of a philosopher than either of us realized. He had discovered a basic principle.

The hall always smelt deliciously of beeswax, and our two young seamen must have spent at least one third of their lives at Simon's Town polishing it.

We had arrived in the middle of the bazaar and fête season, and I had to take the plunge and learn to stand on a public platform and make a speech, something I had never done in my life before. It took me some time to relax and realize that the eggs and tomatoes at church fairs were innocently on sale and not to be used as ammunition. Too many political meetings in my girlhood had left their mark.

CHAPTER THREE

'TOTSIENS, OUBAAS!'

WE had been less than a fortnight in Simon's Town when a great blow befell the country.

On the evening of 12th September the Flag Lieutenant was called to his office. We had just finished dinner, and he rejoined us with a grave face.

'I am sorry to tell you, Sir, General Smuts died at his farm at Irene at seven-thirty this evening. He was out on the veld all day and seemed well. After supper he collapsed of a heart attack and died in the arms of his daughter.'

Two days later we flew to Pretoria for the State Military Funeral.

We left Cape Town at five in the afternoon, and landed at Palmietfontein three and a half hours later. As we drove across the veld to Pretoria the aromatic up-country scents assailed our nostrils – sharp, resinous and grassy. The night was keen and starry.

This was the country the Oubaas had loved most – this and Table Mountain.

Jan Christiaan Smuts had been born eighty years ago on a Cape farm in the Malmesbury district where High Dutch had been the language of his home. He was educated at Stellenbosch as was his friend, Daniel François Malan, who was later to become his bitterest political opponent. During my husband's term as C.-in-C. South Atlantic Dr. D. F. Malan was Prime Minister of the Nationalist Government which ousted the Smuts United Party Government after World War Two. Smuts, the most brilliant student of his year, won a scholarship to Christ's College, Cambridge, where he studied Law, while Malan, in his turn, went to the University of Utrecht to qualify as a minister of the Dutch Reformed Church.

Smuts was called to the Bar and returned to South Africa to practise as an advocate at the Cape, where he married his childhood friend and fellow student, Sybella Margaretha Krige, known to her friends as 'Isie' until the Second World War when the Springbok soldiers she helped so devotedly christened her 'Ouma' (Grannie). The Oubaas, however, referred to his unworldly and faithful helpmeet as 'my child of nature' or 'the steam in my kettle'.

Soon after their marriage he uprooted his bride and took her to the austere new Republic of Oom Paul Kruger across the Vaal, and at twenty-eight years old, the young Cape Advocate was appointed Attorney General of the Transvaal Republic.

When the Boer War came with its terrible inevitability, the State Attorney turned soldier, for every burger and Boer in that raw land was part of its defence, and he was presently put in command of the Boer Forces in the Cape Colony. How bravely he and his men fought on, long after their cause was lost, how he strove to recruit troops from the Cape, is an old story. He was the last to give in. Yet, for all that, he was able to realize that Boer and Briton must become allies if the white race was to survive in South Africa. And in 1910 it was Smuts who, with his friend and leader, General Louis Botha, was largely instrumental in influencing the Cape Colony, the Transvaal, the Orange Free State and Natal into forming the self-governing Union of South Africa. His many dealings with British statesmen in London had convinced him that they preferred co-operation to oppression, and already he was developing that world view-point which was ultimately to estrange him from his own people.

'This is his farm, Doornkloof,' pointed out Mr. Rumbold, the First Secretary to the High Commissioner, who had met us at Palmietfontein. In the starlight we saw a shadowy tin-roofed colonial farmhouse sheltered by willows and gums in the lee of a wooded koppie. 'His children and grandchildren are here now, staying with Ouma.'

His children? There had been twins, still-born during the Boer War when shells were falling in Isie's garden at Pretoria. Cato, Japie, Sylma, Jannie and Louis had followed. Louis was a girl, but she had been named General Louis Botha. Isie had not found it easy to set aside the bitterness left by the Boer War, and there is a legend that those of her babies who came into the world after the sad peace of Vereeniging were nevertheless born under the flag of the defeated twin Republics because their mother draped the *Vierkleur* over her great four-poster when the first pains warned her that her time was upon her.

'You will be punished for your obstinacy,' Jannie had said, his blue eyes laughing. 'Your girls will marry Englishmen.'

Two of them did. But by then the 'punishment' had lost its sting.

It was ten-thirty when we arrived at High Commission House in Pretoria.*

Sir Evelyn Baring had been recalled from one of his tours of the High Commission Territories of Basutoland, Bechuanaland and Swaziland, and he had only returned a few hours earlier. General Dowler, in Command of the East African Forces, and his daughter had come from Kenya and were our fellow guests. Over coffee and sandwiches Sir Evelyn explained arrangements for the next day.

Although not yet fifty, the High Commissioner was a man of considerable Colonial and administrative experience. He had a wide knowledge of Africa and the Middle East, had been Agent General for India in the Union, and Governor of Southern Rhodesia. He was well-informed on a vast

---

* *Before the Union of South Africa became a Republic Britain's Diplomatic Representative was the High Commissioner (now an Ambassador). The three British Protectorates of Basutoland, Bechuanaland and Swaziland came under his jurisdiction. They are now the independent states of Lesotho, Botswana and the Kingdom of Swaziland.*

range of subjects including the flora and fauna of South Africa and the life and philosophy of Mahommed. He was tall and distinguished with an air at times remote and at others friendly and approachable. His wife, Lady Mary, who was in England with the children, also had strong ties with the Union. Her grandfather, Lord Selborne, had been Governor of the Transvaal and High Commissioner of the Cape before Union.

Later, in 1952, Sir Evelyn was to be Governor of Kenya at one of the most desperate moments in the history of that Colony, when the Mau Mau were committing their unspeakable outrages in a wave of anti-White terrorism.

I woke early the following morning and went to look out of my window at the city of Pretoria spread among its flowering trees cupped in the hills.

Today it was a city of sorrow and of mourning for Jan Christiaan Smuts.

On the farm, Doornkloof, messages were pouring in from Kings and Presidents and loving friends. And across the veld rode a withered white-bearded company of *oudstryders*, his old comrades-in-arms, determined to go on his last trek with their leader. In the town the crowds gathered.

The morning light lay mellow on the veld he loved, while down at the Cape his beloved mountain brooded over the Houses of Parliament where he had fought so many wordy battles. How often he had climbed Table Mountain to escape on its heights the endless vexations of political life! Wild flowers and trees he had loved, and the wise old botanist, Dr. R. Marloth, had been his constant companion in these hours of relaxation. The African scene in all its infinite variety was dearer to his heart than any other, yet, much as he had cherished his homeland, he had persisted in seeing it in relation to the universe.

Klaas Havenga, his formidable opponent – who had nevertheless served the Union well in the Hertzog-Smuts Coalition before World War Two – spoke truly when he said of Smuts and of himself.

46

'He rose from height to height and his light was spread far beyond the bounds of his course ... his country was the world, and I had to be content with the more particular sphere of South Africa.'

His country was the world. In that truth lay his success and his failure, his breadth of vision and his blindness. He lost touch with his own people. But on this sad day, for one sublime unknowing moment, he found them again.

We arrived at the plain dignified Groote Kerk shortly after ten. The dense crowds were orderly and silent, and the escort was already drawn up in front of the gun-carriage. Inside the church there was a feeling of intimacy, perhaps because almost everyone there had known him personally. Only Ouma was not present. At Doornkloof she would hear the service that was being broadcast throughout the land. But her flowers lay upon his coffin, the red, purple and white heaths of the Cape – of her birthplace and his where they had fallen in love some sixty years ago.

On her card was written her simple message to him.

'*Totsiens Pappa*' – 'See you soon Pappa . . .'

Men who had fought with him and against him filed into the church.

Dr. Malan, the Prime Minister, entered with his second wife, some thirty years his junior. He looked old and careworn and seemed more than ever to take comfort from her arm clasped closely in his.

'For all of us,' Dr. Malan had said, 'his passing leaves a sense of irreparable loss and emptiness.'

He had lost a great adversary and contemporary, the lad from his own district who had earned the world's love and admiration while his own name had incurred so much disfavour and misunderstanding in other lands.

My thoughts turned upon the still heart beneath Ouma's flowers. How hard Jan Smuts had tried to bring our people together! Why should it be so difficult to reconcile the British and Afrikaner sections of our national life when both possessed such splendid qualities? Perhaps the tenacious affection of certain English-speaking South Africans

47

for the island of their origin angered the Afrikaners who had long since severed the natal cord with Holland or France, while the Afrikaner clamour for a Republic alarmed those who feared a return to the isolationist days of Oom Paul Kruker. Even the basic principle of *apartheid* was no real bone of contention. It was a traditional policy built as much upon the theories of Cecil John Rhodes as upon those of Dr. Malan. Only its application was felt to be too harsh in an enlightened age. It could and would be modified if our two White races would show goodwill and good sense.

God teach us to be kind and to understand one another ...

People rose in their pews and the beautiful Afrikaans words of Ouma's favourite hymn rang out.

> 'Net soos die landman wat geploeg het,
> Die avenskadu bly begroet—
> So bly sien one wat swaar geswoeg het,
> Ons lewensdag ten einde spoed.'*

Through the windows behind the circular gallery we could see the clear blue sky. Little stories about him fluttered through my memory. Trivial things. There had been 'small potatoes'.

After the Victory Parade the Oubaas had been invited to lunch at Buckingham Palace, where he had found himself in the company of a number of young queens, both reigning and in exile. Suddenly Queen Mary appeared.

'Ah,' he had said in all sincerity. 'There she comes – the Queen of Queens! Beside her you are all small potatoes.'

The quip was passed round delightedly, and it is related that at luncheon, the present Queen Mother had said to the footman, 'Don't offer the Field-Marshal any new potatoes.

* *A free translation of this verse is:*
> *'Like the landman who has ploughed*
> *Greets the grateful evening shade,*
> *So gladly we, who long have toiled,*
> *See swift our lifespan fade.'*

He does not care for small potatoes.' She knew his weakness for English new potatoes, and her eyes, even bluer than her guest's twinkled at his discomfiture.

Smuts was well known for his way of looking into space and musing aloud. One day on Table Mountain he had soliloquized to a gathering of young folk.

'Truth. What is Truth? Truth is a vision. Mary Magdalen saw that vision in a garden the first Easter morning. Upon it we have built a whole civilization.'

I believe in the resurrection of the dead, the life everlasting . . .

There was a stir, and then silence fell for Dominee Reyneke to speak in Afrikaans. His was a human and tender funeral oration, for he spoke of a tried friend, and sometimes his voice faltered, only to gather strength again.

'*Liewe Ouma* – dear Ouma, in loneliness upon your farm,' he began, and with the words the sense of her loss became personal to all of us. And then we saw the statesmen, the world figure. 'When God takes away a great leader the life of a Nation is affected and the Lord talks to his people. . . . People of South Africa, our beloved Fatherland, shall we not answer the voice of God and be more tolerant of one another?'

Throughout his career, said the Dominee, Jan Christiaan Smuts had striven for unity between the two White races of South Africa and understanding for the dark-skinned folk whose welfare was a sacred trust upon the White man. We, too, must strive towards that goal.

He told us of the funeral of a poor *oudstryder* who had fought in the Boer War with General Smuts.

'A handful of people had come to show their last respects to this old grandfather of ninety-three. Among them was the man whose memory we honour today. He was Prime Minister of the Union of South Africa then, yet he had time to spare for an old comrade-in-arms forgotten by the world. Jan Christiaan Smuts, you had a place among the greatest of the earth, you had a place among the humblest of individuals. We bid you farewell. *Vaarwel*, Jan Christiaan Smuts! *Vaarwel, Oubaas*!'

There followed the measured English address of the Reverend Webb, who gave us the same message and the same plea for unity and goodwill.

At last we heard the solemn music of the Funeral March and eight Generals stepped down from their pew while eight Warrant Officers shouldered his coffin. My husband left my side to take his place in the procession that would march from the Church to the Railway Station.

Out in the sun the silent bare-headed throngs waited, and in the naked boughs of the jacaranda trees perched the brown boys, stripped for once of their natural merriment, dimly aware that in the passing of this great and sage South African they had lost an ally and a friend.

Later, from my room in Bryntirion, I heard the last salute as the funeral train left the station for Johannesburg, and, in the hollow of the hills, the military aircraft circled and dipped. Along the railway line children strewed flowers for him and the Native school choirs sang *God Bless Africa* in their sombre melodious voices. At Irene his grandchildren and his servants waved to him for the last time, and at Doornkloof Ouma waited.

Now he was no longer hers. For the last time she was sharing him with the world. But when the final prayers had been read and the last mourners turned home he would come back to this place he had loved, and to her. For all eternity he would be part of Doornkloof where he had known a little peace and spent his last living day in quiet contentment on the open veld. He would be one with the red earth of the koppie behind his homestead, with the buck watchful among the thorn-trees, with the rock-pigeons and *dassies*, with the green miracle of the Transvaal spring and its brilliant winter when frost spangles the tawny grass. These were the things his spirit had craved. Soon they would be his for evermore. And one day, not too far distant, they would also be hers.

She would scatter the ashes of the man who had been her

husband for nearly sixty years, and she would whisper the words her simple card had borne.

'*Totsiens, Papa . . . Totsiens, Oubaas . . .*'

CHAPTER FOUR

MIDSUMMER, CHRISTMAS AND
NEW YEAR

DECEMBER came and the stream in the kloof-garden ran dry. Days were hot, and from the stone pier opposite the Secretary's Cottage a shark-net was stretched to our little beach to make safe bathing for the children of the Compound.

We never saw a shark, but quite often Wendy the Whale blew waterspouts in our corner of the bay, and sometimes Sally the Seal frolicked off-shore or pulled herself on to the sands for a sunbathe.

Sally was well-known among the warships. At high tide it amused her to climb on to the wharf and make believe she was a mermaid. But sailors are not as simple as all that, and when they found her there, they usually pushed her good-naturedly back into the sea with a few of those quaint remarks that only sailors may make to seals.

From time to time Percy the Penguin paced up and down our beach and Bertie suggested that he was the spirit of a departed Admiral pacing his quarterdeck. But he looked to me more like a reincarnated head waiter.

Schools broke up for the Christmas holidays and my husband was asked to give away the prizes at Bishop's, Piet's old college. It was a mild sunny day and the ceremony took place under the trees outside the old stone buildings. Afterwards, while we were having tea out of doors, someone came and gave my husband a message.

We had been expecting it, and my heart gave a great happy leap as a smile broke over his face. He looked across at me.

'Another little boy for Bishop's. Ronnie arrived ten minutes ago and Piet says Glen is fine.'

The Headmaster turned to his wife.

'We must congratulate the Commander-in-Chief. A Bishop's boy has just made him a grandfather.'

A few days later I made an entry in my diary. Bertie was playing men's tennis at Wynberg Military Camp. I dropped him there and drove on to Kirstenbosch Gardens alone.

These wild gardens on the southern slopes of the mountain possess a particular enchantment. Only indigenous plants bloom there in an atmosphere of utter tranquillity. The gardens have a beginning but no end. You may enter at the great stone gates and climb up the gorge to the summit of Table Mountain if you wish. Many people go there in the spring and summer, yet it is easy to find solitude. They are gardens for lovers or for those seeking some quiet spot in which to reflect.

'Dec. 10 1950. Alone by a stream in Kirstenbosch Gardens.

'It could all be so lovely if only we had time to enjoy it. Time is one of the few things we never have. The painters and electricians have cleared out of Admiralty House at last. The sea-garden is a dream with its wide lawns and white balustrades. The sparkling sea laps our little beach with a soft slapping sound, there is always a cooing of doves, and across the bay the mountains change with every mood of light and weather.

If only there were time to watch and listen and learn to know our surroundings, time to explore our kloof-garden and climb the Simon's Town hills and discover the old port, how happy I should be! If there were time to write.

'But there is no time.

'Now is the season of fêtes and bazaars, of children's parties, amateur theatricals, races, prize-givings, regattas and a thousand social and welfare activities in which we must take part. We each do our own jobs in this line and there are many which we do together, and our private lives slip away from us like mercury in a thermometer shaken by an impatient hand. ...

'As I write now I am sitting on the banks of a stream. There is the sound of the wind in the trees, of the water flowing over the boulders, of a cricket somewhere, and a frog with its pulsing call. Bell-like grasses tinkle and nod over the paper, there is bird song but no human voice, and already a lovely stillness steals over my nerves.

'On Thursday, Dec. 7, our grandson was born.

'It is curious, I write the word "grandson" with reluctance – though we do most eagerly welcome this baby, And Mum, God bless her, has now moved into the highly senior class of great-grannie! Big milestones if one thinks about it. ...

'Glen is at home and very well and happy. I went to see her yesterday. Piet was with her, and three dogs and two cats. Sister has no objection! "If you turf out the dogs they'll be jealous," she says. When Piet was born at Tees Lodge nobody bothered about dog-psychology. Our poor animal was just considered unhygienic and my Sister would have none of him.

'Ronnie sleeps in his cradle – the same one that Piet and I slept in – blows bubbles, cracks wind, pulls faces and changes colour like a chameleon from one moment to the next. He looks like any Packer crossed with a charming kitten. But of course there's no knowing how any new baby will look later on.

'Piet has already bathed him, and Glen will not hear of a nurse when Sister goes.

' "We are taking care of him ourselves," she says. And is not at all alarmed at the prospect. It seems to me that modern parents have more courage and intelligence than we had, also less imagination perhaps. ...'

That hour alone when I made my first grand-maternal entry in my journal was a happy one. Now, looking back over the past two years, I can recall several such peaceful

hours – time in which to reflect – and the sense of being
relaxed and 'smoothed out' which followed them. They were
too few, and they stand out with the blessed clarity of water
in the thirstland.

No wonder the Oubaas loved the veld and the mountain.
Alone with nature he could adjust his wide outlook on life
and forget the petty pinpricks that would reduce a statesman
to a party politician.

Our Ronnie was only one of a crop of new arrivals. That
summer saw several increases in our little community. It was
a cheerful community, kind and neighbourly, and when one
or another of our naval or dockyard wives went to hospital
to produce an infant or for any other reason there was
always some accommodating wife who would take in the
children or keep an eye on the house in the meantime. This
spirit of help-one-another allowed wives to pack and follow
their husbands when the ships went to some interesting new
port, and, in consequence, the Simon's Town children
became quite communal. One day they would be staying in
somebody else's house, the next somebody else would be
staying in theirs.

A few days before Christmas the Flagship, *Bermuda*,
which had refitted and re-commissioned in England, sailed
into Simon's Bay amid great rejoicing. Sitting on the wharf,
waiting to welcome her, was Sally the Seal.

We gave a dance in honour of the cruiser's arrival. The
moon was at the full, the old house was floodlit and fairy-
lights glowed among the trees. Upstairs my maid, Gladys,
watched over Ronnie and three other very young babies
from 'up the line' who had been brought to the party in their
carry-cots so that the ten o'clock needs of nature should not
be denied.

My mother, who was staying in the house, wore her very
best evening dress, and with two of her favourite friends and
relations, Mittie Marais and Olga Albers, she 'watched the
fun' and declared that never had she enjoyed a dance more.
What memories did it evoke for her? Sixty years had passed

55

since the momentous ball at which she had first met young Dr. Julius Petersen.

For my Cousin Olga Albers it was also a glad occasion. Her only son, the Guy's surgeon, Alfred Albers, had recently returned to settle at the Cape with his bride Prunella Stack of Health and Beauty fame.

'I want to start Health and Beauty out here in South Africa,' Prunella said to me that night. 'Would you be willing to speak at my inaugural meeting.'

'Of course,' I promised. 'If Health and Beauty makes people look like you do this evening there must be something to it.'

Slim and poised, with happiness shining in her eyes, she looked up at her tall athletic husband, and they laughed as they linked arms and wandered into the garden where lovers have walked under the moon for over a century and a half.

On Christmas Eve the Dockyard Church Choir came and sang carols for us on the lawn. Many of our friends were there to hear them and the still summer magic of the evening and the loveliness of their voices is one of the memories that will linger with me forever, a part of the spell Simon's Town has laid upon my heart.

In the New Year Piet and Glen came to stay with us for a fortnight, bringing Ronnie and the three dogs. Fortunately the garden seemed large enough to hold the Packer animals and Veronica's pets – perhaps because Sammy was too big for ordinary dogs to treat with anything except respect and the Pekes were too small to present a challenge.

Before they left us Piet and Glen gave a *braaivleis* on the lower lawn behind the wattle windbreak. A *braaivleis* (which means grilled meat) is the South African version of a barbecue. Piet had got a sheep from the country and chops and sausages sizzled on wire netting grills over three huge log-fires, there were troughs of sliced water-melon, buckets of iced beer, and, on the terrace above, a Coloured Coon Band played Afrikaans *liedjies* or music with accordions and guitars. The guests were in slacks or cotton dresses and ate

56

how and where they pleased by the light of the moon or the fires.

Suddenly there was a surprise and the spirit of the Orient materialized in our midst. Out of the shadows appeared the gilded figure of a Siamese temple dancer in glittering pagoda tunic and sun-burst headdress. He leapt and postured over and round the flickering flames in a wild exotic phoenix dance, and vanished into the night whence he had come. Afterwards we learned that the glamorous performer was our second cook who had been in the Sadler's Wells Ballet Company before he joined the Navy.

Bertie and I said good night and left youth in possession of the garden and the beach.

Through our bedroom window we could see the reflections of the flames and hear the coon guitars above the wash of the waves. We could smell the fragrance of tobacco plants mingled with that of burning wood, and in the very old fir tree by the stoep the rainbow bouquets of coloured lights fell from the homes of sleeping ring-doves.

Bertie said: 'I've told Veronica to save the ash for my carnations. It's just the thing for them.'

In the green room opposite ours Gladys sat quietly knitting, and the carry-cot people made the odd little noises of sleeping infancy while their parents danced barefoot on the grass or swam in the moon-silver sea.

February was a busy and a happy month.

On the 11th Ronald Packer was christened. His behaviour in church and afterwards at Langi Banool was exemplary. A small family party drank his health and during the toast he lay peacefully in the arms of old Nan, and I heard her murmur to herself with wonder and a hint of tears in her voice, 'This is the third generation that I hold in my arms.'

Alfred and Prunella Albers came late to the party, they had been climbing Table Mountain. Every week-end they climbed, it was their favourite recreation.

As I had promised I spoke at the inauguration of the

Women's League of Health and Beauty in South Africa. The Mayor of Cape Town introduced Prunella and a distinguished Professor of Medicine endorsed the theory that a fit body was the way to health and happiness. When Prunella and two assistants had demonstrated exercises to music every woman in the crowded hall was fired with enthusiasm to learn the secret of perfect grace, control and flexibility. Prunella could not have wished for a more responsive audience. When she called for volunteers for a demonstration lesson one shy giggling girl after another ventured on to the platform with asides to friends: 'I haven't really the right sort of undies, but all the same ...' They bounced about happily in gauche imitation of the slim glamorous figure in black briefs and white satin shirt.

'Now keep your heads up and smile,' said Prunella, as they marched off the platform back to their seats. 'That's part of it – pull your neck right out of your shoulders, head back – and *never forget to smile*!'

Alfred Albers said afterwards:

'I was very proud of Prunella Stack tonight.'

Health and Beauty took on. Prunella extended it to Coloured women's institutions, and in the squalor of District Six there blossomed this new movement of comradeship through physical fitness.

Then came the Ides of March, eight months after her marriage.

Alfred, Prunella and Sir Evelyn Baring climbed Table Mountain with another friend. The conditions were excellent and the ascent not particularly difficult. But there was one dangerous ledge along that formidable buttress. Alfred was leading. Someone called out something and he turned his head to answer. Perhaps that small careless movement shifted the weight of the heavy rucksack he carried on his broad shoulders.

The drop to the next ledge was seventy feet.

Prunella was alone with him when the others returned with help two hours later. The stretcher bearers lifted him gently and she walked beside him down the silent kloofs. The grim old mountain had claimed another sacrifice.

Long shadows gathered in the gorges and mist hid the ledge. Presently the rain of early autumn began to fall, sad as tears in the darkness of the night.

One morning, as I slid away the windows of the sun-trap extension of my bedroom to let in all the fresh glory of the new day, I saw in the bay a new unaccountable ship.

'Come and look!' I called to Bertie in his dressing-room. 'What can this ship be?'

His starched tropical uniform was blue-white in the dazzling sunshine as he focused his glasses on the stranger.

'That's the *Galathea*, the Danish research ship,' he said. 'We sold her to the Danes. She's an old Town Class sloop.'

'What's she here for?'

'She's on a scientific expedition round the world to examine the unplumbed depths of the oceans.'

During the next fortnight we saw a good deal of the *Galathea*'s officers and scientists. The expedition had been organized by Denmark's leading scientist, Dr. Bruun, and the writer-artist-sailor, Hakon Mielche.

It would be difficult to find two men less alike in appearance, or better cast for their respective roles. Dr. Bruun, in spite of a long sea voyage, had not lost the pallor of the laboratory. His face, his hair, his eyes were all pale. He walked with a limp and one arm was withered. He had the air of one withdrawn from the world, yet all his efforts were directed towards finding a marine solution to its problems of nutrition which grow graver every year. Hakon Mielche, robust and tanned, was a compelling personality with many adventurous voyages in sail to his credit. His was the task of writing the story of the expedition. Several young science students were doing their military service in the *Galathea* as part of the crew.

Dr. Bruun showed us over the little ship where the student sailors worked in their spare time in a cramped but practical laboratory. He explained his theories to us in perfect English.

'Populations are increasing and food is decreasing, the land of the world has been farmed to a standstill, and we must begin to farm the seas – not for fish alone, but for organic matter on which fish live. We hope to explore the oceans to a depth of four miles and to discover organic matter which can be produced in an edible form.'

New submerged worlds came to the rescue of hungry mankind as he expanded his idea. I asked him how he came to know English so well.

He said, with his pleasing diffident smile:

'Denmark is a small country which cannot afford libraries of scientfic and technical volumes specially translated for the few who require them. We students must learn the languages we need for our reading. Before the war Germany gave us excellent text books and all the latest developments. But, for the time being, no more. England and America are the present great sources of information and learning. It is absolutely essential to know English.'

I wished Dr. Bruun would say as much to the Minister for Education, for it had struck me that the lingual emphasis in the Union was leaning too heavily on the development of the Afrikaans tongue. Children in the *platteland* – country districts – were growing up almost entirely ignorant of English. Afrikaans is a delightful language well suited to South Africa and especially her farming communities, but it is a sentimental and cultural luxury, whereas English, the language of the Commonwealth and the United States, has become a practical necessity. If a young Afrikaner would benefit himself and his country in the world beyond the Union he must have command of the Union's second language. South Africa's importance in world issues has grown too great for her to slide back into the pastoral era of Oom Paul Kruger's isolated Boer Republic.

It was curious how often in our subsequent travels we heard news of the *Galathea*. In Durban, Madagascar, Lourenço Marques and later the Gold Coast, we found that she had been before us and invariably she had added some new contribution to science.

We signed our names in her visitors' book with its shark-skin cover, we looked at Hakon Mielche's log with its amusing sketches and we met Captain Madsen who modestly referred to himself as 'the driver'. Then one morning she went as unobtrusively as she had come, a bold little old ship with people on board who believed that their discoveries might help to save the human race from the starvation which stares it in the face.

When the *Galathea* had gone her eastward way we were visited by the French cruiser *Gazelle* flying the flag of Admiral Philippe Auboyneau, the Commander-in-Chief of all the French Forces in the Indian Ocean.

Philippe Auboyneau, who during World War Two had been at the head of the Fighting French Naval Forces, was a firm friend of my husband's, and we were delighted to have him and his fascinating young wife, Kitty, to stay with us at Admiralty House.

They had flown from Madagascar to the Cape in a French naval plane while the flagship *Gazelle* exercised in company with the South Atlantic Squadron and the South African Navy, and their visit, which happened to coincide with the height of the social season, was the occasion for a cheerful *entente cordiale*.

The new Governor-General, Dr. E. G. Jansen, had recently succeeded Mr. Brand van Zyl, and the Auboneaus went with us to a garden party at Westbrooke, the Governor-General's official country residence in the beautiful Groote Schuur Estate bequeathed to the Peninsula by Cecil John Rhodes.

Dr. Jansen was much liked and respected. He had been for many years Speaker of the House of Assembly and had twice been Minister for Native Affairs. He was tall and straight with narrow features and a benevolent smile. He had a marked dislike for idle chatter. No doubt many years in Parliament had wearied him of the human voice, and his term as Speaker had caused him to weigh his own words and avoid light pronouncements. But when he did speak in public it was always to encourage the elusive quality of goodwill between our warring factions.

Mrs. Jansen, who was descended from Huguenot stock, was stately and fair. In spite of poor health she had been an active help to her husband in his political career, and her most earnest efforts were devoted to the promotion of the Afrikaans language and culture.

As we wandered among the glowing gardens of Westbrooke the eyes of the women followed our French guests with interest. The sophisticated simplicity of Kitty's Paris dress and hat intrigued them almost as much as the attractive foreign Admiral at her side. And, for her part, Kitty wanted to know all about everybody.

There was Dr. Malan, also a descendant of the Huguenots, strolling between the beds of scarlet and yellow cannas, his arm linked in that of his wife. Except when he smiled the old Prime Minister's expression was set in the habitual stubborn mould of one who has battled for half a century to turn a political party into a government, and who was still battling to turn it into a good government. At times he must have felt rather like Mr. Attlee – in danger of being overrun and crushed under the impetuous heels of his headstrong followers. But whenever he glanced at Mrs. Malan his features softened and the pleasant humour of which he is capable came to the surface.

Mrs. Malan, with her fine dark blue eyes and dark upswept hair, was a forceful personality not to be disregarded.

I pointed out some of the Ministers' wives.

'They are good-looking,' announced Kitty, after due consideration. 'Not in the French fashion – more Nordic than Latin – but *enfin* they have something. And they are not so very old!'

'No, they are not old. The Nationalist Government has a young-middle-aged Cabinet – plenty of future leaders!'

'That dark man there – the one with the bold eyes and the stern mouth – who is he?'

'The Minister for Lands, Mr. Strijdom. He is a great orator and an ardent republican. Many people think he will be the next Prime Minister if the Nationalists remain in power and when Dr. Malan resigns. He is supposed to be an honest politician—'

Kitty laughed and wrinkled her pretty nose. Was there such a thing?

We left Westbrooke just after the Prime Minister and Dr. Malan. Waiting for them in the big ministerial car was a lively sprite of six or seven.

'That's Marietjie,' I said. 'She's the little German war orphan they adopted after the war. Dr. Malan has two sons by his first wife, but that little one can twist him round her finger any time she likes.'

As they drove away we saw the child clamber on to her adopted father's lap and lay her soft small face against his – an innocent human talisman against a world of fear.

When Philippe and Kitty bade us good-bye a few days later it was with the assurance that we would soon meet again, for they were going to call at the east coast ports of Port Elizabeth and East London on their return journey to Madagascar, and we hoped to meet them there.

The *Bermuda* sailed for Port Elizabeth early in March and the Flag Lieutenant and Coxswain went with her. So did our luggage. Bertie and I had decided to travel overland in our private car, an easy two day run through the Garden Route and some of the most magnificent scenery in South Africa. Our picnics in the sunny coves and forested mountains of that wild coast are among my pleasantest recollections. To be alone and say and do exactly what we liked had become a rare luxury.

CHAPTER FIVE

BORDER COUNTRY

My husband was to open Port Elizabeth Agricultural Show, and during Show Week we were the guests of the city. A suite of rooms had been reserved for us in a splendid new hotel on the sea-front, and fresh flowers arrived for me daily.

The atmosphere of the port, where the first British settlers had landed in South Africa in 1820, was highly stimulating. In those days it had been savage bush country, today there was a wool-boom and the air reeked of sheep and shekels. Moreover the recent Industrial Revolution in the Union was at its most active in this thriving port so easily accessible to the interior. Its flat hinterland offered ideal factory sites, and the entrance to Port Elizabeth might have been the Great West Road into London. Model villages had been built for the Natives flocking from the Reserves to the new factories, and an exceptionally liberal City Council refused to countenance any repressive controls on its Black community. It believed that good housing, good health and decent working conditions could not fail to maintain the racial amity that has been a feature of life in the Eastern Province for many years.

Yet in 1952, when Kenya was in the throes of Mau Mau murders, Port Elizabeth suffered grave disillusionment. A series of riots blew up for no apparent reason, as is so often the way in Africa, and overnight £300,000 worth of damage was done in the model township of New Brighton. The mob burned down the cinemas, welfare centres and buildings erected for them at the expense of the White citizens and

64

then murdered such White persons as they could lay hands on. Further up the coast, East London followed suit and among the White victims was a medical nun who had devoted her life to the service of the Bantus. She was stabbed to death for her pains and then burnt. Indeed, that night human beings reverted to primitive senseless apes and the Black man's cause was set back for generations. When primitive Africa is worried or afraid she kills.

Those 1952 riots were particularly significant, because they were the first anti-White demonstrations known since Union, and they were clearly fomented from without.

From end to end of the African continent the paid agitator was at work.

But in 1951 Port Elizabeth was carefree, she was riding the crest of the wave.

The day before the opening of the Show Mr. V. H. O. Christian, the President, took us round the exhibits.

Mr. Christian was a descendant of Lieutenant Christian of the ill-famed *Bounty*, and two of his naval ancestors had their names in gold lettering on the mahogany boards in the entrance hall at Admiralty House. He was a fine old gentleman of eighty and for fifty-seven years he had watched the Port Elizabeth Show grow from 'a sort of picnic' to its present high standard.

'Now what would your fancy be?' he asked me. 'Horses, dogs—' My 'fancy' was sheep and big bulls. So we went to the cool cattle-sheds and admired massive Frieslands, blonde Jerseys, curly-headed Ayrshires and bronze Afrikanders developed from the native herds which originally came down Africa from Egypt, long-legged, long-horned and living, like camels, on their humps. The winning Afrikander family had been bred by Mr. Pringle, whose Scottish ancestor, Thomas Pringle, had recorded the trials and progress of his fellow 1820 settllers in a manner both entertaining and informative.

I said to the judge: 'Their horns all grow differently, some like handle-bars and others curving downwards. Does it matter?'

He answered gravely, 'How a horn leaves the head is important. It should not obscure the profile. There should be a nice bulgy forehead in front of the horn.'

'Ears may be worn according to personal taste, like hats,' observed Bertie. 'Either pushed forward of the horn or right aft.'

The wool farmers watched the judging of their valuable sheep with shrewd critical eyes. One of these fortunate individuals, not knowing how best to spend his new found wealth, had bought a Rolls-Royce with a glass partition and, when someone had asked him how he liked it, he had said: 'Man, it's wonderful not having the sheep breathe down your neck!'

'Here's a charming thought,' said Bertie, with his hand on the matted outer wool of a £3,000 champion Merino ram. 'This grey top grease that looks so unattractive is the basis of most of your face-creams.'

In the long wool room we saw the trays of samples.

'The gold of the Eastern Province,' said one of the judges, and his tone wrote off the hard solid gold of the Transvaal and the Orange Free State. His fingers frayed out the raw locks to the texture of a cobweb, then tugged at the fine strands. None broke.

'Delicate as a young girl's hair and strong as wire,' he said. 'That's quality for you!'

And all this was started in 1826 by a few far-seeing settlers. In 1834 Thomas Pringle, journalist and pioneer, had travelled through the district and reported its progress.

'The luxurious pastures of the Zuurveld proper, being from their acidulant quality generally unfit for sheep, have been gradually covered with numerous herds of horned cattle ... (the progenitors of his descendant's Afrikanders). But what is of far more importance to the prosperity of the Settlement, it has been found that fine wool can be produced on the more inland pastures of the

66

district, of a quality fully equal to the best Spanish or Australian. At the period of my last visit in 1826, Lieut. Daniell, Major Pigot, Major Dundas, the new Landdrost, Capt. Campbell, and one or two other enterprising individuals, were raising experimental flocks of merinos, which were just beginning to excite some attention among their neighbours, but which the older Dutch-African colonists then generally regarded with apathy or derision. Now, in 1834, there are about 12,000 fine wooled sheep in Albany, the owners of which are realizing large profits; in so much that the attention of the whole Colony has been vividly awakened to the high importance of this branch of husbandry, which promises to prove a mine of inexhaustible wealth for South Africa.'

When my husband opened the Show he had a full house. The owners of the 'fine wooled sheep' of the Eastern Province, who, like their ancestors, were 'realizing large profits', had come to town in a big way. They were buying tractors for themselves and diamonds for their wives, and everybody was out to enjoy everything, even an opening speech by an Admiral. And what could an Admiral accustomed to seafaring know about farming?

The answer, of course, was Nothing. But the Simon's Town visit of the *Galathea* had borne its own marine fruit, and soon the sailor had his listeners all at sea. Astonished countrymen found themselves being asked to envisage ocean-farming when the earth's surface should cease to grow enough food to sustain life. Schools of great whales like three hundred ton oxen grazed steadily on organic matter as they moved about the seas, he said, and one day this matter would be farmed and turned into palatable food for human consumption.

'For myself,' he admitted. 'I prefer beef.'

Behind him the grand parade of gleaming prize cattle mooed appreciation of this very proper sentiment.

And then, since the Eastern Province owed so much of its present prosperity to the courage and determination of the

first settlers, he spoke of those men and women of his own
country who had come here to South Africa to make a new
life for their families. Those people, he said, could never
have survived without the help of the Boer settlers who had
already partly colonized the border. For every settler's farm
on the frontier of Kaffirland was his fortress and he was
prepared to defend it with his life.

He compared the reasons why a young man goes to sea or
becomes a farmer. Surely the main urge which drove a
young lad to sea was the prospect of one day commanding
his own ship – and when that day came and he stepped for
the first time on to the bridge of his own command he would
know a thrill never to be forgotten for the rest of his
years.

It must be so with a farmer too. He also must long to be
master of his own wide acres, his flocks, herds and crops and
those whose ceaseless task it was to tend them. And this
thought was borne out by the journal of one of those first
1820 settlers who had landed here with his party and then
journeyed twelve days' trek inland. There, in the bush, 'the
roughly kind Dutch waggoners', who had been their transport and escort, had set them down and wished them good-
bye and God's blessing. My husband quoted the words of
that journal. ' "There we were in the wilderness. Towns, villages, inns, hostelries, there were none. We must take root
and grow or die where we stood.

' "*But we were standing on our own ground, and it was
the first time many could say so. This thought roused to
action*, the tents were pitched, the night fires kindled, and the
life of a settler was begun." '

There was a ball that night at the old Feather Market
where once ostrich feathers had been sold for high prices.
Then too there had been a boom. The ostrich farmers had
had their day – a day dependent upon fickle fashion.
Perhaps it would come again. But 1951 was the year of the
Merino, the *annus mirabilis* of the Golden Fleece.

68

One afternoon another descendant of Thomas Pringle – this time the Curator of the Snake Park and Museum – showed me his deadly charges.

In a pit surrounded with running water and furnished with thorn trees and a rockery dwelt skeins and skeins of poisonous reptiles. William, the Coloured Snake-Boy, vaulted into this horrid pit and performed his act for the benefit of a dozen or more onlookers. He wore gauntlets and leggings.

He scooped up several yards of writhing serpents at random and slung them casually round his neck.

'The poison of the cobra paralyses,' he said. 'That of this tree-snake causes haemophilia. The ringhals, which belongs to the cobra group, spits his venom into the eyes of his victims, like this.'

He made a rabbit-face of his hand and held it at shoulder level, darting it to and fro to incite one of the snakes dangling round his neck. The ringhals expanded its hood furiously, and began to weave from side to side in front of the provoking hand. Suddenly it struck and spat a jet of venom into the 'eyes' of the 'rabbit'. William unfolded his hand and seized the snake and flung it down. Then he picked up a flat sluggish well-marked puff adder, and pressing at the jaw hinges, opened the mouth wide to show the long cruelly hooked fangs.

I shuddered, thinking of our kloof-garden at Admiralty House and of the puff-adders who had survived when the wood was dejungled.

'All snakes swim,' remarked William, and divested himself of his sinister garlands of squirming serpents. With a fine gesture he hurtled them into the water runnel round the pit, careless as a woman flinging spaghetti into the pot.

'We've just received a consignment of rattlesnakes from America,' said Mr. Pringle. 'Our first. We do a bit of swapping sometimes.'

'Are you going to unpack them?'

'Yes. Would you care to see them?'

69

'Very much.'

He turned to his white-coated assistant. 'Get me the tins, Charlie.'

'Have you ever been bitten?' I asked.

'Often. One gets careless. But however often you are bitten you are never immune. You must get the treatment at once.'

'What is the first reaction to a bite?'

'Intense fear. I have seen old Johannes, who was our Snake-Boy here for as long as I can remember, collapse at my feet when bitten – out of fear. And he had been bitten scores of times. Yet almost every bite can be cured now if you are quick enough with the serum. Except the mamba. He is usually deadly. The poison works at such terrific speed.'

'And the rattler?'

'I couldn't say. He is a foreigner. We have no experience of his habits.'

Charlie, the assistant, appeared with two cylinders like tennis-ball containers, only rather larger and with holes in the lid. He removed the lid. I nearly jumped out of my skin. But all we saw was a white bag tied at the top.

Mr. Pringle took the bag, which surged madly, and we heard a thin dry rattle, the last vertebrae of the reptiles' angry tails warning us that they were very much alive and kicking.

'None the worse for their flight, it seems,' remarked Mr. Pringle.

He went round to the back of an empty show-case, and, in the presence of an audience which had gathered with hypnotized horror, he put his hands through a trap-door into the case and undid the string at the neck of the bag. Then, still keeping it closed with his fingers, he turned it suddenly and deftly upside down and shook out the contents. Two yellow-brown snakes about six feet long with wide ugly spade-shaped heads flopped out. And very lively they were. Once again he did this trick with another container, and a third snake joined its compatriots.

'Keep the cylinder, Charlie,' said Mr. Pringle. 'We are sending back some cobras in exchange.'

I do not know how the cobras fared, but the rattlers died the following year, mourned only by Mr. Pringle and Charlie. They were, without exception, the least charming of our many new immigrants to the Union.

On our way to East London, a few days later, we stayed the night at Addo, in the elephant bush, with Commander and Mrs. Merewether on their citrus farm.

The flourishing citrus industry of the Eastern Province was started early in this century by Sir Percy Fitzpatrick, the author of the South African classic, *Jock of the Bushveld*, and his magnificent farm near Port Elizabeth is today run by his descendants. Not only do they grow first class oranges, grape-fruit and lemons, but fine polo-ponies as well.

Christopher and Marjorie Merewether had achieved success too, but not easily. Theirs was the story of many settlers between the wars. Christopher had commuted his naval pension to farm under the Sundays River Settlement Scheme. There had been the land and the labour, but the settlers had had to wait too long for the water. Many gave up, but others persevered – living a thirst-land life – until at last a dam was built and the trees saved. When World War Two came, Christopher rejoined the Navy, Marjorie went to London and took a job at the Admiralty, one son was in submarines and the other in the Fleet Air Arm. The precious fruit was ploughed into the ground, and a neighbour 'kept an eye' on the farm.

Now, once again, it was paying its way.

As we drove up to the bungalow Christopher had built himself in those first lean years, the delicious fragrance of the citrus groves came to us on the evening breeze.

Presently one or two neighbouring farmers and their wives came in to sundowners. These men too had been in the Navy, and it struck me that sailors took very kindly to the land. But somehow I could not imagine farmers becoming sailors as my husband had suggested at the show!

Early in the morning we set off on our journey to East London. Marjorie had filled our picnic-basket with good things and the day was warm and bright. She stood with Christopher at the gate to wave us good-bye. Their healthy fruit trees whispered about them with the light chafing of polished leaves, and I found myself thinking of that robust spirit which braves out the bad years, and, given its own ground, even in the wilderness, will somehow manage to 'take root and grow'.

East London is an easy day's drive from Addo through the historic border country which was once the buffer between the old Cape Colony and Kaffirland, and we soon came on to the main Grahamstown road following the line of the old forts and garrison towns where once the settlers' families had taken refuge during Kaffir wars. There are still elephant in the thick undulating bush, which, in days gone by, quivered with the assegais of the savages. But in the late summer the herd wanders away to distant grazing grounds and we did not see any.

Grahamstown, in its wonderful setting of hills and ridges, was less dreamy than usual that Sunday, for her Rhodes University had just been inaugurated as an independent university, and the city was recalling her stirring past with pardonable pride in a century of achievement.

Rhodes University received world attention at the end of 1952 when her Professor J. L. Smith, South Africa's leading fish expert, flew to an island off Madagascar to fetch the unique and famous coelocanth. In an interview at the time he said of this astounding and important catch: 'The coelocanth offers biologists a chance of breathtaking knowledge. It is a relic of the past so remote as to be almost beyond the grasp of the human mind.' For this fish, trawled in the Indian Ocean, belongs not to our day and age but to fifty million years ago. Oddly enough, a few weeks later, the jaw-bones and teeth of an enhominid – or 'near-man' – were unearthed in a Transvaal cave. They are believed to be the remains of the missing link between the ape man and the true man and belong to at least a millennium ago. The scientists have told us that Professor Smith's coelocanth is at the far end of the evolutionary chain and the enhominid at this end – our end.

As we approached East London we met a group of stick-fighters in holiday mood. Stick-fighting is a sort of Native fencing match which often ends in broken heads, but it is a favourite sport and the heads are tough.

These stick-fighters were striking gentlemen in every sense of the word. They wore saffron and ochre blankets, sheepskin spats and bright turbans. Masks of white or blue were painted round their eyes and over their heads they brandished their knobkerries. They were followed by lady-friends in wide saffron skirts, black-banded at the swinging hem, and adorned with beads and brass bangles. The young women carried little mouth organs and played them while the men frisked faun-like. As we stopped to watch them, a girl here or there covered a springy naked breast. That gesture, and the deep carmine lipstick on their broad mouths, were the only indications of the impact of White civilization on these children of nature. In the faces of the girls was an unconcious arrogance which is shy without being diffident and withdrawn without being sulky. The smile, when it comes, breaks furtively before exploding into a fit of delightful and irrepressible merriment.

Against the thorn-bush and the clear cobalt sky, the little band was a study in ochre and yellow – a vignette of tribal Africa.

At East London we were again the guests of the city and nothing was left undone that could have added to our comfort. We stayed at an excellent hotel on the esplanade, and early on Monday morning we woke to see, beyond the great rollers of the Indian Ocean, the *Bermuda* entering harbour in the dazzle of sunrise.

At eleven o'clock the Mayoress called on me formally at

the hotel while my husband received the Mayor on board, and at noon we drove to the City Hall to return the compliment.

Many years ago a very meticulous Commander-in-Chief who was much concerned with dress and ceremonial, wrote, for the information of his successor:

'In ports of the Union the Mayor calls on you. I have endeavoured to get them to dress up a bit more, but they are very unsophisticated. Cape Town and East London know the correct procedure as regards dress. . . . Everywhere in South Africa you will find them hopeless at organization. You arrive to call on the Mayor and though he is all dressed up in his parlour, you will find no one at the door to show you how to get there! This is typical, too, at any function you may have to attend. I have made my Flag Lt. in every case telephone before-hand and get it all taped off – when to arrive, where to arrive, who will meet me, etc. etc. . . . Although some places pretty well know the ropes, Mayors change, and sometimes Town Clerks. . . .'

East London, which had received honourable mention, had not slipped back, in spite of the fact that, since those 'unsophisticated' days, Mayors and Town Clerks had certainly changed many times, and, on the evening of our arrival the *Bermuda*'s officers were made welcome at a very pleasant reception in the City Hall. Among the guests of honour were our French friends, Admiral and Madame Auboyneau and members of the Admiral's personal staff.

At that time a group of French mannequins were touring South Africa to show what Paris could do with Union wool, and several of these gorgeous creatures, clad in Paris creations, happened to be in East London. So it was much to the point when Admiral Auboyneau, in an informal speech, made in perfect English, remarked upon the happy Franco-South-African combination of the beautiful women of France with the beautiful wool of the Union.

The hospitality of East London was as warm and all-embracing as the best Merino wool, and everybody did their best to make the *Bermuda*'s visit a success for the entire ship's company.

From my personal point of view I was touched to discover that my welcome was two-fold, as wife of the Commander-in-Chief and on my own account as a South African and a writer.

The women of East London love their city and they helped me to see it through their eyes. When I met their branch of the National Council of Women it was like being introduced to a social gathering of female Cabinet Ministers.

'This is Mrs. A in charge of Soil Conservation, and Mrs. B looks after Housing. Mrs. C takes care of Native Affairs, and Mrs. D does Arts, Crafts and Culture – oh, and you must meet Dr. E, who is our Health Representative, and Mrs. F, who is Religious Societies. . .'

Down by the seashore is the Marina Glen Tea-Garden run entirely by voluntary workers in aid of the South African Native Tuberculosis Association.

I said to an American woman whose husband had business interests in the port. 'This place is extraordinary. The women here talk about it as if it were their favourite child!'

She was young and cheerful, and she laughed.

'You're telling me! I'm fairly new here myself, but I soon learned to know the difference between an East Londoner and somebody from outside. The outsider says, "Do you think you'll like living in East London?" and the East Londoner says, "Nice to have you here, you'll love it." That's salesmanship!'

Between official occasions we found time to play golf on the beautiful championship course near the mouth of the Buffalo River, and one day I went into the country to tea with two elderly gentlemen, both crippled with arthritis, but more nimble with the aid of sticks than many of their contemporaries who allow their limbs to atrophy from lack of use.

One host had fetched me, and the other took me back.

But, just as we were about to leave, his companion waved his sticks wildly to stop us. With him was a very old, very black Native woman.

'This is the mother of the cook,' he explained, at the window of the car. 'She wants to sing to you.'

The cook's mother clasped a pair of gnarled and ancient hands on her withered bosom and lifted up her cracked tuneless voice in a traveller's blessing of intense feeling. The theme was 'God go with you', and each time she sang these words she focused her old blindish eyes upon me and leaned forward until the song became an incantation. At the final 'God go with you!' I found myself unexpectedly moved.

As we drove down the avenue of gums my old friend turned to me.

'We don't like these trees,' he said. 'We are going to have them down and plant new ones. That one there I planted on my eighty-fifth birthday – the only decent tree in the avenue.'

It did not disturb him that he was unlikely to see his tree grow to maturity. I thought for a moment of the tribesman who gives nothing save his spawn to posterity, of the first Dutch governors who had endowed the Cape with her glorious oaks, and of my hosts who would plant an avenue in the shade of which they would never walk, and it seemed to me that to do such a thing was to earn a moment's respite on that last long pilgrimage between death and eternity.

But my companion was concerned with more immediate matters.

'Look at that!' He pointed indignantly at the road-sign on the highway leading into East London. 'Voortrekker Road! Have you ever known anything so silly? Voortrekker Road here! Why not Pioneer Road? After all *we* conceded Roberts' Heights outside Pretoria, and let them call it Voortrekker Hoogte.'

He had come to South Africa more than half a century ago to fight the Boer War, and I fancied that he had never quite stopped fighting it.

Wherever they might be, from Port Elizabeth to Dakar in French Senegal, these visits, when the *Bermuda* 'showed the flag', were intensely strenuous. A great deal was compressed into a very short time. The port entertained the ship and the ship entertained the port. There was always a cocktail reception on board and the Commander-in-Chief gave luncheons or dinners on the quarterdeck. But the Royal Marines, and particularly the Band, were probably the busiest of all. They were the ship's showmen and we were very proud of them. When they Beat the Retreat at Port Elizabeth Agricultural Show, or anywhere else, for that matter, they evoked a strong nostalgic response. The past came flooding into the present and the time when the colonists had depended for their dubious safety upon the slender garrisons drew near once again. As the Band played 'Abide with me' and the Sunset bugle sounded while the flag was lowered, the spirit of that perilous period stirred in the hearts and minds of the descendants of pioneers and soldiers and sailors. Those had been the days of Empire when British colonial expansion was at its zenith – the days before the scene had begun to change its pattern.

In East London we bade good-bye to the *Bermuda* which continued up the coast to Durban, while we returned to the Cape by car. The Flag Lieutenant went with the ship to make some preliminary arrangements for the three weeks' visit we intended paying Durban in July.

CHAPTER SIX

PEOPLE AND CREATURES

ON our way back we broke our journey at Montague to spend the week-end with Mrs. Caesar Schlesinger.

'My mind feels like a suet pudding,' said Bertie. 'Too many people, not enough exercise, and no time at all for contemplation.'

Montague is a small white town among the Langeberg Mountains on the fringe of the Little Karroo. It is famous for its waters and its bracing air and Flo Schlesinger was well used to having tired friends to stay at her lovely home, *Qui Si Sana* (here is health). A number of her friends were in public life or in Parliament, for she was keenly interested in politics and her point of view was objective. One day you might find her lunching at the House of Assembly with a Nationalist Minister and his wife and the next with the Leader of the Opposition. Her remarkable blue eyes – so shrewd and so kind – missed very little of what was going on.

As she greeted us she said, 'I haven't arranged anything for you. I knew you'd both be dead. Put on anything you like for dinner, it would be absurd to dress up in the middle of the veld.'

We dined in a patio under a trellis of heavy purple grapes and clusters of golden-shower. The veld surged up to the stoep and there was starlight on the wild mountains. Once Flo had planted 3,000 fruit trees on the slope behind the house, but they had died of thirst. Now the hardy succulents took their place.

We talked of many things, particularly the need for better

understanding between the White people of our country, and after a time Flo said, 'It's getting late, you'll want to turn in. By the way, if you'd care to look in and see the Brett-Youngs tomorrow evening they'd be delighted.'

Francis Brett-Young, whose novels I greatly admired, had settled in Montague with his wife, Jessica. We had met them before and looked forward to seeing them again.

Next morning we wakened to the bright pure sunshine of the Karroo, and presently I went outside in my dressing-gown and sat on a little wooden seat under an old *ka-reeboom*.

I closed my eyes, utterly relaxed, and felt the sun hot on my lids.

The senses of feeling, smelling and hearing brought me the spirit of the Little Karroo – a land once drowned and now so sadly waterless beneath the brilliant sky. The aromatic tang of sun-warmed veld grass mingled with the light perfume of thorn-trees and wistaria. Innumerable birds called to one another, wings whirred and there was the intermittent *zoom* of some flying insect. A dry dusty breeze stirred my hair.

I opened my eyes to let sight play its part. The veld spread its pastel carpet of aloes and succulents to the feet of the Langebergen where the baboon and the dassie lived in fear of the leopard and the snake. On their peaks were massed the heavy rain-clouds that would presently shed their moisture west of the range. Speckled butterflies hovered and flitted, and, in the cracked red earth, the busy ants ran to and fro. An emerald lizard sunned himself on a stone and two wary little hunting-cats came round the side of the house – scarcely more than kittens, but the ginger had several rats to his credit and Blackie had killed a cobra. In the kitchen, across the clearing, I could hear the head boy, old Elias, talking in his deep bumbling voice. The smell of breakfast coffee and frying bacon called sharply.

About noon we went to the radio-active baths which are used by White and Brown alike, although each have their own open-air pool.

The brown-gold water was heavy and hot, and above its steamy surface towered a gaunt volcanic cliff. Palms, ferns and flowers blossomed in every crevice, aquiver with butterflies, tiny birds and scarlet skimming dragon-flies. As we swam or floated lazily our tautness and weariness melted away until our limbs and minds were drowsy, desirous only of sleep.

In the evening, greatly renewed, we drove over to Francis and Jessica Brett-Young's cottage, thatched smooth as velvet with Riversdale reeds, and set in a garden which is also a bird-sanctuary. Jessica met us, herself a bird-like being, small and light with a quick turn of the head, a sudden twitter of words and moments of perfect stillness.

Built on to the side of the house is the author's study.

'We bought this cottage, and we like it,' said Jessica. 'But it isn't *us*. This room, which we added, *is*.'

One wall of the studio was almost all window.

'Look!' she said. 'Did you ever see such a view? Those beautiful barbarous mountains, and, over there, our Epsteins.'

The 'Epsteins', on the far side of the little white town, were two long swelling hills cast in a monstrous mould, Nature had caused the massive recumbent thighs of Genesis to rest forever beside some mighty primeval lover.

'But Francis insists on a certain formality,' she added. 'So we have our rose-garden.'

And there it was, fragrant and enclosed. Francis, unlike Flo Schlesinger, refused to allow the veld to come rampaging to his threshold. He kept it at bay.

He was at that time working on a study of the land of his adoption, *In South Africa*, but the books for which he is best known in the Union are *They Seek a Country* and *City of Gold*, two important novels written several years ago with a fine understanding of the human factors leading up to the Great Trek and the Boer War, and a genuine appreciation of both Boer and Briton.

There is about his whole appearance – the tidiness of his dress, the well-kept hands and small clipped moustache – an air of orderly discipline, even a certain severity, and the room in which he worked, the room Jessica described as being characteristically 'us', shared this atmosphere of restraint. There was nothing in it to suggest the Bohemian, but every possession proclaimed the man of letters. The library on either side of the huge open fireplace was evidence of an erudite mind; the pictures were few – a John sketch, a Degas ballet dancer, and a green nostalgic impression of English trees. probably painted in his beloved Worcestershire. There was a large desk, and across one corner of the room, a grand piano. By profession he was a doctor before becoming a novelist, by inclination he is a historian and by instinct a poet. He still retains the air of making a diagnosis when he meets a stranger. As he showed me a few of his books and spoke of his pictures and picked up an antique Italian pottery cat that had once been somebody's hand-warmer, and then lightly touched the open keys of the piano, I was aware of a great cultural vacuum in his life. For South Africa, with all her natural enchantment, is unsophisticated where the Arts are concerned.

Of all his own books the one that satisfies him most is perhaps the least well-known. It is called *The Island* and was written during World War Two when the Island was threatened as never before. It is the story of England suggested in lyrical poetry – a work of great beauty conceived and created in love. His wife never moves without her copy. It is her Bible. It is dedicated to her.

For Jessica
1904–1944

Dearest, in all my life I have known but two
Unwavering loves; for England and for you:
What then more just than that this tribute paid
To one should at the other's feet be laid?

'This tribute' took all he had to give.

'It drained me – left me empty – even of the will to write.'

Absurdly I recalled the French Consul at Cape Town telling us one day that the 'apricot sickness' had emptied his whole system. 'Everything went out of my body with the sickness – even my brain.'

Jessica said: 'We have read your *Pack and Follow*. You'll never guess when we read it.' She always spoke thus, it was always 'we'. She did not wait for an answer. 'Between early tea and breakfast in the mornings. We enjoyed it. It has freshness and life.'

I said, feeling uncomfortable, as I always do when anyone mentions my books:

'If only I had used a big red pencil on half the adjectives and most of the sentiment!'

Brett-Young smiled.

'You *were* rather adjectival.'

'Perhaps experience helps. *Grey Mistress* was a slight improvement.'

'The short words are best,' he said. 'And the fewer used to express a thought, the better.'

His own is a rich vocabulary, he has only to choose the right word from the many and then allow his sense of rhythm to place it most effectively.

'One learns?' I asked.

'One learns,' he agreed. 'I look back on some of my early work with chagrin.'

'You!'

He laughed, and ceased altogether to seem severe. As we went into the garden before taking our leave the young moon swam above the tormented volcanic peaks, thin and adolescent, attended only by her solitary evening star. It was not yet dark.

Brett-Young said: 'She's the wrong way round in this hemisphere.'

'How is she different?' I asked. 'Which way is she in the Island?'

Amazed at such ignorance, he patiently explained.

'Here she is a D, and there a C – facing the opposite way.'

I sighed and laughed. 'So many years of moon-gazing and I didn't know that! Couldn't have been concentrating.'

The birds were quiet, except for a few sleepy *cheeps*. The water in the small bird-bath glimmered.

'Do you miss your English birds?' I asked.

'We have over a hundred and twenty different varieties in this garden,' he said. It was not an answer.

'But no song?'

His very spectacles flashed. 'Many of them have a lovely song! There is one that trills like an English thrush—' To remind him of the Island:

> '... whose mild air
> And gentle skies are sweetened everywhere
> With a winged music by day and night
> Instils an essence of supreme delight
> A secret rapture on the listening ear
> Where is no season of the changing year
> But hath its mead of song.'

Here among the mountains, with the 'Epsteins' gleaming like vast marble effigies on the fringe of the Karroo, where the rains stop dead on the Langebergen and the south-easter breathes its dying gasp, he finds perhaps frail echoes of the scents and sounds of England – roses blooming in the veld and the warbling of a bird that is not a thrush.

Soon after our return to Simon's Town my mother came to spend a few days with us at Admiralty House. One morning she found me in my suntrap with a heap of newspaper cuttings spread before me in great confusion.

'What are you trying to do?' she asked.

'Sort these out. They are oddments I've torn out of various papers about things and people and places that interest me. Some day I may want them for reference.'

'I could sort them for you,' she offered, 'cut them out properly and file them.'

That was the beginning of a home-made reference library

83

that has stood me in good stead. Mother classified the many cuttings that increased their scope steadily during the next two years. When they became out of hand I telephoned Tees Lodge.

'There's work here, Mum – mass of stuff I've collected in need of filing.'

Arend would drive her down, and presently the old lady would be settled in my sun-trap laboriously creating order out of chaos. Sometimes I heard her sigh or chuckle as she pored over my extracts, and after an hour or two she would stand up and brace her shoulders.

'There, that's the lot up to date! For instance, if you want snakes or snails you have only to look here in the MISCELLANEOUS file—'

The MISCELLANEOUS file was my favourite. It was full of enthralling information. Anyone 'wanting snakes' – with rattlers and the Port Elizabeth Snake Park in mind perhaps – could learn from it that:

'The deadly rattlesnakes, said to be more numerous in Oklahoma than in any other state of America, are snared with wire nooses on sticks or in fine mesh nets.

'The Okeene Chamber of Commerce buys them and resells them to zoos, laboratories and canners. After a hunt, the hunters hold a "snake talk" and banquet, with fried rattlesnake on the menu.'

Or one could discover a few side-lights on the life of a retired snake-boy like old Johannes.

'Johannes Molikoe, known throughout South Africa as the man who for 35 years casually dangled a terrifying collection of poisonous snakes round his neck at the Port Elizabeth Snake Park, has married again at the age of 74. Sana, his second wife, is 36. To eke out his pension of £5 a month he does odd jobs. He has been acting as police escort to juvenile delinquents on their way to reformatories, and he also takes charge of lepers who have been committed to a sanatorium in the Transkei.'

It would seem that snake-guarding, like life in the Navy, prepares a man for many strange undertakings.

As time went on I added more reference files to the fascinating MISCELLANEOUS. The Rhodesias, the Protectorates, the Congo, Nigeria and West Africa and a number of others came into existence as our travels took us further afield and my horizons widened. The one I liked least was labelled PURELY POLITICAL and contained what I believed to be more significant pronouncements of politicians on the problems of Africa. Those whose alleged opinions it held were of different nationalities and varying shades of physical and ideological complexion, but after a while I decided that the adverb 'purely' was ill-chosen, and we altered it to 'exclusively'. In any case much of the material this file contained left me exasperated, so that I said to my mother tartly, 'If I want snakes I'll look for them in the POLITICAL folder.'

The sliding windows were wide open, and down in the sunk-garden we could see Veronica working among the dahlias and putting down snail-bait, for snails were Enemy Number One in the sea-garden that year. In fact, MISCELLANEOUS informed us that snails were 'the world's most adaptable colonizers', and that some species had over 80,000 teeth with which to destroy vegetable matter, and that the slime of the snail sullied vast acres of sweet grazing for cattle every year.

'Listen, Mum,' I said. 'This is what Ernest Middlemiss writes about snails. Do you wonder Veronica has her work cut out to keep them down?'

'The world's most spectacular molluscan feats have been achieved by the large African species ACHATINA FULICA. Between 1930 and 1950 it travelled half the circumference of the world. Summarized, its travels were as follows. From Africa it reached Madagascar . . . in 1819 it was in both Mauritius and Réunion. Then it progressed: Calcutta 1847, Ceylon 1900, Straits Settlements 1927, Malaya 1928, Singapore 1930, South China 1931,

Hawaiian Islands 1938, Guam 1945, and California 1947. . . .'

Selfishly I reflected that ACHATINA FULICA and I had reached South China at the same time, and that Achatina's impact had been vastly more impressive than mine.

Suddenly Mother said: 'What's happened to Veronica?'

The tall girl in blue jeans and yellow shirt had leapt sky-high as if Achatina had sunk all those eighty thousand teeth into her ungloved hand. She uttered a strangled cry.

'What's up?' I called down, leaning far over the sill.

She collected herself with a gasp, looked up and even managed to laugh.

'Nothing really – just a thin green snake! It's the sort that eats snails, but I happen to be allergic to snakes of any kind.'

'I don't wonder,' said Mother. 'I had no idea there were snail-eating snakes.'

'Yes,' said Veronica, her calm self once more. 'It's a useful one. We must leave it in peace.'

And so we learned that snakes, like most of us, may be good as well as bad, and have their uses – as, no doubt, have politicians.

At the end of March, Helen Keller, the deaf-blind writer, lecturer and philosopher, visited South Africa.

Born in America in 1880, Helen Keller lost sight and hearing through illness at eighteen months old. A wonderful teacher, Anne Mansfield Sullivan, taught the brilliant tempestuous child the manual language of the deaf by spelling words into her palm. But that was not enough. Helen learned to articulate and even to speak and write French as well as English. She was a world prodigy, an example of perseverance and courage harnessed to a shining intellect. Nothing daunted her. In 1913 she made her first public appearance and so launched her life-long campaign to help others afflicted like herself.

To the deaf and blind of Cape Town her arrival was as the coming of a Messiah.

The night she addressed the packed City Hall is one I shall never forget. The blind and deaf, White or Coloured, occupied the seats of honour, and those dedicated to their service were beside her on the stage. Her address was supported by a programme of music, and both singer and organist were blind.

Helen, in white chiffon, and her splendid companion, Polly Thompson, in scarlet, stood side by side when the moment came for Helen to speak.

An old Senator, sitting beside me, murmured in a wondering voice, 'But, how strange! There is something *childlike* about her!'

Childlike, in its purest sense. Although over seventy, she radiated innocence and an incredible infectious joyousness. She had never seen herself in a mirror and she could not know how charming was the upward toss of her head when she expressed pleasure.

Her voice is mechanical and not easy to understand, so her words were repeated by her friend and transmitter of over thirty years. Polly's own voice was rich and warm, and, as she spoke, she spelt with tapping fingers into the small sensitive hand that lay relaxed in hers.

'Tell us, Helen, why are you so happy tonight?'

Helen's face lit up and a vibration ran visibly through her frame, as if, at Polly's touch, some mental sentry standing at ease within her had sprung to attention.

'I am happy because Cape Town has been so kind to me.'

She told of her visit to the School for the Deaf and the Blind in the beautiful fruit-growing valley of Worcester, and made us believe that she had *seen* the magnificent scenery. Perhaps, indeed, she had through Polly's eyes and fingers. But I wondered what image she held in her mind? It was clear that her imagination was a colourful realm, but what pictures, undreamed of in our sight, would appear if a magic beam could show us the hidden galleries wherein she walked so gaily.

Her choice of words was literary rather than conversational – an echo of the classics she loved to read, and of the Bible which she said 'runs like a great river of light through my life'.

She implored our help for the deaf and the blind. Not charity, but the practical assistance that would find them employment and the chance to work in the company of their more fortunate fellow men and women.

The worst cruelty for the disabled, she said, was the inability to work.

'They *can* do useful and excellent work, and they want to – in factories, in offices, in gardens or on farms. There is a place for them in the working life of the community. Help them – help them, my friends – to find it!'

On the stage, two interpreters, one English and one Afrikaans, were passing her message to the unhearing by the language of the hands. Like tick-tack men, I thought. But my throat was tight as I remembered the two little deaf sons of a young friend of mine, and her urgent voice and shining tear-filled eyes as she said to me: 'They mustn't grow up cut off from other children; they must take their place in normal life – not be isolated.' I remembered their physical perfection, their capacity for enjoyment, their tantrums and frustrations, and the astonishing powers of concentration in these little ones so heavily handicapped.

Next afternoon I met Helen Keller personally at a farewell reception given for her by the Administrator of the Cape Province at his historic gabled house, Leeuwenhof on the slopes of Table Mountain.

She was sitting between her hostess and Polly Thompson in the corner of the large *voorkamer*. The soft afternoon light from the long French doors slanted on to her white dress and across her face which at close quarters possessed a spiritual beauty.

There were only a few people in the room when I arrived, and Polly and Helen seemed to be sharing some small unspoken joke; every now and again Helen lifted a bouquet of flowers to her face to touch and smell them rapturously. As we were introduced Polly spelt my name into her hand.

Helen Keller looked up at me with clear sea-green eyes, and the look was sad, for, unlike the mobile lips, the lovely blind eyes had not learned to smile.

'I am sorry we could not come to see you,' she said. 'There was not time. There is so little time – never enough.'

As Polly began to repeat the words, I said, 'It's all right. I understand perfectly.'

Helen's hand, with a swift gesture, flew to the side of my mouth and with her feather-light touch, she read my lips.

'I had a great friend who became deaf at the age of two. She was taught as you have been taught.'

'The deaf must be taught young,' she answered. 'It is very important.'

Presently the Administrator made a little speech wishing her well in her valiant efforts, and Helen replied. The tick-tack men reported faithfully. After that sherry was offered, and everybody talked at once. Hands spoke and the watchful eyes of the deaf responded with pleasure or amusement, and here and there a man or a woman with dark glasses kept a light hand on a friendly guiding arm. I listened to snatches of conversation. How unlike the ordinary tattle of a cock-tail-party!

Of course Helen and her achievements were the central theme, the wonderful hope-giving inspiration in our midst.

'Isn't she amazing! She can hear music—'

'—or applause – it's vibration—'

'—can feel density, a crowd—'

'She says white horses feel cooler than black horses!'

'And her humour – knows when she's feeling blue!'

'—work, we must give them work, she's so right. In our firm we have a deaf typist who is first rate.'

'concentration—'

'—and observation. When you can't hear you have to—'

'But it's no good saying that the loss of two vital faculties can be compensated by the development of others. If she's

89

wonderful with neither sight nor hearing what would she have been with those as well?'

There was Helen's aura of warmth and goodwill everywhere. It pervaded the room and all those in it.

'As I bade her good-bye Polly again began to spell my name into her palm, but Helen closed her fingers sharply over those of her companion. It was her way of interrupting.

'I know,' she said quickly. 'It's Lady Packer from Admiralty House.'

For an instant I sensed the bright hasty mind caged in unwilling helplessness, craving freedom. That small gesture had cried aloud, *'Leave me every particle of independence you can!'*

Impulsively I took her hand and put it to my lips.

She gave a start of pleasure and that delightful toss of her head. Her blind sea-green eyes looked into mine, clear as jewels and infinitely sad while the lips smiled happily.

The room was growing dark. Someone turned up the lights. Someone else said, 'Ah, that's better!'

But, for Helen, it was all one. The silence and the dark remained unchanged.

During the summer life at Simon's Town was full of fun and variety, and the navy and country formed fast friendships. Nothing pleased the naval people more than a day or a week-end on a fruit farm and the farmers were always delighted to come to the sea. In the tennis and cricket season matches between Simon's Town and the *platteland* formed a splendid excuse for an outing. The teams bundled joyously into their motor-cars with their wives, children, or sweethearts and drove to the lovely fruit-growing valleys inland or down to the sea as the case might be, and a good time was had by all. But in autumn the tempo slowed down. April brought the first rains, the fishing-boats tossed among the white-caps in the bay, and a fine day was all the more perfect when it came.

It was on such a day that we went to Seal Island with Piet,

Glen, Tony, and my brother, Fred, and his son David, who was on Easter vacation from the Witwatersrand University. We went in the Commander-in-Chief's barge with Corney in charge of the boat's crew and his little son, Melvin, beside him at the wheel.

'This is grand,' said Piet. 'It would have taken us twice as long in the old *Nausea!*'

We all trailed fishing lines over the side, but with no great hopes of a catch, for seal-waters are a poor field for human fishers.

'The awful thing is to get a seal on your line,' said Glen. 'They cry like babies, tears and all.'

There was a light south-easter blowing and the sea was br ght and choppy. Gulls and shags rode the swell or dived for fish, swift, vertical and ruthless. After about an hour we saw the abandoned radar-masts of the small island which was used as a radar station during the war, but which is normally inhabited only by seals and sea-birds. Then the first penguins slid past us on the water, and a school of leaping porpoises crossed our bows, landing sometimes with a loud belly-flop to rid themselves of sea-lice. Through Bertie's glasses we could see the colony on the rocks – innumerable birds, and seals of every shape and size basking on the rocks, like humans sunbathing on Muizenberg beach, or plunging into a vortex of mad activity in the surf.

Someone said, 'Christmas! what a smell!'

Fred laughed. 'Your sense of smell tires quickly.'

'Let's hope so!'

The stench of seals and bird-guano was sickening, and Bertie told Corney to keep the barge to windward. Then the sound caught up with the smell, beating upon our ears in great waves. It was like the lowing of mighty herds of cattle and the baaing of flocks of sheep. Big fellows bellowed as loudly as angry bulls, others yodelled, and the little ones wailed in the quavering voices of lambs and young infants.

It was soon evident that we had struck the mating season, for the breakers round the island were alive with thousands of amorous seals and it was literally impossible to make head or tail of them. One moment a smooth round head rose high into the air and the next half a dozen neighbours appeared to be bottoms up. Every now and again a ponderous old man slithered down from his sunny ledge of rock and plunged into the maelstrom.

'Their theme-song reminds me of Port Elizabeth Show,' I said. 'All that mooing and maaing.'

'Yes,' agreed Bertie. 'But I don't need to make a speech.'

'Think of all the fish this colony eat!' I said. 'No wonder Dr. Bruun advised us to do away with our seals and duikers.'

'True enough,' said Piet. 'Let's move on. We haven't a chance of a bite round here.'

As we left the island we passed a lonely seal swimming in the direction of Simon's Town. Little Melvin Corney called excitedly:

'That's Sally! I'm *sure* that's Sally going back to the ships!'

And probably he was right. For Sally-the-Seal never deserted the Navy for long. And the children, as well as the sailors, loved Sally.

A few days later we were honoured by a short visit from the Earl and Countess of Athlone.

This was a great pleasure to us as many of our happiest memories were bound up with the days when the Earl was Governor-General of the Union – surely the best-loved Governor-General South Africa has ever had.

Although he had been very ill he was as straight and handsome as ever, and when this brother of Queen Mary inspected the ships' companies of the South Atlantic Squadron at Simon's Town it was a proud day for them. Pretty witty Princess Alice had, in some magical way, snapped her delicate fingers at time and her vitality was inexhaustible.

'How nice to be here,' she said, as she entered the big inner hall. 'All just as it used to be, except that your covers are more attractive. They used to be white piped with navy blue in the old days – too masculine.'

Her observant glance came to rest on the enlarged photographs of the King and Queen on either side of the big wall mirror.

'Oh, dear, you can't have that! The King and Queen mustn't face away from each other. So unsociable.'

In a few minutes the Chief Joiner had brought his ladder and changed the pictures round. And it seemed as if the likenesses smiled their appreciation and the lofty hall was all the brighter. On the way upstairs the Earl and Countess recognized many old friends among the gallery of past Commanders-in-Chief, and we could see that they were glad to be with the Navy again.

In the mornings Princess Alice often sat in the garden and worked at a petit-point chair cover she was making for her daughter, or she might suddenly spring to her feet and help de-snail the dahlias.

'I can't bear stamping on snails,' she'd say. 'Disgustingly messy! They must go into the road.'

So Achatina Fulica soared from her dainty hand over the high wall, and what fate met her there we neither knew nor cared. She probably hitched a ride to the *platteland* to besmirch the pastures with her bitter slime or clog the wheels of tractors with her endless progeny.

From us the Earl and Countess went to Groote Schuur to stay with the Prime Minister and Mrs. Malan, and Princess Alice discovered in Dr. Malan a lively sense of humour. But then who could fail to respond to the mischievous wit of this royal and gifted lady whose charm, allied with her husband's experience and kindliness, had captivated two great dominions in turn – the Union of South Africa and Canada.

The showers of April gave way to the soaking rains of May, the vineyards turned amber and ruby, and the north-west wind tore the withered leaves from the trees. The pink oleanders and flowering gums in the kloof-garden shed their opulent blossoms and the reprieved pepper-tree scattered its opaque berries on the new sidewalk. Although Bertie's carnations still bloomed, flowers were few, and Veronica eked out her arrangements in the house with original substitutes. Globe-artichoke flowers, like gigantic purple thistles, and even lettuces gone to seed and resembling oriental pagodas, came into the tall rooms and were as gracefully accepted as the pictures by modern South African artists which we had borrowed from Charles te Water to adorn our bare walls.

Many personalities had imprinted themselves upon Admiralty House during the past century and a half, and it had grown tolerant. It was sure of itself, of its beautifully proportioned rooms and fair setting. Admirals and their families might come and go, leaving a date carved here or there to mark some innovation in their time, but the really important things remained the same. There were always doves in the trees, and the tides still washed mother-of-pearl venus-ears on to the little beach; there were warships in the bay, and, up in the kloof-garden slept Midshipman Percival George Duddy.

Fires burned in the hearths now, and the children of the Admiralty Compound played more on the grass and less on the sands. The shark-net had been removed for the winter and Bertie no longer took his early morning swim. The tennis and cricket season was over, and our girl-proof Flag Lieutenant went his way rejoicing in his immunity and playing rough games like rugger and hockey in his spare time, and sometimes golf with his Admiral. Our naval and dockyard community behaved in its usual mutable way and those we had come to know sailed for home and others arrived in their place.

'You people are heart-breaking,' moaned the Magistrate's wife. 'We no sooner get to know you than off you go and we have to start all over again.'

In our Admiralty Compound there were changes and new faces.

The games-playing Staff Officer Operations and his cheerful family had left, and in their stead we had Commander

Peter Norton and his South African ballet-dancer wife, professionally known as Olive Deacon.

'Peter is an artist,' said Kathie Sherwin, who gave me the news. 'And Olive was a solo dancer in the Sadler's Wells Company and the Russian Monte Carlo Ballet! Come and see the Barrows' new baby.'

We strolled across from the Secretary's Cottage to Bush Cottage, the house of the Signal Officer, where a fine new infant lay in his pram on the stoep, a source of interest to his brother aged three.

The other dwelling in the Compound was Veronica's two-roomed hut on the waterfront. It had been a signal office during the war and still bore the forbidding notice 'NO ADMITTANCE' over the door. But Veronica's regular visitors could not read words of more than three letters and were immune to hints, so there were always Sherwin, Norton or Barrow children swarming in and out of her abode to see how she and the pets were getting on.

Up at Belmont House the two daughters of the Captain-in-Charge of the Dockyard had recently arrived from England – Susan, a slim young hospital nurse, and Carol who went daily to Cape Town to learn typing and shorthand and other mysteries at the Technical College. As they usually had girl-friends to stay with them Captain Selby attended church on Sundays with quite a harem.

It was after church that we met the newcomers and heard the gossip, standing outside the old Sail Loft between the Simon's Berg and the sea. Then we strolled back to Admiralty House, which we now thought of as 'home', and there we found Piet and Glen and Ronnie and the three dogs. Our life was begining to settle into a pattern.

But it was an interrupted pattern, for the winter at the Cape was the time for H.M.S. *Bermuda*'s long cruises and for many of our journeys.

In June we flew to the Congo and I had my first experience of Black Africa.

CHAPTER SEVEN

EQUATORIAL AFRICA – LEOPOLDVILLE

My husband was to spend the King's official birthday in the capitals of the Belgian and French Congo* respectively, and this had been easily arranged, since Leopoldville and Brazzaville stare enigmatically at one another across the broad expanse of Stanley Pool, where the great Congo River widens into a lake before narrowing again into the wild fury of over two hundred miles of impassable rapids. It is only a matter of a short crossing by launch to go from one town to the other.

Our plane landed at Mayo-Mayo airport outside Brazzaville at nine in the morning. Overnight we had said good-bye to the stormy snow-capped Cape mountains and the icy sparkle of the high veld, we had crossed over the granite land of Rhodesia and the arid plain of Portuguese Angola in the pink haze of dawn, and we had come down to the lush tropical bush of Equatorial Africa – *l'Afrique Noire*, where there is neither summer nor winter but only the hot season and the cool season, the wet season and the dry season. The rains were over and this we gathered, was the cool dry season, yet my husband and the Flag Lieutenant were wearing their tropical whites, and my thin navy-blue travelling dress clung to me in the steamy heat. A low oppressive blanket of grey cloud obscured the sun.

The Governor of the Belgian Congo had sent his Dove aircraft to meet us, and, as we flew across the Congo River to Leopoldville – known to its intimates as Leo – the pilot swooped in a deep curve over the Rapids. They looked like

* Now independent states of Zaire and Congo-Brazza.

beaten silver as they raged round a tropical islet inhabited only by monkeys. Between Leo and the river port of Matadi the navigable Congo is transformed into 200 miles of leaping death to man or vessel. After Matadi it widens once more into a great waterway flowing clear to the Atlantic.

Our host during the next few days was the British Consul-General, Mr. Wikeley, who, for all his diplomatic *savoir-faire*, was, by disposition, something of a recluse.

His Consulate, on the shores of Stanley Pool, was lofty and spacious and designed to allow through-draughts as well as fans to cool the air. In the lounge were vases of frail mauve and chartreuse orchids, poised against the pastel walls more in the manner of butterflies than of flowers. He had gathered them in the marshes and arranged them himself, for Mr. Wikeley was a naturalist and his was a bachelor household.

While Bertie paid his official call on the Governor, I rested after the night journey, lying relaxed on my bed and emptying my mind in readiness to receive new impressions — always an agreeable and exciting process to me.

Presently Antoine, the little Head Boy, came into my room, his footfall soft and animal on the stone floor. He had the wrinkled brown face of an old intelligent Simian, and he asked me in slurred broken French whether I had any pressing to be done. Before he took my dresses he closed the shutters, explaining that the glare from the Pool would make the room too hot, for the sun had broken through the grey morning cloud and the wide lake was a sheet of burning tin-foil. In the palms and frangipani trees outside the windows little orange-breasted birds with red beaks and long forked tails flitted to and fro.

Antoine said, 'Is there anything else Madame would like?' and, hearing that there was nothing, padded away as quietly as he had come.

He worked for the Consul-General from early morn until such time as he was required, and then he returned to the African town and his wife and family. If duty kept him after nine at night he must show a pass from his master. The

African town is entirely segregated from White Leo after 9 p.m. No European may enter it, no African may leave it.

Apartheid? The pass-system? Yes. But so far Belgium has been able to conduct her African affairs without the hue and cry of dark-skinned Uno at her heels.

The Congo is Belgium's treasure trove. Its raw materials are legion, and include vegetable oils and fibres, coffee, timber, diamonds, tin, copper, cobalt and now uranium. And of course one can add those ancient symbols of Africa – 'gold, and silver, ivory and apes, and peacocks', and 'great plenty of almug trees and precious stones . . .', for this vast territory lies at the very heart of the Dark Continent – the heart that beats with the rhythm of the jungle drum – where the Native still uses 'almug' (ebony) and ivory as the two main mediums of his carver's art.

Yet, in spite of the heat, the heavy fragrance of frangipani, the tattoo of distant drums and the perpetual roar of the Rapids, Leo maintains an atmosphere of solid calculating good sense. The city is the administrative capital of Belgium's prosperous and remarkable equatorial welfare state, and her White business men are as hard-headed and hard working, even in the Tropics, as any 'Birmingham boy' determined to make his fortune by sheer thrift and application well-spiced with initiative.

Leopoldville and Stanley Pool. In the reason for those place names lies the human interest in the story of Congo development.

Leopold II, King of the Belgians, and Henry Morton Stanley, adventurer, journalist and explorer, were the two men whose vision and achievement last century led directly to the present source of Belgium's greatest wealth.

How different they were – Leopold, avaricious and far seeing, and Stanley, the Welsh-born American-naturalized explorer, whose life was one of the most dramatic and physically courageous in the world! Both men took tremendous risks – Leopold with his money, and Stanley with his life.

When, in 1871, the *New York Herald* sent Stanley to seek the missing Scottish missionary, David Livingstone, among the Great Lakes of Central Africa, that newspaper unwittingly put him on the way to the all-important discovery of the elaborate system of navigable waterways that was to prove the solution to the terrible problem of jungle transport.

It is well known that Stanley tried and failed to interest Britain and America in his discoveries, and that their indifference drove him into the arms of Leopold. The King of Belgium financed Stanley's next two epic expeditions, with far-reaching results. And in 1885 the Congo Free State was established under the Sovereignty of Leopold II of Belgium. Thirteen years later a most remarkable feat of engineering created the railway from Leopoldville to Matadi, thus by-passing the 200 mile long Rapids of the great Congo River and linking its upper and lower reaches and the interior of Central Africa with the Atlantic coast.

As was so often the case in the 'Scramble for Africa' at the end of the nineteenth century, private enterprise had carved out the way for a nation's gain. Today the old – and once notorious – Congo Free State is a Belgian colony, the envy of Europe and the United States.

Towards evening Mr. Wikeley took us for a drive through the splendid city of Leo to the site high above the Pool where a new monument to Stanley was soon to be placed among lawns and gardens. From there his statue will look across the river he charted to the French towns of Brazzaville, where de Brazza, the bearded French explorer, staked his country's claim and put a stop to Belgian expansion.

In a little unkempt cemetery nearby we strolled among the graves of yesterday's pioneers. In comparison with the older history of South Africa this all seemed very near and new – a tale of the turn of the century – and yet already so much had been achieved.

As we drove on, the high grasses and trees at the side of the earth road hid our view of the river, but we could hear the thunder of the cataract.

Mr. Wikeley said: 'Last time I came this way I ran over a crocodile. The river was high after the rains and crocs and pythons were all over the place.'

'What happened to the croc – and you?'

'We both had a bad fright. This is where we stop. From here you'll see the Rapids rather well.'

Our host had a sense of the theatre and of timing. He turned his car into the grounds of a tall lonely tower-house as weird as any haunted dwelling in a Disney film. We expected to see bats and ghosts fly out of the windows, as no doubt they often did. The wooden doors and balconies were decorated with native carvings, the story of Eden seen through primitive eyes.

'Adam and Eve are Congolese,' pointed out Mr. Wikeley. 'And you must admit the serpent is a real beauty!'

We wandered through a wilderness garden, where we paused to look down a sheer escarpment of semi-jungle to the great river. On either side of Monkey Island, inaccessible to human beings, except by helicopter, surged the monster mill-race of the Rapids, a thunderous split channel of molten metal reflecting, shattering and scattering the blazing glory of the sunset. Westward, on the far bank, flamed the windows of Brazzaville.

An English voice said behind us: 'So Mr. Wikeley has brought you sight-seeing. We really do get the best view from here.'

The Consul-General introduced us to Mrs. le Jeune, the English wife of a Belgian business man. She took us to a tree-shaded courtyard and offered us an *apéritif*. As dusk fell the glow-worms lit and extinguished their tinker-bell candles all about us and the frogs and cicadas tuned into their metallic symphony. The air was soft and fresh as it can only be during the cool season.

'This is a most beautiful place,' I said to Mrs. le Jeune. 'But could you make it your *permanent* home?'

She shook her head. 'One might live on the shores of Lake Kivu, where it is high and healthy, but here one could not bring up children without taking them home constantly.

This climate is not suitable for Europeans, except in small doses.'

There it was – the difference between White Africa and Black Africa, between the healthy colony of settlement and the tropical colony of exploitation.

Black Africa is fundamentally a Black man's country. Climatically it suits him and it does not suit the European. The White man goes there to develop or administer the territory, to make money out of it or organize it in such a way that other White men may extract its wealth. Then he goes home to settle down and live happily ever after on his fortune or his pension.

White Africa is every bit as much a White man's country as a Black man's. The European goes there to settle and build a future for his descendants. He puts in as much as he takes out, he loves the country and calls it 'home'. The Congo was Black Africa, the Union very definitely White. After a while we spoke of Dr. Malan's violent reaction to the experiment of responsible government in the Gold Coast.

'The fear of African emancipation is very understandable in the Union,' said Mr. Wikeley reasonably. 'The South Africans can't afford to educate their Natives politically. After all, if the English in West Africa don't like the Gold Coast under self-government, they can clear out and go home. They'll do that anyway, sooner or later. But, if the South Africans lose their country to the Natives, they've nowhere to go. For them South Africa is all they have. It *is* home.'

'What is the attitude here?' I asked.

'Neither as reactionary as in South Africa, nor as liberal as the English colonial policy,' I was told. 'The Belgians make no pretence at educating their Natives towards self-government. This is a benevolently administered colony.'

Theoretically there is no Colour Bar in the Belgian Congo, but, in fact, there is a strong distinction between the laws that govern White and Black behaviour. In general the Natives are still very rightly regarded and treated as children, but, as they become better educated, no economic restrictions are put in the way of their advancement. For there is no need to protect White labour against Black competition. For instance, in a town like Leo, with a White population of about 10,000 and over 200,000 registered Blacks, and many more coming in daily, there is manual and clerical work for all who care to apply. The programme is one of swift expansion and there is no unemployment.

Education, which is mostly in the hands of Christian Missions, is given to the Natives on a strictly practical basis and in digestible measure. There is no question of the franchise for Black or White, and no necessity for it. There is little idealism and much realism. The Congo is under-populated, and if big business is to keep abreast of its labour requirements it must increase the birthrate and improve the health of the Congolese, and if, in consequence, the people are healthy and contented they will not clamour for political rights. It is still as simple as all that – or so the Administration believes.

We dined that night at the Zoo Restaurant with Mr. Wikeley.

An exquisite dinner was served to us out of doors on the terrace. Our host, who had spent much of his time in the Middle East, was an accomplished raconteur. He was also experienced in the ordering of a delicious meal. It is a feature of White life in the Congo that almost everything is imported – fish, meat, vegetables and salad. And, naturally, wine. The Congo is so rich that she can afford anything she wants from blue trout, flown from Europe for her restaurants, to the most expensive American X-ray machine in the world for her Native Hospital.

In the dark, outside the garland of lights, we could hear the grunting and coughing of the animals – two restless young lions, an elephant blowing sand over himself with his mobile trunk, prowling jackals, little blue-faced monkeys, and Marcel, the murderous chimpanzee who had killed three of his wives and bitten off the finger of a young lady who had attempted to caress him through the bars of his

cage. We could hear too the strange bestial sounds made by
the dumb Congolese keeper who could persuade his lions to
purr like kittens and pass a lighted cigarette from his own
thick lips to those of wicked Marcel. The Zoo was really
only a transit-camp for animals on their way to Europe or
America. Sometimes rare okapi came in for a week or two,
or precious baby gorillas.

The Congolese waiters had astonishingly pink palms and
rosy nails. Their hands, when they were not occupied, hung
limply at their sides like the hands of Marcel when he was
not engaged in strangling a wife.

When we got back to the Consulate we found the stoep
alive with crawling and winged creatures. Geckos and little
toads were busy among them.

'Last time I brought guests home, we met a snake writhing on these steps,' said Mr. Wikeley. The light attracts the
insects, the insects attract lizards and frogs, and the lizards
and frogs attract snakes. The larger devours the lesser.'

A mammoth shin-bone lay on the balustrade, bleached
white by time and starlight.

'Who ever had a bone like that?' I asked.

'A hippopotamus,' he said. 'That shin-bone belonged to
my sister's dog. He was very fond of burying it and digging
it up again, but when she went back to England she hadn't
room to pack it. You can have it if you like.'

I didn't like. But afterwards I was sorry. It was the sort of
bone Veronica would have loved for her 'props cupboard',
and she might have enjoyed using it as the foundation for a
really formidable flower arrangement.

In the mango tree outside our bedroom window fruit-bats
as big as owls kept up a queer sucking noise all night, and
there were some weird sounds overhead.

'Odd things live in one's roof,' explained Mr. Wikeley
next day. 'There was a twenty-foot python made his home
up there some while ago, but we killed him. I shouldn't
worry, if I were you.'

In the morning the Mayor of Leopoldville showed us

some of the social services for which the Belgian Congo is so justly famed.

A considerable proportion of the Colony's immense profits is ploughed back into the country in Native housing and welfare. For example, no Company is granted a monopoly unless it guarantees to look after its Black employees and house them adequately. Every big business concern has its own compounds, villages, hospitals, schools and recreation grounds and swimming-pools. And the conditions under which the Europeans live would cause any British Government Officer from the West Coast to burst into tears of sheer envy.

But Leo's real pride was its enormous Native Hospital fitted with every modern device known to medical science.

The patients are cared for by European doctors and Sisters of Mercy helped by Native assistant-doctors and nurses trained in the Medical College.

In this College we met the young girls studying nursing, and saw a Congolese medical student strip down a mechanical human model imported from America as if it were an automobile engine.

'They are good mechanically,' said the European Professor. 'If they can see and touch what they are working with it is all right. It is the craftsman's mentality. But although they have much superstition they have little imagination. So our teaching is kept as practical as possible.'

In the course of our future travels I was to see many African hospitals and learn some strange and astonishing facts in the process, but Leo Native Hospital was the first place of its sort I had visited. The Medical Officer in Charge showed us round with great thoroughness, and by the time my feet were falling off and I was melting away in the tropical heat he was not even beginning to wilt. The nuns in charge of the wards had this same cool unruffled demeanour, everything was under perfect control.

The different wings of this huge single-storied building jutted like so many piers into a sea of grass and trees, and in these green leafy compounds were encamped whole families

– men in singlets and striped cotton pants, women in gaily-printed Manchester cottons and children in nothing at all. Some slept in the shade, others cooked or laundered, and everyone seemed quite at home.

'There can't be much wrong with them,' I said.

'There isn't,' said the doctor. 'But in Africa if one member of the family goes to hospital his relatives go too.'

'To see fair play?'

'Pardon?' said the grave young man, and added, 'we cannot send them away, and in some ways they even have their uses. In any case, you will see how well our patients are disciplined.'

As we passed upon our tour of inspection every individual able to scramble to his or her feet did so with a polite *'Bon jour'*. Only those incapable of thought or speech failed to greet us.

In the maternity ward we found the Black mothers squatting beside their beds on tiny low wooden stools, their babies on their laps. One had twin girls.

'Do they like girl or boy babies best?'

'Girls,' answered the nun in charge of the ward. 'They receive a bride-price for their daughters. Sons are merely an expense.'

The doctor touched the small woolly heads of the twins. 'In some villages twins are considered proof that the mother has been unfaithful, and they may be put to death.'

'Not these,' smiled the nun. 'This is a Christian family.'

'In 1925 four babies were born in this hospital,' said the doctor. 'In 1950, 5,500! They have confidence in us now, and, by building up confidence, one develops sympathy between Black and White.'

Sympathy, yes. Equality, no. If ever there was a working example of General Smuts's ideal of White 'trusteeship' for the Black, it was here in the Belgian Congo.

The Hospital was spotlessly clean. Kitchens gleamed as brilliantly as operating theatres. Several of the theatres were in use, and we saw operations performed under local anaesthetics. The idea of being put into the 'deep sleep' of Adam

105

does not appeal to primitive people, for who knows what devil might not take possession of the body in the absence of a spirit which cannot even be recalled by pain. They can endure pain. And they like their medicine nasty. But then most of them have been brought up to accept the initiation rites and abominable concoctions of Native witch-doctors.

The Mayor then took us to the Institute of Domestic Science, where the women are taught elementary hygiene and nutrition. Only their own native foods were being cooked in the wood-burning ovens – manioc, rice, bananas, river-fish and meat fried in palm-oil. Laundering was done in big troughs such as those used in the villages where all water is communal. A young Belgian welfare worker taught expectant mothers to sew and knit for their infants and themselves. They sat on smooth little benches in giggling groups, chattering in the *Lingala*, which is the Congolese Esperanto, as *Fanakola* is the universal language of the mines throughout Southern Africa. Their babies slept in raffia baskets at their feet and the older children played near at hand.

The women obviously enjoyed their lessons and their work, and it was plain that they had also been well schooled in polite and respectful behaviour.

The lasting impression that has remained in my mind is of the clear-cut relationship between Black and White as I saw it in Leo. There was nothing confused about it. The Blacks were carefully and kindly disciplined by their White superiors, and, like children in a well-run school, they were content.

'It interested me to hear that the Administrator of the Cape and various members of the Union Government had visited and studied the administration of the Belgian Congo.

'We will now drive through the old Native Town,' said the Mayor. 'And then you shall see the new one in process of being built.'

In the Old Town among the cassias and flamboyants, the

sewing machines of the Native tailors hummed under open palm-shelters, fashioning bright cottons into gowns for the majestic Black women who strolled home from the market in the shimmering heat. Babies were slung on their backs, and on their heads they carried large enamel basins filled with such delicacies as smoked caterpillars, dried fish like old shoe-soles, dried hippo, elephant or buffalo meat, and palm-oil or palm-wine in Coca-Cola bottles.

'Spirits they dare not buy,' said the Mayor. 'Hard liquor is ruin to Natives – even more than to Whites. We allow them beer.'

He showed us the new Native town, superbly sited above the river with an immense stadium and swimming-bath as its core.

'You can tell an *evolué*'s house by the windows,' he said. 'Windows are a sign of enlightenment. The jungle Native prefers his dark hut.'

Exactly what is an *evolué*?'

'A Native of some education – a clerk or an office worker. He may earn as much as £40 a month by your standards, and he feels contempt for the manual labourers. But the women are still very backward and when he seeks a wife on his own mental level he cannot find one.'

'Why do you do all this for your Natives? It is incredible!'

'We need healthy happy labour. This way we get it.'

The Belgian Congo can afford its social services. They are largely financed by the powerful commercial firms which draw their wealth from this great territory. Its vast resources are still untapped, and labour is needed to tap them. It is today the world's example of a model Central African Dependency. Yet it is chastening to remember that not so long ago the Dutch East Indies were the 'model colonies' of the Far East – the source of Holland's prosperity. Change is life's only unchanging law.

On the following day the Governor, Mr. Eugène Jungers, gave a large luncheon for us.

Mr. Jungers, who had served forty years, on and off, in the Congo, was slight and fresh-complexioned with an air of energetic authority, such as it was surprising to find in the languid Tropics. He held me enthralled with tales of the great Game Parks, where the huge gorillas live safe from the hunter's gun; about experimental schools for elephants, where even the fierce African elephant is being tamed; about the Pygmy country, and the Ruwenzori Mountains of the Moon. He offered to take us to Lake Kivu – 'the best and most beautiful holiday spot in the world' – and the kingdoms of Ruanda Urundi, in his Dove aircraft. I could hardly bear to refuse, but I was reluctantly compelled to recognize the truth of my husband's warning to me: 'Do please realize that it just isn't possible to do *everything*! There simply isn't time.'

My right-hand neighbour at lunch was an art expert who had come from Brussels to organize the preservation of Native Arts and Crafts.

'Their work is best when it is original,' he said. 'When they try to imitate European art its value is gone. We see that with those who study in Europe.'

'Are they influenced by surrealism?'

He shook his head. 'Not by any form of abstract art. With the *Indigène* the imagination embraces only what it observes. *L'esprit* is lacking, there is nothing much behind here—' he tapped his forehead.

The doctor at the Medical School had said: 'They have the craftsman's mentality.' And our own Bantus in South Africa can crack each others' heads in a stick-fight, or open up a huge gash inches long and think nothing of it because the wound is visible and they know the reason for it. But let them get a pain inside them – one which they cannot see and account for – and the old fears and superstitions of Africa rise up in them and they prepare for death. Some enemy has put a spell upon them!

The Belgian ladies at the party were very well dressed and pleasant, but I could not help recalling the mournful plaint of one young British bachelor.

'Everybody in Leo is married, and they all go to bed early. At midnight it's lights out and even the cicadas close down.'

He had gazed wistfully at French Brazzaville across the Pool. There you might dance till the small hours and the cicadas never knew when to pack in.

The Belgian experiment in Equatorial Africa is wide, courageous and logical. It deserved to succeed. Leo was only one example of the progress being made throughout this tropical colony ruled by a conscientious administration and financed by big business. It has put its indigenous population and its elephants to school, its sick into hospitals, its gorillas into reserves, and, in the mining and agricultural areas, it has put nomads into model villages. It is developing fisheries and stock-breeding, and everybody is happy. With one possible exception. The little Native who wears a European suit and spectacles, whose pink-padded fingers hammer a typewriter, and who lives in a house with windows and seeks a wife who can give him companionship. He has the power of the literate over his ignorant fellows, but, even so, there are times when he swings in space between two worlds, and then he is vulnerable to the sinister influence that is stirring up evil throughout Africa, trading upon the pride of those with a little learning and the ignorance of those with none.

If there is a threat to the profits of European enterprise it lies in the mild little man with spectacles – the *evolué*.

CHAPTER EIGHT

EQUATORIAL AFRICA – BRAZZAVILLE

AT eleven o'clock on the morning of 6th June, at an official reception given by Mr. Wikeley at the Consulate, we drank the health of King George VI. At noon we crossed Stanley Pool in the Belgian Governor's *vedette*, and were welcomed on the French shore by the British Consul-General, Mr. Mason, a number of French officials and a brass band in scarlet and gold who played 'God Save the King' in a minor key with a deep roll of drums for *victorious* and *glorious*.

'It sounded like Rachmaninoff,' I murmured to Mr. Mason.

'They can't read music, so they play by ear,' he said. 'That effort was truly terrific!'

The Consul-General was a lean dark man with a restless temperament, a love of music and fine singing voice. He spoke French with a perfect mastery of idiom. His house, on the banks of the Congo, had been built by a modern French architect, and resembled nothing more than a cloistered maze of unusual charm with a beautiful lofty living-room at its core.

At an official evening reception we once again drank to the birthday of His Majesty King George VI. All the French were very gay and the party went with a swing. It went on for a long time. When finally the last guest had gone we had soup and eggs and bacon with Mr. Mason keeping a sharp eye on his staff.

'They can't resist a cocktail party,' he explained. 'If you

let your glass out of your hand for an instant they whisk it away and finish the contents themselves.'

When we had eaten, the waiters returned to their own native town, but first they shook hands formally with all of us.

'They always do that,' said Mr. Mason. 'They shake your hand and each others' and everybody else's. It's their idea of courtesy. They really have great charm – though of course they are inclined to steal. And they aren't at all punctual. They know sunrise, noon and sunset, but for the rest it's guess-work. Their ambition in life is to possess a watch and a pair of shoes. They send for catalogues and do endless window-shopping in that way.'

'Do they ever buy the watch or the shoes?'

'Frequently. That's why they need to do a bit of stealing.'

Next door, the Cercle Civile, the French Club, was playing dance music, and, although it was well past midnight, the French cicadas were still shrilling themselves hoarse. Across the Lake humans and insects were going to bed. Not here.

As we walked along the cloistered terrace to our room the little toads hopped out of the way, the gekkos ran towards the light, and, as I turned down the sheets to get into bed, a large black spider snarled at me indignantly.

'By the way.' I said, as I chased it away. 'Did you hear that story of Monsieur Rollin's this evening? About the python he killed that had three hens inside it.'

'Yes,' said Bertie. 'But the interesting part is that all the hens had gone down the python beak first.'

I shuddered. 'Shows they must have been hypnotized.'

'Or that it's more comfortable for snakes to swallow birds without ruffling their feathers the wrong way.'

'Ssh, you'll give me nightmares.'

At about two in the morning I was wakened by a fine rain of plaster on my face as the biggest and hairiest speckled spider in creation forced her way out of a crack in the ceiling immediately over my head. She was evidently a creature of

111

regular habits, for every morning at two she burst out of her lair with a warning shower of plaster, rushed about the ceiling in search of small insects trapped in the electric light bowl, and was home by daylight. Fortunately she never lost her footing!

The *Administrateur-Maire* took us for a tour of the district and we visited the Pasteur Institute which is leading the world in the fight against sleeping sickness. We saw a cage full of the deadly tsetse flies. They looked innocent, like small very lively horse-flies. From a magnificent modern prefabricated hotel on the hill we looked down at the Native town among its palms – very suitably named Potopoto, which means mud.

'Are the Natives compelled to live in their own quarters?' I asked.

He shrugged his shoulders. 'They can live where they like – if they can afford it. But they prefer to live together. They have more fun and companionship. It is only natural.'

It is – until someone tells you it isn't.

The French, like the Belgians, do not adhere to the British principle of educating backward peoples towards self-government and ultimate independence. They find it absurd. Their African colonies are regarded as Provinces of France, and are represented in Paris by African as well as European delegates. Every Native in the French Congo is encouraged to think of himself as a Frenchman.

One of the more cynical citizens of Brazzaville had his views about this system. 'The *Indigène* may learn good French when he goes to Paris,' he said, 'but he also learns good Communism. The Blacks in Paris are the magnets for the Reds.'

Although the French Congo may be a Province of the mother-country, its atmosphere is far from provincial. It is Bohemian.

The night after we arrived we went to a 'Moulin Rouge party' given in the garden of Monsieur and Madame Rollin. All the guests represented characters from Montmartre. There, on the high bank of the Congo, was le Moulin Rouge,

112

its scarlet sails revolving in a light breeze. There was an outdoor theatre, a dance floor, little bars and buffets under pergolas of roses, and all the artists, taxi-girls and habitués of Bohemian Paris seemed to have found their way into Equatorial Africa for the night – from Toulouse Lautrec to Maurice Chevalier.

Next morning even our energetic Flag Lieutenant looked three parts asleep as we set off for a day's 'peekneek' to Foulakary Falls.

Eighteen of us clambered into various vehicles and off we sped through the jungle with its palm-thatch Native villages among the manioc plants and oil palms. Many of the huts were decorated with silhouettes of white men in helmets and gorillas in nothing. Goats, fowls and wiry little pigs ran around, but no cattle, for this was a tsetse-fly belt. We stopped to wander into a country market with its stalls of medicines, provisions and printed Manchester cottons. Tony and I tried to lift one woman's 'shopping bag' – a pirogue-shaped basket filled with cooked manioc wrapped in banana leaves. Only with the greatest effort could we move it, much less carry it, for it weighed some sixty pounds. But two Congolese men hoisted it on to the woman's head and she walked away carrying it easily by perfection of balance.

The only meat in the market was some unsavoury black game buzzing with flies.

'Are they very short of meat?' I asked one French lady.

'Very,' she said. 'They always have been and the poor things are meat-eaters by nature. That is why they are apt to eat each other.'

'Still?'

'From time to time. One *Indigène* was tried the other day for eating his grandmother. He saw no harm in it. He said he had not killed her, she had died of old age, so there seemed no reason why the village should not benefit. Everybody had a share. After all, it is an ancient custom here.'

'Grannie must have been rather tough and stringy.'

113

'So is a hippo. Another time a Black came before the court when his wife disappeared. He admitted that he had been walking behind her down a jungle path and suddenly he had an overwhelming impulse to eat her. He had been unable to resist it.'

I remembered our London housekeeper telling me one day that her husband had insulted her. He had said, 'When you were young I used to want to eat you. Now I wish I had.' In the Congo the youthful appetite of a man for a maid can be taken too literally!

'The 'peekneek', at the end of three and a half hours' drive, could not have been less like the British notion of such an outing.

Attendants in spotless white uniforms served a delicious three course lunch under a palm-thatch shelter on the lip of the Falls – sardines from Portugal, ham from Denmark, pâté de Perigord, wines and cheeses of France – and afterwards everybody dozed in the spray-cooled shade opposite the evanescent rainbows leaping from foaming waters. The song of the plunging cataract was deep and monotonous.

On our last evening we dined with General and Madame Bourgund. The General was the Commander-in-Chief of all the French Forces in Equatorial Africa – a merry man with a charming family. His daughter nursed at the Hospital, and his son, Jean-Pierre, aged sixteen, was considered too young to join us at dinner, but we met him afterwards when we went into the salon for coffee. At my request he brought his pet, Cheeta-Cheeta, with him.

'Are you really sure you wish to meet her?' asked Madame Bourgund. 'We all love her very dearly, she is like a child in the family, but not everybody feels the same way about a chimpanzee.'

But yes, we were sure. Then Jean-Pierre must fetch her. She was asleep? No matter, he must wake her.

The lad came into the room holding a very sleepy chimpanzee by the hand. A white Pomeranian frisked at their heels.

114

Cheeta-Cheeta was seventeen months old, by no means full-grown. She walked clumsily on bandy legs, her long fur was coarse and black, and, with the knuckles of her disengaged paw, she rubbed limpid sleep-filled brown eyes. Her collar and chain had worn the fur on her shoulders thin in a harness mark. I do not know what I had expected, perhaps something more in the nature of the frowning dog-faced baboon or the sulking murderous Marcel of Leo Zoo. Not this travesty of a human child newly wakened from slumber, pathetic and engaging.

'Shake hands, shake hands!' commanded Jean-Pierre in French.

The young ape, grumbling and chirrupping, allowed me to take her hand. One could not call it a paw. It was very long and supple and narrow, with limp cold fingers that could tear a dog apart without an effort. She drew my hand to her protruding flexible mouth, and I caressed her ears. They were pink and round.

'There's no starch in them,' I said to Tony. 'They are cool and floppy as petals. Feel!'

But the Flag Lieutenant preferred to take my word for it.

Jean-Pierre was impatient with his pet. 'She is too sleepy to show off. *Elle est bête ce soir! Cheeta-Cheeta, embarrasse moi!*'

The ape flung her long hairy arms about the handsome youth's neck and nuzzled the curve of his shoulder, clinging to him and muttering, like a child in unfamiliar company.

As he led her away the Pomeranian danced after them. He was Cheeta-Cheeta's playmate.

Madame Bourgund sighed. 'Jean-Pierre was ashamed of his Cheeta-Cheeta tonight. She seemed dull and brutish when really she is more like a person than a beast. Our son worships her – as if she were his little sister.'

'He has taught her to eat at table,' laughed the General, 'and to take wine from her own glass. When she had dysentery she was taken care of at the Pasteur Institute. We went to see her and we wept. Her expression told of her suffering

115

and her trust. I said to my wife. "Never again will we take an ape into our home. It is too human!" When she came back to us Jean-Pierre had her in his room and woke every two hours of the night to give her the medicine she needed. He loves her too much.'

'Will you take her to Paris when you return next year?'

'An ape in a small Paris apartment? No, it is impossible.'

'What then? A zoo?'

Madame Bourgund made a gesture of horror. 'Never that! Once they have become human you cannot turn them back into animals – it is death.' She half raised her shoulders in that expressive French gesture which may mean all or nothing. 'We have had Cheeta-Cheeta from infancy. My son fed her from the bottle. We found her so amusing. Now she is a problem. But that is life, Madame. One gives one's heart without thinking of tomorrow... Come, it is a lovely night, we will show you our garden and our sloth, who is a clown.'

The sloth hung by his tail from the creeper-covered trellis ceiling of his large cage. Clown he might be, but Cheeta-Cheeta did not like him, so he remained behind bars.

'*Zut*, he sleeps!' said the General. 'Our animals are in bed so early they might as well live in Leo!' He added with regret. 'I wish you could have seen my perroquet. There was a lovely bird! Such pretty colours and always willing to wake up and talk to me.'

Unfortunately Cheeta-Cheeta had not liked the perroquet either, and one day she had simply put it under her arm and twisted its neck.

'One cannot really blame her,' said Madame Bourgund. 'It was one of those little *drames* that can have only one ending. It is the nature of a chimpanzee to kill a bird – and in the end nature always has her way.'

116

CHAPTER NINE

SENTIMENTAL JOURNEY

WE returned to Simon's Town to find the political atmosphere even more explosive than usual during the Session at the Cape and everybody was relieved when Parliament adjourned. But before the cabinet ministers and diplomatic corps returned to their official residences in Pretoria, Mr. Havenga, the Minister of Finance, and his wife dined with us at Admiralty House, and we naturally avoided those contentious subjects that had become so tedious to us all.

'You are just back from the Congo,' said Mr. Havenga. 'Where are you off to next? Durban, I suppose, for the July Handicap.' The Durban July Handicap was the main racing event of Natal's social season, and was always well attended by the Navy.

I laughed. 'We'll see you there!' The Minister of Finance, though no punter, bred blood stock on his beautiful Free State farm. 'We are going by car, through the Free State and Basutoland.* The High Commissioner has arranged for us to see the Protectorates this winter, and Basutoland is right on the way to Natal.'

'You must break your journey at Bloemfontein – at Brandkop Farm, for old time's sake. I will write and tell Gustav Fichardt to expect you.'

So it was planned that we should spend a night at Brandkop on our way to Maseru, the capital of Basutoland, while the Flag Lieutenant and the Coxswain would go by sea and meet us later in Durban.

For me this was a sentimental journey, as some of the

* Now Lesotho.

happiest days of my girlhood had been spent at Brandkop with the Fichardt family.

In those days, only a few years after World War One, the Nationalist Party was just beginning to gain impetus, and Charlie Fichardt was one of its most dynamic leaders. We knew him and his family well, for my father was their family doctor when they were at the Cape for the Session, and sometimes, in the winter holidays, I went to Brandkop to stay with Val, the lovely daughter of the house.

It was there that I first made the acquaintance of General Hertzog, the quiet, thin-faced father of Nationalism, of bland brilliant Tielman Roos, the Transvaal leader of the Party, and of Hertzog's most promising and sincere disciple, Klaas Havenga. Of those three, only Havenga, now nearly seventy, was left.

Charlie's eldest son, Gustav, had then been a tall fair young man courting the girl he subsequently married, and Val had been in the first bloom of young womanhood. Soon afterwards Val had died suddenly and tragically of a short illness, and Charlie, who had idolized his daughter, had turned his face to the wall and abandoned the will to live.

As we drew near the farm every mile of the dusty road through the tawny Free State veld evoked memories of my girlhood. Here the blesbok grazed with the cattle by the windmill, there the green koppie rose to shelter the red-roofed house, and beyond lay the dam where we had bathed, and the plantations where we had ridden our Basuto ponies with the frosty web of early morning dew still on the grass.

'Oh, Bertie, there's the rose-garden – and the big tree where the monkey who ate caterpillars lived! And over there, among the firs, is the little family burial-ground—'

As we drew up outside the homestead with its red-tiled stoep, Gustav came down the steps to greet us with his slow kind smile, and, standing in the doorway, was Frieda, who, just for a moment, might have been Mrs. Charlie rather than Mrs. Gustav Fichardt.

118

Gustav introduced to us his 'young bloods' – three fine sons – and 'the afterthought', an attractive ten-year-old girl called Zaza.

'We have a few people to meet you this evening,' said Frieda. 'About seven o'clock. But now you must have some tea.'

After tea I asked if I might take Bertie for a stroll.

'Of course,' said Frieda, serene and understanding. 'You remember your way?'

Gustav added: 'You'll find Val's stone and my parents' over on the left by the wall – rough-hewn from the koppie. That was what my father wanted.'

My husband and I walked alone down the path between the trees to the little burial-place that had always seemed to me to be the very soul of peace. 'Over on the left' we found the stone we had come to see.

'Valerie Marie Fichardt. 1901–1923.'

We sat on the low boundary wall where she and I had shared the confidences of romantic youth. Nearly thirty years had gone by since those days – the days before my husband was known to me. Yet everything was as I remembered it. The birds twittered in the cypresses, the black and white Friesland cattle stood quietly round the dam, the far flat-topped mountains were topaz in the sunset, and the wide empty pink plush veld affected me with a familiar tender melancholy. I closed my eyes, seeking that young friend of the past, but Valerie Marie, with her bright hair and her brighter dreams, slept unfulfilled beside her parents. 1901–1923 – so brief a watch in the night. . . .

Frieda's 'few people' turned out to be a cheerful party for supper in the true Brandkop tradition, with hot soup, *bobotie*, cold meats and salads, and delicious sweets with fresh farm cream. Some of the guests were descendants of the first Boer Presidents of the old Orange Free State Republic, there was a well-known Afrikaans writer, and almost everybody

119

was Nationalist. Although Afrikaans was their home-language, only English was spoken so that we should not feel at a disadvantage.

Frieda smiled and said: 'You wrote in *Pack and Follow* that when you were at Brandkop you were among the rebels. Well, you still are!'

Everybody laughed, and Gustav added: 'In those old days feeling ran so high that people were always wanting to tar and feather each other. Families were split up and not on speaking terms because they didn't agree politically, but now we have learned sense. We still have our differences but they needn't interfere with our personal friendships.'

Little Zaza was here, there and everywhere, fetching and carrying. When she spoke to us it was in flawless English.

Frieda watched her with amusement. 'When she knew you were coming she asked us if she should speak her "elocution English", and we told her Yes.'

'Elocution English' is not a characteristic of South African children, who more often run all their words gaily together, but now I recollected that Bloemfontein has produced fine elocution teachers and actresses for many generations. For some odd reason this dignified city in the veld – the official judicial capital of the Union – maintans great purity of speech in both languages of the country.

Frieda had put us into the room Val and I had shared so many years ago, and once again I fell asleep in the firelight. Very erratic firelight it was too, because there happened to be a swarm of bees in the chimney, and every now and again a burst of melting wax sizzled and flared. Next morning the house-boy swept up a carpet of dead bees. He was the son of the house-boy who had been at Brandkop thirty years ago, for this beautiful family estate was run on feudal lines, and down in the neat farm location lived the descendants of those who had served Charlie Fichardt and his father before him.

After breakfast Gustav drove us round the lands to show us his blesbok and wildebeest sanctuary. The farm-dogs followed us until they were bored or tired, when they turned back home.

At eleven o'clock we were guests at a formal Mayoral reception in Bloemfontein, and, after an early lunch, we set off for the wild mountainous Protectorate of Basutoland.

The Orange Free State is at its most impressive where it borders on Basutoland and Natal in the shadow of the great Drakensberg Range and along the banks of the lovely Caledon River which constitutes the border between the Union and this British Native Territory. Here, in true frontier fashion, the Boers of the old Republic a century ago had been constantly at war with the Basuto Chief, Moshesh, a crafty old lion who had gathered together the scattered remnants of tribes decimated by the terrible Matabele and Zulu warriors of Natal and welded them into one people – the Basuto. The British of Natal also had their misunderstandings with Moshesh, and many battles were fought under the towering cliffs of Thaba Basui, the Mountain of Night, which Moshesh had wisely chosen as his stronghold.

Brave Boer or British leaders who fell in conflict met an ugly fate at the hands of their Basuto enemies. Their bodies were mutilated to make medicine, for it was the custom of Bantu Chiefs to possess a 'medicine horn' – a kind of cornucopia of power and prestige, filled with unspeakably gruesome ingredients recommended by the witchdoctor. Human odds and ends were regarded as particularly potent medicine – a belief which unfortunately still prevails.

By the late nineteenth century Moshesh had become a gentleman. He had professed Christianity (while naturally retaining a few of his own time-honoured beliefs), learned to ride the horses of the white man that had somehow 'strayed' into his territory, acquired a stovepipe hat and black frockcoat like Oom Paul Kruger, and a fancy for a quiet life. So he patched up his differences with the British and begged for the Protection of the Great White Queen against any other hostile tribes, and, of course, the Boers, and promised to behave himself and see that his people did likewise. The

Basuto, he said, would be 'the fleas in the Queen's blanket'. At that period a good many African fleas were creeping into the folds of the Imperial Blanket, and the bones of British soldiers bleaching on the veld or in the bush bore witness to a constant necessity for keeping Victoria's irritating parasites in order.

Even today the Basuto like a little bit of warfare, because, after all, tribal conflict is as much in their marrow as polygamy. So, on the mines of the Rand, there are sporadic skirmishes between the Basuto and their ancient enemies, the Zulus in which the Basuto, for purposes of intimidation, call themselves 'Russians'. Russians, they have been told, are the most terrifying people on earth – 'bloody, bold and resolute', and quite invincible. But the Zulus fight back well. They do not believe that the Basuto can turn themselves into Russians.

Now, when I look back upon Basutoland, I see waves upon waves of gentian mountains surrounding the pastel plains. There are cattle on the plains, and little boys with blankets pinned at their throats call the beasts home at sunset, and the dearly beloved oxen, which have grazed communally all day, split up like a convoy at a given signal and follow their particular child back to the kraal to which they belong.

On the skyline there is always a man on horseback with a conical hat or jellybag on his head and a blanket like a bandit's cloak pinned at the neck by a monster curved safety-pin such as one might use to secure the nappy of some gigantic infant. The man inside the blanket may be a wizened little creature, and often is, but he is as impressive as a moving tent. He loves his sure-footed mountain pony nearly as much as his cattle. Not quite as much, of course, because it is more useful to him, and utility is not really a lovable quality. He also loves the blanket which he wears in winter to keep out the cold and in summer to keep off the sun. It often has a geometrical aeroplane stamped upon it, or perhaps a coronet, because the Basuto are feverishly loyal to the Crown, especially when they suspect Dr. Malan of casting a speculative eye upon their territory – or upon their behaviour which, in certain respects, is very far from commendable.

This tent on horseback is usually travelling to or from the trading station, which is, in a manner of speaking, his club. There, on the stoep in the dusty sunshine, men and women squat and chat and ponder. Inside the store is everything the human heart could desire, including saddlery and horse paraphernalia of all sorts, iron bedsteads, fleecy blankets suspended from the ceiling in the winged shape of mammoth moths, and outsize bottles of fierce dark medicine guaranteed to cure all ills. But terrible as this medicine may look, smell and taste, it is not compounded of cat's entrails and cow-dung and other animal and vegetable products such as those cooked up by the witchdoctor, and it is certainly innocent of the most powerful ingredient of all – the dreadful shocking *diretlo* that has come back into fashion and turned the Territory into a land of fear.

Outside the store men go about their business in a sociable way and you may see a man skinning an ox expertly with a razor-sharp penknife. The people watch him a little warily. Today it is the ox – tomorrow, who knows . . .?

Because it is winter the women remain near their kraals. In spring and summer they hoe and plant and reap and there is laughter and song in the fields. At all times the men go in their thousands to work in the mines and on the farms of the Union. Basutoland, which is about the size of Belgium, is entirely surrounded by the Union and economically dependent upon it. Without its mines and farms the Basuto would perish, and without the Basuto the mines and farms would suffer. Each needs the other – always a fairly satisfactory state of affairs.

The only Europeans in the country are in Government Service, or they are traders or missionaries or officers in the Native Recruitment Corporation who sign men on for work in the Union and arrange for the remittance of part of their earnings to Basutoland. Most of the trading posts have been in the hands of the same family for over a century. The Missions are many and varied, and, throughout the wide scene, like quills on the back of a porcupine, there bristle the little pink sand-stone churches where dedicated and undaunted men and women strive to show these dark folk the light. But the church and the school house do not really belong to the landscape. They stand out and beg for attention, while the thatched huts and twisted cattle-fold behind wild seisal hedges melt into the grey-green kranzes as naturally as the smoke of a cooking-fire melts into the mist or a buck into the thorn bush.

There are no buck in Basutoland, only a few rock-rabbits and no jackals, for the Basuto have eaten the indigenous fauna of their land just as their cattle have grazed it bare. Only field-mice abound in the stubble, and the snakes that live on mice and birds.

So the Basutoland Hunt has to follow a scent instead of a jackal, and what fun they have just the same!

That is another of the things that sticks in my mind – the fun those few Europeans have in a very lonely land. Taken all in all, there are not more than two thousand White people in the territory, and about six hundred of them are concentrated in Maseru, 'The Place of Red Sandstone'. For the rest there are only 'camps' – a handful of bungalows, an inn, and, of course, a club. There is always a club, with a tennis court or two, perhaps a polo-ground and even an embryo golf-course, because the British, who are natural born colonists, are sportsmen in the literal as well as the figurative sense of the word, and so are their women. The French and Belgians are never able to achieve this wholehearted affinity with life in the blue. They have not been brought up with an overwhelming sense of duty towards all primitive people, no matter how unsavoury, nor do they possess an ingrained Pagan worship of fresh air and animals. Moreover, their women feel more at home in a 'little black dress' than in jodhpurs.

Another thing I shall never forget is the kindness we received in Basutoland. Our visit could hardly have been

124

worse timed from the point of view of the Administration, although it was admirable from ours, yet not one soul allowed us to feel that we *were* rather a nuisance at just that particular moment.

And it was a difficult moment – in some ways even heartbreaking – for those whose duty it was to govern and help a people who were in many ways so likeable, and in others so incomprehensibly and uncomprehendingly cruel.

CHAPTER TEN

BASUTOLAND – REIGN OF FEAR

THE Resident Commissioner, Mr. Forsyth-Thompson, was due to retire the day after our arrival in Maseru, so we were to stay with Mr. G. J. Armstrong, the Government Secretary, who became Acting Resident Commissioner on his departure.

Mr. and Mrs. Armstrong had their three young sons – George, Mark and Paul Winston – home from boarding school for the winter vacation, but they assured us that the house could 'stretch' and that it had not yet reached its full capacity. It was the usual homely colonial bungalow with a wide stoep and tin roof, and it stood opposite the Residency on the rise outside Maseru. And, when Mr. Forsyth-Thompson left, the sentry-box and visitors' book were simply carried across the road to the Armstrongs' gate and the Union Jack came too and flew bravely from the flag-pole in their garden. It was odd not to see the orange, white and blue South African flag flying beside it.

Mr. Armstrong was South African. There are many South Africans in British Government Service in the High Commission Territories, and our host and his two brothers were all in the Administration. They had been brought up in the Union Native Territory of the Transkei, and they all spoke several Native languages and knew the mentality of the Bantu by instinct as well as experience. We were to meet Mr. Armstrong's younger brother later in Swaziland.

It was late afternoon when we arrived, and the little boys, who were playing on the lawn with an unidentifiable grey dog of winning personality, immediately rushed indoors and

126

gave a shrill penetrating alarm which brought their parents hurrying out to meet us.

Mr. Armstrong was lean and wiry with a springing crest of white hair and a pair of piercing brown eyes under black brows.

'You'll need to empty your radiator, Admiral,' he said, as he helped Bertie to unload the car. 'It freezes hard here at night.'

In fact, the icy night wind was already beginning to whisper over the veld.'

Mrs. Armstrong said, 'You take this,' and gave Paul Winston, her youngest, the light brief-case in which I kept my diary. George and Mark were bustled off with coats and an attaché case, and two Native girls took our heavier bags, urged on by their mistress in their own language.

'You musn't judge these Basuto in the winter,' she said, turning to me. 'They hibernate. In the summer they come alive.'

The faces of the two plump maids were sealed with an expression of costive stupidity, and Mrs. Armstrong's efforts to stir them into activity reminded me of Priscilla, the terrier, trying to dig out our somnolent tortoise. Their features were about as responsive as the thick unyielding shell as it settled deeper among the agapanthus lilies.

While Bertie put the car away we stood looking down the great sweep of the valley to the far snowy peaks. The veld was seamed with *dongas* (deep ditches worn and widened by erosion) but they had been planted with birches and poplars, and we could see the contour ploughing of the foothills.

'When the snows melt and the swollen rivers come down, they carry away all the top-soil,' said Mrs. Armstrong. 'This part of the world is so vulnerable to erosion, with all the mountains round it. But the Agricultural Department is doing wonders.'

I knew that she was right, for I had heard members of the Union Ministry for Native Affairs give generous praise to the work that had been done for soil conservation in Basutoland during the past twenty years.

I shivered. 'How quickly it gets cold! Ten minutes ago the sun was shining.' With sunset the temperature had fallen like a plummet, and already the air was freezing.

Presently, over tea in front of the fire, we heard some of the plans that had been made for us.

'We have a farewell cocktail party here for the Forsyth-Thompsons this evening,' said Mrs. Armstrong. 'You'll see everybody then. Tomorrow we thought you might like to go to Machacha Mountain with Mr. Deal, the Government Engineer. He is pushing a new road through the mountain and he has a forward camp up there. And the Chapmans want to take you to Thaba Basui—'

'Or you may care to meet the Regent,' suggested Mr. Armstrong. His eyes twinkled. 'She's quite a character! But if she's in a bad mood – *well* . . .'

We met 'everybody' at the party – kind hospitable people who made us feel welcome and at home.

'We share each others' guests,' said Mrs. Chapman, the wife of the Head of the Native Recruitment Corporation in Maseru. 'After all, we don't get many strangers here. Why, if a car with a new number plate is seen in the territory, everyone is agog to know whose it is!'

The Chief Medical Officer told us many interesting facts about the chain of clinics through the wild inaccessible mountains, about the medical missionaries who do such excellent work, and about the encouraging results of sulphatrone, the new cure for leprosy. We made the acquaintance of a young pilot who operated the new air service into the heart of the Maluttis. And we arranged with Mr. Marwick, the Assistant Government Secretary, to visit 'Mantsebo Seeiso, the Regent for the boy Paramount Chief, Bereng.

Mr. Marwick, who was quiet and amusing, had written a distinguished treatise on the Swazi, and his attractive wife gave lessons to the European children of Maseru.

Presently we were introduced to a dark athletic young Colonel, the Chief Police Officer in charge of a Force of about three hundred and fifty mounted Native police

128

officered by Europeans. He was proud of his men, but somewhat 'browned off' with the type of crime they were called upon to handle.

'Nothing but stock-theft and medicine murder – and I haven't a strong enough stomach for some of those!'

Medicine murder. There it was – the skeleton in Basutoland's cupboard. But not as pretty as that. Oh, dear, no! Nice clean Mr. Bones in his cardboard coffin on a shelf in Admiralty House was full of homely charm compared with the mutilated horrors that regularly cronfronted the Basutoland police at the base of cliffs and crags.

Medicine murder. The word carried a special shame and stigma – not only for the Basuto themselves, but for every White man in the territory. Here was the big let down – the ultimate negation of the work of missionaries and administrators who had tried, for close on a century, to inculcate the laws of God and man into the people of old Moshesh. And the worst of it was that the killers were the aristocrats – the so-called enlightened members of society, the very channels of government itself. For the High Commission Territories are governed on Britain's time-honoured and hitherto successful method of indirect rule through the chiefs and headmen, with the Paramount Chief at the head of the Native Administration.

This particular wave of crime had reached its climax in 1949. And in that year a specialist was called in to diagnose and prescribe for the morally sick Protectorate. This specialist was Mr. G. I. Jones, Lecturer in Anthropology at Cambridge University. He was sent to South Africa by the British Government to inquire into and report on medicine murder in Basutoland, and his findings were presented to Parliament at Westminster in 1951. The Report was published in a White Paper by His Majesty's Stationery Office, and a dry, lucid analysis of human woe and torment it turned out to be.

Mr. Jones studied and enumerated scores of cases described the 'pattern', and diagnosed the cause of the disease.

129

Cause and effect in Africa are often very strange and baffling to the European mind. What really goes on inside the peppercorn head of the Native (call him African or Bantu if you will) is one great monkey-puzzle to most of us. Even Mr. Jones, who had made the study of primitive man his life-work, had not got all the answers. Nor had people like Mr. Armstrong, although they had dealt with Natives from their childhood onwards and loved and understood them. Both men might be able to diagnose the disease easily enough, but to ensure a cure was another matter. Especially as the 'patient' in this instance refused to recognize the extent of his illness and eradicate the cause from his system.

The cause? Ancient African beliefs, superstitions and sorceries that come to the surface in time of stress.

What stress? Mr. Jones attributed it mainly to certain political reforms implemented some ten years earlier to curtail the power of the chiefs while increasing their responsibility. Such reforms were just another logical step in Britain's consistent and avowed ideal of educating her backward dependencies towards democratic self-government, but somehow the step had not gone quite according to plan. The chiefs and headmen disliked losing their autocratic powers and were uncertain of their ability to carry out their new obligations. A lack of 'face' had been incurred.

'Face' is as important in Africa as it is in the East. If a man loses 'face' in the East, he might just as well lose his whole head and be down with it. A Japanese who has lost 'face' kills himself. An African does not. He has no liking for suicide. He prefers to kill someone else. If something happens to make an African feel insecure, *pouff!* and away blows a century of Christian teaching and civilized example. And the witch-doctor – that sinister figure for ever in the African background – steps out of the shadows, rattles his bones and consults his dreadful oracles, and away in the veld some innocent child herding cattle is condemned to a ghoulish death. Or it may be a young mother, or a mad old

130

man – anyone his wide and terrible nostrils have 'sniffed out' as a desirable victim. From then on there is no reprieve and no pity.

When a member of the ruling class has been advised by the witch-doctor to 'enhance his prestige' by taking human life, a whole district may find itself drawn into the ugly business. Moreover the district accepts the situation, because it believes that a chief so 'strengthened' will bring attendant blessings upon his people – better crops, fatter cattle and good rains. And those few who may be sceptical know very well that to drop a hint to the police is as good as asking to be the next sacrifice.

We have glanced at *cause*, let us consider *effect*.

What Mr. Jones describes as the 'pattern' of the crime is fundamentally unvarying. It is always premeditated. The sacrifice must have the flesh required for medicine (*diretlo*) sliced from the living body, and if the operation fails to produce death, the throat must be cut. The medicine is made by the witch-doctor. The fumes from his cauldron are inhaled by the killers to give them courage, part of the stew is eaten by the person to be 'strengthened', and ointment is made of the rest, to be smeared where required. Obscene and brutal doings may complete the ritual. After a few days the pitiful remains are thrown over a cliff to be found by the police and the vultures. That is part of the magic. As people are drawn by the magnetism of a shocking sight, so they will be attracted to the individual for whom the medicine has been procured.

Mr. Jones demonstrated the 'pattern' with the case of Mochesela, his friend, Dane, and the Chieftainess of his District.

Picture the circumstances! Mochesela was a cheerful young man, well-liked in his village. After a wedding feast he is drinking beer in a hut with his friend and relative, Dane. He does not know that the Chieftainess of his District has just arrived accompanied by sixteen strong-arm men and two female attendants. But Dane is better informed.

131

'Come, Cousin, let us go outside a while,' he suggests.

As they leave the hut Mochesela is seized. He cries out aloud in dread and anguish.

'You are going to kill me! Let me go and I will give you my black ox!'

His captors reply: 'It is you we want, not your ox.'

As he is dragged away, village boys, attracted by his screams, follow, and someone throws stones at them. They slink back to the kraal like beaten dogs. They too know what is going to happen.

Mochesela is taken to his Golgotha. He is gagged, stripped and held on the ground. Dane, his friend and cousin, is the man with the knife. Mochesela is a satisfactory victim, he takes an unconscionable time a-dying. Even after his eyes have been plucked out, and, as a final gesture, his entire face skinned, it is necessary to cut his throat.

The Chieftainess, beside whom Lady Macbeth is Little Eva, expresses her thanks to Dane and his able assistants. But her gratitude is not unmixed with a note of warning.

'I thank you, my children, for having killed this man for me,' she says. And adds, 'I know the police will come to investigate the matter, and, if anyone talks, I will kill him as I have killed Mochesela.'

She then arranges for the body to be concealed for a few days before being exposed. After which she walks calmly home with portions of Mochesela's flesh, his vitals, his eyes and his tongue in a billycan carried by one of her stalwart female attendants. She is followed by the witch-doctor, who will make the medicine that is to 'strengthen' her son, a dissolute young chief.

Mochesela was only one of scores of similar sacrifices. Quite often the murderers were professing Christians and close relations of the murdered. For instance, one old woman was slaughtered after a baptismal feast at which killers and slain had celebrated together: a young man sold his old blind mother for *diretlo*, and yet another ambushed the girl who had given birth to his child. Many children were kidnapped by adults they trusted, hundreds of people were

involved, and yet every crime was wrapped in the same conspiracy of silence.

No wonder the police and the authorities on the spot were
feeling just about as rattled as a witch-doctor's unholy
bones, while Mr. Jones had drawn his conclusions with the
nice objectivity of the theorist back in the seclusion of his
professorial study.

'The Southern Bantu [ran his Report] had been in con-
tact with European culture for over a hundred years;
during which period he has had ample time to assimilate
those features which he considered of advantage to him.
The fact that he retains certain features of his own culture, is an indication that he attaches considerable value
to them; it cannot be dismissed as the reaction of a
"primitive" mentality that will change as soon as he can
read and write and go to church. The major figures in
these DIRETLO killings belonged to the more advanced
and not the more reactionary Basuto chiefs.

Quite so, I thought, as I closed the grim dispassionate
White Paper, which I had been reading in bed on the night
of our arrival in Maseru. And, as I switched off the light, I
could not help wishing that some of the Fabians and critics
of my country, who know the African only as a University
man and think of him as one of themselves with a different
shade of pigmentation, could come to this troubled land and
learn for themselves that there is a wider difference between
Black and White and African and European than colour
alone. Today Kenya's Mau Mau are teaching them that
lesson, but they might have learned it just as well in Basutoland and Swaziland some years ago. The Bantu is still
our responsibility and not our equal.

I drew the blankets up to my chin and watched the firelight paint crazy pictures on the white walls of the little
room. Outside, the icy wind wailed round the house, and the
earth froze hard as the heart of man.

Poor Sacrifice upon the Cross! I thought. How many

deaths have You died since Calvary – how many deaths have You died in Africa?

Next morning the sun shone with its cold winter brilliance and out in the garden the convicts worked in their red jerseys. The little Armstrong boys scampered off to play with their grey dog, expressing loud hopes that it would snow so that they could make a snow-man, and soon Mr. Deal came to drive us to his road camp on Machacha.

We saw the great bulldozers at work on the virgin mountain-side, and, up near the snow-line, we found the little European settlement of tents and prefabs. The single men lived in the tents and the families occupied the prefabs. The women were making brawn, biltong, and salt beef and pork of an ox and a pig they had bought from the Natives. They were mostly South African girls, merry and adaptable.

'There's a fine spirit among these people,' said Mr. Deal. 'And we need it in an outpost like this. They'll be here for a year or more before we press on.'

The mechanic's wife, who was in charge of the pickling, by virtue of her farm-training, broke off to give us eleven o'clock tea in her cosy hut.

'We love it here,' she said. 'We ride and walk and the kids do splendidly. Look at my three! Did you ever see such apple-cheeks? Soon the Mission in the valley is going to get us a nun to give them their lessons – you see, there are about twenty kids here of various ages. And we are going to make a tennis court and lay out gardens, so that when we go we'll leave something nice behind . . .'

'The nucleus of a rest-camp,' said Mr. Deal.

'It would make a wonderful holiday camp,' I agreed. 'Just the place for people keen on riding or climbing, or in need of peace.'

Far below us spread the dry mealie-lands and the tall pink grass so good for thatch – soft as a pink and beige Basuto blanket – and always on the horizon rose the mountains, more and more blue mountains against a blue sky.

In the afternoon Eric Chapman and his wife took us to

Thaba Basui. They had recently come from Portuguese East Africa, and for Mrs. Chapman, who did not play games, Maseru must have seemed like the end of the world. But her husband was Master of Fox Hounds, and he was pleased because he had managed to arrange for the Argentine Polo Team touring the Union to visit Basutoland, so that everybody was even more horse-minded than usual, and a set of sturdy Basuto polo ponies were being groomed and trained in honour of the foreign guests.

To make our expedition to old Chief Moshesh's Mountain of Night more interesting, the Chapmans took one of his descendants with us, a little clerk from the office, called Mahassi.

Mahassi was full of charm and enthusiasm, and pointed with happy pride to the poplars growing in the *dongas*, the flood-water dams, and acres of pasturage being 'rested' from grazing. His people were learning! In the distance the sheer cliffs of the wedge-shaped natural fortress of Thaba Basui gleamed naked in the fierce light. Moshesh had used it as the ancient Greeks used the Acropolis, gathering his tribes and herds on its summit at the first hint of danger. And, though often attacked, it had remained impregnable.

Mahassi and I climbed the heights ahead of the others, and he talked about his great ancestor. On the summit were several big heaps of stones.

'These heaps mark the graves of the Chiefs,' he explained. 'But Moshesh does not lie under his boulders. He is buried in a secret cave, sitting up straight in his ox-hide shroud with his shield and his spear beside him.'

Mahassi told me how once some communistic young men had killed an ox and called a *pitsu* (meeting) on Thaba Basui.

'But our people are not interested in Communism. They were interested in the ox. When the Communists talked the people soon became bored. They said to each other, "This talk makes no sense. How can all men be equal? We know that they are not. We will now go and eat the ox and let these fellows talk to themselves!"'

We discussed the young Bereng Seeiso, who will be the Paramount Chief when he comes of age.

'Will he go to a University?' I asked.

'He goes to Roma now, the Catholic Mission School, and later he will probably go to Fort Hare University in the Union. But it would be better if he could go to an English University. Our Nation can afford it. A Basuto family could go with him to keep him in touch with his own country, and that family could be changed every two years. I would go with him myself. I want very much to go to England.' His wistful expression made it clear that his plans for young Bereng were not unconnected with his own ambitions.

'He should mix with royalty,' said Mahassi, entirely without presumption. 'That would broaden his mind.'

The Royal visit to Basutoland, when the whole nation had gathered in a mighty *pitsu* at Maseru to welcome the King and Queen and their daughters had left a deep impression, and I do not believe that it occurred to Mahassi that the Royal House of Windsor might have obligations that would allow it little time to bestow upon the young scion of the Royal House of Seeiso.

I mentioned the horny problem of Seretse Khama, whose English education had proved rather too extensive for the good of the Bamangwato.

He cried out in consternation. 'But that could never happen here! The Basuto do not like mixed marriages. We prefer to keep our race pure. The nation will choose the wife for the Chief. They have the right, for they must give the cattle for the feast.'

Fair enough. Yet the words, 'That could never happen here!' had a hollow ring. Only the very naïve dare speak them.

Little Mahassi was anxious that I should appreciate the full depth of Basuto loyalty to the Crown.

'Last war,' he said, 'the Paramount Chief called a *pitsu* to tell the people of Britain's danger. All he said was "Men, the Queen's house is on fire!" There was not a man or a boy who was not ready to go and fight that fire.'

'The *Queen*?'

'Yes,' said Mahassi. 'To the Basuto nation there is still a Great White Queen across the sea.' Yet, when he spoke, in 1951, there was a King.

On the following day we went with Mr. Marwick to visit the Paramount Chief in her Native capital of Mahtsieng.

'Mantsebo Seeiso was the tribal wife of the late Chief Griffith Seeiso who had died some ten years earlier. She had therefore been elected Regent for the child Bereng, his eldest son by a junior wife. She herself had only borne him a daughter. The family professed to be Roman Catholics.

'Mantsebo Seeiso was not by any means an ideal Regent, and her efforts to put a stop to the wave of medicine murder that had risen steadily since her accession, had been neither as whole-hearted nor as effective as the Administration had reason to hope. Mr. G. I. Jones described her thus:

> 'The Regent was not a person of strong or masculine character. Her health was poor, she had no political experience and little aptitude for ruling. People, particularly some of the older chiefs, felt that she was very much a woman, and that any chief who succeeded in becoming her favourite councillor would be able to exercise undue influence in national affairs.'

I was deeply interested to meet this 'very much a woman'.

Mahtsieng was a mud and sandstone village at the base of a rocky buttress soaring into the dazzling sky. Two eagles wheeled overhead with slow deliberation, seeking a young lamb or a chicken. The thatched huts, surrounded by acacias, beeches and willows, hugged the precipice in a horseshoe hedge of blue-green seisal, as if withdrawing from the raw new buildings of the Native Administration on either side of an earth road.

We were greeted by one of the Regent's three advisors, Griffith Moneheng, a little old man with a shaven head, a European suit, good manners and a quick sense of humour.

137

He had served in France in the Labour Corps in World War One and had carried back indelible memories of cold, damp and excruciating sea-sickness.

The Regent's office, which was also her reception room, was furnished with a large desk – clearly not for use, since 'Mantsebo Seeiso was not one for reading or writing reports – three chairs with arms, three without, a coloured photograph of the Royal Family, a framed snapshot of old Chief Griffith Seeiso on horseback, looking like a Mexican bandit in his blanket and sombrero, and a post-card of one of the lesser male film stars.

Through an open door leading into a dusty compound we could see the Regent's house from which she could contemplate the mushroom huts of her relatives, their naked children, their livestock, and all the homely aspects of the kraal. On the verandah was a derelict iron bedstead, perhaps as a reminder to all and sundry that the best people no longer sleep on the floor. Invisible to us were her glittering American motor-cars in which she drove about her domain with her swarms of hangers-on.

A ponderous silhouette appeared in the doorway, and 'Mantsebo Seeiso lumbered in with a nautical roll. A beige blanket covered a somewhat soiled gingham dress and on her head was a black erection which Mr. Marwick, with a nice flair for fashion reporting, described as a 'Cossack cap'. Her complexion was milk chocolate and her features surprisingly small in a broad face about as expressive as a damp sponge. From time to time she stole furtive glances at the coat I wore slung about my shoulders – summing up the value of my 'blanket' – and occasionally she allowed a coy, rather pleasant smile to flit across her countenance. Now and again she raised her hand vaguely to pick her nose, but, missing the right orifice, she let it drift aimlessly over her features before it fell once more into her vast lap.

Somewhere under the Cossack cap nature had placed a GO SLOW sign, and a little conversation took a long time.

An ebony interpreter in a check suit and mustard pullover introduced my husband as 'The Commander of all the Seas round Africa' at which she graciously inclined her headgear. He admired her beautiful country, inquired after her health and spoke of her warriors whom he had seen in the Pioneer Corps in North Africa. And in return he learned that the Regent hoped to call upon the King and Queen at Buckingham Palace in the near future. After a little more polite and formal conversation the Regent took her leave and swayed back whence she had come.

In fact, 'Mantsebo Seeiso and twelve of her Chiefs went to London in the following October bearing an address of loyalty to the King. The King was far from well, but the Regent and the address were received by the Queen at Buckingham Palace. So the Acting Paramount Chief had her wish.

As we left Mahtsieng we saw a gangling youth in khaki shorts wandering up the hill, with a dusty little mongrel dog at his heels.

'That's Bereng, the boy who will be Paramount Chief,' said Mr. Marwick. 'I am told that he is shaping well.'

He also mentioned that the Regent had been in a good mood that day. Her best.

On the morning of our departure from Maseru the sky was overcast, and the convicts in the garden stamped their feet as they worked, and blew on their hands. And the Armstrong boys whooped for joy because they were sure it was going to snow.

It did – a real snow-storm – and, as we drove along a ridge amid the whirling flakes, we looked down and saw the veld wearing a beautiful Siberian blanket of glittering white. But not for long. By noon the sun was out and the snow melting.

We reached Leribe Camp in time for tea. Mr. Butler, the District Commissioner, and his wife, put us up for the night with true Basutoland hospitality. They gave a party for us at which we met most of Leribe and several people from across the border in the Free State. Basutoland and her neighbour in the Union got on very well together, and in all inter-provincial sports meetings the Protectorate and the Free State join forces and play as one team.

It was even colder at Leribe than in Maseru, and we slept under nine blankets, with two hot bottles each and a fire in the room, and still we were not too warm.

At daybreak we left for the long run through to Durban.

Postscript.

I finished typing this chapter yesterday, 28th November 1952, on board S.S. *Capetown Castle*. This morning, in the ship's Radio News, I read the following item.

'MASERU, Basutoland.

'A Headman, who was stated to have murdered a mental defective to replenish his medicine horn with human blood, was sentenced to death in the High Court here yesterday. He was Headman Quanaka Moiloa, who, with four other Natives, was found guilty of murdering Lejone Thanyane. The four others were also sentenced to death. It was stated that Quanaka needed medicine to counter the activities of a man who was troubling him with court cases.'

Why a mental defective? This – like so much else – is beyond me. It must go into the tray Tony used to mark 'TOO DIFFICULT'.

CHAPTER ELEVEN

'YESTERDAY, TODAY AND TOMORROW'

WE crossed the Caledon River back into the Union and climbed up and up to the Golden Gate where a mountain had split asunder, the wounds of its cleavage still red as blood. Through this gap the Voortrekkers had taken their great tented wagons down into Natal where so many of their number were to meet a violent death from the clubs and spears of Dingaan's Zulu warriors.

On Van Reenen's Pass we outspanned for our picnic lunch, and then said good-bye to the stinging cold of the high plateau to descend into the warm sub-tropical sugar belt on the shores of the Indian Ocean.

We were to spend the week-end with Douglas and Renée Saunders at Tongaat, the beautiful sugar estate that had been in the Saunders family for over a century. Now it had been formed into a Company with Douglas Saunders as Chairman.

Their home, Amanzimnyama, which means 'Black Water' after the nearby river, was set in lush gardens draped with dense curtains of white, magenta and scarlet bougain-villaea and shaded by palms and flowering trees. Prettiest of all perhaps was the lovely sweet-scented tree called 'yester-day, today and tomorrow' because it bears white, mauve and purple blossoms all at the same time.

On the pediment over the porch of the old colonial house was a bas relief of a Native boy and his oxen in a cane-field. In one corner was a hare. Nogjawa, the Hare, is Douglas's native name because he is liable to pop up here, there and everywhere. The whole family were in when we arrived; Douglas, his wife, Renée, slim as a boy in her perfectly cut slacks and satin blouse, and their three children – Chris, soon going to Oxford, Georgie, a magnet for young naval officers, and dreamy musical little Edward with a golden cocker puppy in his arms. The Saunders had communal dogs and personal dogs. The Alsatian and Scottie were communal, but Sherry, the baby spaniel, and Mr. Pim, the black poodle, were very personal indeed. Mr. Pim never took his eyes off Renée's pretty face, except to go to sleep or go-a-hunting, and Sherry shadowed Edward.

'Come on in and have a drink to wash the dust out of your necks,' said Rene. 'You must both be dead!'

We followed her down the passage into a big modern lounge. There were many valuable things in that room, but loveliest of all was the picture painted by nature and framed by a huge plate-glass window. Through this window a hedge of carmine poinsettia gave point to a vista of undulating emerald sugar plantations, soft as swelling velvet in the cobweb dusk. It was all Tongaat, as far as the eye could see – the heritage of settlers who had come to the land of Natal a century ago and made good.

Presently Edward took me to his playroom to see his treasures. Already he was developing his father's 'Quinney sense' – the special instinct of the connoisseur – and many of his tiny porcelain and silver jars and snuff-boxes were of real value. But, for the moment, he was absorbed in constructing a miniature theatre with the aid of 'Robbie', the governess-companion of the entire household. The spirit of the theatre was strong in all the family and at any time they might decide to raid the 'dressing up box' and persuade their guests to join in an impromptu variety show.

After the bleak cold emptiness of Basutoland it was curious to wake next morning in the warm lazy air of Natal, with mynah-birds chattering in the palms. I heard a splash as Bertie dived into the swimming-pool, while I lay in luxurious contemplaton of this great land of contrasts where you

142

can always seek and find the sun and pick your climate throughout the year.

After breakfast Douglas suggested that we go round the estate with the General Manager, Mr. Watson. 'He knows more about it than anyone else.'

This was an understatement. We soon realized that Mr. Watson and Tongaat were one. To this tall spare man, fashionable Durban was a fine port which owed its prosperity to the sugar industry. And Durban's three-cornered European-Indian-Native problem was a vivid reflection of the problem of every sugar-belt village. Sugar was not only Natal's life-blood but the source of her major modern headache – what to do about the Indians. In Tongaat they were trying to find a satisfactory answer to that problem.

'I'll take you through the fields first, then the mill, and finally the township,' said Mr. Watson.

In the sea of tall green leaves the sweating Pondo boys, naked save for their loin-cloths, cut and stripped the cane in one sweeping movement. In the mill some 90,000 tons of sugar were produced every year. Then we came to the township and its satellite villages – the social experiment of Tongaat, which is, in fact, practical *apartheid* applied by private enterprise with goodwill and good sense.

To appreciate what is being done, one must go back in time.

The sugar industry belongs to the cradle days of Natal, which was first colonized in the middle of the nineteenth century by the Boers infiltrating from the interior and the British coming in from the sea. Their mutual peril was the ferocious Zulu warrior. When the British settlers of 1848 began to grow sugar the only labour they could get were Native fugitives from the Zulus. So, in 1860, it was decided to import Indian coolies. These coolies signed on for five years, after which they could either be repatriated or stay on. Most of them stayed. Close on their heels followed the commercial Indians, bent on making money out of their humble compatriots.

143

Today there are about 290,000* Asiatics in the Union, and most of them are in Natal. Indians breed at a rate which alarms even Pandit Nehru in his own country and alarms Dr. Malan and every thinking South African still more. There are no longer Indian coolies cutting the cane, they have long since advanced as they could never have done in their own caste-dominated land, and they have become artisans, traders and land and property owners with flashing cars and fine houses. The Native is the field labourer. Between Indians, Natives and Europeans there is tension. The Natives loathe the Indians who exploit them commercially, the Indians despise the Natives and resent the Europeans. The Europeans fear the Indians and Natives collectively and are determined to maintain what Professor André Siegfried has described as their 'small European island in a rising tide of colour'.

To reconcile these uncomfortable human elements is no easy task. Tongaat has attempted it.

'We avoid unnecessary friction by having three separate model satellite villages round an International Area,' said Mr. Watson. 'The Natives, Indians and Europeans each have their own village, where they develop according to their own social, religious and cultural standards and with a proper pride in their own achievements. In the International Area are our Civic Centre, our Health Centre, our gardens, swimming-pool and sports stadium. The general store is Gandhi and Co. and has been in Tongaat for over fifty years. Members of the Mahatma's family – the Desnais – serve on

* The Cape Times of 4.1.73 quotes the following population estimates drawn up recently by the Department of Statistics in Pretoria which 'show that in the past eleven years the White population has grown by a mere 792,000 from 3,166,000 in 1962 to an estimated 3,958,000 last year. But in the same period the non-White population has increased from 14·5 m. to 19 m. . . . The figures show an increase in the African population from 12·3 m. to the 16·2 m. figure. Asiatic population increased from 502,000 to 668,000 while the Coloured population increased from 1·6 m. to 2·1 m.' The total population is estimated to be 22,987,000. Strong food for thought here!

the Town Board, so do leaders of the Native community. We all work together very well.'

But Douglas Saunders had been out to do even more than establish model villages and racial goodwill. He had enlisted the co-operation of his friend, the late Gwelo Goodman, South Africa's brilliant artist and architect, and, under Gwelo's inspiration, the traditional white gables of the Cape graced the green exuberance of the sugar-belt.

On the façade of the Health Centre in the International Area was a bas relief representing racial co-operation, and, in a corner, of course, Nogjawa, the Hare.

At Tongaat, Europeans, Indians and Natives have certain important things in common – the knowledge that their welfare is of paramount importance, that their interests are fairly represented, and pride in their township. During the Durban Riots, when Natives began burning down Indian properties and many lives were lost, the model townships of Tongaat remained calm.

As we drove back in the cool of the evening we could hear the Natives singing and strumming on their guitars, while Indian women in gaudy saris strolled home to their village, graceful and leisurely. The shadows of palm and cypress lengthened in the beautiful gardens laid out by Dr. Labuschagne of Tongaat, and the white, mauve and violet flowers of 'yesterday, today and tomorrow' distilled an essence as sweet and nostalgic as their name.

Yesterday, today and tomorrow?

Yesterday Tongaat had been virgin forest, the home of the hunter and the hunted; today it was a flourishing sugar industry with an ideal of racial unity; and what of the purple flower of tomorrow when Nogjawa, the Hare, would pop up no more in cane field or Civic Centre? Tomorrow is the heritage of today, and today in Tongaat was good.

From the moment of Tony's decisive knock at our door, an hour after the *Bermuda* docked in Durban on a brilliant Monday morning early in July, all was gaiety – official functions, private parties, and, for my husband, a great deal of speech-making. The Navy League, Missions to Seamen and Seamens' Institute were at their busiest and most helpful, and if anybody in the *Bermuda* or the two Frigates, *Nereide* and *Actaeon*, did not have a good time it was due to their own personal fault or misfortune. A number of naval wives had managed to lend their children to accommodating friends or neighbours in Simon's Town and had come to Durban to join in the fun.

During July this sea-port goes mad. It is a carnival round a series of race-meetings, with the Durban July Handicap as the most important event, and, as everyone knows the owners of the various horses, the excitement has a personal flavour which adds to its intensity. No other subject is discussed by anybody from the Native house-boys and the Indian waiters to the Cabinet Ministers, Leaders of the Opposition and Diplomats who honour the season with their presence. Even politics are overlooked.

The city, on its flowering hills above the splendid harbour, is blessed with a perfect winter climate – warm and sunny by day and cold at night – the people are kind and prosperous and live up to the legend of South African hospitality and the whole atmosphere is one of 'Let's enjoy ourselves!' We stayed in a hotel on the Esplanade, and every morning we breakfasted on a sunny balcony overlooking the mild Indian Ocean.

The beaches were crowded with sunbathers and the sea dotted with surf-bathers riding the great rollers that pounded on to silver sands. The candy-coloured saris of the Indian women and the bright clothes of their children were as exotic as the Zulu rickshaw boys were barbaric, loping and prancing between the shafts, with furs, feathers, beads and horns to enhance their muscular magnificence. There were European beaches, Indian beaches and Native beaches. The Indians said the sea should be free for all everywhere, and overflowed happily on to the European beaches, but if a Native showed his broad nose anywhere near theirs he was ducked and promptly slung out.

Sometimes we played golf, and, thanks to the jungle-charm of our surroundings, my concentration was even less than usual. But it is a little disconcerting when a pretty grey monkey picks your ball off the fairway and scampers into the bush with it.

'What do I do now?' I asked my Indian caddy.

'You play another from back there. Free. No penalty.' He talked in a high quick voice.

'Do monkeys often steal balls?'

'Sometimes steal, sometimes give. Monkeys give me two Dunlop sixty-fives. They were playing with them. When I come they give.'

Little faces peered at us from the trees as we putted, then suddenly, with a hoarse chatter and flurry, a flock of aquamarine behinds disappeared among the leaves.

'They don't think much of our putting,' said Bertie.

'Not that,' said the caddy. 'They talk about dog. When dog is near they tell each other, "Look out! *Dog!*" '

'Do dogs hunt them?'

'Dog terrible animal,' said the caddy. 'He chase them till they turn and bit him.'

'If they bite him why does he chase them?'

'Dog is fool. Plenty dogs here monkey-bit.'

'Are monkeys fools?'

'Monkeys very clever. Monkeys fond of Indians and White people. Can't stand Natives. When Natives come monkeys go.'

'Why?'

'Natives eat them. Yesterday monkey was killed by car, and, quick, Native was skinning him in the road.'

'Are there snakes in the jungle too?'

'Plenty snakes. Pythons, cobras, adders, mambas—'

'Heavens! And a mamba's bite is deadly!'

'Twenty minutes after mamba bite you dead. Python all right, he only crush and swallow.'

'What do snakes live on? Monkeys?'

'Not monkeys,' said the loyal youth, to whom monkeys were evidently sacred. 'Monkeys too smart. Rabbits, frogs, rats, mice, birds, small buck.'

147

'Have you killed any snakes?'

'Not me. Some boys catch snakes and sell alive to Snake Park. Get 7s. 6d. a foot. Snake Park like big snakes. I think better caddy.'

I recalled the Port Elizabeth Snake Park where enterprising boys scaled the wall and stole snakes from the pit at dead of night and sold them back next day. The hazards of a caddy's life were certainly less than those of a seller of serpents.

The day of 'the July' was as dazzling as it always is, with the pretty course overflowing with punters from all over the Union, with busy bookies, women in Ascot dresses and, above all, the burnished horses on whom so many hopes were set. Everybody was in a good mood. Her Excellency, Mrs. Jansen, consented to have a bet on the big race and, like a true feminist, backed Gay Jane, the only filly and the winner. It was a typical 'Durban July' with no thought for yesterday and little for tomorrow. Only today mattered.

But Durban is a feminine city, and, like everything beautiful and feminine, she has her past.

We found a great deal of her 'yesterday' concentrated in the small quick capable hands of Miss Killie Campbell, a dynamic personality burning with enthusiasm for her self-appointed task of collecting everything to do with the history of her beloved Natal. In her fine library are hundreds of original documents and letters written by early British settlers over a hundred years ago, all carefully typed, annotated and filed. Her beautiful old home is a museum for all sorts of Africana – old pictures and books, thousands of Native weapons, beads and masks, and a large collection of paintings of tribal life and custom by that excellent artist, Barbara Tyrrell.

Killie Campbell is a descendant of those first British settlers herself, and in seeking out and preserving their archives she and her helpers are accomplishing a work of real value to posterity.

As for the 'tomorrow' of this fair province – who can foretell the future? Many shapes mingle in the crystal and too many of them are the dark forms whose forebears crossed the ocean nearly a hundred years ago in the coolie ships for the sugar-fields – the fertile polygamous people of India.

CHAPTER TWELVE

WOMAN IN A WARSHIP

WHEN H.M.S. *Bermuda* sailed from Durban for Madagascar two females sailed with her – the Commander-in-Chief's wife, by kind permission of their Lordships, and the ship's cat who took it for granted that she belonged to the Navy and was always welcome on board a warship. I envied the casual way she possessed the ship from bows to stern. Even Captain Philip Currey, who could shiver the timbers of the best, was gentle with this sleek young thing in the black fur coat.

As we left harbour in the heaving south-east trades she sat on the rail and watched the vanishing bluff.

'What do you suppose Durban meant to her?' I asked Corney, the Coxswain, who had been deputed to keep me out of people's way.

'Blackie has a family of kittens in the capstan engine flat,' he said. 'That helps tie them a bit.'

'Like most women,' said Cameron McClure from the South African Broadcasting Corporation, who was my husband's guest on board, and who soon came to know the ship nearly as well as Blackie. He might have been called Nogjawa, the Hare, for he and his portable recorder popped up here, there and everywhere at all hours of the day and night, sensing the metabolism of the ship, her life-rhythm – recording her many voices, human and metallic.

'How right Bertie was to call her a Steel Box with the lid down,' said Mac. 'Especially at the moment!'

And indeed the lid was down, for the decks of the warship

were constantly awash as she plunged and rolled in the south-east trades, and every hatch was closed.

Chief Petty Officer Corney, who was our guide in the small compressed world of the Steel Box, excused her antics. 'It's the superstructure makes her lively, the weight of all the armaments – and her thin bottom. She can't sit down in the water.' Sometimes the racing screws leapt clear and then she shuddered from stem to stern.

Blackie didn't care, she was as casual as a bird on a tossing twig. She set her fellow female passenger a stout example. But exploring the innards of the Steel Box was like taking a very giddy trip through the Haunted Castle at the Fun Fair. The order of the day was 'Watch your head, and 'ware your shins!' Fearful blasts of hot or cold air bellowed out of unexpected places, grimy jack-in-the-boxes popped up from holes at our feet, gun-turrets became whirling towers, men and boys appeared at the double from nowhere, and, but for Corney going ahead as shock-absorber, even more surprises might have startled us. 'You never can tell with sailors,' he explained mysteriously. 'They don't expect ladies between decks.'

Odd smells assailed our nostrils at every turn – paint, polish, rope, tar, fuel-oil, baking bread, roasting meat and rum – and many and strange were the sounds Mac picked up on his mike – the high keening of pipes, melodious bugle calls, bells, guns, engines, the throb of the pitometer, the ceaseless hum of the ventilators, orders barked, hymns sung, the thrum of a guitar at a concert party or the Captain's clipped voice dictating a signal.

And once, when the mike on its long lead was lowered down a ladder to pick up the rumble of the anchor chain in the bowels of the ship, it recorded, as well, one of those little overtones of life at sea.

Miaow-brr-miaow . . . rumble-rumble-clank-clank-clank, and then the stentorian tones of a ham-handed seaman with a saucer of milk for Blackie and the kittens. 'All right, you — little —, if you don't want your — milk, I'll — well take it away again.'

'Too Elizabethan,' said Mac, delighted. 'If only I didn't have to edit it!'

During each of the next five days we increased our experience. We visited the shipwright's shop, clean, airy and smelling of wood-shavings, and the 'garage', where the spare torpedo lived in company with the Chief Diver who was an artist when he was off duty. Desert Island scenery for the Ship's Concert Party leaned against a bulkhead. A sailor painted SOUTH ATLANTIC on a lifebelt, and another polished the headpiece of a diver's suit.

'Feel the weight of the helmet,' said Mac.

It seemed to me to weigh as much as a Congolese woman's market-basket. The Chief Diver brought out a pair of diving-boots.

'Try these!' he suggested.

'A ton of bricks! You couldn't kick anyone with these on.'

'Just as well, perhaps,' said the Chief Diver. 'But it's all light under water. You'd be surprised.'

In the Blacksmith's Shop we found everything except a horse.

'This is a nice quiet place,' said the Blacksmith. He looked round at a number of men who did not appear to be engaged in any vital activity. 'It's a sort of club where everybody comes to read their books and write their letters home and be peaceful. Till we light up the forge. Then, with the noise and the fumes, they all run like rabbits.'

The Machine Shop was hot, smooth and oily – more Mac's fancy than mine – and I was glad to go into the Sail-maker's den with its timeless atmosphere and odour of canvas. The Sailmaker was plugging enormous brass eyelets into a sail, and behind a little canvas curtain I caught a glimpse of the jerseys and boots of a football team.

Trays of crisp white newly-baked bread and lemon-curd tarts were ready in the Bakery, and in the galley the cooks were putting out the hot substantial dinners for the various messes. We heard 'Up spirits!' piped, and a sailor from each mess queued with his billy-can to receive the grog ration dished out of a huge oak barrel with 'THE KING, GOD BLESS HIM' in brass lettering on it.

'That barrel is every sailor's joy and pride,' said Corney. 'Nothing but rum goes into it, and he keeps it polished and takes care of it always.'

Now, once again, as in the days of the first Elizabeth, when English seamen were discovering new worlds, the rum barrels of the Royal Navy carry the words 'THE QUEEN, GOD BLESS HER'.*

Corney took us into the different messes. Each had its own personality. Some had saucy pin-up girls, others preferred pictures of members of the Royal Family. In these messes men ate, lived and slept. On the boys' mess-deck there was something of a crowd, for twenty-four Rhodesian sea-cadets, who had never been to sea in their lives, had joined the ship for the Madagascar cruise. At first some had been sick, but they had settled down surprisingly quickly in their hot cramped quarters. My husband told me afterwards that in American warships there are no messes, only a central cafeteria.

'Men take their food and eat it where they like.'

'Is it better to have messes?'

'We think so. They are like families in a village, each with its special character and pride. There is rivalry between them – competitions, boat-races and so on – and within them is companionship. That's the most important thing, the companionship – the meaning of the word *messmate*.'

'You could be lonely without it?'

'More than that. Your messmates are good for you. If a chap is tiresome or ill-tempered his messmates work on him. Buck him up.'

'It's the closeness one notices,' I said. 'The steel-box feeling – nowhere for anyone to be alone – no privacy at all.'

'Yes,' he agreed. 'In a ship, where there is literally none for most people, you begin to realize how precious privacy is! People cherish it. Even if it's just having a place two by

---

* *This traditional R.N. rum tot ritual with its 'Yo-ho-ho' flavour of the Spanish Main is today replaced by a humdrum issue of canned beer.*

153

four of your own. The Petty Officer in charge of the quarter-deck stores, for instance. It doesn't matter that all he has is a dark hole, with the noise of the fan, and the temperature at ninety-eight degrees – it's somewhere he can get to by himself – to write a letter perhaps, or to read one – it's a place to be alone when he feels the need.'

One morning Corney suggested that I steer the ship. I agreed with innocent enthusiasm, thinking of the bridge of a liner, and some amiable officer saying, 'Would you like to take the wheel?' But here one had to earn the privilege. Nothing could have alarmed me more than when Corney pointed down a manhole with one of those naked vertical steel ladders dropping on to a narrow platform above a bottomless pit.

'We go down there,' he said. 'To the lower steering position.'

'I can't steer down there,' I protested panic-stricken. 'I must look where I'm going!'

The Coxswain's white teeth flashed. 'Not these days, you needn't. This ship isn't the Victory.'

'I'm sorry,' I said. 'I can't go down there. It makes me giddy just to look into those depths.'

Corney, who was already on his way down, skimmed up again, his expression genuinely pained and shocked.

'Your Ladyship, this is something special! No Wren has ever steered a warship. What woman has? Tell me that.'

'Probably Princess Margaret,' I said feebly, my palms damp.

'And probably not,' he retorted. 'This is the chance of a lifetime, and you throw it away on account of a little ladder.'

I appealed to Cameron McClure. 'You explain, Mac. You know I can't.'

Mac also had no head for heights. His face was friendly and understanding as he said, 'I know you *can*.'

The shock of his answer killed further resistance. The descent was accomplished. A bearded Quartermaster called up

154

the voice-pipe to the bridge, 'Permission for Lady Packer to take the wheel,' and the 'chance of a lifetime' was seized. But in a very few minutes a brisk order came down from the bridge: 'Quartermaster, take over the wheel!'

When the coxswain said 'Now we can go to the engine room', my courage finally failed me. Mac and his mike were bolder. He was fascinated. Once was not enough. At night he often went on to the bridge and kept the middle watch – finding his way through the belly of the Steel Box with difficulty, stumbling over bodies, bumping into hammocks and being jabbed in the eye more than once by some unconscious big toe.

Sometimes all the anti-aircraft artillery went into action at once. Up on the bridge, I held my ears.

'This noise is nothing,' said the Captain crisply. 'You should hear the eight barrel pom-poms. Your spirit leaves your body.'

The Frigate *Actaeon* was in company with us and it was decided to send the Gunnery Officer over to discuss the shoot with her. Also a net of our delicious white loaves. The *Actaeon* came parallel with the *Bermuda* and in spite of racing seas a line was successfully shot across with a chair suspended to it.

'I hope the Gunnery Officer will wear a lifebelt,' I said anxiously to Bertie.

He looked at me with the deadpan expression he reserves for women talking nonsense about men's activities. 'And warm underclothes,' he said.

The tossing chair with the considerable weight of the Gunnery Officer looked abominably dangerous swinging over the foaming chasm between the two ships steaming side by side in the swell.

'He'll fall in!' I gasped.

'Or break like an egg-shell against the side,' suggested Bertie.

But all went well with the man and loaves, and the Chief Baker showed me the signal he received from *Actaeon*. 'Thanks for your fine bread.' Across it he wrote 'Well done', and pinned it on the notice-board for the benefit of his bakers.

Wherever you go in a warship you bump into hammock stowages. As Corney and I passed one of these near the boys' mess deck, he paused and said solemnly: 'If this was the Admiral's ship and he came past here he'd go off his head.'

'Why should he go off his head just here?'

'The way they stow them these days. Boys aren't what they were. They expect a chocolate bar and an ice-cream before they stow a hammock properly.'

'How long does it take to lash up one of these?'

'About two minutes it took in my time. Now a boy can take up to fifty minutes. Hasn't got his heart in his work.'

We were on our way to the Paint Shop in the bows, and to go there we went through the capstan engine flat. There was a large notice forbidding anyone to touch the engine. It was the sort of engine several people could have sat on comfortably, as it had nice smooth surfaces.

'I wonder why you mustn't touch it?' I said.

Corney said, 'You know what sailors are – they go mad all of a sudden. You can't have a sailor going mad on the capstan engine.'

What with Admirals liable to go off their heads about hammocks and sailors going mad all of a sudden, life at sea sounded far from monotonous.

Next door to the capstan engine flat was the cat and kitten flat, complete with sand-box. Blackie came purring out to meet us.

'Through here,' said the Coxswain, 'is the cells. There's a man in one picking oakum. Just make as if he isn't there.'

This was difficult as the oakum-picker's cell door was open and I practically fell over him. Blackie for her part greeted him warmly.

'This,' said Corney, with a sweeping gesture at the Paint Shop, 'is the most important place in the ship. Where would she be without paint to keep her all dressed up and smart?'

The grey paint-pots evoked memories of the past – of

Wei-Hai-Wei Island in North China when my Admiral had been the Commander of a slim cruiser and the man responsible for keeping her all dressed up and smart. There had always been little figures suspended over the sides of the *Kent* painting ship as she lay in the lovely harbour between the cardboard mountains of Shantung and the little winged temples and pomegranate trees of the Island.

As we went back aft we found the Royal Marine band playing rousing music on the Quarter Deck. In the middle of 'Pomp and Circumstance' a great green wave swamped the deck and nearly washed them overboard, but so superb was their discipline that they continued to play their instruments under water. The Marines never faltered.

The Commander-in-Chief's quarters were in the stern, and in rough weather many mysterious things went *boomp* in the night. I woke often and listened to the roar and thrash of the propellers, and, it seemed, as I lay wedged into my bunk with pillows, that my ear rested upon a mighty pounding heart. In the moonlit circle of the closed scuttle the white crests surged and every now and again all was dark as a wave broke against the thick glass.

How strange to be on board my husband's ship – *a ménage à trois* with the Grey Mistress! Yet this was different – and somehow a little sad. 'If this was the Admiral's ship . . .' the Coxswain had said. . . . Well, wasn't she? I found myself wondering about the relationship between a Commander-in-Chief and his flag-ship in time of peace. Perhaps it was something like that of her own to Gay Jane, the winner of the Durban July Handicap. Gay Jane's owner did not groom her, train her, or sleep in the stable with her, but she took a tremendous pride in her filly's achievements. Maybe an Admiral felt a bit that way too. His flag-ship wore his colours proudly and bravely, and he knew her to be a winner.

In Nelson's time, of course, an Admiral could even expect to make money out of a 'good win', but the great days of prize-money had gone with so much else.

When sleep was elusive in the rocking turbulent clanging night, I read a book I had borrowed from the Captain which brought the bold days of sail very near. It was the Journal of Lieutenant Thomas Boteler, R.N., who, in 1821, set sail from England to explore the seas which H.M.S. *Bermuda* now sailed so confidently. In those days the perils of the pioneer mariner were so great that few survived to tell the tale. Pirates, shipwreck, storms, disease and encounters with savages ashore all took their toll. Lieutenant Boteler's Log made enthralling reading. It had been incorporated in the official account of the expedition.

'Narrative of Voyages
to explore the shores of
Africa, Arabia and Madagascar
performed by H.M. Ships *Leven* and *Baracouta*
under the direction of
Captain W. F. W. Owen, R.N.
by command of the Lords Commissioners of the
Admiralty
published in London by
Richard Bentley, New Burlington Street
publisher in ordinary to His Majesty
1833'

In the business of charting the coastline of Madagascar they sometimes found the natives friendly, sometimes not, and often treacherous. The names on the chart still indicate the fate of many members of that expedition, such as 'Graves Island', and 'Murderers' Bay' where two young midshipmen were killed by the Malagasy while surveying ashore. Boys of sixteen, perhaps, like Percival George Duddy in the kloof-garden of Admiralty House.

Lieutenant Boteler, who took command of the sloop *Baracouta*, when her Captain died, saw many of his comrades swept overboard by storms, perish at the hands of savages or succumb to fevers.

Already on board the *Bermuda* we were taking our palu-

158

drine, but in 1821 the anopheles mosquito was as deadly as the mamba, and far more common. Boteler grieves for one of his young officers who, curiously, had a South African name, Lieutenant Reitz.

'A burning brow, sudden prostration ... unquenchable thirst and continued restlessness, are the constant attendants on its course. Delirium ensues, when the body, exhausted by the wild ravings of the mind, sinks an emaciated skeleton to the grave.

'Such was the frightful picture exhibited by so many of our comrades in their passage to the tomb. Their bones are mouldering in a distant land; the savage tramples over their lonely resting place. ... But there are hearts which, though thousands of miles are between them, turn in memory to the lonely spot, and dwell again on recollections of the dead.'

In those words the young man wrote of his own fate, for, although he survived the East Coast Expedition, he sailed again in 1827 to chart the West coast, where he too died of fever, having lost nearly all his crew from illness and mishap.

But for the sailors of Europe there would have been no settlers to colonize the Dark Continent and no Voortrekkers to set the great wheels rolling into the interior. Women sailed with their seamen husbands on these hazardous voyages. On September 16th, 1821, Boteler notes that:

'The gunner's wife, Mrs. Vasey, was delivered of a girl, being the third native of His Majesty's Ship *Leven* born since our departure from England.'

Strangely enough, the Gunner of His Majesty's Ship *Bermuda*, a hundred and thirty years later, also became the father of a daughter on the way to Madagascar. But *his* child was born safely in Simon's Town and the glad news relayed to him by wireless. As we drank the health of mother and

159

baby in the Wardroom, I could not help thinking about Mrs. Vasey. Who had been *her* accoucheur in the dark discomfort of the *Baracouta* between the little-known coast of East Africa and the less known shores of Madagascar? And what fate had befallen the new addition to the ship's complement? On that score the 'Narrative of the Voyages' told me no more than I have quoted.

CHAPTER THIRTEEN

MADAGASCAR INTERLUDE

WHENEVER the *Bermuda* visited a foreign port, the Instructor Lieutenant-Commander, known as 'Schoolie', gave a brief broadcast about it for the benefit of the ship's company.

We learned that Madagascar was the third largest island in the world, situated on the trade route to the Far East, and therefore a popular haunt of pirates in days gone by. It had been discovered by Portuguese navigators, and had become a French Colony in 1896. It was mountainous, with a high central plateau, and the tropical climate was influenced by the south-east trades. The inhabitants, collectively known as Malagasy, were of mixed origin – Negroid, Arab, Indian and Melanesian – and their language and religion varied from one district to the next.*

After the Napoleonic Wars (in the time of H.M.S. *Baracouta* and *Leven*) Britain's influence in Madagascar had been considerable. The Hovas were the ruling race, and their King, Radama I, was a Christian who assisted the British in quelling the Slave Trade. Unfortunately, at his death, he was succeeded by his wife, Ranavalona, who martyred the Christians and closed the island to foreign trade. From then on, it seemed, Madagascar was opened and closed like a door in a house where there are dogs, and, like dogs, the European trading nations were kicked out as often as they were let in.

Products were salt, coffee, pepper, tapioca, rice and minerals, and there was a flourishing export of hides and tinned

* *Madagascar became the Malagasy Republic in 1960.*

beef from the South. At this point Schoolie abandoned the encyclopedia and told us that during World War Two, when Madagascar was Vichy controlled, the island was occupied by Britain and South Africa in order to prevent a Japanese invasion.

He said: 'The success of the original operation at Diego Suarez was largely due to the initiative and dash of a landing party of Royal Marines taking the defenders in the rear and creating a disturbance out of all proportion to its size.'

The island was governed by a High-Commissioner with Administrator-Mayors in charge of the various districts. And, like the French Congo, it was represented in Paris, where the Native delegates were able to make an exhaustive study of Communism. (That final qualification is not Schoolie's but my own.)

Soon after sunrise on Saturday, 21st July, the *Actaeon* left us to anchor off the island of Nossi-Bé, and at eight o'clock the mountains behind the glorious enclosed harbour of Diego Suarez echoed with the reverberations of our twenty-one gun salute.

Unfortunately our friends, the Auboyneaus, were not there. It had recently been decided that Admiral Auboyneau should conduct his operations from Paris, so they had returned to France with their two baby girls.

However our kind hosts had arranged a week of intensive entertainment for the British ships, with every hour accounted for in advance in an elegant souvenir programme.

That evening the *Bermuda* gave a reception for about a hundred and fifty people. There were Monsieur Pileni, the Corsican Administrator, and his wife and daughter; the French Naval Officers and their wives; a number of Malagasy; some wealthy Indian traders, and a miscellaneous collection of dusky ladies who smelt of all the perfumes of Arabia or allowed nature to take its course. The Indians were the flock of the British Consul-General, Mr. Arning, and a prosperous flock they were.

Not long before our visit, Aly Khan and Rita had flown to

162

Madagascar so that Aly might remind the Faithful that they owed certain obligations to his father, the Aga Khan, the direct descendant of the Prophet. The French women were still sighing over the allure of Aly and the glamour of Rita and the sad fact that such an exotic union should prove so impermanent.

Indians gave Aly a fortune!' I was told. 'But then why not? They have the money. They own the best houses on the island, they can afford to buy any property they want, and their papers are always in order. They are a power in Madagascar and we cannot keep them out.'

India, it seemed, was well established on the springboard for East Africa.

Quaint snatches of conversation came to my ears. A pretty girl, trying out her English, said to the Flag Captain, 'Do you smell much?'

Phil Currey wrinkled a fastidious nose. 'Not much, I hope.'

'I do not smell at all,' she announced. 'My mother does – all the time.'

'Have a cigarette,' said the Captain hastily.

The young lady gave him a patient look. 'I have already explained that I do *not* smell.' As he lit his own cigarette, she added, '*Alors*, you *do* then! I have remarked that most gentlemen do.'

Phil caught my eye, and handed me his case. 'Will you smell?' he asked briskly, his face expressionless.

Mr. Arning joined us. 'I hope you're not taking too much baggage in the plane tomorrow,' he said. 'I'm taking two cases of whisky, and nothing will part me from them.'

We were to fly to Tananarive, the capital, at seven next morning, a four hours flight in a naval Junker. The Flag Captain, Flag Lieutenant, three officers and my husband's valet were to accompany us, and, of course, the Consul-General.

Cameron McClure had arranged his passage to Tananarive in a naval plane which was going to Nossie-Bé first to pick up some of H.M.S. *Actaeon*'s officers. It had been

163

understood that once ashore he would be independent of us, and what became of him in Tananarive was always something of a mystery.

When we arrived at the airport the pilot threw up his hands in horror at the number of passengers and weight of the load, but Mr. Arning was adamant about his two precious cases. He would be entertaining in our honour at the Consulate and a reception short of whisky would be unthinkable. The pilot, who had been invited, shrugged, groaned and finally said, '*Eh bien,* bring your cases! We are so much overweight already that a little more or less makes no difference.'

Phil Currey muttered as we took our places, 'The Commander-in-Chief has a look of sullen courage.'

'He mistrusts all air-travel,' I whispered, 'especially when there are strap-hangers!'

Bertie strove to fasten his seat-belt and failed. It was of no importance, said the French wireless officer, crouched over a dusty machine. None of the belts fastened, he added, one did not worry. A roar, a few backfires and sprawling strap-hangers, and we were airborne, whisky and all.

A desolate but beautiful scene spread below us. Swamps and plains gave way to jagged mountains and presently we were flying over the high plateau 4,000 feet above sea-level. There were few villages until we were near Tananarive when the valleys began to glow with cultivation and the luminous green of rice-padi. The town of Tananarive straggled from one hilltop to another in a rosy fantasy of red clay houses, very tall and narrow with steep tiled roofs. In the hollow at its heart was a toy race-course and a lake. In the meadows little brown boys tended the humped cattle, and overhead the big Madagascar eagles wheeled lazily.

As soon as we landed, Bertie was swept away to call on Monsieur Martine, who was the Governor, Secretary General and Acting High Commissioner all combined, I was taken in charge by Captain and Madame Seguin who were our constant companions during the next few days. The Captain, who was the High Commissioner's Military Aide, had a laughing faun's face and a gift for organizing people without any fuss. His wife was a cool green-eyed blonde, poised and considerate. As we rattled merrily through the narrow, winding, up-and-down streets, they showed me the fine Naval and Military Headquarters and parks and playgrounds and the picturesque market where the Malagasy went about their business in the shade of the umbrellas or parasols without which they never moved. Over an odd assortment of European clothes they draped white or scarlet togas. Scarlet implied descent from the royal house of the Hovas, and, as the early kings were polygamous and fertile, there was plenty of scarlet in the island.

'At present the Hova throne is a museum piece in the old wooden palace up there on the hill,' said Captain Seguin. 'The last Queen was exiled more than fifty years ago.'

'Do they hope to restore the monarchy?'

He raised cynical eyebrows. 'It is hard to know what they hope. But after the war there was a rebellion. It was ineffective and quickly put down. But then they chose April 1st to launch it!'

Madame Seguin changed the subject. 'Your party is to stay at Mahazoarivo. It is the summer residence of the *Haut Commissaire*. I hope you will be comfortable.'

Mahazoarivo was a tall old stone house standing in lovely gardens. The Union Jack flew over it in honour of the British visitors, and, as we drove past the sentry-box at the gates, a native guard in blue skiing trousers and red boleros and tarbooshes sprang smartly to attention on dusty bare feet.

Our rooms were high and spacious with great bowls of mimosa and sweet-peas everywhere. Raffia rugs made by convicts were spread on the tiled floors, and, from the little balconies outside the tall French windows, we looked down upon a lotus lake. I noticed mosquito-nets over the beds and remembered that here one must never forget to take an anti-malaria tablet.

After an informal lunch out of doors with Governor Martine and his animated daughter, 'Jackie', I said to Madame

Seguin: 'Our programme is very full, but I wonder if it would be possible for me to steal an hour to have my hair shampooed.'

She studied the official programme earnestly.

'There is *nowhere* a free hour,' she said – and I felt, rather than heard, a faint sigh from my husband – 'unless we curtail our visit to the gardens of Tsimbazaza this afternoon ...'

'Do that then,' commanded the Governor, who had interested himself in the matter.

She turned her green eyes upon him, smiling. 'There is another small difficulty. It is Sunday, and the *coiffeur* is closed.'

'Open him,' said the Governor. 'He will be enchanted.'

'Naturally,' agreed Jackie, and she and Madame Seguin excused themselves to give the *coiffeur* '*un coup de telefon*'.

'Five o'clock,' they said as they returned. 'He is honoured.'

A few moments later our party was piled into cars and we were on our way to Tsimbazaza, where Professor Millot, the Director of Scientific Research, awaited us.

'He is a *savant*,' Madame Seguin explained. 'A famous scientist, naturalist, geologist and philosopher. He knows the earth and all its potentialities. Tsimbazaza is only a sideline to him.'

The Professor was small and lame with a pale humorous face, pale wise eyes and an air of amiable detachment towards human beings and of easy intimacy to fauna and flora.

We saw snakes and giant tortoises horridly entwined, and, as I shuddered, Professor Millot smiled.

'The snakes of Madagascar are entirely inoffensive,' he said in his perfect English. 'You may make pets of them. Would you like to take one back with you?'

'If the Flag Lieutenant will make it his special charge,' I said. But Tony, who had once been shipmates with a man who kept pet snakes, would have none of this suggestion.

Monstrous livid chameleons clung to bleached boughs and

166

rolled goiterous eyes at us, and, in an aviary, we saw brilliant peacocks, parakeets and crested cranes. Most endearing were the lemur monkeys with their long ringed bushy tails and their pretty faces jewelled with great round eyes of dazzling gold or green or melting brown. They were grey, tan or black and white, and, as they saw the Professor, they set up a happy chattering and came swinging down from the trees to the bars of their huge cage, and thrust out their little black hands for the crusts he drew from his pocket as inexhaustibly as a conjurer draws flags from a top-hat.

'So much love!' said Phil Currey to me. 'Have you ever seen anyone love his creatures like this little man?'

And indeed the expression of St. Francis of Assisi must once have been filled with this same tenderness for his wild birds and beasts.

When Professor Millot showed us his aloes it was clear that he regarded them as human.

'Many of these are foreigners,' he said. 'We have some of your South Africans here. They like Madagascar. See, this bell-like succulent comes from the Karroo, but this star-flower here is a native, unique to this island. How lovely she is with the small red stars at her finger-tips! If you wish, I will let you have some plants. She will be happy in Simon's Town.'

'I would love some of the star-flowers,' I said, knowing how they would rejoice Veronica's heart. 'But some of these others give me the creeps.'

They were out of a nightmare. Weird spiked obelisks, leathery bottle-aloes, leprous rhizomes and tormented arms holding out sulphur yellow torches. It only required our herbalist Bantu, Mamputa, with one of his head colds, and twigs sticking out of his ears and nose, to complete the surrealist picture.

But the Professor found his freaks brave and lovable.

He said reproachfully: 'They are desert plants. They endure the heat and thirst of the day. They are unshapely but long-suffering, and they bring forth their own strange beauty.'

Someone asked, could he show us orchids?

'Unfortunately it is not the season. It is a pity. There are over nine hundred known orchids in the world, and one fifth of them are indigenous to Madagascar.'

Wherever we went, a crowd pursued us faithfully, and the long brown gaze of Melanesia, India, Arabia and Africa followed us from beneath raffia hats, black umbrellas and bright sunshades.

Captain Seguin said: 'It is the officers who are on view today. Even the *lémuriens* admire the British Navy!'

At five o'clock I was introduced to Monsieur François, the *Coiffeur*. He bowed as charmingly as if his Sunday afternoon plans had not been turned topsy-turvy on my account, and, while setting my hair, he showed me snapshots of Durban. Here was the City Hall and there the Post Office. What a magnificent city! So clean, so spacious! And how remarkable that the Europeans, Indians and Natives were not all housed together higgledy-piggledy in one great insanitary confusion like Tananarive. But then, one must make allowances, *évidément* Tananarive had never been planned, it had simply evolved.

A drowsy half-hour with the hum of the drier in my ears and then the voice of Monsieur François recalled me from near sleep.

'There, Madame, they are quite dry. I will comb them for you.'

Madame Seguin, who had taken the opportunity to have her hair reset, slipped her small burnished head out of the steel helmet and glanced at her watch.

'You will not have much time to repose yourself. We dine at the *Amirauté* with le Capitaine Patou at eight o'clock.'

I said it did not matter and asked what I owed.

Monsieur François performed one of his sweeping bows and said:

'Madame is the guest of Madagascar.'

On the high plateau it grows cold at night, and, as we left

the *Coiffeur*, a chill evening breeze had begun to blow. The Malagasy in the narrow streets drew their togas close about their shoulders as they hovered round the wells – a slender secret people, the descendants of slaves and chieftains. Since the abortive 1947 rebellion there had lingered in the air a suggestion of unease for some twenty thousand French among three million natives.

At Mahazoarivo the guard was drawn up for the sunset ceremony of hauling down the Union Jack, the crows shouted hoarse good nights to one another and the Madagascar eagles settled in the trees. The red and green landscape glowed with a soft opalescent light and there was a faint whistle of wings as an arrow-head of ducks rose from the pearly lake. Down in the valley the egrets deserted their hosts, the humped cattle, and came to rest among the branches in the garden like bouquets of great magnolias glimmering in the dusk. The moment between day and night in Madagascar was briefer even than in Africa, it was the single sweep of a flaming sword.

Upstairs in our suite I found my husband's valet trying to draw water from a bath. None flowed.

'I've rung for the head boy,' he said. 'But nobody here talks English – not one word!' He sounded aggrieved.

Michel, the Hova head boy, in his white tunic and broad vermillion sash, appeared, smiling and courteous.

'*Mais oui, l'eau ne coule pas – on va faire quelque chose* . . .'

Alternately he blew furiously up the bath tap and sucked down it, then he turned on every tap in sight. And behold there was water! Michel beamed, bowed and withdrew. Marie, the Hova maid, brought in my evening dress, carefully pressed. She closed the shutters and drew the hand-woven curtains, going about her duties with a curious light-footed light-handed deliberation. Here was none of the slow stateliness of the African Negress, here was seduction and a stealthy animal caution.

Next morning we visited the wooden palaces of erstwhile

kings and queens on the heights above the town. These are now museums strongly influenced by the spirit of Napoleon and Queen Victoria. Radama I had aped the Corsican General down to the last detail of his dress and even unto the wayward lock over the forehead. And Victoria's Malagasy contemporary was photographed in a close-fitting bodice and voluminous bustle. Madagascar would have liked to have come under the protection of the Great White Queen, but Victoria had contented herself with sending the Hova Queen a massive illustrated bible and a gold loving-cup engraved with a Highland deer-stalking scene.

Even more extinct than dead Radama and wicked Ranavalona were the first inhabitants of Madagascar whose bones graced the Natural History Museum. The complete skeletons of a dinosaur and an aepyornis (a gigantic ostrich) evoked fearful visions of the era when the island was the home of prehistoric monsters. A naval friend of ours, Captain Jack Borrett, who had been in command of a British warship during the occupation of Madagascar in World War Two, had been presented with an aepyornis egg by a local chief but unfortunately, this unique gift became cracked during the blitz like so much else. Pre-history, always strangely near in Madagascar, leapt suddenly forward into our own time when Professor Smith's living coelocanth was caught off a nearby island. One knew then that creatures of the remote past could survive the millenniums, so perhaps an aepyornis egg may one day hatch out some monstrous chicken. Such eggs are still occasionally found in the island.

The Palace of the Hova Prime Ministers had been transformed into a School for Arts and Crafts, where we saw girls making raffia goods, or shrouds as gay as Spanish shawls. The Malagasy – like so many of the human race – love their relations most when they are no more. So they dig them out of their graves after three years to give them a party. And what a party! They clothe them in a new festive winding sheet and there is much feasting and dancing, after which the defunct are re-interred and the period of mourning is lifted.

The young French teacher in charge of Arts and Crafts was as gay and pretty as a Malagasy shroud, and she took us on to a high balcony where any of us might well have qualified for such an article. The wooden rail was crumbling and most of the floor boards were missing. We stepped over yawning chasms. She said '*Attention!*' in an unconcerned sort of voice. And made a sweeping gesture to embrace the hills and valley.

'The best view in Tananarive! From here I watch the races. You see the little course? There, beside the Palace of the Kings and Queens, is the chapel built to commemorate the martyrs.'

'What martyrs?'

'Queen Ranavalona threw all the Christians over the precipice.'

'Many Christians?'

Mademoiselle tossed her charming head and laughed aloud.

'Who can say? With martyrs it is of no account. Perhaps twenty, perhaps two hundred. In any case it was some time ago, and now we have the chapel!'

Early next day we flew to the hot springs of Antsirabe, five thousand feet up among the whispering pines. The waters, we were informed, had all the properties of Vichy. The air was clear and pellucid and the place was wonderfully peaceful. On our return we circled low over a fathomless green lake in an extinct volcano – lonely and sinister.

'Unhappy lovers make excursions there to disappear,' said Madame Seguin. 'It is the rendezvous for *les suicidés.*'

It seemed a long way to go when all they needed to do was to climb on to the balcony of the School for Arts and Crafts and fall through the missing planks, or lean against the insecure railing.

Once again there was little time in which 'to repose ourselves' on our return, for we were to dine with the Governor.

The heavy fragrance of the garden filtered through the

open French doors, the Hova boys waited at the Governor's table, white-gloved and soft-footed, exotic in their blood-red boleros. The glasses were charged with champagne and Monsieur Martine rose to say a few words.

'England and France – your country and mine – are like an old married couple, *un vieux ménage.* They love each other, they quarrel and make up, and quarrel again, but in the long run they cannot do without each other . . .'

Bertie replied in French in the same warm vein.

'Today France and England remain the two great powers for good in a sad and struggling Europe . . . we must keep our *vieux ménage* intact and devoted. Upon that depends the future of Europe. . . .'

Europe – so far away that one had almost forgotten her bitter tribulations, Europe with her iron curtains, her inflammable borders, and the menace of the Kremlin lengthening as inevitably as a shadow lengthens at close of day – drew nearer with the words that had been spoken. Suddenly we were aware of a sense of exile, a shiver of fear and a surge of friendship. Madame Seguin's green eyes were moist as she turned to the Flag Captain. 'I have the lomp in the throat,' she said.

Once again we set off in the early morning to fly from the bracing air of Tananarive to the tropical jungle isle of Nossi-Bé. Captain and Madame Seguin and Mr. Arning were with our party and would remain with us until we sailed from Diego Suarez.

It was a three hour flight. Below us the mountain peaks crowded, one beyond the other, the colour of grey-green lichen, softened by cloud shadows, and clawed everywhere by erosion and the axe of the Malagasy wood-cutter, so that where a grove of trees should have trembled in the wind there was only a scarlet wound. We followed the course of the Betsiboka, jade in the hills but muddy as it flowed through the plain with its sad harvest of red earth and its evil crocodiles.

'Isle of Fear' the French had called Madagascar before

they called it 'The Red Island' after the colour of its soil, and 'Isle of the Moon' the Arabs had named it. If it were not for the efforts of the French this island might soon have become depopulated, for the Malagasy were a dwindling race, both in numbers and stature, owing to the fever and disease inherent in them. But nowadays every Native was tested for malaria, venereal disease and tuberculosis, and every house was sprayed annually with D.D.T. Yet the sanitation of Tananarive had struck me as primitve and there were many patches of stagnant water where anopheles might lay her eggs.

As we followed the coast with its hidden coves and anchorages it was easy to see why the pirates of old must have found the 'Isle of Fear' an ideal base for their activities. Captain Kidd, Long Ben, Bartholomew Roberts and many others had reigned here like kings. Yes, for a pirate, a poet, an artist or a naturalist, this must be a wonderful place, but for ordinary people with no particular resources, it might seem more like a beautiful tropical cage.

The Administrator of Nossi-Bé met us on the air-strip – a thin young man in white shirt and shorts, with a sallow sensitive face. Bertie, Tony and I were to stay with him at his house, the Seguins and Mr. Arning were going to the local Bank Manager, and the *Bermuda* officers were being put up in the *Actaeon* which lay in the harbour.

The drive across the island to the port of Nossi-Bé took us through plantations of coffee and ylang-ylang, the long bright leaf from which the essential oil of perfume is distilled; and, clinging to the jungle trees, like ivy, was wild pepper. In the forest we caught glimpses of the little furry faces of the lemurs.

'The *lémuriens* and serpents are sacred here,' said the Administrator 'They are protected, and one would not think of harming them.'

He had a soft voice and he spoke partly in English and partly in French, and often he used the words of a poet.

'Do you write poetry?' I asked.

'Ah, no,' he disclaimed. 'But naturally when I was younger I wrote verses like all French students.'

'You paint?'

'To amuse myself. One must do something here . . .'

The Residence, with the Tricolour flying, was high above the bay. Behind it was the little port and the green steamy jungle. The heat was suffocating after the high clear air of Tananarive, and we would have liked to swim, but there were sharks

'With sharks in the sea and crocodiles in the rivers it is never wise to swim,' he said.

There were no clubs or bathing-pools in these out of the way places, for the French are not driven by the British urge to make some sort of home and social centre in their place of exile.

In the tank in the garden were five baby crocodiles, which the Administrator would, at a suitable stage in their development, transform into serviceable shoes, valises or note-cases.

That evening there was a cocktail reception on the quarterdeck of H.M.S. *Actaeon*, and, among the guests, was the King of the Island, who looked like the Aga Khan, but he was a King with a token throne and no authority, and he could certainly not have exacted rich tribute from his subjects. Suddenly a tropical storm blew up, the deluge came, and everybody went home drenched to the skin.

Before dinner that night, about thirty young women of Indian origin and clad in tinsel *saris*, gathered on the front verandah of the Residence, and, urged on by horny matrons, sang in loud tuneless voices, making up the words as they went along. They shuffled their feet to the rhythm of their song – two steps to the right, and two to the left. From time to time they clapped their hands. Since neither song nor dance varied from stanza to stanza there seemed no reason why they should ever stop.

'Who are they?' I asked.

'They are the girls who sing for the King,' said the Administrator. 'But he is too old to be interested any more. It is disappointing for them. In any case, they are not up to much.' He dismissed them with a wave of his hand.

On the following morning he took us to a ruined Arab village among the mangrove swamps on the sea-shore. Once Arab traders or pirates had dwelt here in luxury. Now all that remained of a moment of prosperity were a few studded doors, some delicate fluted wooden columns and carved copings already clasped in the hungry embrace of the white-barked trees. Just so had the jungle taken back the Kingdom of the vanished Khmers in far Cambodia.

'Who were these Arabs who lived here?' I said 'When did they come and why did they go?'

The young man pushed his straw hat back a little from his perspiring brow. 'One cannot say. There are no historians among the *Malagasch*.'

A Native village huddled in a banana grove behind the ruins. Children fished for shrimps in the swamp and old men worked in a primitive shipbuilding yard. But, in the derelict palaces of long ago, Indian traders had set up shop, and here and there, from the shell of an upper storey, a keen dark face stared down unsmiling in its ruined frame.

Back at the house my husband's valet was packing. He had come ashore from the *Actaeon*, where he had spent the night. He said, smiling:

'Coming off in the liberty-boat we had eight of those monkey-things running all over the place! *Eight* of them swinging around. One was pure black with a snow white waistcoat. I must say he was smart!'

'Lemurs? I wonder how the sailors got them? They are supposed to be protected – sacred '

He folded a white dinner jacket and laid it carefully in the suitcase.

'They are so tame, Milady. You can catch them with no trouble. The sailors got them ashore yesterday, and of course they want to keep them. But the Captain said they were to be returned to the island. The sailors were very upset, they were mad on the monkey-things.'

So the little sacred lemurs had been returned to their green jungle, where they could swing so prettily on the liana monkey-ropes. I thought once more of the *Narrative of the Voyages*, in which sailors over a century ago had also been 'mad on the monkey-things'. Lieutenant Booteler had written of the Madagascar lemurs:

'It was delightful to watch the graceful manner in which, as if formed by nature to please, they sprung through the air from bough to bough, performing the most fearful leaps with the utmost facility. ... Many of these little animals were brought on board by the seamen, and, from their affectionate manners and harmless disposition, became great pets. But as we got into colder climes they soon died, when the sailors might be seen mourning over the lifeless bodies of their little favourites with all the regret attendant upon a deceased comrade.'

So perhaps the eight lemurs of Nossi-Bé were spared a sad end.

On the night of our return to Diego Suarez the Administrator, Monsieur Pileni, gave a wonderful evening party for the officers of the *Bermuda*.

Monsieur Pileni was Corsican, and, in common with King Radama I, he was an ardent admirer of Napoleon whom he closely resembled in appearance. His wife was charming and merry with cameo features and, like her husband, she spoke in the quick Corsican fashion.

The gardens and fountains were illuminated and we dined out of doors round an improvized dance-floor. The southeaster had dropped at sunset and the air was balmy. The house, tall and floodlit, was on the landward side of us, and an elfin figure on a scooter careered madly up and down the terrace, six-year-old Marie-Paule Pileni, who could melt her father with a glance, even in his most Napoleonic mood. A moon-path glimmered over the sea between the palms.

The officer next to me at table spoke slow and determined English, disgorging each word with a painful effort.

'You will go to see the sacrifice to the crocodiles tomorrow?' he asked.

'It has been arranged,' I said. 'Tell me, what do crocodiles normally eat – when there is no sacrifice?'

He thought for a while. 'Ox, cow, people, poison, and finally, of course, they eat themselves.'

I heard Phil Currey, opposite me, say: 'Beginning at the tail, no doubt, and washing yourself down with a nice mug of poison. What a diet!'

' "Each other", is what he would say,' corrected Madame Seguin. 'And *poisson* fish.'

'And tomorrow? I asked, ignoring the interruptions.

'It should be a young virgin,' said the officer with dreadful deliberation. 'But that naturally has been impossible since Madagascar was colonized by the French. So now it is an ox. But it will be a veritable sacrifice.'

'What is the origin of the ceremony?'

'The people of the village behaved badly, so one day it disappeared into a lake and each body was transformed into a crocodile. Now the people believe the crocodiles to be their ancestors. So the lake is sacred, also the crocodiles. Each year there is the sacrifice, but no longer the virgin.'

We set off early in the morning on the long drive to the Sacred Lake. Bertie remained on board to attend to his correspondence. 'You can go,' he said to me. 'You are a journalist. But I don't like horrors.'

I found myself in a car with Madame Pileni and Madame Seguin. We were followed by quite a convoy which included a number of our officers and Mademoiselle Pileni and her small sister, Marie-Paule. Lorry-loads of sailors had left the ship at dawn to be sure of being at the rendezvous in time. We whizzed past their broken down vehicles in a cloud of red dust.

There seemed to be a gremlin in those lorries.

'Oh, la, la,' said Madame Pileni, as we swerved past unheeding. '*Encore une panne!*'

The sailors wandered about among the coconut and raffia palms with the philosophical resignation of their kind. The lorry stood dejectedly on three legs and the native driver shook his head. He had no spare tyre.

'Do you think they will be in time?' I asked.

The ladies shrugged their shoulders and said it was of no importance. I did not agree. They pointed out the great variety of the scenery indefatigably, and we all went into raptures about the purity of the light, but after a while the conversation turned on matrimony and infidelity, and I learned that in the French view what a husband does when he is absent from his wife is, within reason, his own concern, but if he interests himself in another woman when they are together *that* is insupportable, *that* is infidelity. Then they found it rather absurd that the word 'flirt' in the French language should have derived from English. 'For the English women are not much *flirt*, they are too occupied with *le sport*.' I did not see fit to disillusion them.

In a village much *en gala* we were given an early lunch, and, thus fortified, we drove down to the Sacred Lake which was, in fact, the crater of an extinct volcano and very beautiful in the cup of the wooded hills.

On a grassy slope at the water's edge stood a single small tree to which was tethered a black ox whose hump was as limp as the comb of a sick cock.

'*Pauvre bête,*' said Madame Seguin. 'He seems to know his fate.'

'*Maman,*' piped six-year-old Marie-Paule. 'What is one going to do to the ox?'

To my astonishment her mother told her.

On the crest of the bank squatted a native female chorus in brilliant many-coloured *saris*. The Master of Ceremonies, in a felt hat, striped pyjama trousers and a red shirt worn on the outside, was urging them to sing to their ancestors, and, after a good deal of giggling, a little tentative yodelling and crooning drifted across the lake like a somewhat uncertain dinner-gong.

Sailors wandered round the sacrifical tree with cameras at

178

the ready, and we all looked with mistrust at a sinister path through the rushes on the fringe of the water.

'*C'est le passage des crocodiles*,' explained Captain Seguin.

Suddenly the stranded lorry-loads of sailors arrived in a relief bus which precipitated them into the midst of the chorus, scattering it in wild confusion.

The sun burned fiercely, the ox kicked about aimlessly under its tree, and, on the lily-covered lake, water-fowl swam cheerfully, regardless of the submarine saurians. Small birds peened in the rushes and I wondered if any of them had been engaged to pick crocodile teeth later in the day, for every self-respecting crocodile has its own personal winged toothpick.

The Master of Ceremonies advanced upon the sacrifice with a long sharp knife in his hand. Two of his henchmen carried rope and a blunt instrument.

The Flag Captain said, 'I have no stomach for this sort of thing. Behind us is one of the prettiest birds I have ever seen – a sort of bloodfinch.'

'We call him a *cardinal*,' said Madame Seguin.

The little bird was entrancing as he flitted here and there among the reeds or paused to swing delicately every now and again.

'I think Marie-Paule would like to watch him,' I said to Madame Pileni. But she laughed and said:

'Marie-Paule is a stoical colonial child. She interests herself in the sacrifice.'

The ox uttered no sound as it was pole-axed and hamstrung, and I only knew that its throat had been cut when Marie-Paule said loudly to her pretty elder sister:

'Look at the flies! How quickly the flies have gathered to drink the blood of the ox!'

'Shades of Saki and Giles,' murmured the Captain.

The girls of St. Trinian's should be here,' I said.

The Master of Ceremonies sliced off the hump of the ox, and, with this and a bowl of blood, made his way to the water's edge. On the bank the chorus set up an ear-splitting

179

warbling, literally calculated to wake the dead, and at the same time clapped hands with a metronome beat. The water was anointed with blood and the hump placed in an enticing position at the entrance to the *passage des crocodiles*.

Almost immediately the water was disturbed by an armoured shape, and an enormous ancestor rushed through the reeds. The shrilling of the chorus became slightly hysterical as the vast hinged cavern opened wide with a shocking array of teeth and seized the hump. The ancestor reversed into the shallow water where it flung back its abominable head, showing the pale under-belly, and, with great gulps of muddy-bloody water, it washed down the tasty morsel. No other crocodile appeared.

'Perhaps the telephone system is out of order,' suggested Captain Seguin, his eyes laughing. 'Or the ancestors have heard that there is no virgin.'

'They prefer to kill their own meat,' said Madame Pileni.

In spite of the shrill efforts of the chorus and the delectable offerings of the Master of Ceremonies it became apparent that the ancestors had gone on strike. No virgins, no crocodiles! The one black-leg had vanished, and what the strikers did to punish him for letting down the side we never learned. For all in a moment dark clouds gathered, lightning flashed and thunder rumbled round the hills. The Pagan Deities were expressing disapproval, they had been slighted; things were not what they were in the good old days of succulent damsels. Torrential rain fell from the furious heavens, and, as the Malagasy umbrellas went up, we ran for our cars.

As we sailed for Lourenço Marques, exactly one week after our arrival, the mountains of Diego Suarez were flushed with sunrise, and, at the entrance to the beautiful dramatic harbour, the line of surf along the coral reef was shot with leaping gold. In 1942 a Japanese submarine had braved that surf in a suicidal – and successful – effort to torpedo H.M.S.

Ramillies at her anchorage. Another Japanese submarine had been smashed to pieces on the reef.

I stood on the bridge beside my husband.

'No guns?'

'No guns,' he said. 'We don't shoot our way out of a foreign port. We only shoot our way in – to establish friendly relations.'

I could see Blackie washing herself on the fo'c'sle, neck arched, dainty tongue busy. No Madagascar 'monkey-things' had joined the ship to put her nose out of joint and lure the sailors with their 'affectionate manners and harmless disposition'. What had Blackie thought of Madagascar? What had the sailors thought?

In Durban my husband had thanked the Missions to Seamen and Seamen's Institute for the good work they did – work so important to those men who sail the seas far from home.

'Sailors the world over are a cheerful lot,' he had said, 'always ready for a bit of fun, kind and good-hearted. But in many ways they are rather a lost tribe. They go ashore in strange ports, and, if there isn't somewhere like this to make them welcome, there are only the bars and the dubious quarters of the port. Then perhaps they get silly and up to mischief. You give them a club, you find friends and entertainment for them, and you make them feel that somebody cares about them . . .'

A vignette of Diego Suarez flashed into my mind.

An early and charming dinner ashore with the Captain in Charge. A little after ten o'clock we go down to the jetty where the barge throbs in readiness to take us back on board. Already the shabby port is dead. The hot wind raises a whirl of dust and the moon swims in a sky like curdled milk. A Group of *Bermuda* men stand about the jetty, waiting for the liberty-boat to fetch them. No Seamen's Institute or Missions to Seamen here. No club to make them welcome.

'Our poor sailors – nowhere to go, nothing to do.' My

husband turns to the Coxswain. 'Corney, tell the Chief Petty
Officers and Petty Officers we'll give them a passage.'

On board he asks the Officer of the Watch, 'When is the
liberty-boat going off?'

'In about half an hour, sir.'

'Send it now. There are men hanging about. It's a
wretched place for them.'

'Aye, aye, sir.'

Seeing them that evening, standing about in the heat and
the wind, one lighting a cigarette for another with a joke and
a smile, the dark forbidding dwellings in the shabby street
behind them sealed and unwelcoming – which was probably
just as well – it came home to me that my husband had
meant by sailors the world over being 'rather a lost tribe'.

CHAPTER FOURTEEN

LOURENÇO MARQUES AND SWAZI WARRIOR

WE 'shot our way' into the magnificent Portuguese harbour of Lourenço Marques on a dazzling day, and while Bertie received his official callers, Mac and I disembarked to go to the fashionable hotel where his wife, my cousin Cicely, was to meet him. Cicely was with Charles and Maisie te Water, so, when Bertie joined us later in the morning, it was a real family reunion, for not only were Cicely and Maisie sisters but Charles was one of our oldest friends.

Charles, who continued to serve his country with energy and distinction in the fields of culture, education, town-planning and soil-conservation, was taking a well-earned holiday.

'Poor Kiki has been frantic,' said Maisie. 'She was quite sure Mac was going to be washed overboard—'

'Or devoured by savages or crocodiles,' added Charles.

In fact Mac had turned the tables neatly on savages and crocodiles by bringing Kiki a Malagasy winding-sheet embroidered in every colour of the rainbow, and the underbelly of a crocodile guaranteed by the Indian trader to be in perfect condition, supple in texture and elegant in shade.

We sipped our *apéritifs* on the terrace by the swimming-pool under a gaudy beach-umbrella, and, while we talked, we watched the antics of a very small Portuguese boy in red satin trunks baiting an imaginary bull with his bathing towel.

After lunch Bertie and I read our mail upstairs in our room, and, as we opened letters from the Cape, the harsh white glare of East Africa faded and we saw again the amber winter sun slanting through the bare tracery of oak and beech and weeping pepper-tree.

Piet and Glen had gone for a fortnight's holiday to the Drakensberg Mountains, and Nannie had taken charge of Langi Banool and Ronnie.

Mother wrote of her great-grandson:

'I have seen Ronnie three times since Piet and Glen left. One sunny day I took him and Nan to Constantia Nek for tea. The child is too adorable for words, full of beans and laughter, all rosy cheeks and bright eyes. My word I did fall for him. Nannie handed him to Arend to hold for a few minutes and when she wanted him back he smiled and clung to Arend who was so thrilled that he laughed and said "Oh just see how he likes the brown man!" I think myself Nan finds it rather much for her, but she would sooner die than admit it. She hugs and adores the child and says "What love can do!" Nothing is too much trouble for her where Ronnie is concerned. . . .'

So the third generation was staking its special claim on the great heart that had given so much faithful devotion to the other two.

With a half sigh I turned to a letter from Veronica giving us news of the garden at Admiralty House.

'I wished you could have been here today. I put old Mamputa on to weeding above the Midshipman's grave and when I went to check up on him he was looking decidedly grey and wide-eyed. "Oh Lady," he said, "I have had a *skrik*" and he pointed with a long stick to a patch of cannas in which reposed the top of a human skull! I am pretty sure it is a human one – looks too big for anything else. Anyway old Mamputa was even more upset when I picked it up with my bare hands and he is quite convinced that its owner is going to "come to me" tonight. I must find out more about it before I add it to my prop cupboard. One never knows, it might be a *Homo Rhodesiensis* or something. I don't think it could have been Midshipman Percival George Duddy, it was too far up. This is the most fascinating garden to work in, one never knows what one will find next!

'The admiral's carnations are doing well, and our stream is in full spate. . . .'

There was Tony's double knock on the door. An official engagement claimed us. I folded the letters and shut them away in a drawer, and with that gesture, put away truth and reality in favour of the comedy of manners.

The Portuguese were as charming and elegant as their city, and the Governor-General, Captain Gabriel de Texeira, was well known and popular throughout Southern Africa, especially in Rhodesia which is on excellent terms with her Portuguese neighbour-state.* The Governor-General, who came from the lovely island of Madeira, spoke fluent English, and was a first class horseman. Before taking his present appointment he had been in the Navy and had risen to the rank of Flag Captain. It seemed only poetic justice that a mariner should govern Portuguese East Africa, for Portugal owes her far-flung colonies to the seamanship of her courageous early navigators who led the world in voyages of discovery. Madame Texeira combined classic beauty with gentle dignity, and Government House was enlivened by the presence of a young daughter with enormous sparkling black eyes.

There is no official colour bar in the Portuguese possessions. The educated Native can go where he pleases, marry whom he pleases, and advance himself socially and economically as much as his ability permits. The test of his acceptability is his degree of education and good manners. The French hold the same point of view. If a Black man

---

* *Portugal in 1973 still controls her three African territories of Guinea-Bissau, Angola and Mozambique at the price of continuous guerilla warfare. They are regarded as part of Portugal and any suggestion of racism or colonialism is emphatically denied by Portugal.*

thinks, talks and acts like a civilized human being, he will be treated as such. The British are more sentimental in their African colonies. The Black man can fall very far short of what is generally regarded as a reasonable standard of behaviour, and still be accepted socially. The Union, of course, finds it difficult to distinguish between the Native as a whole and the cultured individual.

But, with their Natives in the mass, the Portuguese are much more severe than the Union or Southern Rhodesia. The police are always armed and every Black man knows that they do not wear their revolvers as ornaments.

I asked one official whether the Natives here indulged in ritual murder. He said there had been one case, and there were unlikely to be more.

'We deported *all* the suspects – about fifty people. They were very important while they were here, but they are not at all important where they are now. There will be no further trouble.'

'Are your Natives contented?'

'Certainly. They understand us and we understand them. The natives used to understand the English too, when the English governed them. But now that the English want them to govern themselves they do not know where they are.'

In the road beyond the terrace where we sat, Black men wielded picks, and chanted as they worked.

'What do they sing?' I asked.

My companion smiled with his mouth drawn down at the corners.

'They sing: *'The White man has taken our country . . . We will take it back . . .'*

'Will they?'

'They wouldn't know what to do with it if they did. It would revert to the days of tribal warfare, of slavery, and ultimate starvation, for who would bother about conserving the soil? It will be a sad day for them if they take it back.'

As with the Basuto, a vast number of Natives from Portuguese East Africa are absorbed into the mines of the Union. They are so anxious to work in the Union that the border has to be constantly patrolled by South African police to prevent them from entering illegally.

The trader who makes money out of the Natives – and the Europeans too – is the Indian. Here too, as in all East Africa, he has a sound footing.

But nobody was worrying about Natives or Indians when we were in Lourenço Marques. A really important issue had set the whole place by the ears.

To kill, or not to kill, the bull?

The Spanish kill their bulls, the Portuguese do not. And less than a week ago a famous Spanish matador, fighting in Lourenço Marques, had broken the law and killed his bull! He had immediately been arrested and imprisoned and released again on a very considerable bail. His defence was that in the heat of the moment he had forgotten that he was not in Spain, but it was assumed that he had deliberately provoked a test case. There was no other topic of conversation, and the controversy raged this way and that, and was still unsettled when we left. One night at dinner in a fashionable restaurant like a mediaeval baronial hall, a fiery Italian offered me his views on the subject.

'I am neutral,' he declared. 'Neither Spanish nor Portuguese, and *I* say it is kindest to kill the bull. This Spaniard – this man from Madrid – he proved it! Ah, what an artist! How superbly he did it – expert, instant and painless! Now the squeamish NO KILL must be altered here. In any case, a bull can only fight once – and I tell you, I assure you, Madame, it is *kindest* to kill!'

'That's as it may be,' I said. 'But with or without killing, I think any man who fights a bull is remarkably brave.'

'They start as children – waving little flags at little bulls on wheels, then a small real animal, and so on until finally it is a true fighting bull. It is gradual, and not particularly brave. Now *I* started three years ago, and straight away with a fighting bull. *That* is courage!'

'What made you do it?'

'A wager.'

'Weren't you frightened?'

He laughed lightly. 'I fear nothing. In the war I gained many medals for gallantry. In my first bull fight, I call the bull to me. I say *'Come, toro, toro – bull, bull, come!'* He rushes at me – I side-step him – he rushes again! I stand with my feet in my hat – *that* is something really artistic – and, as he charges, I move my body to avoid him, like this, and this, weaving like a serpent! He knows I am fearless. At last, as he thunders towards me, I put on my hat and fling myself between his horns! I hold him *thus*. He is powerless, I am his master!' He added casually, 'Of course, if his horns turn inwards, such a feat is not possible. A man's body could not pass.'

'But even if his horns turn out, what if the matador misses the passage between them?' It sounded even more dangerous than to fling oneself into the *passage des crocodiles* on the shores of the sacred lake.

'Ah, then he is impaled. I have seen two men die so.'

At this point, the excellent gipsy band which had been accompanying my companion's exposition on bull-fighting, with and without hat, was compelled to stop playing, as an enormous party of Portuguese and South African footballers and their satellites had reached the speech-making stage of a ceremonial dinner. The South Africans spoke little and seldom, perhaps because the Portuguese spoke often and long and with the utmost abandon. The fact that they were addressing not only their guests but the entire restaurant was only an added stimulus to their fervour.

'They adore speeches,' said the Italian. 'They have violence and tenderness and all the gestures. See, the speaker now! He flies into a passion – he weeps – he makes a mockery! It is a play. I too – I adore to make speeches.'

'Do you make good speeches?'

'But yes, very good. I was at dinner the other night. The Governnor-General was there – you know His Excellency?'

'Yes – charming, handsome, speaks perfect English, lovely wife and—'

'Ah, yes, yes, *yes*.' He waved away the Governor-General's attributes. 'There were many speeches at this feast in his honour, and suddenly I could bear it no longer – not to be one of the speakers. So I spring to my feet and make an oration of fire! Everybody is delighted and claps their hands.'

When one has lived with the modest inarticulate British for some time it is a refreshing experience to hear the uninhibited boasting which is usually only associated with innocent little children and Chinese soldiery. Presently our Italian friend left us to speak to one of the football team, and I knew that soon he would be making 'an oration of fire' – but the competition was keen, for indeed, as we learned that night, the Portuguese are indefatigable orators.

My husband added one rather unusual event to his entertaining on board while we were at Lourenço Marques.

He invited Sobhuza II,* the Paramount Chief of the Swazi nation, to come on board the *Bermuda*. The necessary arrangements for the visit were made by Mr. Vaughan, the British Consul-General and Mr. Morgan, the Resident Commissioner of Swaziland. The Portuguese authorities raised no objections providing that the Paramount Chief and his retinue came and left on the same day and that they were conventionally dressed. As Mbabane, the capital of Swaziland, was only just over three hours' journey by car from Lourenço Marques, and as Chiefs and their councillors possess conventional attire, the stipulations presented no difficulties.

The party arrived on the quay shortly before noon in several car-loads. First the Government officials – Mr. D. L. Morgan (the Resident Commissioner), the Chief of Police, the Government Secretary, the District Commissioner from Stegi, and Mr. R. Armstrong, the First Assistant Secretary and brother of our kind host in Basutoland. Next came three of the Paramount Chief's

* *Sobhuza II, still monarch of the Kingdom of Swaziland, has announced his intention of establishing a one-party-state – under his rule, of course.*

189

Senior Councillors, very neat in European suits and stepping rather high in extremely new shoes. And out of the final car stepped the Paramount Chief. Sobhuza II was forty-eight years old – spruce, alert, quick in the uptake and intensely expressive. He wore a sparse fringe of whiskers round his chin, like a Chinese warlord, and, under his felt hat, his hair fitted as snugly as an astrakhan cap. He spoke in little rushes of good, but gusty, English and often ended on a burst of stammering like machine-gun fire. Sobhuza had never in his life been on board a warship, and the Acting High Commissioner, Mr. Turnbull, had suggested to my husband, some time before, that he would probably like very much to come on board while the *Bermuda* was in Lourenço Marques. It was an excellent idea, and, from the moment he appeared on the quarterdeck, the Swazi warrior's whiskers were electric with excitement, for there were many surprises and marvels in store for him.

But he too had surprises in store for us, and three of them followed him up the gangway. Sobhuza had brought his young ladies. They were buttoned up to the throat in tweed coats and on their heads were felt hats. The first of the three was the Paramount Chief's sister, a comely matron whose petunia hat had come to rest upon the dense superstructure of her hair like a butterfly upon a guardsman's busby. For the Swazi married woman wears her hair in a fashion that might well have derived straight from the Horse Guards Parade. As she handed her coat to the able seaman on the quarter-deck, she displayed a beige costume, for she had adhered strictly to the 'conventional attire' order of the day. But the two younger belles, Sobhuza's latest wife and favourite daughter, both aged about seventeen, were less sophisticated. They were not used to being whisked out of their own country into a magnificent city, they had never seen the sea, much less a ship, and on their way to the harbour they had been overwhelmed by their first sight of a train. So they unbuttoned their coats and removed their hats with nervous fingers, and put them into the equally nervous hands of the able seaman. For, if the Swazis had never seen a sailor, nor had the sailor ever seen a Swazi – and these were worth seeing.

To begin with, their hair-do was striking. Bleached and stiffened, it stood out from the centre of the crown in well teased reddish strands, framing their demure, broad-featured faces in the manner of the round thatched roof shading the little mud hut. A prodigious hairpin stuck out over one ear, and right on top, like a delicate weather-vane, nodded a single peacock feather. One bronze shoulder was exposed, and the other was covered by a gaily printed shoulder-cloth falling across a bizarre *sarong*. Their beads and bangles, and copper anklets, inches deep above their bare feet, were as bright and shining as a pheasant's courting plumage in the spring. It was explained to me later that young Mrs. Sobhuza was not yet entitled to put her hair up busby-style, because a Swazi bride does not alter her status overnight. She is married little by little, and each stage has its accompanying rituals. The busby is the final symbol of wedlock.

Although Sobhuza was an enlightened and well educated Chief he had not adopted the Christian religion, and it was known that he had many wives throughout the land and many sons to watch over the interests of the dynasty. But he was on good terms with most of the missions that abound in Swaziland and often sang lustily in their churches.

It must have been quite an experience for him to find himself being entertained under conditions entirely foreign to him, but he conducted himself with poise and managed his party with easy authority. The girls sat like good children on two stiff little chairs, immobile, except for their toes with the square alabaster nails, curling and uncurling under the chairs, immeasurably expressive and appealing. Since they spoke only their Native tongue, the Chief and his sister translated for them, and, whenever he addressed them, they raised their eyes shyly and answered in long soft *ooohs* and little squeals and giggles.

Before the buffet lunch Mrs. Vaughan, the Consul-General's wife, and I took them down to the Commander-in-Chief's quarters. All three were terrified of the ladders and moans of fear accompanied their journeys up and down.

But Sobhuza was afraid of nothing and interested in everything, and his conversation was punctuated with long ringing *aaaahs* straight from the stomach as if blown up by some mighty bellows. It occurred to me that he would have been invaluable in the Marine Band, performing on one of the more formidable wind-instruments.

For my part, I was fascinated to discover that he was a great reader and student, and had built himself a study-hut out of range of the daily hub-bub of the kraal. He was very anxious to classify the herbal remedies of his people.

'But it is not easy,' he said. 'Every herbalist has his own secret preparations and refuses to tell them to anybody. Yet many of these should be given to the world.'

He told us about one herbalist who claimed to immunize his clients against snake-bite by making a small incision in the wrist and rubbing some special ointment into it. As Natives, who go through the grasslands bare-foot, are naturally frightened of snakes this doctor had many grateful patients – because, it appeared, his immunization really worked! It was also effective in cases of tape-worm. The most persistent parasites of the worm-family fled at the first application of the special ointment.

'When I heard of these things, I sent for the man,' said Sobhuza. 'But he had died a week previously – and his secrets with him. It was sad, for these cures should be known.'

Later, in Swaziland, we heard of a woman dismissed from hospital with incurable cancer, so that she might die among her own people as she wished. She returned to the hospital some months later apparently cured by a Native doctor. Cowdung had featured prominently in the treatment.

Herbalists are not to be confused with witch-doctors. Many herbalists have a genuine and wide knowledge of the medicinal and antidote properties of veld plants combined with an intuitive understanding of the psychology of their patients, with the result that they do real good. The witch-doctor is a much more sinister figure.

We did not discuss witch-doctors with Sobhuza, nor the incidence of medicine murder, which was almost as prevalent in Swaziland as in Basutoland, and for similar reasons.

A few months earlier a certain British Labour Minister had toured the Union, and particularly the Protectorates. He told me that he had met many of the chiefs and had found them 'good fellows, and intelligent'.

'A little old-fashioned – some of them,' I suggested. 'Inclined to indulge in medicine murder . . .'

He took his pipe out of his mouth and regarded me gravely.

'Medicine murder is a specially unpleasant form of private enterprise,' he said. 'The individual puts his own interests before those of the tribe, and even persuades the community that it may benefit by his activities. When we catch him, we hang him for it.'

This Minister had liked Sobhuza. He had realized that the Swazi Paramount Chief's passion for preserving the tribal customs of his nation did not extend to those evil deeds that had their roots back in the old days of tribal warfare and the mutilation of a brave enemy's body. In any case, no responsible Swazis ever admitted to a belief in *diretlo – that* was an importation from Zululand, they declared. As to the crimes – they were incomprehensible – *tsk, tsk, tsk . . .*

After lunch we visited all the more accessible portions of the *Bermuda*, but we avoided the elaborate internal network of ladders and hatches. The young ladies covered their eyes with their hands at the mere idea, though the councillors, who were ready to try anything once, would have risked their lives on the unaccustomed steel rungs in almost equally unaccustomed new shoes. But to have allowed them to do so would have been tantamount to expecting the officers to skim up and down the ladders on skates – which, indeed, they often appeared to do.

But the party clambered in and out of gun-turrets with aplomb, and the high light came when the Paramount Chief sat on a little saddle, revolving rapidly, as he turned a wheel to train and elevate the power-controlled Bofors anti-aircraft guns. The councillors expressed admiration and respect for his achievements by blowing air up from their stomachs and emitting it from between their teeth with a sound like a loud escape of steam. His young ladies just marvelled expressively.

When he reckoned that he had about fifty direct hits in the bag, he vacated his seat for his wife and insisted that she too ride the merry-go-round and aim the guns at seagulls. But not for pleasure alone – oh, dear, no! – Sobhuza wished to demonstrate the mechanism. Wherever we went he adopted the same procedure. As soon as he had mastered the way things worked, he called his councillors and young ladies round him and gave them a dissertation in their own language.

'Talks to them like a gunner's mate,' murmured the Commander to Mr. Armstrong and me.

'They are all enjoying the gun-mountings,' I whispered. 'What wonderful merry-go-rounds they'd make!'

'They do,' said the Commander. 'At children's parties on board, all the gun-mountings and the capstan are used as merry-go-rounds. They are always a great success.'

Mr. Armstrong said: 'They are loving *everything*. The young wife said to me just now. "These White people! When will they come to the end of their inventions?" '

Mr. Armstrong closely resembled his brother in Basutoland. The Swazis called him *Ntendele*, 'the crested partridge', because his crisp grey hair grew stiffly *en brosse* and refused to lie down. He too, knew Native lore and languages well. In fact he was an authority on Swazi customs, and so many and so strange were the true stories he had gathered throughout his experience that his friends hoped he would write a book about them.

Before the party left, my husband presented everybody with a framed photograph of the ship. And the Paramount

Chief promised that when we should visit his country in the following week he would stage a dance of his warriors for our benefit and we would all meet again.

'But you may not recognize us,' he added, with his explosive laugh. 'We will not be dressed like this!'

The councillors stepped sedately down the gangway, and I am sure that the moment their car was safely out of sight, they removed their fine new shoes. Sobhuza's young ladies followed at his heels, and paused a moment on the quay to wave their little pink-palmed hands. In the breezy sunshine the peacock feathers on their heads danced a delicate glittering dance, and the petunia felt hat on the matronly busby suddenly took playfully to the air and cavorted merrily along the wharf until it was captured by a sailor and politely returned to its owner. All three ladies squealed and giggled and clasped their hands over their mouths to control their mirth.

And then the shining door of the royal car slammed to, and gone were the beads and bangles and shy smiling faces and fluttering fingers. Wheels turned and gathered speed, bearing our Swazi friends away – back to the beehive huts in the Lebombo Mountains, and the dusty sunny kraal, and the dark sorcery of their own people.

I stood at the rail and watched them go – touched, amused, and somehow a little sad.

The seabirds cried raucously as they planed slowly over the complex armaments of this modern engine of war, and the shadows of the White man's death-dealing magic massed and lengthened on the deck. A chill of half-formulated foreboding ran down my spine. The old cruel ways of Africa and the murderous devices of the twentieth century merged in a verse by some cynical philosopher.

> 'Ape's inhumanity to ape—
> Laugh this off, brother, if you can—
> Is not so anthropoid a shape
> As man's inhumanity to man . . .'

'Well,' said Bertie. 'That's that. I think it was a success, don't you?'

Mr. Morgan said, as he took his leave. 'They'll never forget this day.'

Nor, for that matter, would we.

CHAPTER FIFTEEN

SWAZILAND – THE BEAUTY AND THE PITY OF IT

FROM Lourenço Marques the *Bermuda* sailed for Durban once more and the Flag Lieutenant with her. Tony was working for his promotion examination, and for the next month would be steeped in Military Law and the other subjects he must master if he was to become a major in the Royal Marines. Meanwhile, an unofficial tour of the British Protectorates of Swaziland and Bechuanaland, and of the two Rhodesias, had been arranged for my husband and me.*

We travelled as before, in our private car – a medium-sized British make – with our luggage for a month, our golf clubs and tennis rackets, and our precious picnic basket. On the long runs we shared the driving, with Bertie taking the rough stretches.

The winter climate of all this north-eastern part of South Africa is gloriously sunny by day and cold at night, and we set off for Mbabane, the European capital of Swaziland, on one of those crisp blue and gold days when the world feels new-born. At the border we had to run the car through a dip-trough to cleanse the tyres of any foot-and-mouth germs they might have picked up in Portuguese territory. We found the customs officer very busy answering his telephone.

'It's ring-ring-ring all morning,' he said. 'The school bus from Mbabane to Lourenço Marques passes here in the

* *Bechuanaland now Botswana. Southern Rhodesia the independent state of Rhodesia since Ian Smith's Unilateral Declaration of Independence. Northern Rhodesia now Zambia.*

next half-hour, and all the parents keep calling me up to find out of it's been through yet.'

Many of the children of British and South African parents in Portuguese East Africa went to boarding school in Mbabane, and, soon after leaving the border, we passed the bus which looked rather like an illustration out of a *Tiger Tim Annual*. The children, hanging out of all the windows, yelling and waving in a cloud of golden dust, seemed just as crazy as Tiger Tim and his friends going off on one of their wilder excursions. Master Vaughan, the Consul-General's young son was among them, and I remembered Mrs. Vaughan saying, 'They go raving mad on their way home for the holidays. On the way back they are quite reasonable people.'

Mr. Forsyth-Thompson, the District Commissioner of Stegi, and the Police Officer in charge of the area, met us along the road. We were to lunch at Stegi with the Forsyth-Thompsons, so I changed over into his car while the Police Officer went with Bertie.

This part of Swaziland was middle-veld, the sort of landscape one sees in *safari* films. One felt it should abound with game.

'But it doesn't really,' said Mr. Forsyth-Thompson. 'The game is down there in the bushveld – Jock's country. We only get the little duiker here and sometimes koodoo. And mambas. When we cleared the land to build our present house thirty snakes were killed, many of them mambas.'

We were driving along a tawny ridge of thorn scrub, but, in the blue of the valleys below, was the denser bushveld falling away towards the Kruger Park. And, separating Swaziland from Portugese East Africa, was the amethyst range of the Lebombo Mountains. Brilliant birds flew suddenly from the branches of the winter trees, and every now and again the blood-red flowers of a leafless kaffir-boom were painted against the cloudless sky – a beautiful, menacing splash of colour in a pastel scene.

Down there Percy Fitzpatrick's Jock, the dog hero of every boy and girl in South Africa, had lived his life of adventure, the friend and servant of a great hunter. Already I felt the spell of this land upon me.

Mr. Forsyth-Thompson explained that Swaziland differed from the Basutoland Protectorate in that Europeans could own land here.

'It is a patchwork – about one-third European ranches and two-thirds Native territory. The Natives own about four times as much cattle as the Europeans.'

It was interesting to see the difference.

On one side of the road might be the fenced lands of the European farmer, and on the other the communal grazing of the Swazi. The Native lands were grazed as threadbare as worn beige plush, while the European lands were covered with rich grass.

'Look!' say the Natives. 'The White man always takes the best land!'

And the White men say: 'There you have it – the typical result of Native ownership. Overgrazed pastures, no rotation of crops, no effort to conserve the soil.'

The White men are right. Whatever may be said at U.N.O., or anywhere else, it is the White man of South Africa, not the Native, who holds his finger in the dyke to save half a continent from erosion and starvation. The Native is, by nature and of ancient necessity, a nomad herdsman. As he wanders with his cattle he uses up the pasturage and leaves wide acres bare. Only great patience, perseverance, and persistent supervision can change his habits. Gradually results are being achieved, but not without a bitter heart-breaking struggle on the part of the White Administration.

Yet, if the Swazis mistrust the Europeans, it is hardly surprising. At the end of the nineteenth century, in the bold days of the concession hunters in Africa, the Swazi King, Mbandeni, signed away his people's birthright for rather less value than a mess of pottage. For greyhounds and champagne, the White men bought a pastoral paradise about the size of Wales, from a Black Chief who knew not what he sold.

Sometime after the Boer War, when many matters were

adjusted, Swaziland became a British Protectorate, and two thirds of the territory was given back for Native settlement. And it is now so integrated that, wherever he may be, the Native has the example of European agricultural methods constantly before him.

The Forsyth-Thompsons were a delightful young South African couple, who had recently returned from Cambridge, where they had both taken a course in Colonial Affairs. Sobhuza II, unlike his cumbrous colleague in Basutoland, had no objection to South Africans in Government Service in Swaziland. 'Give us *good* men – that's all we ask!' he said. And good men were needed. For here too the shadow of Pagan crime lay heavy.

In the Stegi area, less than a year ago, had happened one of the most tragic cases of child medicine murder it would be possible to imagine. Two men had been hanged for it only a few days before our visit. The case haunted me, and I shall tell the story briefly, because it throws its own sad sinister light upon the mentality of Africa which is still so deep a mystery to those Europeans who know it well enough to understand how little they know.

It is the story of a Swazi mother, her two sons, and the wicked uncles, and of the dark web of witchcraft.

The mother professed to be a Christian. Her name was Lomisi. She was married to a Chief who died, leaving as his heir their son, Mahlabindaba Dhlameni, who was still a boy. At the Chief's death Lomisi was taken over by her brother in the Native custom. This man became Acting Chief. By him Lomisi had another son, Solinye – a child born under an evil star.

Her eldest boy grew up wild and dissolute and lacking in any sense of responsibility. It was clear that he would not make a good chief. Whereas Solinye, then twelve years old, was a happy, healthy child, herding the cattle according to the ways of his people, laughing in the sun with the other boys and especially with his cousin, Lomlete, a few months his senior.

200

Mahlabindaba acceded to the Chieftainship, and very soon his weakness and drunken behaviour gave cause for grave anxiety among his relatives and to the tribe in general. Finally two of the young man's influential uncles came to the conclusion that something drastic must be done.

These two men – the wicked uncles, who, according to their lights, meant well – came to Lomisi. They found her in her store-hut, and they told her that they wished to 'treat' her elder son, Mahlabindaba, to give him the strength and prestige he so sadly lacked. She knew full well what they meant, though she only knew the half of it. Even so, she cried out:

'Get out, you cannibal dogs! Do you think you can make your tricks and treat my child? His father was never treated by killing a person! I will tell the elders what you mean to do.'

They answered her. 'If you do that, it will mean that you do not wish to live.' She was silent and afraid.

At that moment the boy, Solinye, came to the door of the hut carrying milk for his mother. He heard his uncles say that he would be a suitable victim for *diretlo*. Child as he was, he knew, at that moment, something of the terrible fate destined for him. Lomisi knew it too. Yet she held her peace – so stern is the Rule of Fear.

Three months passed. The ploughing season came. Solinye went with his cousin, Lomlete, to help plough near the Nzimpofu River. Perhaps by then his fears had been forgotten, for children are as gay as puppies, and the name of Nemesis is unknown to them. Perhaps that day in the fields was a happy one – a child's carefree day with its mead of labour and laughter. Solinye was a merry ingenuous boy, and the world of the kraal and the veld, of cattle and companionship, was all that he asked of life. That night he and Lomlete brought the oxen home to the fold and slept soundly as boys will after long hours in the open air. But the cold shadow of his doom was upon him.

At the trial of *Rex v. Mahlabindaba and 5 others* in the High Court at Mbabane the grim tale unfolded, sentence by

201

sentence, as the witnesses said their say, their dark faces sullen at this intrusion of the White man's law upon their own.

It is hard for Lomisi to speak. She has lost one son for the sake of the other, and now that other is threatened by the deed done to 'strengthen' him. She stands in the witness box, expressionless, the mask of stupidity over her pain.

'Next day was dipping day,' she says slowly. 'It must have been near Christmas. Solinye took the oxen to the pastures with Lomlete. I never saw him again.'

Weeks pass. Yet the mother does nothing about her child's disappearance. Again and again she says, 'I was afraid. If I reported what I knew to the police, I was afraid accused would kill me.'

Every witness says the same thing. 'We are telling now because Government has caught us. We were afraid to tell before. Accused were our betters. We had to do as they told us.'

But, at last, after two or three months, Lomisi reports the disappearance of Solinye to a Native Constable, and calls in the help of a Diviner.

'I sent for Diviner Sidakwa from Gtseni in the Hlatikulu District. Sedakwa said Solinye was in the veld, but had become an animal. He said Solinye would be killed at the next ploughing season and his flesh used to fertilize the crops. . . . We clapped hands for Syolinye as for a ghost. . . .'

In fact the poor child *had* become an animal and a ghost, as the tragic evidence continues to relate.

Lomlete is called to tell what happened on 'dipping day', when he went with his cousin, Solinye, to take the cattle to the pastures.

'I was told that Solinye was to be surrounded while he was herding the cattle. Accused said I must shout for him, so that he would not run away. He would run from the others. . . . When they caught Solinye the witch-doctor poured powder from his medicine-horn into his nostrils and ears. He grew limp, only the whites of his eyes showed, he shivered. . . . I called him when they told me to, because I was afraid. I had not yet reached the age of puberty, and I knew they would take me if they did not get Solinye.'

The rest of the tale is as curious as it is pitiful.

There is no quick cruel death. The conspiracy of silence and fear surrounds the captive child like a cloak of invisibility. He is taken to a dry *donga* and tied to a fig tree. He is fed from time to time in order that life may be preserved until the day chosen by the witch-doctor. For eight months the phantom of the little herd-boy exists, emaciated and bereft of its senses. The rope tying him to the tree rots, and the child crawls into a cave. A woman passing by sees this creature that was once a merry little lad. She goes to Lomisi.

'I have seen the ghost of your child,' she says. 'He is all white, even his eyes are white – and he walks on all fours with the backs of his hands on the ground like an ape.' Lomisi makes no comment. 'She did not seem interested,' says the witness.

At last the wicked uncles and their henchmen release Solinye from the frail bonds of life. The dreadful ritual is performed. The medicine is made in Lomisi's hut, and all partake of it, save only the mother, who turns her face to the wall.

Another African tragedy has been played out to its fearful conclusion.

The two wicked uncles were condemned to death, but the young Chief, Mahlabindaba, who had genuinely tried to disassociate himself from the whole business, was set free. In his summing up, Sir Walter Harrigan, the Chief Justice for the High Commission Territories, cast a penetrating beam of light upon these dreadful doings. In his wisdom and experience he understood what, to most of us, is past all comprehension.

'However reprehensible civilized people may think the action of these people to be, the fact is that this was done by close relations in order to do good to the young Chief, and, incidentally, to the whole village. *In fact, from their point of view, their intentions were not malicious, however cruel they may have been to Solinye.*'

The Swazis are a gay and attractive people despite their dark beliefs. Their country is soft and beautiful and the influence of civilization is everywhere in evidence. Missions abound – so much so that there is cut-throat competition for souls, which is a pity and confusing for the proselyte who can only distinguish between the various sects by comparing the material benefits they are able to offer him. Swaziland is being developed, it has a future, and Europeans fall in love with it. Small wonder. It is a well-watered land of infinite variety, with high forested mountains, deep valleys and wide vistas of veld. On the skyline the tall long-horned Afrikander cattle plough the rich furrows, or they graze in the pastures with the little herd-boys near them. In all our African travels Swaziland stands out as the most beautiful. Yet, for me, its enchantment had a *belle dame sans merci* quality, and, behind the friendly greetings of the children, naked save for their loincloths, there hovered a small pale ghost – 'all white – even his eyes' – the ghost of a child doomed by savage sorcery, a child who had known his dread destiny, and guessed that neither father, mother, brother, cousin nor friend would help him in his extremity, for, among his people, there was neither love nor compassion great enough to cast out fear.

The White settlers and Government Officers are a cheerful crowd in Swaziland.

'We are all sorts here,' said Mrs. Forsyth-Thompson. 'British South Africans, Afrikaners, English, Canadians, and even some Poles, and we all get along splendidly. A great many people in Government Service retire here, and there are a good many privately owned ranches. This country gets you once you've lived here. We are all mad about it.'

Of course there was a Club, and a very adolescent golf course. Mr. Forsyth-Thompson persuaded the young lady who owned the General Store to abandon her post for an hour after lunch and we played the six holes.

'Next time you visit us the other three will be ready,' promised the District Commissioner as he put us on the road to Mbabane.

As we ascended the long pass up to the high plateau and the little town of Mbabane, the sun was already sinking over the rim of the world. The chill of evening slid down the darkening flanks of the mountains, the dense swathes of the pine forests sighed as the night breeze whispered among the resinous needles, and the rolling grasslands sank into sombre dreams. The kraals and Native villages, spaced far apart, and hidden behind their high reed stockades, were scarcely visible in the dusk, and, then, one by one, the lights of the lonely town embroidered the vast curtain of approaching night with a close human pattern.

'Could be Katmandu in the Himalayas,' said Bertie, who has never been to Katmandu, but who had been brought up in the Rudyard Kipling tradition. And it was true that the long white Residency, flying the Union Jack on the roof of the world, had a Kipling touch about it – a touch accentuated by its occupants.

Mr. Morgan, the Resident Commissioner, came of a military family and many of his forbears had served in the Imperial Indian Army. He himself had the brisk direct manner of one accustomed to exerting authority, and the easy way with strangers that comes of meeting all sorts and conditions of people in out-of-the-way places and circumstances. His wife, too, had been brought up in Army surroundings, and her slim figure in tweeds was characteristically English. Their young daughter, Jill, was engaged to be married to tall Sub-Inspector Sam Browne of the Swaziland Police, a direct descendant of the original Indian Army Sam Browne 'of the belt'.

With sunset, cold takes command of the high plateau, and we were glad to warm our hands at the huge open log-fire in the lounge. To one side of it was a Thibetan fire-screen. Young Sam Browne, rangy and aquiline, poured us sundowners, little fair Jill offered cigarettes, and Mrs. Morgan saw that our luggage was taken to our rooms and unpacked, while the Resident Commissioner told us what plans had been made for us to see something of the country.

When we had bathed and changed we sat down to an exquisite dinner in surroundings made charming by the excellent taste of our hostess. Later, while we were enjoying our coffee by the fireside, Sam was called to the telephone. When he came back he made his excuses, and, after a few words privately with the Resident Commissioner, he left us. It was only long afterwards that we realized that it had just been reported that the body of an old White woman, who lived alone on a small farm, had been found under conditions suggesting medicine murder. In time this was proved to be the case, but the killers were never brought to book.

If the Katmandu effect was impressive at sunset it was even more wonderful in the morning light. As we looked across the velvet veld to the far blue peaks, Mrs. Morgan said, 'It would be hard to find a view to touch this.'

The red jerseys of the convicts working in the garden and the red flowers of the *kaffirbome* flamed in the hard clear light.

'It makes one long to be a poet,' I said.

Yet now I sometimes wonder. Perhaps there is more real poetry in one small Chelsea churchyard than in all the wide savage scenery of Swaziland.

Mr. Armstrong – *Ntendele*, the crested partridge – whom we had already met on board the *Bermuda* with Sobhuza, was to be our escort on a day's drive round southern Swaziland. And, after twenty-five years in the country, what a knowledgeable escort he was! He held us spellbound with his tales of the people and their customs.

'They are so nice,' I said. 'So merry and friendly, yet they do such unspeakable things – like the killing of little Solinye . . .'

He shook his head sadly.

'Those things are almost impossible to explain. Some beliefs are born into these people, and all the missionaries

206

and government officials in the world can't seem to eradicate them. Any more than they can stop a Native believing in ghosts.'

(In 1952 the Swaziland Administration appointed a mixed Commission of Europeans and Africans to report on the ever-increasing medicine murders, but it is doubtful if their findings were of any very great value.)

Mr. Armstrong took us into a Native kraal.

Within the stockade of tall reeds there are sleeping-huts, cooking-huts, and store-huts, and a boys' hut and a girls' hut. For, when the boys and girls reach the age of puberty, they leave their mothers and go to their respective dormitories. Most important of all, probably, is the cattlefold of thorn branches. Several families may live in one kraal, but women predominate numerically because a man has the number of wives he wants or can afford. Each wife has her own hut and cooks for her own family, but a substantial helping of the meal must always go to the husband, so a husband with four wives can count on four meals at one time, which means that he feeds four hangers-on. The men are nothing if not frank, and when a wife is too old to interest them they tell her so, and she accepts the verdict as a matter of course and welcomes the new young wife who will help her work in the fields and round the kraal.

'Would you like to go into a hut?' asked Mr. Armstrong.

Bertie's eye fell dubiously on the low U-shaped door in the beehive hut. Was the manoeuvre possible? I had to giggle at his expression, and several elderly hags in cow-hide shoulder-cloths tittered too. Some had their venerable breasts dangling in the sunshine, others not. Their hair was done up in the traditional dense woollen busby. One mother nursed her two-year old child indifferently.

Mr. Armstrong explained:

'She must not stop nursing till father gives permission or nature steps in, or should I say out?'

The older children were at the nearby mission school, most of the young women were in the fields, and the men were absent, either with the cattle or working for Europeans, or in the Union, and those who remained were withered ancients squatting contentedly in the sun, or a few happy naked toddlers with round mealie-swollen bellies and sparkling eyes playing about among scrawny chickens and a goat or two. There was a rather agreeable odour of cattle-dung, hide, grass, cooking fires and humanity in the raw.

'Well,' I said to Bertie. 'Shall we make a dive for it?'

'We could try,' he said cautiously. 'But I did know a horse once who bent his knees and crept into a corrugated iron shed through a low door. And, when it came to getting him out again, he lost his nerve and wouldn't budge. We had to lift the shed off him.'

'No wonder these old folk don't get rheumatism,' I said, as a great-grannie squirmed nimbly through the opening to give us a lead. 'Bending more than double day in day out must keep you supple.'

We performed the necessary gymnastics to get into the hut, though Bertie gave us some anxious moments when it seemed that he would carry the whole edifice away on his broad shoulders. Once in the cool shadowy interior we had to wait till our eyes adjusted themselves to the windowless gloom. Then we became aware of the extreme cleanliness of this primitive abode. In the middle was a rough brazier.

'The night-fire ventilates through the reed thatch and kills all the vermin,' said Mr. Armstrong. 'Smokes them out.'

The place was bare save for a central transverse pole over which hung the family blankets. The little wooden head-rests that serve as pillows were neatly put away. 'And look at this!' exclaimed Bertie. 'A lovely stow!' He touched the cord slings against the convex sides of the hut, each with a sleeping mat neatly folded in it. And I thought of Corney in the *Bermuda* and his views on the modern boys' stowing of hammocks.

The workmanship of one of these Native huts is beautiful. First the strong flexible withy framework, then the reed thatch, and finally a network of plaited cord to keep it tidy – like a woman's hair-net. Four poles support each hut and a

208

top-knot adorns it. If the man of the house dies, one pole and the top-knot are removed and also one of the four horizontal supports of the reed windscreen outside.

This was the hut-building season – the dry season – and everywhere homes were going up, as much a natural part of the veld as the nest is part of a tree, for only nature's fabrics are used by the raw Native and the wild bird.

The following day was, for us, a keen delight. Sobhuza II had been as good as his word. He had staged a dance for our benefit.

His Native village was not very far from Mbabane, and the stage and the performers would have turned Hollywood green with envy.

The amphitheatre was enclosed by a range of violet hills curved like the horns of some mighty beast. Within the encircling horns some four hundred warriors waited on the pale winter veld. The sunny wind brought us the scent of dry grass and hot warrior – the scent of Africa.

Mr. Morgan, Jill and Sam Browne, the Government Secretary, Mr. Stebbing, and Mr. Armstrong were with us; and, rather surprisingly, our distinguished friend, Monsieur Gazelle, the French Ambassador, who also happened to be touring Swaziland.

When the Paramount Chief came forward to greet us, I did not at first recognize him. Here was not just another Native dressed in European clothes, but Sobhuza II, *Nkosi Ingmenyama*, the Lion. About his loins he wore a leopard skin over a short bead embroidered skirt, across his bare torso was a sash of pink beads, and he carried a cowhide shield tufted with fur and feathers and laced with assegais. Stuck in his woolly hair, like darts, were a semi-circle of scarlet lory feathers, the emblem of the royal clan. He had dignity and an air of command, he was on his 'quarter-deck'.

Sobhuza presented his 'mother', *Indlovukati*, the She Elephant, a stout body in her cow-hide costume and high headdress. We learned presently from Mr. Morgan that she was not really Sobhuza's mother but his aunt. His mother was dead, and, since a Queen Mother is as essential to the life of the people as a Queen Bee is essential to the hive, there was nothing for it but to promote a close relative. In any case, relatives among the Swazis are fairly interchangeable. For instance when a man dies his brother adopts his widow and children and also his connubial rights. When Christian teaching forbids this custom the widow is deprived of security and often takes to an immoral way of life. Polygamy, of course, adds to the complexities of relationship, and also makes it possible for a virile Chief to establish a frame-work of family rulers throughout his country. His sons are automatically chiefs and his daughters marry chiefs, thus, in Swaziland, the royal clan is everywhere. Because the tribal wife is selected for the Paramount Chief by the nation, he feels quite entitled to indulge his personal fancy as well.

When Sobhuza's warriors had paraded past our chairs, prancing and chanting, with their knobkerries raised on high like a phalanx of number-four woods face up, they formed into two long ranks and we all inspected them. They were a fierce-looking crowd. They carried their knobkerries in one hand and in the other their cow-hide shields and throwing assegais. They wore beads, and sporrans of baboon, civet-cat or monkey fur, and their stiff bleached hair was frayed out gollywog style and stabbed with peacock feathers or the royal red of the lory bird. Many of them had served in two European wars, though not in this primitive regalia. As we returned to our seats they all whistled shrilly through slit-like mouths – a piercing blast intended as a compliment, but one that might well, in other circumstances, make one's blood run cold. Astonishingly, the French Ambassador turned in his tracks. And, putting two fingers in the corners of his mouth, he too uttered the same wild terrifying sound. The warriors yelled with delight and redoubled their efforts till the blue hills behind them shuddered in atavistic ecstasy.

The ceremonial began. There was a song so sad, resonant,

melodious and triumphant that it made me think of Chaliapin singing the Easter Mass in St. Petersburg Cathedral.

'That is what they sang at the inauguration of my father as Paramount Chief,' said Sobhuza.

The mountains threw back the echoes of the voice of Africa, as dark and deep as their own mysterious kranzes.

'It's a most beautiful song,' I said, moved by its mournful strength.

'Yes,' agreed the Paramount Chief. 'I wish I could get all our songs recorded – and our ancient ceremonies too. We have beautiful customs to mark different times of the year and events in the life of the tribe and of individuals. When the young girls gather and bring in the reeds there is some wonderful dancing, and again at the time of the First Crops.'

Sobhuza is a traditionalist and proud of it. His people are pastoral and everything happens in its appointed season. When the boys become men there is a ceremony known as the 'pummelling of the bull'. A young bull is let loose and the boys chase it and pummel it to death. The leader is the hero of the day. When a representative of the Society for the Prevention of Cruelty to Animals tried to interfere with this custom the Paramount Chief told him firmly but politely to put a stop to bull-fighting across the border first and to abolish fox-hunting in England before concerning himself with the traditions of Swaziland.

And now the warriors were singing battle-songs and dancing – advance, retreat, stamp, circle, crouch behind the shield, leap high into the air! Every now and again one stepped forward out of the ranks and performed a *pas seul*, singing aggressively.

'What does he sing about?' I asked.

'About himself,' said Sobhuza. 'He boasts to make himself brave. The words are what he pleases.'

Four small boys appeared, stamping, wiggling their legs, blowing little tin whistles, and, as they pranced along in front of the warriors, their shining black buttocks were bellicose and swaggering.

Then four young girls danced past.

'They dance to excite the warriors,' said Sobhuza. He was watching my face with amusement.

The scarlet feathers quivered in the bleached thatch of their hair, their resilient naked breasts bounced with every cavorting step and their deportment was arrogant yet enticing, drawing wild whistling from the responsive warriors. Tiny bead sporrans, necklaces, bangles and anklets were all the girls wore.

'Good gracious, your daughter!' I exclaimed.

Sobhuza roared with laughter. 'I told you you wouldn't recognize her! They are all my daughters, but the leader was the one who came on board the warship.'

Presently the Paramount Chief said: 'Now we will go to my mother's kraal for refreshment. It is no good waiting for the dance to finish. It will go on for hours, they never get tired of dancing.'

Before we left nature's great amphitheatre, Bertie stepped forward with an interpreter and congratulated the warriors on their performance.

'I have arranged that there will be a feast for you,' he concluded. 'I hope you will enjoy it.' An announcement which evoked another rousing burst of whistling.

The She Elephant's kraal was on the rise looking across the arena we had just left to the horn-shaped hills. The huts clustered round the huge stockade for the herds. We sat on a rough wooden bench in the shade of a reed shelter, though Indlovukati, the She Elephant, preferred to squat on the mud floor. A councillor brought a loving cup of maize beer and offered it to my husband, who drank first, then Sobhuza took a long draught, and, with his whiskers dripping with the beverage, he handed the calabash to me. I played my part and passed it on to Mr. Morgan, wondering, with an inward smile, what my old-fashioned mother would think if she could see us now.

Outside in the sun squatted the elders and a few dames in cowhide. Anyone coming to speak to the Paramount Chief literally crawled to him, and, wherever he moved, paeans of praise were loudly chanted. In a primitive Native community there is no such thing as equality. There never has been and never will be.

Gifts were brought forth. Sobhuza presented Bertie with a cowhide warrior's shield laced with throwing assegais. I was given a charming bead necklace and bracelet made by the daughter. Bertie gave Sobhuza a signed group taken on board the *Bermuda*, and to the She Elephant a Van Der Hum liqueur bottle filled with sea-water. This inexpensive present was of the utmost value. The sea-water, which must be bottled before dawn, forms an important part of the rain-making ritual. Before the Festival of the First Fruits it is customary for Indlovukati's medicine men to take a ceremonial gourd and make a pilgrimage from land-locked Swaziland to the coast to fill it with the water of the Indian Ocean. My gift to the old dame was less magical but more practical. It was a sunset-coloured blanket of fine quality, which pleased her greatly.

The shadows lengthened on the veld and the pink light deepened in the hills. From the valley we heard the singing of the warriors preparing for the feast. As we returned to Mbabane dusk enfolded the thatched huts and the folk who believe that if you clap your hands with a certain rhythm a ghost will answer the call, that a child may be transformed into an animal and that a killer can inhale safety with the fumes from a cooking-pot filled with the flesh and blood of his victim.

Next morning we left for Pigg's Peak high in the mountains near the Transvaal border. On the way out of Mbabane Mrs. Morgan took us to see Mr. Hendy's birds.

Mr. Hendy was one of those Europeans who had lost his heart to Swaziland. He had built a beautiful home with a wonderful view, and he had gradually acquired a very remarkable private aviary. His wife looked more like Paris than remote Africa, and she had a nice sense of humour.

'A ship was your rival,' she said to me. 'A Grey Mistress. But come and see *my* rivals – all of them! When I want a new dress my husband says, "But that's the equivalent of a new golden pheasant!" Even my plum trees are trained to give shade to the aviaries, and we have nine boys to take care of the birds. All the same I love my rivals. You loved yours too, didn't you?'

Mr. Hendy, tall and lame, was not unlike one of his own dignified cranes. Like Professor Millot of Madagascar, he knew every bird individually – its disposition, habits and personal eccentricities. He imported them from all over the world, and exchanged them like Mr. Pringle, the Curator of the Port Elizabeth Snake Park, who swapped cobras for rattlesnakes. In Mr. Hendy's garden we met pure white and pale pink flamingos, exotic crested cranes, mallards as colourful as children's celluloid bath-ducks, parakeets and peacocks. Pheasants from India, China, Tibet and England tossed burnished judicial wigs in the sun and preened their lovely tails, but, to my eyes, the prettiest of all were the indigenous kingfishers who flash their gleaming enamelled wings among the thorn trees of the veld.

We tore ourselves away reluctantly, bade a regretful good-bye to Mrs. Morgan, and turned our car towards the distant mountains.

Pigg's Peak is in the timber country which is being developed by private enterprise, and the Colonial Development Corporation, which has lent the Swazi nation £40,000 for afforestation of Native lands. Still farther north is the Havelock Asbestos Mine, another highly successful private enterprise which takes the lion's share in balancing the Territory's budget.

On the summit of the mountain we found Kipling again. There was a notice 'TO CLUB' and another 'TO HOTEL' and the Union Jack flew bravely from the Residency. The Lebombo ranges rose and fell like the waves of a purple sea, the conifers marched down into hidden valleys empty save for a few Native kraals, and there was nowhere any trace of civilization apart from that small sound core created by men and women whose work had called them into the blue.

Reg Oldham, the District Commissioner, had been in the

Navy during the war and had married a slender Wren called Nikki who had a quiet way of getting things done. The District Commissioner had learned a great deal about Swaziland very quickly, and he kindly lent me a most able and helpful report he had written about the country and the people.

When we arrived, two-and-a-half-year-old Rodney Oldham was in a state of high excitement and could only talk about the 'dwums'. And, in fact, the rarefied mountain air was throbbing with the beat of approaching wardrums.

The Oldhams had turned a disused tennis court into a stockade, and when night fell great log fires were lit, and the Native dance-teams of Pigg's Peak and Havelock Mine collected with their warbling and whistling and the queer eerie bird-noises that had once sent them hot-blooded to the slaughter of their enemies.

Little Roddy wept at first, afraid of the pounding persistent drums, but soon he grew accustomed to them, and fell asleep.

Everybody from far and near came to the Oldhams' party, doctors, police, inspectors of stock and agriculture, the folk from the Havelock Mine and from the Timber settlement, and a crowd of admiring Natives arrived to support the dance-teams.

The dancing was even madder and more abandoned than that of Sobhuza's warriors, the stamping more savage. Knees were drawn up quick as lightning, and down came the hard bare feet – *stamp, stamp*! The whole court shook.

Bertie said: 'Do you wonder that the whole earth trembled at the stamping of Chaka's impis!'

Convicts stoked the fires and sat on a log to watch the fun. The Southern Cross hung low in a frosty sky between two tall trees, and the moon was almost at the full. Ever and anon the breeze fanned the flames and a cascade of sparks rose into the night like a myriad fireflies. From time to time a small Native child toddled in a drunken baby way to the log on which the convicts sat. They accepted his presence absent-mindedly, sat him on their laps and petted him. The child was happy with them.

Next morning Roddy demanded that the drums come back. 'Daddy go office, fetch dwums.' But the drums had long since throbbed their way to a beer drink, and could not be recalled.

Nikki put up a superb picnic basket for us.

'Don't you get homesick?' I asked her.

'Not any more,' she smiled.

I remembered Bertie speaking to his Wrens at Whale Island during the war. Rather harsh he had seemed.

'Everybody tells you you are wonderful. But you are doing no more than your duty. I shall say you are wonderful if, after the war, you go back to your ordinary lives and make a success of the jobs you have to find for yourselves, or of taking care of homes, husbands and babies – perhaps under difficult conditions. If you can do those things well and cheerfully, you *will* be wonderful . . .'

CHAPTER SIXTEEN

GRANITE LAND WITH GROWING PAINS

OUR night-stop was to be Mountain Inn, not far from the Rhodesian border, and we had a long day's drive before us through some stupendous scenery.

But the long day became even longer, because up in the mountains round Barberton the car suddenly turned sulky and refused to pull. It was Sunday, the country garages were shut, and in any case there was no town or village within fifty miles.

My husband is not a mechanically-minded man and I know as much about engines as Sobhuza's daughter knows about 'the White man's magic'. We both groaned and said, 'If only Piet were here!' But, since he wasn't something had to be done.

Between us we unpicked everything under the bonnet and blew into whatever had a hole in it. We cleaned every part of the mechanism and transferred all the dirt and oil on to ourselves in the process. Then we put the jigsaw together again and set off. But the long zigzag road, steep as Jacob's ladder, simply mocked at us, the fir-trees shook their heads and laughed in the wind, and down in the plain the pale grasses rippled with mirth while the car came to a mulish standstill.

'Must be a stoppage in the exhaust,' said Bertie at last. 'Anyway I'm fed up with it, and I'm going to knock a ruddy great hole in the silencer!'

'Isn't that a bit drastic?'

'Yes,' he said. And lay on his back in the fine red dust and began to ease himself under the car. 'Now pass me the hammer and chisel.'

When we started again, we almost flew. A roar like the bellow of a racing Bugatti went with us. We discovered later that a baffle in the silencer had shaken loose and set back against the exhaust, and I was sorry when the exhilarating noise of our home-made cut out was stilled by the necessary repairs.

So, instead of reaching Mountain Inn before sunset, we found ourselves some hours distant as night began to fall. Our earth road through the bushveld ran parallel with the Kruger Game Reserve, and suddenly, in the half-light, there loomed out of the thorn scrub the most fantastic shape. Long legs, a long neck and the gentle head of some prehistoric deer swayed towards us in the gloom. Bertie put the wheel hard over and avoided the apparition by a few feet.

'Hell's delight! We nearly collided with a giraffe!'

That same night, near the scene of our encounter, another car *did* collide with a giraffe – perhaps the same animal – and the husband, who was driving, broke three ribs as his body struck the steering wheel. His wife, who sat beside him, was flung against the windscreen and killed instantly. The giraffe shrugged its long sloping shoulders and disappeared.

Next morning, on 13th August, we crossed the Beit Bridge over the 'great grey-green, greasy Limpopo River, all set about with fever-trees' into the British self-governing Colony of Southern Rhodesia.*

We were issued with a generous supply of petrol coupons – for in 1951 petrol was still rationed in Rhodesia – and received instructions on how to use the strip-roads. The earth roads were seamed with two tarmac strips to ensure that they would not become a mire after the rains.

As the little sailor mascot on our bonnet set his course for the north we entered the granite land of a great Empire-

_____

* *Now independent state of Rhodesia.*

builder, Cecil John Rhodes, the man with the granite will and the golden touch.

Rhodesia is a land of sparsely wooded veld, of grass that burns like paper in the dry season, of koppies studded with monstrous smooth granite boulders carved by nature into weird idolatrous forms, and of great distances veiled by a delicate gauze curtain of smoky African blue. It is the land of Kipling's High and Far Off Times, of his Elephant's Child and all that inquisitive mammoth's relations – his tall aunt, the Ostrich; his tall uncle, the Giraffe; his broad aunt, the Hippopotamus; his hairy uncle, the Baboon; the Ko-lokolo Bird; the Crocodile and the Bi-coloured-Python-Rock-Snake. It is also the land of opportunity, a young man's land, as it was in the days of the Colossus who gave it his name.

The achievements of Cecil John Rhodes cannot be compressed into a paragraph, but they can be suggested. He was a financial genius, a spell-binder, an opportunist and probably the greatest Imperialist in Britain's long history of Empire. He believed that an English-speaking master-race should rule the world for the world's good, and he wanted a United States of South Africa under the Union Jack from the Cape to Tanganyika – or, better still, a United States of Africa, all British pink, from Cape to Cairo. His views on the Native problem were in harmony with those of Dr. Malan. The tribes must be segregated in their own reserves so that they might develop their own Bantu culture and be responsible for their own people in time. 'There must be class legislation, Pass Laws, and Peace Preservation Acts', he declared. He went further. Native land, he considered, should be inherited from the father by the eldest son, and the younger sons should go to work for the Europeans in the mines, in industry and in agriculture – thereby ensuring an endless labour reserve for his manifold schemes and interests.

Rhodes used all sorts to help him acquire the land that bears his name – his old friends and colleagues of the early days in Kimberley; Selous, the mighty hunter; Moffatt, the missionary; soldiers, adventurers and traders. He formed his Pioneer Column of 200 enterprising young men to open up the country with the aid of a force of Bechuanaland Police. They were to establish Forts, plant the Union Jack, and eventually settle on grants, hardly and bravely won, to grow tobacco, grain or cattle on their own ranches. And what minerals might this harsh land reveal? Today we know some of the answers. Gold, tin, and, above all, copper – the real 'gold' of Northern Rhodesia. Tobacco is the wealth of Southern Rhodesia.

But this rapidly developing country owes her early growth to the old Cape Colony. With the help of the financier, Alfred Beit, Rhodes persuaded the Directors of de Beers to finance his beloved new venture. The diamonds of Kimberley paid for Rhodesia's first roads and railways, her telegraph system, her police and her administration. The British South Africa Company, which grew out of the original Chartered Company, drew its life-blood from de Beers, and, in the fullness of time, paid its debts.

All this because one man knew what he wanted. If Rhodes had been born ten years later, Oom Paul Kruger, Portugal, Belgium or Germany might have moved into the territory of the Barotse and of Lobengula's Mashona-Matabele. But, as it was, Rhodes, whose destiny had already made him Prime Minister of the Cape Colony, was able to present his Motherland with a new healthy colony, already well subsidized – the nucleus of White Africa north of the Limpopo.

At four in the afternoon we entered Fort Victoria, where the Pioneer Column placed its first Fort in 1890. We stopped for petrol in the garage in the main street where we were to meet the Magistrate, Mr. Bruce-Brand, who was to lead us to the famous Zimbabwe Ruins. Mr. Bruce-Brand and his wife both came from the Union, but they loved Rhodesia.

'It's an exciting country,' they said.

In the next weeks we found it so.

We followed the Magistrate's car into the heart of the

220

bush, where, among the tall tambootie trees, we saw the
stone temple and Sacred Place of Great Zimbabwe. What
Gods were worshipped there none know.

> 'Who were the dwellers in Great Zimbabwe?
>> No man can say
> Nor what dark dynasties
>> Of blood and fear
> Held, as they should not cease,
>> Dominion here. . . .'

Near the Temple was once a town, and, looming over the
site of this and many similar ruins in the surrounding bush,
is the Acropolis, a fortified hill where gold was smelted long
ago in a cave on its summit.

We had tea with Mr. and Mrs. Sands, the Curator and his
wife, and then Mr. Sands took us and the Bruce-Brands up
the Acropolis to the golden cave. Mr. Sands, sturdy and
practical, had served many years in the Navy and had been
an inspector at Scotland Yard. He was a man of good sense,
comfortably impervious to the strange ghostly influences
which are known to haunt this broken shell of a vanished
civilization.

Up and up we climbed to the walled top of the ancient
citadel with its mysterious caves and gateways, and there,
among the wild fig-trees and blossoming shrubs, we rested a
while in silence and contemplated the wild open country of
bush and forest at our feet, cupped by hills glowing with
resplendent rose in the light of the setting sun. In the near
valley lay the last traces of some royal city given over to the
leopards, the baboons, the wild pig and leaping buck.

You can take your choice of the theories about Zimbabwe. Like Angkor, in Cambodia, it is one of the world's
mysteries. You may place it three hundred years before
Christ and call it the Kingdom of Ophir, whence Solomon's
Navy brought those entrancing cargoes of 'gold, and silver,
and ivory, apes, and peacocks', or it might have been built
anywhere between the fifth and fifteenth centuries A.D. by

people of Bantu or Dravidian origin. The latest tests suggest the sixth century A.D., but, dreaming on the Acropolis, my thoughts were upon the lovely unlikely notion of vanished Ophir.

As we picked our way down the rough winding stone steps between the rocks and trees, a covey of partridges clacked loudly in the undergrowth and flew suddenly into the air; every now and again the wings of bird or bat whirred past us, or the rustle of rat or snake made a scary sound in the grasses. On the koppie opposite, a troop of baboons scampered to their sleeping-place safe from the prowling leopard or lion.

'They don't come *here*,' laughed Mr. Sands. 'They are afraid of the ghosts!'

The moon, still milky pale, hung in the darkening sky, but soon she would spill her radiance over the great walls, and silver the conical tower of stone set upon stone – the phallic symbol of the seed of life, man's only immortality.

The Bruce-Brands put us on the way to Glen Livet, and, as they said good-bye, they warned us that we might find it necessary to make a detour on the morrow.

'A rogue elephant was shot on the Umtali road yesterday,' they explained. 'It's a bit of a job moving five tons of dead elephant, so you may still find him there!'

If the ghosts walked at Zimbabwe that night we were unaware of it. We slept soundly among the orange groves and woods of Glen Livet on the shores of the moonlit lake. Next day we travelled east to the beautiful Umtali district among the Vumba Mountains on the Portuguese border. We were forced to make our detour. Five tons of elephant still lay across the road.

At Umtali we were joined by Colonel Sir Ellis Robins, D.S.O., Resident Director in Africa of the British South Africa Company, the modern development of Rhodes' original Chartered Company. The wide interests of B.S.A. touch every aspect of life in the Rhodesias, and its activities spread even further into the African Continent. It is private enterprise at its most successful and ambitious, and even the representatives of the Labour Government then visiting Rhodesia had to admit that the Commonwealth would be a mint the poorer without the prodigious enterprise of that remarkable individualist, Cecil John Rhodes, and those who came after him.

From now until we bade good-bye to the Rhodesias, Ellis Robins was our companion, guide and adviser. And it is still extraordinary to me how anyone with as many irons in the fire as he had, could maintain his tireless good humour and thoughtfulness under any conditions. He is in his sixties – tall, with a rather cherubic countenance. But the eyes are not at all cherubic. They are brown, kind and intensely observant, narrowing readily into laughter.

Ellis Robins was born in Philadelphia, U.S.A., and educated in America. He won a Rhodes Scholarship, went to Oxford, took British Nationality, and served his adopted country in both World Wars.

Umtali's fine modern buildings are set in avenues of mauve jacarandas and red flamboyants. It is the lovely core of a famous scenic area, and has the advantage of being comparatively near the Portuguese port of Beira.

Settlers were pouring in, and industry was beginning to rear its ugly head among the soft blue hills. The older settlers were a little saddened, for they had loved their paradise as it was.

A number of retired British officers had chosen to make their home in Umtali, among them Captain Herbert, R.N., known locally as 'the Bo'sun'. He was something of a legend in the Navy.

'He has nine lives like a cat,' said Bertie. 'But his narrowest shave was in the First World War when he was the sole survivor of a submarine disaster in the days before the Davis escape apparatus. He was fired to the surface through a torpedo tube and it is a miracle that he lived to tell the tale.'

In that same war – after an episode known as 'the *Baralong* affair' – the enemy put a price on Captain Herbert's head, and, when it was known that he was once more at sea in World War Two, that price was renewed, and I actually heard Lord Haw-Haw announce it over the radio '*Chairmany calling . . .*'

Captain Herbert and his wife were living in an attractive bungalow on a ridge in the lee of a koppie. We went to see them at about half past six one evening. Already the moon was enormous above the horizon while the western hills were silhouetted against a sultry sunset. Down in the valley lights began to twinkle.

'Rhodesian moonlight!' I said. 'How well I remember it from my romantic youth! So bright, it was almost blinding!'

But Captain Herbert was a wiry white-haired realist who spoke his mind, a veteran well acquainted with the practical disadvantages of moonlight.

'I curse that magnificent full moon! It brings the buck. They come down from the koppie and gobble up all our young vegetables and lettuces!'

'Aren't they afraid of human habitations?'

'Not they! They think my vegetables and my wife's flowers have been planted specially for their benefit. I've put up a burglar-alarm with wires and bells to warn me when there's a raid on.'

'Here comes Major Mercer,' said Mrs. Davis. 'You probably know him as Dornford Yates.'

Dornford Yates, for many years an established best-selling novelist, was very spare with deep-set disillusioned brown eyes in a thin face. His narrow feet were encased in the best-polished shoes I have ever seen.

Between the wars he had lived in the Pyrenees, but now he found France changed and less to his liking. During World War Two he had served in Kenya and Rhodesia, and he had discovered Umtali and decided to bring his wife to this beautiful place to start life all over again.

'Are you writing about Rhodesia?' I asked him.

'Not yet. I am still absorbing the atmosphere.'

'It must be wonderfully satisfactory to write a novel.'

224

'It is. And you should try it. Anyone who can write at all, can write a novel. And you can write.'

'But to imagine characters – a plot—'

He impaled me with his intense gaze.

'All you have to do is to get the *beginning* of your novel mapped out. Never mind the end. Take a few characters – half-a-dozen – the others will follow, they will find their own way into your book. You must be prepared to let the book take charge. Kipling used to say, "There is a ghost at my elbow when I write, I dare not deny the ghost".'

'But I am accustomed to dealing with reality. You are creative.'

'*You* could be. Your characters will come alive if you let them. They will build houses and furnish rooms, they will tell you a little of their past – just enough to make the present credible – they will go their own ways and write your book for you. And, when it is over and written, you will be left empty and friendless. You knew them all so well, you lived with them, and suddenly you are abandoned – a dreadful feeling.'

Frances Brett-Young had said, 'After writing *The Island* I was drained – empty . . .'

'Is this a good place for writing? It must be quiet enough.'

'It is quiet, but relaxing. In France I could do as much as eight hours at a stretch – that's too much, of course – creative brain-work is fatiguing. But here I can't manage more than five.'

Major Mercer did not begin to write until he was thirty-five, since when he has written thirty books – an average of one a year. Before World War One he was a promising young barrister with a great career before him, but, when he was demobilized from the Army, he decided to become a professional writer. His success proves that a writer is the better for having a second profession behind him. 'A ghost at your elbow' may be all very well, but a knowledge of medicine or the law is not to be despised.

Umtali may be relaxing, but it must be healthy, for Ellis

told us that two of Rhodes's original 1890 Pioneer Column were still living nearby. The one was ninety, the other ninety-two. Even now 'Ninety' rode into town to do his shopping, tethered his horse outside Meikle's Hotel, and rode home again with his provisions stored in his saddle-bags.

When I drew my curtains wide before going to bed I wondered if Captain Herbert's Heath Robinson bells were tinkling up on the ridge to tell him that delicate cloven hoofs were trespassing daintily among his lettuces. Maybe they were, but down in the Native Quarter that night a moon-struck hippopotamus was certainly wandering in search of monstrous romance – and wandering in vain . . .

We were to spend a few days at Ellis's home, June Hill, in Salisbury, the capital of Southern Rhodesia, so he sent our luggage ahead in his car by the direct route, while he came with us on the spectacular tour through the glorious Inyanga country. Inyanga Mountain brooded over the rich plantations of B.S.A., over deep green valleys and the magnificent gorge of the Tungwe Falls. At Troutbeck Inn, beside an artificial lake, well stocked with fish, we stopped for lunch.

As we sat on the stoep at the water's edge, a tall sun-burned man with a pith helmet and khaki shorts joined us. He was a high officer in the Government Medical Service. He was grimly humorous and a realist to the core. Before long we were discussing Southern Rhodesia's differences with her sister in the north. Our new acquaintance summed up the situation briefly.

'Our main difference is our attitude towards the Native. Here, in Southern Rhodesia, we accept responsibility for our Natives as a whole. You do the same in the Union. But in Northern Rhodesia they concentrate on their bright boys. . . . They send them home to learn more than is good for them and then bring them back to *guide* their fellow Africans. We believe in caring for the masses and letting the bright boys look out for themselves. They are quite capable of that, you'll find, whereas they are not yet capable of guiding others wisely.'

He told us how difficult it was in the hospitals to train the Native staff not to exploit the patients. (I was to learn more of this in West Africa later on.) And he made a remark which I believe to be deeply penetrating.

'The Native, by and large – there *are* exceptions, mind you – still lacks two important qualities. *A sense of responsibility and a sense of compassion.*

'In hospital both are important.'

'Very important. And, unfortunately, only one of those qualities can be instilled by teaching.'

Only one. The other – compassion – is a small part of Divine Love. I could not help thinking of little Solinye, the herd-boy, who will haunt a *donga* in Swaziland for ever with the spirit of his lonely anguish. A child forsaken by compassion.

We reached Salisbury in the evening with that incredible moon coming up over the sky-line. This thriving open city, with all the veld to expand in, was unable to expand fast enough. Umtali's growing pains were mere tweaks compared with those of the bigger Rhodesian cities. Settlers were flooding Salisbury alone at the rate of over a hundred and fifty families a month. The men had jobs, but nowhere to put their wives and children. Builders were frantically putting up houses, but the more they built the more they needed skilled labour, and the more skilled labour arrived in the country the more houses had to be built.

As we drove through the shady Coronation Park we saw hundreds of tents and caravans under the trees. Camp-fires burned in the dusk, radios and gramophones blared and children shrieked as they played joyfully. Camping out indefinitely was like one grand holiday to them, but to their parents, waiting for a home in a strange land, it was not such a joke.

In 1951 17,561 settlers entered Southern Rhodesia. The country needed this White life-blood, but she could not absorb it at such breath-taking speed. In 1952 she was compelled to restrict immigration. Strangely enough, more than half her immigrants were from the Union. Several South African settlers told me that they had decided to make their future in Rhodesia because 'we can't stand the racial atmosphere of the Union. It's too bitter'. But we learned also that the Rhodesians were afraid of 'Afrikaner infiltration'. We even heard it called 'a fifth column'. North of the Limpopo there exists a real fear of South African 'Imperialism'.

Yet Southern Rhodesia was not happy with some of her new British settlers. One old stager talked to me.

'People who have always behaved perfectly reasonably at home lose their heads out here. For instance, one firm put up a model settlement of labour-saving cottages for its employees – assisted artisan immigrants and their families. Women who had never in their lives contemplated having help in their homes were at first delighted with their bright, easy-to-run cottages, where they had only to press a button to get their light, fuel and hot water. But very soon they were discontented. They said "Other people in this country have Black men working for them. You must give us Native Quarters." So it was done. But they had no idea how to treat their new Black servants. Their cook-boys sat down to meals with them. And if the young bachelors wanted extra girls for a party they called in Native girls. You can't do those things out here – it's crazy!'

I said, 'Wouldn't it be possible to have the Rhodesian way of life explained to these people before they come here? They can't be expected to know that one observes certain different standards in a place like this.'

He groaned. 'My dear lady, they are brought up to believe that all men are equal. You have only to look at human beings to see the fallacy of it – but some folk look without seeing anything!'

But, in spite of her frustrations and her occasional irritation with her British-born settlers, Southern Rhodesia's loyalty to the Old Country is as true as steel. And, although she is a great land-locked territory, she loves the Royal Navy and has close links with it.

We were entertained by a most active branch of the Navy League, and also by a naval group known as the Central African Naval Officers' Association, which included a number of ex-Wrens. Bertie found many old ship-mates among these ex-Naval officers, and he inspected the Sea Cadets who had been on board the *Bermuda* on her Madagascar trip. All these Naval men and women were determined to return to the Service should their country need them. In the meantime they were growing tobacco, farming, mining or contributing to the growth of the new young land in some other useful way.

June Hill, Ellis Robins's home, was thatched and gabled, and shaded by cypresses, gums and flowering trees. The wide lawns were pale till the coming of the rains, and round about spread the veld with its stunted thorn trees.

Lady Robins was in England, visiting a married daughter, so Winifred, the Scotch housekeeper, took charge of us. She brought me my breakfast in bed of a morning with scones so light they melted on the tongue. Sun streamed over the coverlet, and the air – at four thousand five hundred feet above sea-level – was strong, dry and aromatic. On my tray were letters from the Cape, breathing the soft air of the mountain mists and the salt spray of storm-lashed sea. Still winter there – and here it was already early spring. In England it was late summer – London's 'silly season'.

A day or two later we continued on our way, this time alone by car, to Lusaka, the capital of the British Protectorate of Northern Rhodesia, a day's hard driving from Salisbury. Ellis was to fly up and meet us there later and we would go on together to the Copper Belt on the frontier of the Belgian Congo.

It was a long tiring day to Lusaka, growing steadily hotter as we descended from the high escarpment into the plain. From the escarpment we could see the immense tapestry of green and gold Africa veiled by its elusive blue.

Long stretches of the road were shocking, for a bigger and

better road was in course of construction and we were constantly skidding through the deep dust of 'diversions'. We seldom met another vehicle. Mountainous droppings and broken boughs told us that we were in elephant country, while a notice in the morning's paper had caused me some concern.

'Aug. 19th. Snakes waking now are full of venom after their winter sleep and liable to be particularly spiteful with the approach of the breeding season. ... Rhodesia's most common poisonous snakes are the banded cobra, puff-adder, mamba, ringhals and boom-slang.'

We had our snake-bite outfit with us, but it would have been a bad day for Bertie if ever I had been compelled to use it on him, because I would certainly have lost my head.

'It says "*Boil the syringe*",' I read aloud. 'How can one boil a syringe in the middle of nowhere – and a mamba bite takes twelve minutes to kill!'

'You could suck the puncture while the kettle's boiling,' said Bertie.

Yet it was not the elephant or the snake that threatened our lives. It was the dread dance of Loki, the Fire-God.

At Chirundu, on the Zambesi, at Otto Beit's Bridge, we crossed the border into Northern Rhodesia.* The young police officer – as in Rhodes' day – wore the badge of the B.S.A.

'You ask me if elephant have been this way!' he said. 'Too many! There are several herds, and they are destructive brutes. If you lived in elephant country you wouldn't want to see them.'

'Are we likely to?'

'Not at this time. It's early mornings and evenings they come down to the river to drink. By day they stay up there in the bush.'

About ten miles on we chose a picnic spot in the grass

* *Now Zambia. Lusaka the capital.*

230

under the scrubby trees. As soon as we had unpacked our basket little flies began to swarm round us.

'I can't stand these!' I said desperately. 'For heaven's sake, give me a cigarette and a light!'

Bertie handed me a cigarette and a box of matches and occupied himself with opening our thermos flask.

I still find it difficult to credit the speed with which things happened then. I lit the cigarette hastily and puffed the smoke at the horde of flies buzzing round my ears, and carelessly I threw the lighted match into the bone-dry grass. In a trice, full-grown flames were leaping from tuft to feathery tuft at our feet. The hot mid-day breeze fanned them and their crazy crackling was louder than the *zoom* of the flies.

Bertie beat at the flames with the empty picnic basket, I beat with the canvas tarpaulin on which we had spread our lunch, but they sprang on in an ever-widening fan, licking at the dry bark of the trees, consuming the parchment-coloured grass. I was panic-stricken. Nothing could stop this thing I had begun – all Northern Rhodesia would presently be one sheet of flame – and my fault! From the Zambesi to Lusaka and beyond there was nothing but dry thorn veld, fuel for the fire!

'What can stop it?' I gasped. 'Quick, let's make for the car – let's go back to the border and report it—'

'Wait', said Bertie. 'The wind's shifting . . .'

The fickle noonday breeze had changed as quickly as it had come up, and in a few moments the flames turned and ran before it, over their own blackened spoor. We beat upon the living fringes, but the heart, with nothing to feed upon, was dead, and soon Loki breathed his dying gasp. But I was severely shaken by my brief lesson.

We stayed in Lusaka with Major Harry Grenfell of the B.S.A. at Charter House, and, in so doing, made the acquaintance of one of the best liked men in the country. Harry Grenfell was the traditional English Army officer, a man of charm and distinction and unconquerable personal courage. He had lost both legs in the Burma Campaign of

World War Two, yet he drove a car, played games and took part in all the activities of life in a young Colony swiftly advancing towards Dominion Status. He liked good music, good pictures and good reading, and if Lusaka failed to measure up to his cultural standards he made the most of its compensations.

Lusaka had been brought into being to serve the Copper Belt. The great business companies were putting up hotels, cinemas, stores and offices on a grand scale. They were gambling, or rather banking, on the future of Lusaka. Men had their work and their interests in this city of the future. But women, always more prone to home-sickness, and with a deeper need of the known and familiar, had a harder task to adapt themselves. True, their houses were charming, and they could get Black servants. But when the hot wind blew the fine red dust across the unfinished roads and the gardens that needed such persuasion to grow, it filled those charming houses with a powdery deposit and played strange high tunes on nerves stretched taut. The trouble wasn't being *in* Lusaka, it was not being able to get *out* of it – except into the endless veld under the hot African sky.

'If one could go for a day to the sea!' said one young wife.

But Rhodesian families can't pile into the car for a picnic at the coast. They must take their amusements in other ways.

In Lusaka I was constantly reminded of Ankara, the capital of Turkey artificially created by Mustapha Kemal Ataturk in the face of bitter opposition. The fine Embassies of foreign nations had sprung up on the lonely Anatolian plain like national pavilions at a World Fair, and everybody had grumbled. *This* after Istanbul! No water, no trees, no gardens – nothing! 'There *shall* be water, and there *shall* be trees, and there *shall* be gardens!' the Dictator had said. And behold, a dam soon gleamed in a fold in the bleak hills, trees were born and kept alive, and gardens bloomed in the aching glare of Kemal's city in the wilderness. And gradually people began to make an admission. 'Ankara is

232

healthy! See how rosy our children are!' The unloved ugly duckling grew proud and splendid, the symbol of New Turkey turning West towards progress – a proclamation of faith in the future of a nation able to take its place in the modern world.

Is Lusaka too symbolic – a proclamation of the White man's continued stake in the Dark Continent?

CHAPTER SEVENTEEN

COPPER COUNTRY

From Lusaka to the Copper Belt on the border of the Belgian Congo is only a flip of three quarters of an hour.

We began to get the 'feel' of the Copper Belt even before we took to the air. The airport was like a club, and Ellis Robins – who was a Director of Central African Airways – introduced us to a number of our fellow passengers and the pilot and crew of the Viking which was to take us to Ndola, the commercial distributing centre of the wide area of great copper mines collectively known as 'the Copper Belt'.

A plane landed while we were being weighed up. It was a real holiday plane. Men in khaki shorts and bush-shirts got out and took babies and toddlers from the arms of hatless young women in cotton dresses with sandals on their bare feet. Their luggage was cluttered up with golf-clubs, tennis-racquets, kiddy-cars and carry-cots. Everybody looked pleased with life. We were seeing the human reflection of a happy and prosperous mood. We had seen the same thing in Port Elizabeth during the wool boom, and now we saw it here. Once again we were stimulated by the atmosphere of an area in luck. And the copper mines, like the wool farmers, had been through their bad times. But, for them, too, the economic wind had shifted into the right quarter.

Air passages are cheap by Central African Airways, and there are special concessions for families. Our Viking was quiet and comfortable. It was thundery weather, and we flew through a pink haze. The earth below looked like a coloured slide I had seen at Leopoldville Medical School to demonstrate a typical case of small-pox. Africa's skin, seen from the air, was angrily flushed, with black pustulating sores. Later it recovered a healthy green as we flew over bush that twenty years ago had teemed with game – a happy hunting ground for the lion. To us the lion is still the King of the Beasts, but in Rhodesia he is classified as 'vermin', which only goes to show how opinions may vary as to the definition of 'vermin'!

It was six o'clock when we left Ndola for Kitwe, forty miles by car through the fast darkening bush. It had grown appreciably hotter with every mile that had taken us north of Salisbury and nearer the Equator, and now the air had lost the last of its sting. In a few weeks it would be the hot season. On either side of the tarmac road the msasa forests were in young coppery leaf – all the shades of autumn beech-woods in England – and the sky glowed with the pink-gold of well-burnished copper. Near Nkana Mine we began to be aware of the acrid emanations of the smelter and the sky burned with a fiercer glare.

The Rhokana Corporation* is responsible for the housing and welfare of some fifteen hundred White mine employees and ten thousand Africans. We passed through the African township and into the pretty town of Kitwe with its fine buildings, the Government School, the Chamber of Mines, and airy bungalows in flower gardens made fantastic by enormous ant-heaps which human hands had planted over or carved into shapes even more curious than those achieved by the termite. Many of these ant-hills were more than twenty feet high.

The Rhokana Corporation Guest House is one of those astonishingly luxurious habitations one sometimes finds in the wilds. This large bungalow with its wide furnished ver-andahs might have been a private home arranged with ex-quisite taste of a highly personal order. Mrs. English, the white-haired housekeeper, had put gay cottage flowers in every room, including the biggest and brightest Iceland poppies I have ever seen. The meals she ordered for us were

* Zambia nationalized this 'heritage' and many others after independ-ence and the policy of Africanization inevitably inhibits White opportunity.

235

delicious, and when she brought me my breakfast tray, there was a tiny posy on it.

Presently Mr. and Mrs. O. Bennett came in for a sundowner. 'Ob' Bennett was the Mine Manager for the two big mines of Nkana and Mindola. He was a broad-shouldered young man with boundless vitality, not yet forty, and earning a salary of several thousands a year, with a free house and car and entertaining allowance. His income tax, being Rhodesian, was, by English standards, negligible.

'Tomorrow I've arranged for King, the Underground Manager of Mindola, to take Admiral and Lady Packer down the shaft. After lunch we could go over the smelter, and in the evening we hope you'll all dine with us,' he said to Ellis. 'On the following day I thought you might all like to go over to Nkana. Pope, the Mine Manager, could fix up golf for the afternoon, and Lady Packer could see the welfare and hospitals in the morning.'

The Bennetts both enjoyed life on the Copper Belt. They had two small children who did well in the climate.

'The winter is perfect,' said Mrs. Bennett, who was slim, with hair of the same pale gold as that of her spaniel puppy, Pippa. 'And in summer we can go away to the Great Lakes for a change. Kivu, Nyasa, or Tanganyika – you can get some wonderful fishing! Oh, Rhodesia is a fine country – if you like outdoors and aren't too conventional.'

Next morning, while Ellis attended a conference, we went down Mindola Mine. Mr. King, the Underground Manager, was a cheery man who feared nothing except holy matrimony. But he had nerved himself for the plunge and was to be married to a young English school-teacher the following week. She had been six months in the Copper Belt and liked it.

'She may be able to manage me,' admitted Mr. King. 'She can keep fifty children in order without any trouble, so one man should be easy enough—'

For his part, Mr. King was in charge of quite a family too

236

– two hundred Europeans and two thousand five hundred Natives . . .

There were gardens at the shaft-head watered by the flow pumped hourly out of the shaft. The gardeners were African miners who had suffered some injury or illness which made it inadvisable to employ them underground.

Mr. King took us into his office, where we were offered enormous cups of tea while he explained a diagram of the mine in which appeared the name of every shift-boss – young men earning handsome pay-cheques and living in attractive modern houses provided by the Corporation for a small nominal rent.

'These fellows are paid according to output,' said Mr. King. 'For instance, this man here got £270 this month. It isn't always as good as that, but they can expect about £1,500 a year.'

He saw me pick out the South African names – Nels, Malan, Uys, Molyneux.

'Yes,' he said. 'Many of our chaps come from the Union, but we also have British, Rhodesians and Canadians – all sorts – and a good team they are.'

We were given overalls, tin hats and torches, and then we walked over to the headgear soaring into the hot blue sky like a gigantic meccano model. We stepped into the cage. A few miners, Black and White, glanced at us curiously. Down we dropped to two thousand feet, and, as the doors opened, we stepped into an airy tunnel with a railway line down the middle.

'Could be a London tube,' I said.

'You could walk three and a half miles down there,' said Mr. King.

But mercifully we didn't. We soon turned down one of the many dark seams that led to the rock-face.

As I know as little about mining as about warships, my impressions of Mindola Shaft are not intended for the initiated.

Jonah, in the belly of his whale, must have felt much as I

did that morning – a sense of fearful claustrophobia in the hot, steamy night of the monster's intestines. There was the continuous windy roar of the ventilation system, and every now and again the hollow abdominal rumbling of blasting. Parasites inhabited this gaseous interior – Black men, clad as we were, but invisible in the gloom, save for the white gleam of their rolling eyes and great teeth, and the sudden flash of their torches. Here and there some flimsy skeleton structure indicated a thousand foot drop into the dark bowels of Mindola, and ever and again, at the end of a seam, glittered veins of gold and blue.

'See this gold and blue in the ore-body?' said Mr. King. 'That's copper and cobalt. *Fool's gold*, some call the copper. Come and see the diamond drill – it drills out the ore-body ready to receive the dynamite charges.' He led us into a dark dripping cavern at the edge of one of those bottomless pits. Aimed at the rock-face was something which, in the gloom, resembled a gigantic rocket. 'Like to see it work?'

Bertie said yes.

There was a loud hissing sound. A few seconds later the diamond-studded mouth of the drill bit into the rock with a noise that made me think of Captain Currey's description of the eight-barrelled pom-poms – 'The sound makes your soul leave your body!' Every particle of the rock so relentlessly attacked seemed to shudder, shriek and groan, and the echo of this fleshless agony ran up and down the seam, reverberating and gathering intensity. Unable to escape, it was forced back upon itself in a crescendo of nightmare sound.

I closed my eyes in the sweating dark and held my ears. Through my shut lids I was aware of a torch flashed upon my face, and of my husband's voice shouting above the tumult.

'Thank you! Could you stop it now?'

'Enough!' bellowed Mr. King.

The drill fell silent and only the fans roared on.

As we made our way back to the main tunnel, strange tales we had heard went through my mind. Tales of haunted seams where boys refused to work because of 'spookaspooks'. There was the story of the *induna*, or native boss, who was alone in a seam when he saw a figure with a light running towards a drop of a thousand feet to certain death. He called after the figure, thinking it might be a new native who had lost his head, but the other ran on, unheeding. The *induna* gave chase, hoping to catch the fleeing figure in time to avert a tragedy. Then suddenly the runner disappeared, and the *induna* found himself panting on the very lip of the abyss! He collected his wits and hurried to the surface to report a man killed. He described the incident, the figure and the type of torch the runner had carried.

The torch was of a type long since abandoned. And no man was missing.

Mr. King was proud of his *indunas*.

'They have been trained to a very high sense of responsibility. Not long ago one was awarded the George Medal. Do you know anything about methods of blasting? No – well, it's like this, one shift places the charges, lights the fuses and leaves the explosive to do its work. The next shift comes down and clears away the debris. On this occasion the shift boss had a bit of trouble getting his fuses lighted, and while he was still struggling with the last one, the first charges began to go off. It's terrifying when that happens. It's a deafening noise, and bits of rock blow out all over the place. Your one idea is to take to your heels and get to hell out of it!'

This they had all done, with the *induna* in the lead. But, as he looked back over his shoulder, he saw that the White shift boss had been injured and had fallen, and so had another African. Without hesitation the *induna* did the one thing most calculated to strike terror into any heart. He ran back into the lethal showers of exploding rock and dragged the European to safety. Then he returned to do as much for his fellow African.

'It's a miracle he wasn't killed! He deserved his George Medal if ever a man did. But I wish you could have seen his face the day the Governor gave him his award! *Then* he might have been going to the gallows!'

239

(The tall doctor we had met at Troutbeck Inn in Southern Rhodesia had said, 'The Native lacks two important qualities – a sense of responsibility, and a sense of compassion. And only one of these can be instilled by teaching.' Here had been a shining example of an acquired sense of responsibility, culminating in heroism – as is so often the case with Native troops. Perhaps one day compassion too might be instilled by teaching?)

The Africans on the Copper Belt do not live in compounds. They have their own model townships where they can lead a normal family life if they wish. But they seldom wish. Few of them bring their kraal wives to a mining area. Someone must stay at home to till the land and send the young boys out with the cattle, and, in any case, for a young man, work in the mines is his initiation into the sophistry of the White man's world. The bright lights and jitterbug dances are not for his pastoral women-folk, they are for the temporary liaison he finds in the town. And how he loves to dance! All the madness of his African blood pounds in his flickering feet and rippling legs as he dances, and his eyes roll like the eyes of Sobhuza's stamping warriors. But the fur and feathers of the veld are not for the Copper Belt. Here the African wears the White man's tails ordered from London, from the Fifty Shilling Tailor, by post, and altered by the little Indian tailor who squats outside the Native Stores and plies his sewing-machine on an old packing case and thinks his Oriental thoughts about his flamboyant clients. The Black man may wear a red tie with his evening suit, or an emerald waistcoat, or he may fancy his tails down to his heels or up to his knees, but no one can make them fly faster or higher than he, for jazz was born of the rhythm in his African blood. And when he goes home to the kraal with his gay little trunk on his shoulder, filled with trinkets and lengths of material for those at home, what a hero he is! That is, of course, if the wantons on the way have not stripped the poor pilgrim of all his gifts.

'Now we go up five hundred feet to the Pump Room,' said Mr. King. He guided us into the lift, which whisked us up into the heart of Mindola – a huge pulsing chamber in which monstrous electric pumps throbbed day and night. I felt like Jonah listening to the heart-throb of his whale. *Chook-chook-chook, chook-chook* ...

'We have a five hour life,' said Mr. King. 'If these pumps failed for longer than five hours, the mine would be flooded – and dead for a long time.'

At last, like Jonah, we were safely disgorged. How good it was to feel the sun again – hot and glaring though it was! How good to breathe real air!

'Think of it – eight hours at a stretch down there!' I said.

Mr. King laughed. 'Why not? Eight hours work, eight hours play, and eight hours sleep. Seems fair enough to me.'

'Don't your Africans ever get claustrophobia?'

'Not they! They haven't enough imagination. They have plenty of superstition, but that's a different cup of tea.'

In the afternoon we were taken over the smelter – Dante's Inferno, all fire and brimstone.

'The more I see of machinery, the more I love nature,' I said.

'Then we'll go out to the dam,' said Mr. Bennett, his eyes amused. 'We'll pick up my wife first.'

Each Mine Manager on the Copper Belt impresses something of his own personality upon his surroundings. It may be a cricket field, a polo-ground, a golf course or an artificial lake. 'Ob' Bennett's contribution was this beautiful lake filled by the water pumped hourly from the mines. And the Sailing Club. It was the cool of the evening when we went out, and there was not a breath of wind, so we had to use the outboard motor.

The sheet of silvery water was broken by ant-heap islands covered with rushes and weeping willows. The msasa trees, in their young copper leaf, were reflected among the opalescent lights of the sunset, and, in the tall reeds, the cormorants spread heraldic wings to dry after fishing. It was so peaceful on the water after the industrial roar of the mines

241

that one relaxed almost without knowing it, giving oneself over to a serene human process of regeneration. Even the dynamic personality of Mr. Bennett was at rest. His glance followed the lovely flight of geese across a pearly sky, and the happy skimming of baby ducks still too young to fly.

'One needs this at the end of a hot day,' he said. 'It means a lot.'

His wife pointed suddenly. 'Those are new ducks! They weren't here before.' She turned her head to where I was sitting in the stern of the boat. 'It was amazing how the birds came when this dam was finished. They came from everywhere and nowhere – more and more of them. We are only afraid the crocs may get to hear of it. They'll trek for miles overland if they think it's worth their while. But we hope for the best.'

When we went back to the little wooden pier, Pippa, the spaniel puppy, was waiting for us. She had been swimming and her coat was soaking.

'Dry yourself! Dry yourself, Pippa!' said her mistress.

The little dog rushed round and shook herself frantically.

'There, that's better. Now you can come in the car. It's time to go back.'

We dined with the Bennetts that evening.

Northern Rhodesia has the hot climate habit of a long session of sundowners before a late dinner, and we had plenty of time to talk to people and learn something of life in the Copper Country. Socially, it was gay and democratic, with the sort of comfort women at home have forgotten exists.

Bertie rediscovered an old acquaintance that evening in Mr. Arnot, who had been in mine-sweepers during the war. He and his wife had three little boys. The younger ones were at school locally, but their ten-year-old son went to Grahamstown in the Union – five days by train!

Another guest was a young man with a dazed shocked look still in his eyes. He was the father of two motherless children. Only a few weeks ago life had been full of promise and happiness. He had been promoted from a Government post in Salisbury to the Copper Belt. He had gone ahead of his family to prepare their new home. His wife had packed up their house a few miles out of Salisbury, and, on her last night there, a neighbour had taken the children to enable her to get the place quite ready for the new occupants. She had only to turn the key in the lock next day, collect her children and catch her train. But she never caught that train. Her murdered body was found in her empty home. The Native gardener confessed to the crime.

'In America he would have been lynched,' somebody said. 'Here justice takes its course, no matter how terrible the crime.'

On the following morning we drove over to Nchanga, where the Mine Manager, Mr. Pope, had nursed a delightful eighteen-hole golf course into being. The water pumped from Nchanga shaft had the rare quality of having no ill effects on plants or grass, and the fairways were excellent. Mr. Pope's daughter, Priscilla, had been the lady gardener at Admiralty House for some years, and many of the lovely flowers that thrived in the sea-garden had been introduced by this artistic girl from land-locked Rhodesia.

Before we flew back to Lusaka Bertie inspected a parade of the African Mine Police. They were very smart in their khaki tunics and shorts and red tarbooshes; and the band, trained by a retired Royal Marine bandmaster, performed superbly on drums, cymbals and trombones. As they padded away from the hot dusty parade ground on their bare feet they sang in deep voices – 'And now we say good-bye . . .' – a melodious nostalgic marching-song, one verse in English and the next in their native Chiwemba.

And now we say good-bye – the song of the Copper Belt, of here today and hence tomorrow, of those who stay a while to seek 'fools' gold' and go their way, of the wind in the msasa trees, the flighting of wild duck against a sunset sky, and the powerful heart-throb of the mines . . .

CHAPTER EIGHTEEN

WORLD'S WONDER, WANKIE, WORLD'S VIEW

AT Ndola we turned our faces south towards Simon's Town – but it was still a very long way to go!

Once more we flew through the pink haze to Lusaka, where we stayed a night at Government House with Sir Gilbert and Lady Rennie before picking up our car and continuing our journey to the Victoria Falls. Sir Ellis Robins went straight on to Salisbury, promising to meet us again in Bulawayo before we should finally leave the Rhodesias and enter the Bechuanaland Protectorate.

Government House in Lusaka is on the same grand scale as most official buildings in this new city. Spacious and modern, it seemed to have been dropped by some genii into the middle of the veld.

The wide main staircase of black marble was the genii's joke.

'The staircase is dangerous,' said Lady Rennie, in the voice one uses about a fierce dog – *be careful, he bites!*

When I had nearly killed myself on it I noticed that the family never used it. They must have had some safe secret approach to upstairs. It was a relief to recall that the Governor's wife was not only very good-looking but had received a medical training. She would know how to set the broken bones of the casualties. It was a mystery to me how our fellow guest, Professor Macmillan, negotiated the marble menace, for he walked with the aid of sticks.

Professor Macmillan, the Director of Colonial Studies at the University of St. Andrew's, was one of the three observers sent to Bechuanaland by the British Labour Government to study the knotty question of the Bamangwato succession. He was South African born and had been educated at Stellenbosch as a boy, as had Dr. Malan and the late General Smuts a decade earlier. He was also a Rhodes Scholar and a distinguished student of the Colour problems of Southern Africa. The Professor had been the neutral member of the unhappy trinity of observers, for the other two had been politicians of divergent views who at times had appeared to be more concerned with their own quarrels than with those of the Bamangwato. *Punch* summed up the situation aptly in its 'Charivaria' of 5th September, 1951.

'The Bamangwato are believed to have offered to send observers here to investigate the differences between the observers we sent to investigate theirs.'

The fact that Professor Macmillan had found himself in Lusaka after visiting Seretse Khama's home town of Serowe was not surprising. In Africa people think in terms of thousands of miles. I had met him and his family a few months earlier when they had called at Admiralty House, where Mrs. Macmillan's father, Admiral Tweedie, had once been Commander-in-Chief. The Professor's was not a personality it would be easy to forget. His hair stood up in a canary-coloured aura round his wise head, his eyes flashed pale fire and his activity – at rising seventy – was enormous. He must have made a considerable impression on the Bamangwato, but what impression they made on him he did not divulge.

In the evening, before changing for dinner, we sat out on the terrace, where the Governor joined us. Sir Gilbert Rennie had wide experience of colonial administration, and he certainly needed it in his present post, for the future of Northern Rhodesia and a large block of the African Continent hung in the balance.

Across a parched lawn, under an umbrella-shaped tree, was suspended a canvas swimming-bath where his little daughter splashed happily with her elder brother. The mango-trees and orange groves were in full flower and their fragrance was wafted to us across the garden.

Lady Rennie said, 'We have everything in our garden – plums, peaches, cherries, apples, strawberries, and, of course, vegetables and flowers – but the soil needs endless compost.'

Flowering shrubs and bushes glimmered in the swift dusk, burning stars pierced the sky. This was Lusaka at its best.

We left at dawn for the long run through to Livingstone and the Victoria Falls – a tiring dusty day's journey.

At the Falls Hotel we occupied the charming little suite which King George VI and *his* Queen Elizabeth had used during their visit. From our window we could see and hear 'the smoke that thunders', one of the world's wonders first discovered by the Scottish Missionary, David Livingstone, who trekked through Africa with his Bible, his binoculars, his pack and his pith helmet.

Much has been written of the Falls, none of it exaggerated. No one is ever disappointed by the superb majesty of the wide blue Zambesi, flanked with tropical trees and plants, suddenly plunging headlong over the horseshoe-shaped fissure three hundred and fifty feet deep, and then surging off at a sharp angle through a series of narrow zigzag canyons – a boiling tormented volume of water thrown dramatically out of its course by some long-ago upheaval of nature.

We stood in the 'Rain Forest', opposite the sheer basalt cliffs overgrown with ferns and tropical orchids, and watched the many vagrant rainbows dancing in the flying spray, and at sunset we saw that spray tinged with fiery gold, and clouds of little birds soaring up over the Falls to their nests up-river.

We could have gone on many sight-seeing excursions, but we idled away our forty-eight hours on the beautiful banks of the Zambesi in peaceful contentment.

Our journey south took us through the Wankie Game Reserve. The moment we left the banks of the Zambesi we were back in the safari thorn-veld. We entered the northern end of the Reserve in time for an early lunch with the Chief Game Warden, Mr. Davidson. At the gates a giraffe's skull and cross-bones surmounted a notice, 'STAY IN YOUR CAR AT ALL TIMES!' No rain had fallen yet and the air was crisp and clear after the heat of the Copper Belt. The veld wore its winter gold and the trees were in young coppery leaf.

We were introduced to the Davidsons' three sons – two schoolboys and a toddler – and Mrs. Davidson gave us an excellent cold lunch in their pleasant bungalow in the heart of the elephant country.

'It must be fun for the boys to come to a place like this for their holidays,' I said.

'It doesn't mean as much to them as it might to many youngsters,' said their father. 'I'll never forget the thrill of seeing my first elephant! But these chaps can't remember a time when Jumbo wasn't part of the scenery.'

Immediately after lunch we left for the hundred mile drive to Main Camp at the southern end of the Reserve, where we were to spend the night.

'I'll come in your car,' said the Warden. 'And Rodney and Gerry can follow in our jeep with your luggage and our Native driver.'

Mrs. Davidson waved her husband and twelve and ten-year-old sons a cheerful good-bye. 'See you boys back about midnight!' she called. She seemed quite unconcerned at being left alone with a small child and no telephone, miles from her nearest neighbour.

'It's safe enough,' explained her husband. 'Our Natives are all right here. Your rape and murder cases occur near the towns. A Native seldom becomes a criminal unless he is taken out of his natural surroundings and deprived of his own women.'

Our trip through the Reserve was intensely interesting. Mr. Davidson was an expert on wild life and a good racon-teur. His eyes, accustomed to penetrating nature's camouflage, missed nothing. He would break off a conversation suddenly to say in a low voice – 'Stop a moment! There's something over there—' It might be the rare oryx (the *gemsbok*, with the narrow straight horns supposed to be the origin of the unicorn), or the soft-eyed koodoo with great leaf-shaped ears, a flying troop of impala, or a family of giraffes.

'The big darkly dappled fellow is the bull giraffe, his mate is the blonde, and see how pale the baby is!'

The deer-like head, with its curious little snail's horns, was at tree-top height, and birds hovered about it as if they were kissing the tall fellow.

'They like the moisture round his lips,' explained the Warden. 'He doesn't mind that, but he hates them getting in his ears. Except when he's drinking. Then he doesn't bother about them or anything else. They nibble at the wax in his ears and the salty parasites on his head. When he's finished drinking, he just flicks them off.'

'Drinking uphill like a giraffe must be the hell of a lift,' said Bertie. 'I don't wonder he can't worry about birds.'

We were amused at the ugly trotting wart-hogs with tails erect, and Mr. Davidson told us about a tame pair who had lived in their garden when Gerry was four. The boy, the dogs and the wart-hogs were great friends and went on excursions together.

'But wart-hogs never follow, they lead. Gerry used to follow them till he was tired, then he'd stop and so would they, and the whole party would play together for a while, and off they'd go again. Sometimes we'd track them down miles from home, and when we asked Gerry why he'd wandered so far, he'd say, "I went with the wart-hogs". So my wife put her foot down, and the wart-hogs had to go. In any case, they rooted up her garden.'

Sleek zebras cantered through the thorn scrub.

'They look so plump!'

The Warden smiled. 'You ought to know why. They're wearing their stripes the wrong way – round and round – it's a fattening fashion.'

Along came a troop of baboons to remind us of Simon's Town. And towards evening we came upon a herd of buffalo grazing in a depression on the side of the road. Some were already crossing our path on to a koppie.

'Stop!' said Mr. Davidson. 'Buffalo can be nasty. Now go very slowly towards them and don't time it so that you split the herd. There must be about four hundred there!'

The frowning fierce-looking animals were staring at us suspiciously, and a few guards on the flank came at us in a threatening manner. Bertie was having difficulty in low gear as the wheels refused to grip the thick powdery Kalahari sand. Behind us came the jeep with the two boys and the Native driver.

'This Kalahari sand is the devil,' said the Warden, 'but you can increase speed to stop skidding, the animals are crossing the road faster now.'

As we passed within inches of the rearguard, Bertie said, 'Keeping astern of that big chap was quite tricky.'

'I know,' agreed the Warden. 'And he might have been disagreeable.'

They stood on the rise glowering down at us and at the jeep. How terrifying a charge of the herd would be! I thought of these beasts stampeding before a forest fire. How shocking could be the result of a match carelessly thrown on the dry grass in a Reserve!

The two boys waved at us, and presently the jeep was lost in our wake of thick grey dust.

At a turn in the road, Mr. Davidson said, 'Go easy here, and we'll see how the land lies. There's a windmill and a water-hole round this bend.'

As we came in sight of the drinking-place I had to blink my eyes to be sure that I wasn't 'seeing things'.

Vast creatures from another era had gathered here – the living ivory of ancient Africa – some two hundred elephants. Fathers, mothers, babies, aunts and uncles were within a stone's throw of us. Sinuous trunks moved snake-wise to the water, or blew sand over gigantic shoulders. Immense ears flapped like rugs shaken out of windows. These were African elephants, far larger and wilder than their Indian relations, who could be tamed and trained. Never would the mighty feet of Wankie Jumbo tread the sawdust ring, or his massive rump balance on an upturned barrel, never would he work for his living or dance to a human tune.

We spoke in whispers.

'Why aren't their tummies rumbling? I thought elephants' tummies always rumbled.'

'They do a good deal,' said the Warden. 'The water shakes about, but sometimes what you might think is rumbling is really their way of warning each other of danger. They aren't worrying about us. The wind is in our direction and they haven't got our scent.'

'Do they ever harm anyone?'

'Not if people are sensible and stop their cars till the herd moves on. But we have trouble with our boys occasionally. There was a boy in a road-gang who was killed. As you can see by the droppings, elephants like to walk along a road and this boy was evidently careless and didn't realize an elephant was near. The animal got his scent and picked him up in his trunk, dashed him to the ground and knelt on him. There was mighty little left except a smear. The boy's brother was one of our trackers and we went after the killer – up there on the ridge. But we found a pair, and, as we didn't know who was to blame, we shot both.'

'Must you shoot an animal after a fatality?'

'Yes. For two reasons. If we didn't we'd never get boys to work for us. And an animal that has once killed a man may do so again.'

'Where do you aim to shoot an elephant?' asked Bertie.

'The brain. Between the eardrums.'

'Where exactly would that be?'

The Warden hesitated. 'When I aim at an animal I'm not shooting at his *outside*, but at something *inside* him – his brain or his heart. And it depends on the angle. But, if the elephant were charging, you'd aim dead between his eyes. It's difficult to get him in those circumstances because he

250

brings everything with him – whole trees and branches act as camouflage and defence.'

'They've finished drinking,' I said.

The monsters had begun to move away from the waterhole – a grey ghost army losing itself among the trees in the gathering gloom.

Only a few miles farther on was Main Camp, where Mr. Kemp met us – a tanned forthright man – the Warden for the southern part of the Reserve.

'I have a big fierce wife,' he said. 'She'll be here in a moment. Come along in.'

Our luggage was taken out of the jeep and the two boys came in and were given lemonade and cake by small pretty Mrs. Kemp. Their father had a well-earned Scotch and then off they went again, on the long homeward journey through the night and the terrain of the wild beast.

Main Camp was still primitive with outdoor sanitation and no electricity, but the Kemp's bungalow was warm and pleasant and the lamb we ate for dinner was delicious. 'A nice little bit of wart-hog,' said our host as he carved it.

In a basket by the fire slept Tinkerbell, a little smooth-haired terrier like Piet and Glen's Priscilla, delightfully homely and friendly after the great animals we had recently seen.

The Camp woke at six a.m. and a Native brought us tea. Tourist cars were going out, each on its appointed route through the Reserve. At certain hours Main Camp would be in communication with other camps to check the safe arrival of each party. If any car was missing the wardens would go in search of it.

I went into the fresh dewy garden and sat under a giant giraffe-acacia, so-called because the giraffe nibbles its leaves as a rabbit nibbles lettuce. Birds filled it with song.

Mrs. Kemp came out and joined me.

'Aren't you lonely here?' I asked.

'I love it,' she smiled.

We saw the Kemps again at Simon's Town a year later. The Warden had retired and built himself a house by the sea. But every year they planned to go camping in the wilds among the birds and beasts they understood so well.

As distances go in Africa, from Wankie to Bulawayo was not very far – rather less than a full day's journey by car.

The bushveld here was haunted by echoes of the remote long-extinct past of Africa. In fact, at the end of 1952, just about the time when Professor Smith of Rhodes' University at Grahamstown was being introduced to his newly pickled coelacanth in the lonely island near Madagascar, the remains of a young dinosaur, some hundred and fifty million years old, were being discovered in a dry river-bed near Bulawayo. Africa yields up her secrets slowly.

At 'Sunrising', B.S.A.'s guest house in Bulawayo, we were rejoined for a few days by Ellis Robins. Here, too, we found an active Naval Officers' organization, which took care of us and gave us a very happy time. My husband was deeply touched by the affection this city, so far from the sea, felt for the Royal Navy – an affection generously proved when the Mayor presented him with a cheque for over £700 to help the dependents of those lost in the submarine *Affray*.

I spent most of my first morning at 'Sunrising' in bed, collecting my thoughts and writing up my diary.

'Aug. 30 1951. *"Sunrising". Bulawayo.* Having driven many hundreds of miles through this raw land with its tobacco and cattle ranches, its endless *bundu* and rocky koppies, its bright hot sun with the threat of greater heat to follow in the "suicide month" of October before the rains break – having felt the quality of its breadth and loneliness, I find myself longing for the varied landscape of the Cape – for the velvet softness of wheatfields and for old homesteads with their feel of an earlier more leisurely settlement. It seems to me that the "tablecloth", pouring 3,000 feet over our great mountain in a soft silent avalanche, is as impressive as the Zambesi foaming 350 feet into a wound of nature wrought by some fearful primeval convulsion. Above all, I long for a breath of the sea – to

252

sniff salt in the air, to hear the unmelodious cry of sea-birds and the ever-changing thunder and murmur of the ocean, so much moodier than the continuous roar of the Falls. My eyes crave our wide green lawn at Admiralty House and the arums that will be coming into bloom under the pines. At this time of year Flora, our figure-head, will see the tortoise wake from his winter sleep, and busy little moles will tunnel under the grass behind her fine white back, and, in the air all round, the birds will be courting, wild and urgent in their flight and sweet in their calls, and presently they will be building their nests. Wankie is welcome to its elephants!

'It is a year today since we arrived in South Africa.

'And, if I am capable of this passing nostalgia, what of the new settlers in this great young land? I do not mean the wealthy investors who buy a ranch, put in a manager, and come and go as they please, but the *real* settlers who have dragged up their British roots because they believe Rhodesia has more to offer their children. How danger-ous for them to dwell upon the charms of their own dear island – the silvery light of long summer days or the apri-cot bloom of a winter's afternoon, the spires and towers of Westminster reflected in the wide grey Thames, old towns and hamlets steeped in history, and small green meadows safe within their hedges.

'Today, more than ever, the settler must be robust, for his courage is no longer that of desperation. No six months perilous sea-passage stands between him and his homeland if his spirit quails. His line of retreat is open, and he will never write in his journal, as did his counter-part on the borders of the old Cape Colony over a century ago: "*There we were in the wilderness . . . we must take root and grow or die where we stood.*" But if he can resist the temptation to look back – and persuade his wife to resist it too – the future will be established. The children of the next generation, born in the Granite Land, will find no heart-ache in the sentimental picture of the beloved mother-island, for in them will be begotten a new nostalgia. Their eyes will seek the far horizons and the open veld, they will look forward, not back. . . .'

(It seems strange that today, as I transcribe these words, the quality of the twentieth-century settler is being tried and proved in Kenya by men and women fighting day and night against the Black Terror of Mau Mau. Like the frontiersmen of the old Cape Colony, and the first Pioneer Column of Cecil John Rhodes, they are fighting for the future of a White way of life in the African Continent. And their farms, once again, are their fortresses.*)

At eleven o'clock Mrs. Max, the housekeeper at 'Sunrising', brought me a cup of tea and a huge slice of featherlight cake.

'You must eat it, my dear. I made it myself. When you are in Rhodesia you must do as Rhodesia does.'

'Does Rhodesia lie in bed and eat cake at eleven in the morning?'

'It eats always and anywhere. Rhodesians *really* eat – and then they go out into the *bandu* and come back with babies.'

'Well,' I said. 'As far as the eating goes I'll do my best to oblige.'

She moved a vase of freesias and violets on the dressing-table.

'Don't take them away!'

'No,' she said. 'I was only moving them out of the sun. I don't like seeing flowers suffer. Now you relax, my dear – there's not a soul to disturb you. There's nobody here – nothing but the birds and the wind in the trees.'

Through the open window poured the sun, and the breeze rattled the long dry seed-pods of a naked tree and the narrow hard leaves of a blue-gum. The birds flitted to and fro about their inconsequent business.

Next afternoon I had promised to address the combined members of the National Council of Women, the Women's

* White settlement has lost out in Kenya, and now Rhodesia is fighting terrorism for the survival of her White settlers and their descendants.

Institute, and the League of Business and Professional Women.

'It's awful,' I said to Bertie. 'I haven't got the right sort of hat. You wouldn't let me bring a hat-box—'

He just shook his head, and said 'Women . . .'

But luckily Ellis had invited two ex-naval officers and their wives to lunch at 'Sunrising' that day. On one of them I recognized a gift of the gods. She did not flinch when I approached her.

'Try it on!' she said.

Confidence flowed through the light, navy blue straw. Her hat was blessed with the qualities of a Wagnerian helmet. I faced my audience gaily, and told them what little I knew of writing and writers and they received my confidences with heart-warming enthusiasm.

Afterwards I said to one of my new friends: 'It was the hat made me feel so brave. I borrowed it from one of Sir Ellis Robins's guests at lunch today.'

'I know,' she smiled. 'I lent it to her for the occasion.'

'Please let me return it to you at once!' I gasped.

'It isn't mine,' she admitted, 'I borrowed it from my sister.'

I handed it to her with a sigh.

'Somebody once told me that every really good hat must *do* something for its wearer. This does. Please give it back to your sister with my thanks.'

She laughed. 'I'll give her your *message*.' And that was clearly as much as she intended to give.

On our last day in Rhodesia we drove out to the Matoppo Hills above the 'chaotic grandeur' Rhodes so dearly loved. The bronze plate let into the rock over his grave bears an inscription arrogant in its simplicity. 'Here lie the Remains of Cecil John Rhodes.' No date. No epitaph. The words cry aloud 'I am timeless! I am this land which bears my name and is spread at my feet!'

The tribesmen believe the ridge to be ' a place of spirits'. Perhaps it is. At Rhodes's wish 'those who deserved well of their country' are buried there near him. Sir Leander Starr Jameson, his faithful friend and disciple; Sir Patrick Coghlan, the first Prime Minister of Southern Rhodesia, and, most moving of all, the Shangani Memorial dedicated to Major Allen Wilson and thirty-three members of the Shangani Patrol who died in battle in the Matabele-Mashona Rising of 1893. *There was no survivor.*

Rhodes was, at heart, a man of peace. But there is no birth without the spilling of blood. The land he developed with the diamonds of Kimberley and the gold of the Transvaal exacted also the lives of brave men.

CHAPTER NINETEEN

SEROWE AND ITS GHOSTS

ALTHOUGH we left Southern Rhodesia behind when we entered the Bechuanaland Protectorate,* the spirit of Cecil John Rhodes continued to accompany us. For it was he who was mainly responsible for placing this vast territory under British Protection in 1885, and for the building of the railway which runs the length of its eastern border; and many men of the Bechuanaland Police fought and died to help him gain and keep his new country.

Bechuanaland is largely cattle-country. There are a few European-owned ranches, but, for the most part, the country is divided into Native Reserves, such as that of the much-publicized Bamangwato, and the Bakwena – where the ex-Regent of the Bamangwato, Tshekedi, has gone into voluntary exile – and many others. In parts it is beautiful, with lakes and mountains, but much of it is bushveld, and south-west lies the Kalahari Desert and the grasslands where the little Bushmen still shoot wild game with poisoned arrows.

The main road south follows the single-track railway, and you may travel all day, as we did, and seldom see another vehicle except near an occasional siding.

Everything that day seemed to me oppressive and unreal.

* Now independent Botswana under the enlightened rule of English-educated Seretse Khama aided by his English wife, Ruth. In 1951 Seretse's marriage was not yet acceptable to the tribesmen and dilatory British authorities left vital decisions in the 'Too Difficult basket' for too long a period.

For one thing, there was an eclipse of the sun, and this, combined with an out-of-season drizzle, gave us our first dark day in many weeks.

Then the stock farmers were suffering new hardships. Our earth roads through the cattle-lands were not only heavily scored with the hoof-prints of oxen but also with the mighty spoor of elephant. Trees were mutilated and the prodigious steaming droppings told us that Jumbo had passed that way recently.

When we stopped for lunch with Major Bent, the District Officer at Francistown, he told us that the settler-farmers were in despair. In fact, Mr. Davidson of Wankie had been asked to come to Bechuanaland to give his advice on these displaced herds seeking new water-holes.

'The wretched elephants pass through Native villages and simply lift the thatch roofs off the store-huts and help themselves to grain; they ruin crops and kraals, and graze where they please. They go down to the drinking-dams and trample the cattle to death. Last year the poor farmers had a plague of mice, this time it's elephants. Anything can happen to farmers!'

Major Bent knew the Protectorate and its people well. He had served with the Bechuana Royal Pioneer Corps throughout the war in the Middle East and was engaged in writing the story of these campaigns. He was shortly to be transferred to the beautiful, but solitary swamp country.

'Is Serowe easy to find?' we asked.

'No,' said Major Bent. 'It's rather elusive. And you won't make it before dark.'

He gave us directions and told us where to get petrol on the way.

'It doesn't do to run out of fuel. You may be absolutely stranded!'

At the filling station, some eighty miles away, we noticed a new type of Native.

'But these are beautiful people!' I said. 'And look at their clothes!'

The man at the pump smiled.

'They are not local Natives. Those are Hereros. When the Germans set about exterminating the Herero people in German South West a great number fled into Bechuanaland, and old Chief Khama gave them sanctuary. Distinguished looking folk, aren't they? And don't demean themselves by working overmuch!'

No Kaffir blankets for these aristocrats! The women wore voluminous printed Victorian skirts, wasp waists, and high bright turbans. They carried themselves with dignified pride, as did the tall Herero men. We were to see these dark *herrenfolk* again in their own thirst-land, a nation with a proud past which has known suffering.

During the afternoon we watched the eclipse through our coloured glasses. The drizzle had ceased and the sun above the camel-thorns was obscured, save for the outline of a gleaming silver sickle.

The cattle, driven by the little Black herd-boys, plodded home through the heavy clinging dust. We no longer saw the mark of the elephant, but a pride of lions prowled down from the Swañen Hills to slake their thirst at a shining dam. Dusk fell and we began to wonder whether we were lost. There was still no sign of Serowe although we had taken the route Major Bent had described. As our eyes grew accustomed to the gloom we discerned more and more kraals by the wayside, and I was reminded of a Bushman cave on the Matoppo Ridge.

Mr. Jenkins Jones, the Curator of Bulawayo Museum in Charge of Antiquities, had taken us to the cave. He had pointed out the ochre rock-paintings of the little Stone Age hunters. Even after millenniums the faded animal and human silhouettes sprang, warm and life-like, from the cool hard rock.

'Look well,' Mr. Jenkins Jones had said. 'The more you look the more you will begin to see the pattern. You will discover the shapes of men and animals you never guessed were there.'

In the same way, the living pattern of Africa must be studied intently before it will emerge from nature's camouflage. And, in the wide sense, too, the pattern of Africa is hard to see. On that strange dark day of the eclipse I found myself wondering how long the White man's cities and culture could survive before the desert, the jungle, the forest and the veld obliterated them. How soon would this western civilization be devoured by the atavism of the Dark Continent? Would this great savage tapestry, sequined with the thin dazzle of his alien lights, shake itself free of their brilliance and settle again into the twilight where there is no law for man or beast save the law of survival?

The parklands had given way to bush, and a cold night wind had risen. Bertie stopped the car.

'There seems to be a European house over there in the bush. I'm going to look for someone to ask if we are on the right track.'

I shivered, oppressed by the uncanny loneliness of the place. What could Ruth Khama have thought when her African husband brought her here to his primitive kingdom? I noticed then that we had stopped near one of those kraals that are so much a part of the bush as to be almost invisible. I got out, hoping to find somebody who might tell me where we were, but there was no sound save the wind moaning across the waste. There must have been life in that kraal, yet the huts crouched, silent as death, behind the hedge of wild rubber. No human voice laughed or called, and only the yellow eyes of a goat stared at me, while a fowl scratched in the dirt near an empty cattle stockade. Land and sky were cold indigo; low overhead the Southern Cross flew its diamond-tipped kite, and stardust, thick as Kalahari sand, blew along the Milky Way. The life of the kraal seemed suspended in some queer moment of ebb when day has receded to its far limit and the night tide has not yet begun to flow.

I saw Bertie come back across the bush. He called above the wind:

'We haven't passed Serowe. We go on round the next long hill and then we'll probably find someone to show us the way.'

'Who did you talk to?'

'An old Black man hunched over a fire in a shed. There wasn't a soul in the house although it was open. I just walked in and shouted. But no one answered. It was rather eerie – a bit like the beginning of a ghost story. Doors banged in the wind, and my voice echoed back from the deserted rooms.'

'Whose place was it?'

'I have no idea. The old Native spoke no English, so we used signs to make ourselves understood.'

The house, we were told later, belonged to Seretse Khama – the wilderness home to which he had brought his English wife.

The Bamangwato, like most Native tribes, are given to disputes about chieftainship, and the rights and wrongs of the succession have puzzled wiser heads than mine. But one thing is certain. When the young Chief defied tribal tradition and married Ruth Williams, a European woman, he split the unity of his people and caused the British Government of the day to lose much face by its inability to find an acceptable solution to the problem. Seretse's uncle, Tshekedi, who had been Regent during his nephew's minority and student days at Oxford and in London, was profoundly shocked, and the tribe reacted as one man against the marriage. Assembled in *kgotla* to discuss the matter, they had demanded Seretse's abdication unless he should be prepared to give up Ruth. Yet the Government allowed him to return to Serowe 'to state his case' – and, incidentally, form a 'king's party'. Tshekedi, though an enlightened ruler, was autocratic, and, during more than twenty years as Regent, he had made powerful enemies. These began to plot against the possibility of his becoming the permanent Chief in default of his nephew, and, when it became apparent that nothing would induce Seretse to abandon his bride, they reluctantly agreed to support him on his own terms. Plot and counter-plot is a favourite African pastime, and the Bamangwato, finding themselves leaderless and frustrated, cast aside all thought of work and threw themselves whole-heartedly into the game of intrigue.

261

The British Government, in a White Paper of March 1950, described the 'purely temporary expedient' to which it had been driven.

'... the District Commissioner will continue closely to supervise the administration of the Bamangwato Reserve and will exercise the functions of the Native Authority ... Steps will be taken ... steps will be taken ... steps ...'

Yet no decisive step was taken until 1953 when a Conservative Government appointed Rasebolai Kgamane as the Native Authority under whose leadership it was hoped that the Bamangwato would settle down and resume their normal easy-going lives. A temporary expedient.

In 1951 the mood of the people was dangerous, and it was this mood which hung over their land like an approaching thunderstorm.

The headlights of an oncoming car flashed and dimmed as it drew level with us. A strong-featured face with a dark Vandyk beard leaned towards us. 'Glad you're all right, sir. If you'll follow me I'll lead you in.'

The District Commissioner, Mr. Germond, went ahead through devious drifts and tracks, past Serowe's huddled huts, the trader's store, the mission and the hospital to the top of a ridge where the Union Jack, whipped by the wind, flew bravely over the Residency.

The District Commissioner's home was cosy. A fire burned merrily, for here, three thousand feet above sea-level, it was colder than we had known it since leaving Swaziland. Helen, Mrs. Germond's eight-year-old niece, played on the hearth-rug with her doll, and an Afghan Hound rose to inspect us, spilling a white kitten out of the curve of its belly where the little creature had been sleeping.

'Will you wait and have a drink, or would you rather bath and change right away?' asked Mr. Germond, who knew the needs of tired dusty travellers. 'Dinner is any time we want it, so don't bother about that.'

Dinner was at eight-thirty – and it was excellent, with a choice of roast guinea-fowl or mallard duck.

'We shoot for the pot,' said the District Commissioner. 'Not for fun.'

He knew the lore of the wilds and told us many strange tales. Bechuanaland is lion-country, and the lion kills in his own ritual fashion. He disembowels his victim surgically with a neat abdominal incision performed with a sharp dew-claw, then the tips of the ears are bitten off and buried before the meal is begun from the rump upwards.

'When you go for a picnic here it's always as well to be sure there's no fresh lion-spoor about,' smiled Mrs. Germond. 'Even Helen knows that she must keep her eyes open for those big pad-marks!'

The silence down in the kraal-town had cracked, and we could hear voices and music drifting towards us, and that curious warbling-whistling note that has its own sinister overtone.

'This is the biggest African town in the Southern Hemisphere,' said the District Commissioner. 'Thirty thousand people live in that valley. Normally on a Saturday you'd hear ten times this noise. The Natives love to dance. But they are in a queer frame of mind at present. Everything has come to a standstill. Until this Seretse business is resolved they'll just sulk and intrigue.'

'The men are very ignorant,' added Mrs. Germond. 'Partly because they begin herding cattle at about five years old, and grazing grounds are far afield. It makes education difficult. The girls are intelligent and the mission schools are always crowded with them.'

We went into the keen air to listen to Africa's song and dance.

Once again I found myself wondering about Ruth Khama, née Williams of London Town. Enormous stars glittered in the southern sky, and the syncopation of this savage measure was very different from the hey-nonny-no of an English folk song. What had she thought about it?

Presently Mrs. Germond took me to the adjoining rooms

we had been given. She put a torch on each bedside table, and made sure my hot-bottle had been filled. Before saying good night, she hesitated.

'You understand these oil-lamps?'

'My husband does. He was brought up in the wilds of Shropshire!'

She laughed. 'Well, that's all right then. By the way, if you hear creakings overhead, don't worry. These roofs contract and make a queer noise. Or sometimes there are leguaans up there. We pay no attention.'

'Nothing could keep me awake,' I assured her.

The leguaans were having a good party, or the roof was contracting violently, but I fell asleep quickly. It must have been an hour or more past midnight when my husband's voice called to me through the open door between our rooms.

'Joy-Joy, if you can't find your way, I'll bring my torch.'

'Whatever for?' I asked through the veils of sleep.

'Why are you padding about your room in the dark?'

A shiver ran down my spine, and now, fully awake, I heard the soft footfalls moving furtively round my bed. I put out my hand and found my torch and flashed it. Nobody, nothing. Bertie came into the room with his own torch and began to make a thorough search. It was a bare little room and there was no hiding-place in it. I saw the light bobbing about on the verandah and out into the garden as he pursued the unknown owner of those furtive bare feet that had wakened us. In the roof the leguaans were holding their breath.

'Funny,' he said, as he came back. 'I could have sworn there was somebody here.'

Next morning at breakfast we asked Mr. Germond how old the house was.

'About fifteen years. Why do you ask?'

I said: 'No good reason, really ... It was just that last night somebody was walking about in my room – somebody we couldn't see ...'

A look passed between husband and wife.

Mrs. Germond said, 'If they heard it we might as well tell them.'

And her husband added: 'There *is* something that walks, as you put it. It's not malevolent, and we just accept it.'

'A ghost?'

'*Something*. As a matter of fact I *have* seen it – once – some time ago. A little figure. It was going down the passage towards your room. I thought it was Helen for a moment, and asked her what she was doing out of bed. She wasn't out of bed. She was sound asleep.'

Presently we went in the District Commissioner's car to see the town and the burial ground of the Khama family up on the koppie among the rock-caves where the *dassies* swarmed. These beady-eyed, small-eared 'rock-rabbits' with rough khaki fur are more like guinea-pigs. They are seldom tamed and their long front teeth can deliver a nasty nip. Their labyrinth beside the Khama burial ground stank powerfully.

Old Chief Khama III, Seretse's grandfather, had embraced Christianity, and an angel with a broken wing guarded the graves. Chief Khama had been a firm character who reckoned he knew what was best for his people. Upon his own conversion he had commanded the Bamangwato to be Christians whether they liked it or not. But, since the suspension of Khama rule, there had been a good deal of backsliding among the conscripts.

At the foot of the koppie was Tshekedi's European house – burned out by his enemies.

In the morning sunlight there was a certain charm about the scene in the valley below us. Dusty carefree children, naked save for their little hide loin-cloths, played behind the wild rubber stockades, and their shrill voices carried through the pure air. Across the bush the twin blue hills of Pa Swañen and Ma Swañen, and the ridge of Baba Swañens looked down upon the shining cattle-dam. A wild thistle with a buttercup flower flourished in the sand of the kraals.

On our way back to the Residency we stopped at a European cottage. In the garden was a young lioness sleeping under the hedge. Margaret Macintosh, the schoolgirl daughter of the owner of the cottage, tried to lure the lazy lioness out of her morning siesta.

'Come on, Thing! Wake up and play!'

The Macintosh family had picnicked near the dam under the Swañen Hills and there they had found and kidnapped the cub. They had named her Thing, 'because we thought she was just the thing', and had brought her up with their dogs.

'She adores the dogs,' said Mrs. Macintosh, coming into the garden. 'We lost two of them recently with snake-bite, and Thing missed them terribly. She's very affectionate. You should see her with my husband – Oh, good, here he comes!'

The lean dark man called the cub, and she instantly bounded to meet him, making strange little welcoming sounds. As he stooped to pat her she rose on to her hind legs and flung her huge paws about his neck, biting gently at his nose and chin. When he had fondled her, pulling her ears this way and that, she rubbed herself backwards and forwards against his legs in sinuous feline ecstasy.

Little Helen watched the animal, fascinated, and Mrs. Macintosh, observing the child's longing eyes, laughed and said: 'Go on, touch her! She won't harm you.'

Timidly the child ran her little hand through the tawny fur, matted with burrs. 'She's lovely, isn't she?' she said breathlessly. 'What does she eat?'

'Porridge and raw meat,' said Mrs. Macintosh. 'But she's getting rather big and we must get rid of her soon. She hates and fears the Natives. She won't eat from them, and when they come near her she growls. The Johannesburg Zoo want her and will pay us fifty pounds for her, but we can't get a permit to export her owing to rabies restrictions.'

266

The family, followed by the young lioness, saw us to the car. Three Native women passed us, carrying calabashes on their heads. Thing cringed and showed her teeth.

Mr. Germond looked troubled. 'There'll be a tragedy one of these days. She's getting too big to be safe.'

Poor Thing! How would she fare in a zoo without human friends and her canine playmates? She was used to love and to living with people, to riding in the station-wagon with the dogs sitting up beside her on the front seat, to the run of house and garden, to freedom. I thought of Cheeta-Cheeta, the Chimpanzee we had known in the French Congo, and of Madame Bourgund's words: 'Once they have become human you cannot turn them back into animals – it is death ...'

After lunch we played golf. Even in Serowe the staunch-hearted British had wrung nine holes out of a slope known as 'the waste of Judah'. The greens were desert dust and the caddies carried a wooden T-square with which they smoothed away the recent spoor of bird, beast or man before the player attempted to putt.

Our fourth was the Assistant District Officer, Mr. Atkins, a young man who had served in the Royal Marines during the war. He played a good game, chiefly because he kept his head down, and he kept his head down chiefly because 'the wastes of Judah' were scattered with relics of the Palae-olithic period. Every now and again he picked up some odd-shaped stone or flint to show me.

'Probably a weapon or an implement – they must have had some sort of factory up here millenniums ago in the Stone Age.'

In a literal and immediate sense, Mr. Atkins was nearer the stone age than he guessed. Less than a year later the 'queer frame of mind' of the Bamangwato exploded into rioting during a *kgotla* at Serowe. The District Commissioner (at that time Mr. P. G. Batho) and Mr. Atkins and several other government officials were nearly stoned to death by angry tribesmen. Three Native policemen were killed. Mr. Atkins, who was severely injured, received the George Medal for his bravery.

Back at the Residency little Helen showed me her aunt's remarkable collection of sea-shells. Mrs. Germond had lived in the Solomon Islands in the Pacific for some time when her husband was stationed there. She loved the sea, and here – so far from it – we listened to its forgotten murmur in giant conch-shells.

In the evening the small European community came in to sun-downers. They were interesting people with a wealth of unusual experiences. One woman trader, who had been fifty years in Serowe, told me that when the Residency was built a heap of tiny skeletons had been found on the site.

'No one can say whose they were – perhaps Bushmen from the Kalahari—'

I laughed. 'Perhaps. I think one of those little folk was padding round my room last night!'

She peered at me, as if to see whether I was serious.

'You saw it then?'

'Let's say *heard* it. It was barefoot, whatever it was.'

She said slowly, 'Serowe has its ghosts – and there will be more . . .'

Another guest was Miss Pepper, the Matron of the Hospital, and I can believe that, if necessary, this crisp little lady could have lived up to her name.

Ruth Khama's baby – the infant 'Princess Gold' – had been born in Serowe Hospital, as had the four children of Tshekedi's wife.

'In the royal ward,' smiled Miss Pepper. Her eyes softened as she spoke of Mrs. Tshekedi Khama. 'Charming and enlightened, deeply interested in the welfare of her people – and a trained hospital nurse into the bargain!'

From remarks made by one person and another I was also able to build up a composite mental picture of Ruth Khama, the strong-minded young woman whose marriage had so severely disrupted the peace of her husband's subjects.

Nice-looking, obstinate, proud – and brave too. It must

have taken courage for her to remain in Africa as a voluntary 'hostage' when Seretse was summoned to England for talks with the Commonwealth Relations Office not long before her baby was due. It must have been very lonely – the cold cautious attitude of the government officials; the furtive amiability of traders, who depended upon the tribesmen for a living; the virtuous friendship of the missionaries, who owed a perpetual debt to the House of Khama for having imposed forced Christianity upon the Bamangwato; the hostile muttering of the elders, and the strange sense of being in a no-man's-land between savagery and civilization.

Perhaps she enjoyed her spell of publicity while it lasted. Certainly opposition increased her defiance. As somebody put it, 'She seemed all the while to be saying inwardly "I'll win over the Blacks and make these Whites sit up!" And, come to that, she did both for a while!'

Someone else said, 'I'm sure she really *did* love Seretse, and she could have liked Serowe too. It meant something to her.'

'No,' said one young man, in answer to a question. 'She wasn't exactly pretty. Attractive in an unspectacular way – yes. But wait a minute, there *was* something arresting about her face – something you remembered! *She had one blue eye and one brown.*'

An eye for her own world, and one for Seretse's. Almost symbolic.

We left early next morning, for it was a long way to our night-stop at Mafeking.

As we stood in the freshness of the new-born day to say good-bye to Mrs. Germond, the strange charm of Serowe imprinted itself upon my memory.

Dew spangled the grass, the flowers of the kaffir-boom raised blood-red hands to the cobalt sky; ground-mists clung in the valley at the foot of the big koppie round which the Native township sprawled, and, filtering up through the tingling air, came the smoke of cooking-fires. Voices called to one another in the hollows and echoed in the hills, there was the lowing of cattle going to distant grazings, the tinkle of cow-bells, the crack of rimpie-whips and the arrogant crowing of cocks.

The District Commissioner gave us a lead to the main road. When he turned his car to go back, the great kraal kingdom was already out of sight.

Pa Swaňen, Ma Swaňen and the ridge of Baba Swaňens fell far behind and the sun rose high and dispensed its welcome warmth. I was silent – haunted by the place we had left and by its troubled ghosts, by the little long-ago phantom of a Bushman, and the pale modern spirit of a young White woman caught in the dark web of Africa.

CHAPTER TWENTY

GOLD AND DIAMONDS

WE had arranged to return to Simon's Town via the Orange Free State gold fields and Kimberley. From Mafeking to Odendaalsrus was partly across country and rough going.

'Poor car on the corrugations!' sighed Bertie. 'There won't be much left of our shock-absorbers by the time we get home.'

'We've been a long way – nearly six thousand miles since we left the Cape – like driving over the sea to England!'

Six years earlier, during my husband's war leave in South Africa, we had passed through Odendaalsrus, then a tiny dorp in the newly discovered reef, with a shanty hotel and a general store. Now we found a busy modern town.

But it is the recently planned town of Welkom that really lies at the heart of the reef. Welkom has been designed to serve the six gold mines of the Anglo-American Group, and the South African mining magnate and wizard of finance, Sir Ernest Oppenheimer, believes that one day it will be even more prosperous than Johannesburg. Already the avenues of young trees are struggling against the wind that blows across the flat tawny grainlands, and hotels, shops, cinemas, housing estates and compounds are springing up in the skeleton shadows of the soaring iron headgears of mines in production, bestriding the veld like Don Quixote's windmill giants. Much of Welkom's inspiration is borrowed from the Congo and the Copper Belt. There is nothing haphazard about this city of the future. It is planned down to the last mine hospital and sports ground. A Native Township and married quarter is part of this great new design intended to stabilize the miners and develop a hereditary mining community among the Natives. But whether such a social evolution of the tribesman will come to pass remains to be seen.*

It was lunch-time when we visited the cafeteria of Welkom Compound.

'It is a new idea,' explained the Compound Manager. 'Usually the mine Natives buy their own food and cook it over communal fires, but this innovation is taking on.'

To me it was sheer Black Bedlam. There were Basuto in pastel blankets, Xhosas in their traditional ochre, Shangaans, Swazis, Zulus, and tribesmen from Rhodesia and Portuguese East Africa. Every clicking Native tongue rose and fell all round us, crossed by deep-throated *Fanakola*, the Esperanto of the mines. A powerful smell of hot cooking competed against that of hot Native, and hot Native won hands down. The rations are generous. Every man is entitled to three and a half pounds of meat a week, plenty of fish, greens, soup, mealie-porridge, and four and a half pints of kaffir-beer or mealie-brew. The long trestle tables were crowded with men, their plates piled higher than those of the hungriest schoolboys. The woolly heads bent over the food were all adorned with some type of hat. There were jelly-bags, berets, tweed caps, cones and skull-caps, but the height of fashion was an emerald green boater. This line of millinery was made out of detonator wire by an enterprising Lesuto. It was good business, for he stole the wire and charged 12s. 6d. a piece for his wares. In sunny corners we saw little knitting bees, and, while the men worked at gaudy complicated pullovers, they gossiped like a mothers' meeting, but their gusts of rumbling laughter implied that the conversation might be spiced with dubious jests.

Although eating was communal, dormitories were tribal, with about eight or ten men to a large room. The tribes, it seemed, were better kept apart lest they fall into their ancient custom of taking each other to pieces. But, should this happen, in spite of all precautions, damaged warriors could

* *Welkom has now become a flourishing and important mining town.*

272

be put together again in the palatial Native Hospital, fully equipped, and staffed by Roman Catholic nursing sisters swept out of the Dutch East Indies by the Communists. These women had the advantage of being able to learn Afrikaans easily, for bilingualism is essential to any profession in the Union.

Everything was on a tremendous scale – a study in superlatives – and it is interesting that Ernest Oppenheimer is going to use the diamonds of Kimberley to help develop his pet projects in the Free State. Just so, and with justifiable success, had Cecil John Rhodes borrowed from De Beers to establish the young land of his heart – Rhodesia.

From Odendaalsrus and Welkom we went south to Kimberley, passing through a corner of the great 'maize triangle' of mechanized farms upon which the Union depends for her daily bread.

The Diamond City of Kimberley – in that stretch of arid sheep country even lonelier than Serowe – was as conservative and old-fashioned as her sister City of Gold, Johannesburg, was racy and flamboyant. In some strange way, Kimberley, the birthplace of glittering temptation, has remained at heart homely and unsophisticated.

The hotel, at which we were the guests of De Beers, still has its linoleum floors and communal bathrooms with quaint demoded baths. The glamour and the glory of the diamond is not to be found here at its fount. That comes later in the playgrounds of the world, and reaches its climax on an occasion such as the coronation of a young and lovely Queen with the two parts of the great Cullinan diamond flashing in her crown and sceptre.

The day we spent in Kimberley had for me a restful quality utterly unlike the atmosphere one expects in a mining town. Here was none of the roar and heat of the Copper Belt, none of the opulence of the Rand reaching for the stars, nor yet the eager clamour of the new young Free State goldfields. Here an elderly city led a quiet life in the bright white sunlight of the veld.

Mr. Beck of De Beers met us, and asked us what we wanted to do and see.

'Living things,' I said, 'and anything that is specially interesting, but not machinery.'

He smiled at that, and discussed the matter with the Mine Manager, Mr. Taylor. They understood perfectly.

The 'living things' fascinated me.

Diamonds are easy to steal. They can be hidden under the nails or in the cavities of the body, and, as it would be impossible to search and X-ray thousands of miners daily, the system of the 'locked compound' must be used. This compound, which sounds like a prison, is more like a self-contained bachelor village. The Natives sign on for three months and then have the option of renewing their contract or going home. Most of them renew it, many stay on for years at a time, and those who go home generally return. They have good living conditions, playing-fields, swimming pools, shops, cinemas and, above all, they make good money by their own standards, and, if they wish, they can go to school or learn trades in their compound.

The core of the shopping centre is a square with a long shelter bisecting it. Beneath this shelter glow the cooking fires in the great ovens that are kept going day and night, so that any man coming off shift can cook himself a hot meal if he wants one.

We saw the miners queueing at the butcher's.

'Not quite the queue you are used to,' said the Compound Manager. 'But what do you think of our special prices – eightpence a pound for prime beef, and ninepence for the best mutton?'

As each man left the shop he took his meat to the cooking-fire and joined his comrades.

'There are over two thousand men here,' said the Manager. 'They form their own messes, and take turns at cooking. Then they squat in the sun with their bowls, and eat and talk. That's the way they like it.'

I was amazed at the quality of goods for sale in the store. I held up a trilby hat marked £3.

'Surely you have no customers for expensive things like this?'

'We can always sell quality,' said the Manager. 'The Native likes the best of everything. He despises cheap stuff. He always knows what he wants, and he doesn't haggle.'

He showed us lengths of material bought by men about to go home – the best gaberdine and barathea folded ready to be packed in their little gilt trunks.

'They'll go home and buy a wife, and lead a life of ease for a while, and then they'll be back, lured by the old magnet – the mine.'

Our next 'living things' were dogs.

De Beers mine-dogs are famous. We sat in the sun and watched the magnificent Alsatians in training – chasing a thief, bringing him down, holding him, leaping through flames, rescuing or attacking at the word of command. There was one memorable study in slow-motion and concentration. The trainer held out a rod with a ball on the end of a line. He moved the rod very slowly round, at the same time raising and dropping the level of the ball. The dog followed it round at the identical slow pace, and never for one instant did his eyes leave the ball.

'His concentration! One can *feel* it!' I whispered. 'He's like a deaf person watching the lips of somebody who has something very important to tell him.'

Bertie said: 'If you'd take a lesson from that dog, and keep your eye on the ball as he does, you wouldn't play the golf you sometimes do.'

Suddenly the trainer flicked the ball into the air. 'Right!' he said.

The Alsatian leapt and seized the ball.

'This, I suppose, counts as machinery,' said Mr. Taylor. 'But it is also specially interesting, I think.'

We stood looking at the pulsator, a long, greased, pulsating slide down which coursed a stream of water and a number of grey pebbles.

275

'You'll notice that the diamonds stick, and the debris is washed away,' he added. 'See those five near the top. Those are diamonds.'

And there they were – five precious stones dancing in one place, while the dross jitter-bugged past them down the slide into limbo.

For every eleven thousand tons of 'blue ground' crushed in Kimberley the yield of diamonds is approximately one pound. And not all will be of gem value.

We drove to the sorting office in the city. There, in a heavily guarded room, we saw the sorters – girls or men – leaning over the long counters grading the stones, handling them with delicate pincers, and weighing them on diminutive scales. The little heaps of rough diamonds glowed with incandescent lights – yellow, green, crystal-white and the steely glint of industrials. Later the skilled craftsmen of Amsterdam and those trained by them would reveal their true glory.

Mining copper or gold must be a dull business compared with diamonds. One length of copper wire is as long and strong as the next and one gold brick no heavier than its fellow. But diamonds demand the human touch, the individual treatment due to their infinite variety. The gem diamond, dancing its light *pas seul* on the thick grease of the pulsator, holds a dream of fair women in its heart, and it keeps the tantalizing secret of its value as intact as the grey living oyster guards the secret of its hidden pearl. Every diamond has its own personality and separate destiny, it is born solitary as a star.

That night the Directors of De Beers gave a dinner in our honour at the Kimberley Club, which was, for both of us, a very happy and special occasion. Unfortunately the Chairman, Sir Ernest Oppenheimer, could not be there, but I sat on the right of Mr. H. P. Rudd, who had been fifty years a Director and at one time 'alternate' for Rhodes, a close friend and associate of his father.

Percy Rudd had been a keen sportsman and owner of racehorses in his day, but the best race ever run to the honour of his name was run on two legs and not on four, when his son, the late Bevil Rudd, won the Olympic 400 metres for South Africa.

Mr. Rudd had known my grandfather, 'Lang Piet' Marais, in the feverish days of young Johannesburg, and later at Wheatfield in the Cape Peninsula when my mother had been at the height of her radiant youth.

'Your mother was a beauty,' he told me, and his distinguished features relaxed into a reminiscent smile. 'In fact, I played an awful lot of croquet with your grandfather!' And, just for a moment, I believe Wheatfield was more vivid to him than the Kimberley Club. Then someone leaned across the table and said: 'Come now, Percy, give it to her!'

As he stood up he seemed to shake long-ago memories from his shoulders. He drew a folded piece of paper from his pocket and presented it to me on behalf of De Beers.

I unfolded the stiff white paper on which diamonds are placed for examination, and there lay a cut stone, sparkling with the pure glitter of the first water – and there, staring at it aghast, was I – more astonished than I have ever been in a life full of exciting surprises!

Afterwards I discovered that Bertie had known the secret, but he did not belong to the Silent Service for nothing.

One more night stop at Beaufort West and then, at last, we were in the passes of the velvet Cape Mountains, looking down upon fields of arums and the valleys of the vines. We stopped for our picnic lunch on du Toit's Kloof high above the plain of Paarl. Butterflies and bumble bees hovered on the swaying chalices of sun-drenched flowers, and birds flitted in the wild erratic way of birds in spring. The air was alive with wings – the soft bright Cape air. But we were tired, and our car was tired too.

'She'll just about make it,' said Bertie. 'But we'll stop in and let Piet have a look at her. I need his advice on one or two of her troubles.'

Piet and Glen were gardening when we drew up outside

the gate, and Ronnie was crawling very rapidly round the lawn with his seat surprisingly high in the air.

'Good heavens!' I said when we had done with greetings. 'He gets around these days!'

'Too fast – and too far,' laughed Glen.

While Piet examined the car I rang up Admiralty House. Everything was all right, the Chief Steward said, except Steward Etheridge. When accidents happened at Admiralty House they happened to Etheridge.

'What is it this time?'

'He was watching Findlay clean the Flag Lieutenant's golf clubs, Milady, and Findlay showed him how to get a ball out of a bunker. Etheridge got his face in the line of fire, so to speak.'

'Was he much hurt?'

'It might have been a calamity, Milady. The Chief Joiner – who knows a lot about golf – says the Flag Lieutenant's blaster is a very powerful club. It just missed Etheridge's eye. He'll be out of hospital next week.'

'We'll be home in half an hour. Let Gladys know – and have tea ready.'

I telephoned Mother and heard that all was well at Tees Lodge, and, as soon as Piet had pronounced his diagnosis, we were on our way.

'See you Sunday – that's tomorrow!' they called, and Ronnie waved one of his over-enthusiastic farewells.

As we turned into the coast road at Muizenberg the joy of home-coming seized me again.

'Thalassa!' said Bertie, his eyes on the white-capped sea.

The sea! To see it, hear it, smell it, after all these many weeks! The long breakers curling on to the wide sands, or bursting over the rocky promontories, and there, in the curve of False Bay, the Naval Dockyard huddled at the foot of the Simon's Berg. How welcome was that sight! A frigate stood out to sea, and the *Bermuda*, recently returned from her cruise, lay alongside. We could see the old white house, repainted in our absence, gleaming among the trees in the afternoon sun.

The pepper tree nodded to us from the corner of the kloof-garden, and sailors were hurrying down the hill at the double to catch the train 'up the line', laughing and joking as they went. And suddenly I knew that it wasn't just the homecoming thrill that was so good. Not just the Cape and the sea and my own folk. It was more than that. Something else was catching at my throat. Here was the Navy. We were coming back to the Royal Navy. No wonder the Rhodesians were building a huge holiday hotel here in Simon's Town – Rhodesia-by-the-Sea – to be paid for out of the great yearly profits from their State Lottery. How kind they had been to us when we were in their country, how glad they had been to be in touch with the Navy again!

Warships in the bay, sailors in the port, God's in his heaven, all's well with the world. . . .

The big teak gates of Admiralty House were wide open. Bertie pressed the horn twice – his signal. Tony was there to meet us as we drew up under the Georgian porch. The Chief Steward mustered his young stewards and the two seamen to unload our dusty bags. Corney received the battered car into his safe-keeping, and the Commander-in-Chief told him what Piet's diagnosis had been. The great hall smelt of polish and was bright with spring flowers. Everything was welcoming. As we went on to the stoep for tea, Veronica came across the lawn to greet us, the sun on her pale hair and Sammy loping at her heels.

'How are my carnations?' asked Bertie.

'They're fine, Admiral. And there's a new one – silvery purple, and very full. . . .' There was a smile on her lips and in her friendly eyes. She knew how he loved his carnations. Presently he would stroll over to the kloof-garden and admire them a little and get to know the new ones.

Upstairs Gladys was unpacking my crumpled dusty clothes. Nothing more to worry about, no more constantly changing scenes – for a short spell there would be just this house and this garden, respite and peace.

When I went up to my room Gladys said: 'I found this in your luggage, Milady. Shall I throw it away?'

279

Perhaps her dark blood suspected in the withered brown twig some herbalist's recipe. She held up a faded branch I had picked from a plant that grows on the Matoppos – the Place of Spirits.

'Oh, no!' I said. 'We must keep that.'

'But it looks quite dead, Milady.'

'Put it in water,' I said. 'It will live again. It's been dead nearly a fortnight, but it's called a Resurrection Plant; it comes from the hills near Rhodes's grave, and the people say that it does not die.'

When I went up to my room at nine o'clock – weary, happy and very ready for bed – I heard, across the garden from the sea, a clear haunting bugle call – the call that has sounded down the ages across so many waters far from home – the Last Post.

In the morning the Resurrection Plant had performed its small miracle, and little dark green leaves had unfurled, as if to say, 'There, my friend! Don't believe in death! Life comes and goes like the spring.'

But, in the end, the little wand from Rhodes's great hinterland obeyed the laws of nature and died for the last time.

When I told Veronica, she only said:

'It has scattered its seed on the Matoppos, so it isn't really dead.'

Perhaps gardeners learn more about the eternal verities than the rest of us.

PART TWO

Our Second Year,
October 1951–September 1952

NORTH AND WEST

CHAPTER TWENTY-ONE

PAUSE AND PERSONALITIES

THE season of tourists had begun, and, since South Africa is in the sterling area, many of our English acquaintances decided to seek the sun by sailing south.

One day Louis Kentner came to lunch with us, and brought his manager with him. They were going to Worcester the same afternoon where Kentner was to give a recital.

This famous pianist had married one step-daughter of our friend, Admiral Cecil Harcourt, and Yehudi Menuhin had married the other. Like farmers, who may be plagued with mice one year and elephants the next, anything can happen to sailors! But two world renowned musicians in one family is a remarkable balance on the credit side.

It was a glorious day, and we sat on the lawn in the sun to enjoy our after-lunch coffee.

Kentner is Hungarian, short and fair, with a benevolent expression and a pleasing speaking voice with only a trace of foreign intonation. His gifted hands, the instruments of his genius, were relaxed, the blunt, cushioned finger-tips resting lightly on the arms of his chair. His eyes were intensely observant, his wit subtle and responsive.

He told us some of the tribulations of a touring pianist.

'A violinist is so fortunate,' he said. 'For instance, Yehudi takes his beloved Stradivarius with him everywhere. I cannot carry my Bechstein! So what happens to me? I assure you, I have to play on pieces of furniture which could only be described as piano-shaped objects. Sometimes the notes, when struck, remain down and refuse to rise again!'

Louis Kentner and his manager were swept out of

Admiralty House by a tide of naval and dockyard wives come to see Veronica give a demonstration of flower decorations. A few hours later he would be anxiously trying some 'piano-shaped object' in Worcester, wondering, no doubt, whether he could hope to find it properly tuned and the notes in no way afflicted with rheumatism.

One week-end our friends D'Urban and Freda Cloete came to visit us, bringing with them D'Urban's cousin, Stuart Cloete, the South African author, and his American wife, Tiny.

He is an odd fellow – this handsome middle-aged farmer-writer, who started his career as an officer in a Guards Regiment. He was twice badly wounded in World War One, and, when he was invalided out of the Army, he took to farming and writing in South Africa. The success of his books in America drew him to New York, where he and Tiny had lived for many years. Now they had settled on a lonely farm near Cape Agulhas, and called it 'Libris'. Stuart – who writes his personal letters in red ink – wrote to me of 'Libris', 'This place is our *love*.'

We spent a day with them there among the hills and the groves of exotic trees he had imported from far parts of the world. The air smelt of the sea and the country both together. As we entered the gate we nearly ran over a flock of peacocks, peahens and ugly little brown pea-chickens. The small Dutch farmhouse was over a century old, and the wild birds flew in and out of the *Voorkamer* through the upper half of the 'stable-door' that was always left open for them. Swallows had nested between the wall and an old ceiling beam, and, when we went into his cool entrance-room, we heard the twittering of the baby birds. There were ten cats and a bull mastiff in the house, but they never worried the birds.

Stuart came to meet us, wearing blue jeans and a red shirt which hung loose and open.

'It's his carrying-shirt,' explained Tiny, in her high tiny voice. 'He has put it on as a compliment to you, but he's dying to take it off.'

Her long hair was tied back with a black bow at the nape of her thin little neck.

'I wish he would let me cut it,' she complained.

'I like it with the bow,' he said. 'That's how you wore it when I first met you.'

Her trill of laughter was caught up with a burst of bird-song from the garden.

'That was fourteen years ago. I can't go on wearing bows forever. I'm over forty!'

Stuart abandoned his 'carrying-shirt', and said: 'George Washington wore a bow like that till he died at the age of sixty-seven.'

On the right of the *voorkamer* was his study. The open window was festooned with cobwebs.

'He adores his spiders – I am not allowed to dust a thing. Look at his lovely pin-ups! Isn't this one a gem?'

'To darling Stuart . . .' was written across the lovely strip-tease artist's photograph. She was one of a gallery of glamour.

'Stuart's just finished his elephant book,' said Tiny. 'And he's already begun another. Sometimes he gets into a panic and wonders what we'll live on—'

'Naturally,' said Stuart. 'Tiny is too old to go on the street, so I have to write.'

'And how! You should see him fly at his typewriter! He's at his best in the mornings – just gets up and rushes for the study, and hammers out words with two fingers. He never looks back to see what he's written, or corrects anything, but goes right on till he's finished a story or a book. After that he *works* on it. Then he gives it to me to see how much I cry. If I cry a lot it's good.'

'But if *I* cry while I'm writing it's even better,' said Stuart. 'And here's a tip for you. Get your high lights written first – as they come into your head. If you suddenly feel a love-scene or a murder cooking in you, get it down. Then throw it in a drawer and forget it till you need it.'

He showed us his collection of psychological works – most of the standard textbooks, and many others.

'My writing is cerebral – it deals with ideas,' he said. 'To keep your characters consistent, you must know why they are as they are, and what might change them.'

He began writing during an unhappy period in his life.

'I had lost confidence, and I felt the need to build a fictitious world, where I could control the beings I had created.'

He likes to keep a fiction and a non-fiction book going at the same time.

'All this – and farming too . . .' I said.

A year later we heard that 'Libris', with its cats and dogs and farm animals, its peacocks and beautiful shrubs and trees, and the spiders Stuart 'adored', was for sale, and we were sorry. We knew that this place was indeed their 'love', and that to part with it would be to die a little.

South Africa makes a strong appeal to writers, yet little that is really worth while has been written of this rewarding land.

H. V. Morton, however, came 'in search of South Africa' and gave us a delightful travel book about the Union. Cameos of history and human interest graced every page. In the end he fell in love with his subject and decided to settle at the Cape, where he built a beautiful Georgian house on a rise above the vineyards and roses of Somerset West.

Harry Morton has a charming pretty wife and a young son at school at Tara, not far from Cape Town, and he also has a most remarkable library of rare and fascinating historical volumes, the source of his unlimited fund of information, which is never dull or stereotyped.

So many people imagine that an author just sits down and writes. If only it were as simple as that! When I saw Stuart Cloete's psychological and philosophical works and Harry Morton's tomes on history, ancient and modern, I realized how much a professional author should study and learn if he is to be worth reading.

October drew to its golden close, and once again we prepared to leave Simon's Town – this time for the West Coast, for Black Africa.

It had been arranged that we should fly to Kano, accompanied by the Flag Lieutenant and join H.M.S. *Bermuda* at Lagos.

We flew from Johannesburg at midnight by B.O.A.C. – up the map of Africa and over the Equator to the ancient city of Kano.

Early in the afternoon the soft green parklands began to spread beneath us, and then we were circling over a rosy walled city of mud and straw among tall palms and indigo trees.

As we stepped out of our aircraft the heat rose up and hit us a physical blow. The Resident Commissioner and his wife, Mr. and Mrs. B. E. Sharwood-Smith, came forward to meet us. Behind them were the three Senior Councillors of the Emir of Kano. They might well have been 'three Kings of the Orient', so imposing and stately were they in their voluminous white robes and immense turbans with flowing chin-cloths.

The Resident Commissioner presented them to my husband, and they bowed gravely and deep as they welcomed us into their own mysterious Moslem world – the ebony world of Black Africa.

CHAPTER TWENTY-TWO

KANO – EMIR AND EARWIGS

KANO, the Capital of Northern Nigeria, is as little like the Cape as Siberia is like the South of France. The wind that tosses the palms and whips the long robes of the men in the cold dust-laden *harmattan* blowing in from the wastes of the Sahara and obscuring the tropical sun. The mud cities, with their mosques and palaces, tell of an ancient Moslem culture, and the sooty Negroid features of the Northern Nigerians are refined by many alien influences – Berber, Arab, and that of the proud cattle-owning Fulani tribe, who, for centuries, dominated Hausaland.

Here had been, and still was, the terminus of desert camel-trains trading across the Sahara from Tunis and Tripoli. Here had been the great slave junction of Africa – the depot whence the heartbreak human merchandise set out for Egypt, Arabia, Persia and the Mediterranean. Kano is still famed for its indigo dyes and iron-work, hides, salt and grain – but if slaves pass that way no man speaks of it.

Northern Nigeria* is the deep hinterland of the British Colony of Lagos Island in the Bight of Benin, and it became a British Protectorate early in Book Two of the sorry saga of the White man in West Africa.

Book One of that Saga relates the story of the growth of the slave trade, and Book Two tells of its suppression.

The Portuguese had established trading bases in West Africa during the fifteenth century for gold, silver, ivory and spices, but it was not until the New World was opened up during the sixteenth century that the most profitable trade of

*Now all Nigeria is independent.

all was launched – the slave trade. Labour was needed for the plantations of America and the Caribbean, and the Black chiefs of Africa were keen to sell their subjects or their enemies for the White man's guns and gin. So, in that shameful, but unrepentant period – for the principle of slavery was then universally accepted – vast fortunes were made by the merchants of Holland, Britain, Denmark and France. So much for Book One.

Book Two takes a pleasanter turn. The great humanitarian trend of the early nineteenth century gathered its forces to crush the slave trade, with Denmark and Britain well in the lead, while, for obvious reasons, the United States of America was the last important nation to join the revolt against slavery. And unfortunately, so long as there were buyers for slaves in the New World, there were sellers in Africa. Thus Britain's Navy, which had once guarded the sad sea-routes round Africa against piracy, now found itself patrolling the same waters in search of Black contraband.

Blind Fate has an odd way of balancing her scales, and at the very moment when it looked as if Britain's interests in West Africa had been killed by the abolitionists, there came the Industrial Revolution, and with it the need for fats to make more candles, grease, lubricating oil and soap for the grimy servants of the Machine Age. So those who had recently brought Black flesh from Africa turned their attention to palm kernels. What about the Niger Delta? Gradually the 'oil rivers' – the delta network between the oil-giving palms – became a vital source of supply.

By the middle of the nineteenth century all Europe was awake to the potentialities of Africa's raw materials. And in 1884 the Berlin Conference of interested nations established various spheres of interest, and laid down the basis for the 'Partition of Africa'. France, Germany, Belgium and Britain assumed the responsibility for the peaceful control of considerable areas which could be effectively developed and exploited. Portugal did not have to 'scramble', for she was already entrenched both east and west of the great continent.

Britain's slice of West Africa was generous, though not as large as that of France. It included the Gambia, Sierre Leone, the Gold Coast and Nigeria.

Curiously enough, she had not seized her opportunities in Africa eagerly, but reluctantly. Rhodesia, in Southern Africa, had been pressed upon her by Rhodes; and the immense territory of Nigeria, with a population of twenty-two millions, came to her through the trading activities of the Royal Niger Company. Like Rhodes's Chartered Company in Rhodesia, the Royal Niger Company had its own constabulary, which was under the command of Captain Frederick Lugard. This brave officer cleansed the whole region of the persistent slave trade, unified it, and implanted that form of 'indirect rule through the chiefs and headmen' which has since become a model for Native administration. His reward was to be appointed the first Governor-General of a United Nigeria in 1914.

In many ways the Royal Niger Company was the example for the British South Africa Company of Cecil John Rhodes. *With one vital difference.* The Royal Niger, with its armed constabulary and lines of communication, made a primitive, dangerous and unhealthy country safe for trade. Whereas Rhodes, with his Pioneers and Police Force, developed a savage area for White settlement – a healthy Colony which European men and women would one day call 'home'.

Vultures perched on the roof of the Resident Commissioner's large stone house, and the heat shimmered among the palms; lizards led their flickering evasive life on wall and parapet in company with monitors, large as baby alligators. 'The vultures are household pets,' said Mr. Sharwood-Smith easily. 'They sit on the cookhouse roof hoping for scraps like robins on your window-sill at home.'

The Resident Commissioner, who was soon to be promoted Lieutenant Governor of the Northern Region, was a big man with a habit of standing or pacing rather than sitting, which had earned him the Hausa name of 'The Man in

290

the Iron Trousers'. His wife was slight and fair, and their two younger children, Geoffrey and Angela, aged six and three, were in Kano, while the third, a nine-year-old boy, was at school in England. As a girl, Mrs. Sharwood-Smith had been at school in Paris, and during World War Two she had acted as her husband's assistant in a small intelligence unit formed in Kano when the neighbouring French territories came under Vichy control.

When she showed us to our room, she said, 'This is the month of the earwigs. The corn has been cut and they come into the houses. We have a plague of them, so if they get out of hand just ring for the boy and he'll cope. They lurk round window-frames and in cupboards.'

To me an earwig is 'out of hand' the moment he emerges from the petals of a dahlia, and I was quite unprepared for the dense shower of insects which spilled on to the bathroom floor when I opened the window. A tall smiling Hausa boy came in answer to my summons, 'flitted' the active creatures and swept them up while they were still unconscious. The innumerable survivors took a fancy to my cosmetics and face tissues. Crushed earwig (or, worse, *uncrushed* earwig) in one's face cream is even less savoury than a fly in the ointment.

The high plateau of Northern Nigeria is subject to violent temperatures. The thermometer touches a hundred and fifteen degrees in April and May and forty in December and January. November, when we were there, is considered the best season – between the rains and before the cold dusty *harmattan*. But to us it seemed excessively hot.

Before breakfast next morning we were going to see a Police Parade at which my husband and the Emir of Kano would take the salute. And, as we were tired after the air journey, we went to bed early. Our host and hostess came to our room to investigate the earwig situation. A fair number were curled up sound asleep with their heads on our pillows. Mr. Sharwood-Smith gave them a rapid stir and they bustled indignantly up inside the mosquito-net at top speed. He caught a few and flung them out.

'You mustn't worry about them?' he said. 'They have sweet natures. Whoever heard of an earwig doing more than tickle?'

'I thought they went into people's ears and wouldn't come out.'

'A fanciful notion. All they really love is a bit of mountaineering. They'll dash to the top of the mosquito-net, and there they'll stay.'

Mrs. Sharwood-Smith was equally reassuring. 'We don't mind earwigs. It's stink-bugs we hate.'

Stink-bugs we were to meet later in a big way.

It was that perfect hour just after sunrise when the Resident Commissioner drove us to the rosy city with its domes, minarets and horned turrets. The queer fishy smell of indigo rose from the dye-pits in the hot sun, and lengths of material or fibre were spread in the air as they had been for centuries, dyed every shade of blue from pale azure to dark navy.

A crowd had gathered in the huge open square between the Emir's Palace and the huge Government Buildings designed in perfect conformity with their setting. We were shown into an open palm shelter furnished with chairs, rugs and cushions. One of the Emir's kingly Councillors greeted us with a deep obeisance. The Nigerian Police were drawn up under the Palace wall in immobile contrast to a troop of grey monkeys frisking along the top. Round us squatted scores of the Emir's personal bodyguard in the royal red and green robes and high turbans. The *hoi polloi* wore many different costumes and headgears, and most of the women were veiled. The children, so blue-black that they might have been dipped at birth in their own indigo dye pits, laughed and played stark-naked or clad only in a loin cloth. Many were deformed.

'That child with the twisted feet,' I said to Mrs. Sharwood-Smith, 'Surely something could be done?'

'Perhaps,' she agreed. 'But the parents will prefer him to grow up a beggar. Begging is a good money-making concern in a Moslem country, and deformity pretty well establishes your career.'

Yes, the influence of the Middle East was strong in this part of Africa.

Here and there we observed a face of surprising beauty.

'A Fulani,' said Mrs. Sharwood-Smith. 'The Fulanis were the ruling race in the North for centuries – cattle-owning nomads, with fine features.'

There was a ripple of excitement. The Emir was emerging from his Palace. A dignified procession walked slowly across the square led by a giant with a long staff which he tapped constantly upon the earth, intoning as he did so and pausing now and again to remove some stick or stone from the path. The Emir followed him, a dignified old warrior with a solemn countenance which seemed carved from fine-grained mahogany. His burnous was snowy white in contrast to the parakeet scarlet and green of his attendants, and his immense turban was intricately embroidered in pure gold. At his approach, the crowds fell prostrate uttering loud cries of adulation and blessings. When he spat, a man rushed forward and gathered the illustrious spittle and buried it so that no ignoble foot should tread it into the ground.

'African democracy,' murmured Bertie.

The Emir entered the palm shelter with ceremony, and presently he and my husband inspected the Police Guard, who were very smart in red jackets and tarbooshes. When they had drilled, they marched past, with the band playing 'Over the Sea to Skye'. The band was new and a source of pride to the Emir. They could not read music, and it was odd to hear the African interpretation of a nostalgic Scots song, deep and ominous in its minor key.

After the Parade the Emir received us in the Palace. The audience chamber was domed and cool, decorated all in black and gilt, with angular cubist designs of aeroplanes side by side with flowing inscriptions from the Koran. The Emir sat cross-legged on the cushioned dais with his Councillors at a lower level, but we were given conventional chairs. A formal conversation between the Emir, the Resident Commissioner and my husband, was conducted through an interpreter.

The Emir expressed pleasure in welcoming us, and mentioned that he was glad that B.O.A.C. now stopped at Kano, as he hoped that his city might give travellers a truer and happier picture of Nigeria than they received on the coast.

The dignified Moslem of the North has little time for the wide-mouthed explosive Negro of Lagos. The Northern Region is conservative and in no hurry for Self-Government. It is the stabilizing influence in the great Protectorate, and it is satisfied at present to work gradually towards a Central African Parliament by gaining experience of local and provincial government first. And, under the New Constitution, there is every opportunity for the different regions to do this.

The Emir had recently returned from a pilgrimage to Mecca made mainly by air, and he had been much impressed by the speed and comfort of the journey, so different from the hazardous desert crossings of his ancestors.

· The Resident Commissioner told the Emir that we were going to Katsina by car next day – an Emirate some hundred miles north of Kano. The Emir asked us to convey his compliments to the Emir of Katsina who was also his son-in-law. And he offered to send a messenger to inform the Headman of Bichi, a village on our way, that we would be passing, so that we might stop off there and get some idea of a rural centre.

After breakfast the Resident Commissioner's Assistant, Mr. Nelson, with whom Tony was staying, showed us over the market.

Mr. Nelson reminded me of one of those lions at the base of his namesake's monument in Trafalgar Square. He was powerfully built with a thick tawny mane and wonderful whiskers curling up all round his adventurous feline nose, for he was one to sniff out new adventures. He was due for leave, and he had decided to go home the hard way – across the desert to Algiers in a French bus. He had been warned of the discomforts, including plagues of fleas, but what lion worries about fleas? Certainly not a Nelson lion!

294

The enormous teeming market was blazing hot, and I envied the tailors and cobblers who plied their trade under shelter. It seemed that all the products of Africa, Europe, America and Japan were on sale. I was tempted by hand-woven cloth, leather work and python skins, but air travellers are disappointing shoppers. Mr. Nelson told us that the enormous python skins came from the area round Lake Chad, where the Natives have original methods of snake-catching. Certain hunters used their own legs as bait, and the story goes that they put one leg down a python's hole and wait till he has swallowed it up to the hip, then they slice off his head with a hunting-knife, draw out the limb so neatly stockinged in serpent, peal off the reptilian nylon, and, lo and behold! there you may have a twenty-foot python skin unmarked by snare or bullet.

'How about a swim at the Club?' suggested Mr. Nelson. And we drove to the shady pleasant Kano Club where you can play golf and tennis or swim. Mrs. Sharwood-Smith and the children were already there and we were glad to join them in the cool clean water.

In the afternoon Tony and I visited the General Hospital – a long domed and turreted edifice filled with resigned Black men and women in spotless wards. The overflow lay outside on the verandahs wrapped in red blankets. Their presence there proved their faith in the White Doctor's medicines, for, although the hospital is officially free, it is not so in fact. No one exploits his brother man with greater enthusiasm and industry than the African. His country is, in every sense of the word, the land of palm-oil. If a patient would get past the doorman to the clerk, he must 'dash' that individual something, and, if he would proceed upon his way into the presence of the doctor, the clerk must naturally be rewarded – in advance. Then, if the sufferer is fortunate enough to get a bed, the orderly must be kept happy to ensure that food and medicine are faithfully delivered. *No 'Dashing', no nothing!* And, even when the patient has paid for the injection he is entitled to receive free, he cannot be sure that he is not getting a dose of coloured water. For instance, a certain cure for yaws (tropical ulcers) had been proved to possess aphrodisiac properties, an asset generally conceded to be as important to the ageing husband of several young wives as to the yaw-victim. So, quite frequently, the yaw-cure disappeared into the black market, where it was administered at considerable expense to vitiated chiefs and headmen, while the hospital patient wondered why his ulcers were taking so long to heal.

There is another, subtler, danger to which a hospital patient may be subjected – one in which the White man's magic and the Black man's sorcery have become strangely interlaced. If you would injure your enemy mortally you need a drop of his blood, parings of his nails and strands of his hair. The *ju-ju* man will do the rest. Such little odds and ends may easily be obtained from a patient and sold to his enemy. In fact, hospital employment is full of fascinating and lucrative possibilities.

Yet, in spite of these hazards, the sick African prefers to take his chance in hospital than at home.

Needless to say, the Administrator-Surgeon who was kind enough to show us round, as cheerfully as if he had not already more than six men's work on his shoulders, told us none of these things. I learned them later from various sources as my experience of West Africa widened.

Medical Service in Africa is a growing problem. How will it keep pace with the demand for drugs to cure the prevalent pulmonary, intestinal and skin diseases of a population which breeds at a rate undreamed of in the West? Nevertheless, it presses on boldly into the bush, seeking out the sick and suffering, and striving to substitute hygiene for *ju-ju*.

I saw a great many hospitals in West Africa, and it was only, bit by bit, that I learned of the difficulties under which responsible staff have to work; and great and selfless work it is. The Director of Medical Services in Nigeria is Dr. S. L. A. Manuwa, an African. His White staff admire him and work willingly under his administration. Dr. Manuwa, who is not yet fifty, is the first Nigerian who has risen to be

296

the Head of a Government Department. His appointment was, frankly, revolutionary. It is interesting that his European Medical Officers have given him absolute loyalty. He is fortunate in having a charming and unassuming wife.

CHAPTER TWENTY-THREE

KATSINA – PANDORA'S CASKET

WE saw the spirit of modern Nigeria next day when we drove to Katsina with Mr. Nelson and the Flag Lieutenant. Tony had been put up by Mr. Nelson, and was clearly enjoying himself. There are people who love deserts and those who fear them, just as there are people who love or fear the sea – though love of either should be tempered by fear, for the sea and the sand are the lonely burial grounds of man. Tony was a desert-lover. He had served in the desert and in the Canal Zone, and the nearer we drew to the great wastes of the Sahara the more he seemed to respond. His red hair flamed more fiercely, his freckles blazed in the dry heat, and if he had suddenly commandeered a grazing camel and disappeared into the distant dust it would scarcely have surprised me. I am sure he would have given a great deal to have set off across the waste with Mr. Nelson in the French bus for Algiers, fleas and all. A fortnight's journey.

There were many 'overlanders' after the war, when it was impossible to get a sea-passage to Southern Africa, and many tragedies in the shifting shadeless sands. Even today, along the regular seasonal desert route from Zinder to Algiers, things may go well or ill. We met one party in Kano who had made the crossing in a land-rover without mishap – a young District Officer, his German wife and little girl. Another party had met with disaster. A husband, wife, child, and doctor friend had set out. Two days out the husband died of heat-stroke. The others returned to Zinder where the doctor collapsed and died of heart-failure.

We broke our drive from Kano to Katsina at Bichi, as the

Emir had suggested. We were met at the gates of the shady walled village among the palms by the Headman and two Elders. We asked to see the school, and the Head Master, upon being presented to us, flopped down at our feet as if his legs had suddenly given way. This is an old-fashioned greeting and gesture of respect which must keep the limbs of the older generation wonderfully supple.

Negro children, like young animals, have particular charm. They seem livelier, coyer and more exuberant in every way than their White contemporaries. Their rolling inquisitive eyes, liquid black in swimming whites, their great gleaming teeth, always quick to laughter and their woolly well-shaped heads entranced me. These school-children were aged between six and eleven. They sat on palm-mats and rested stick-like elbows on their low little desks, their hands cupping small intelligent faces. I picked out among them the consummate elegance of a Fulani child. Brass bangles adorned her tiny wrists, brass circlets hung from the lobes of her delicate ears, a little bright turban set off the proud head, and a flowered skirt was disposed about the bare feet she curled so neatly under her.

As we entered, they all stood up and chanted a Hausa greeting. Then Mr. Nelson introduced my husband to them in their own language. They looked deeply impressed, and no wonder. He had told them that Bertie was 'an august General who fights upon the sea with many ships, the victor of many battles'.

'They wouldn't understand the word *Admiral*,' he explained to us. 'After all, they have never seen the sea, and few of them are ever likely to.'

The lessons were taught with the happiest blend of humour and learning. The Head Master wrote upon the blackboard in Hausa, 'A MAN GOES OUT'. The class, which was just beginning to learn the elements of reading and writing, gazed at the words.

'Whoever understands what is written here, let him do it!'

The children pondered intently. Then a boy at the back of

the class, beaming widely, got up and went out into the play-ground. Another followed, and then another, until only a few numskulls remained, hypnotized by the writing on the wall which they could not fathom. The children loved it. Throughout all West Africa school is the fashion. With edu-cation in your head you are no man's monkey, with edu-cation the White man came to Africa and drew the wealth from the country, with education the Black man would throw him out again and extract the wealth himself. In towns and villages, and away out in the bush, the Africans were going to school to receive the invisible all-powerful defence and weapon of the future – education.

As we travelled further north the parklands became spar-ser, and the feel of the great desert beyond seemed to fill the air with its dry harsh solitude. A signpost pointed the way to Timbuctoo. The ancient caravan routes were opening before us – to Mecca, Casablanca and Cairo. We skirted the walled city of Katsina and drove up an avenue of pink star-flowers to the house of the Acting District Commissioner, Mr. Stephenson, who was the son of a retired Admiral with whom my husband had served.

Mr. Stephenson was the liveliest man I have ever seen in the Tropics. He exuded energy, and his Scottish wife was as cheerful and vital as her husband. They had two small daughters, Caroline, aged four, and Joanna who was not yet two. A 'baby-boy' took care of the children when their mother was otherwise occupied.

'I really do everything for them,' she said. 'But the boy just walks after them and sees that they don't come to harm. He never stops them doing anything that is not actively dangerous, because he says that if they are thwarted they will cry!'

We never heard them cry, and they did as their parents told them, so a little spoiling on the side evidently did no damage.

The African staff was considerable for a house and garden about the size of a small villa on the Riviera. There were two 'indoor boys,' two 'outdoor boys', two 'horse-boys' (for the District Commissioner kept polo ponies) and a 'bug-boy'. The 'bug-boy' was temporary.

When Mr. Stephenson went on tour he piled his family and what staff and baggage was necessary into a lorry and a car and they took to the bush. This they intended to do during the following week – 'partly to get away from our plague,' said Mrs. Stephenson. 'We'd better tell you about it straight away. It's not very nice.'

Mr. Stephenson said, 'we are in the middle of the worst invasion of stink-bugs we have ever experienced – even in Nigeria. The house has been fumigated time and again but we can't get rid of them, and we'll just have to put up with them till the season ends. There, on the arm of your chair, is one of them.'

The bug was winged, grey and rather sluggish on its feet.

'There *are* a few,' I said. 'But hardly enough for a plague, surely?'

Mrs. Stephenson laughed a little bitterly, 'Oh, no? Come out here into the porch,' There, clinging to the wall, was a nest of the creatures, millions of them in slimy clusters, like bad caviar. 'They are all right now,' she said. 'But this evening, at about sunset, they will be swarming. They will come into the house from everywhere. The air and the walls will be thick with them, and they'll get into your clothes and every corner and crevice. From then until midnight it is impossible to go into the house. After that the flying will be over and they will only be crawling. Then we can go to bed.'

'Won't they be in our beds?'

'Not many. We put the mosquito-nets down early and tuck them in very tight. And we get the children to bed before the swarming begins. The nets are perfect protection. And by morning most of them have disappeared.'

'Anyway there's no harm in them,' said Mr. Stephenson breezily. 'They don't even bite, and they only smell revolting if you crush them.'

I said feebly, 'They had earwigs at Kano.'

301

'We've had earwigs,' he said. 'They are finished. Now earwigs *nip*!'

It struck me that everybody was loyal to their prevailing plague. Mrs. Sharwood-Smith had found earwigs gentle creatures and stink bugs abominable.

'The month before earwigs is really very trying,' said Mrs. Stephenson. 'That's when you get the cantharides. That's bad. He brings up a blister, and, if you touch it, it bursts and the liquid out of it brings up another, and so it goes on. You can be one mass of blisters in no time.'

'Why aren't your houses entirely wired in?'

'There's a division of opinion about that. Most people think they'd be too hot. We need every scrap of breeze we can get in the hot season.'

'There's a polo game this afternoon,' said Mr. Stephenson. 'The Emir plays and is as keen as mustard. I expect you'd like to come.'

So, after tea, we drove through the old city to the polo-ground on its western side. Baby Joanna remained at home in charge of her 'baby-boy', but Caroline came with us, for the weekly polo game was the occasion for a rendezvous of the handful of Europeans in Government Service and their families.

A little mud wall backed the homely stand where the spectators could watch the game in comfort protected from the evening sun at their backs.

I was amazed at the number of children playing about.

Taking wives and children to West Africa has only become customary since the war. For two reasons. Firstly, medical science has made West Africa comparatively healthy, and malaria, the great killer, no longer takes its toll of the White man. Secondly, economic conditions at home, and lack of domestic help, make it impossible to park children on relatives, or for a young man in the Colonial Service to maintain a house in England as well as abroad. The Government pays for wives and families to come and go and provides them with accommodation, so today 'the White Man's Grave' is more like a White children's playground.

302

The Elder Dempster West Coast Shipping Line recognizes this change in conditions and its new liners are fitted up with special nurseries and help for mothers.

While the dust flew on the polo-ground I talked to several young wives. One of them had started a Kindergarten for the little ones.

I have never taught before,' she said. 'But I love it, and it gives one an interest.'

It also gave the other mothers a break, and they did not look forward to the end of her husband's tour.

Leave is good in the Colonial Service – approximately a week to every month. But it is needed.

Only three of the polo-players were European. Most of the others were Nigerian Police, mounted from the Emir's stables. The two keenest players were Mr. Stephenson, and the Emir in his white turban and scarlet vest.

The Emir of Kano and the Emir of Katsina, his son-in-law, were characteristic examples of ancient and modern. Kano, slow and stately, remote and unapproachable, and Katsina, athletic and friendly, educated in England and liberal in thought.

He was standing among his ponies when we were presented to him – sturdy unshod ponies more of the Basuto type than the Arab one might have expected. In his shadow a very small boy wearing a long white robe hit at a wooden ball with a miniature polo-stick. The child had the same lizard-swift movements and glances as his grandfather, the Emir, and a jaunty self-confidence that showed in the bold mischievous expression of his enormous liquid black eyes framed in long thick curling lashes. His smile had a dazzling brilliance as it flashed constantly across his little dusky face. His name was Basha and he was four years old. He lived up to his name by accidentally bashing Caroline smartly over the head with the polo-stick. No one, except Caroline, was interested. The antics of Basha were as familiar to the Emir as the movment of wind through palm leaves, or the flight of swallows darting through the sunlit air around us. The boy was part of him, his dancing shadow, and I was reminded of days gone by in Turkey, when we had seen the Dictator, Mustapha Kemal Ataturk, with Ulku, his child mascot, always at his side, even in the night haunts he frequented till the small hours.

There is a vignette of Katsina which lingers in my memory.

Dust clouds, golden in the sunset, rising from pounding unshod hooves, a scarlet vest and a white turban always in the thick of the fray, and, beyond the fast-moving chukka, the eternal African frieze engraved against the pink crenellated city wall – a camel-caravan moving with timeless majesty towards the night encampment.

When the game ended we noticed little Basha waiting eagerly on the fringe of the polo-ground – expectant. The Emir cantered up to where the boy stood, leaned right down and scooped him into the saddle in front of him. Then he galloped full tilt down the length of the field and back again before joining us for an informal tea served by his personal attendants. The child's eyes glowed like living coals.

We drove home through the winding earth streets of the old city, past the deep indigo wells and turreted mud houses. Goats and fowls wandered about in company with the tall cattle, wide-horned and humped, the prototypes of the highly-bred Afrikanders of the Union. Here and there a blind man tapped his way to the Quarter of the Blind, and every now and again we saw groups of students outside a mud house sitting on the sidewalk round the teacher, gravely attentive to his words. Sometimes the students were men in white gowns and turbans, and at others they were girls, unveiled and gaily clad.

'Ladies of the street,' said Mrs. Stephenson, 'otherwise they wouldn't be out here, but safely tucked away in the harem.'

There is a pool outside the southern city gates where crocodiles are reputed to live.

'Are they to be seen?' Mr. Stephenson asked the keeper of the gate in Hausa.

'Not now, Master. At five o'clock in the morning they are

to be seen. If you wish, I will mount my horse the moment a nose appears and gallop to your house to inform you of it.'

We urged him not to trouble.

At the Residency Mrs. Stephenson hurried upstairs to get Caroline to bed and herself changed before the ordeal by bug should be in full flight. Already the creatures had begun to swarm and the air was vibrating with the loud sinister hum of cellophane wings.

'I advise you not to try to take a bath,' said Mrs. Stephenson. 'We've got a bit late from the bug point of view. Just change as quickly as you can and get out of doors into the garden. The Emir is coming to dinner after our little sundowner party but, as we won't be able to enter the house by then, we'll have dinner in the garden on trays – like B.O.A.C. Fortunately the kitchen is the only place reasonably clear of our plague.'

As Bertie zipped up my dress, he was flickering the creatures off my bare arms and shoulders. They were everywhere – on the walls, in the curtains, in the bath, and in the cupboards and drawers. If you crushed one it exuded a sickly sweet stench.

'Pandora's casket! All the winged evils in creation!' I fled into the garden.

It was fresh and quiet there and the sound of swarming had faded. The hand of Allah had snuffed out the mighty candle of the sun, and instantly the stars had begun to blink in the luminous sky. Northern stars.

About half a dozen young couples came in to sundowners. All the men had been in the Navy during the war and were still on the Reserve list, and the District Officer's wife had been in the Wrens. Wherever we went, it seemed, we could find links with the great Service so dear to British hearts.

When the Emir arrived, this time unaccompanied by Basha, and dressed all in flowing white, Mrs. Stephenson produced an excellent dinner for us, served on trays on our laps in the cool fragrant darkness of the lawn lit only by starlight and the glow of the verandah lamps. All her shopping – even meat and groceries – had to be done from Kano or Lagos, and her house was suffering a severe and pestilential invasion, yet she remained cheerful and unruffled. Mrs. Stephenson could take most things in her stride, as I learned later, when she told me how she and her husband had escorted the Emir's twelve-year-old son to school in England on their last leave. 'The poor little laddie had never worn European clothes in his life,' she said in her soft Scots voice, 'and the tailor here had never made any. But he copied one of my husband's suits in miniature, and it wasn't too bad! Somehow we got him fitted out for the voyage till we could get to London and buy his school outfit.'

More complications had arisen when it came to filling in the boy's passport. No one had known his exact age.

'But you must *think, Sereki!*' Mrs Stephenson had urged the Emir. 'Surely there is some way in which you can recall the year he was born.'

The Emir had racked his brain. 'I was in Lagos. It was a very dull Session – yes a quiet year . . .' It is seldom that the Session is dull in Lagos – any more than it is in Cape Town – so its lack of incident had made it memorable. Even so, it was impossible to be precise about the month and the day.

'Very well, then,' Mrs. Stephenson had said firmly. 'Hamsa must choose his own birthday. What birthday will you have?'

The lad had not hesitated. 'I will choose March the twenty-eighth for my birthday – the day we sail from Lagos to England.'

An interesting and spontaneous choice – the day the African boy would be born to a new way of life and a new outlook.

As he was leaving, the Emir invited us to meet his wives at the Palace next day – a rare honour which we greatly appreciated.

When we woke, soon after dawn, we saw that in some strange way the flying and crawling pest of the night before had vanished. Only a few stragglers remained. But downstairs the bug-boy was sweeping up millions of tiny corpses, the casualties of those sprayed by insecticide after the flying stage had passed into the crawling phase.

On our way to the Palace we met a wedding party of women, in gala robes and led by drummers, going to the house of the bride. They sang and danced and giggled gaily as they went.

Mr. Stephenson stopped the car and called them over in Hausa. They came readily, and told him that they were carrying bales of cloth and thirty pounds in cash to the bride. He wished them luck and gave them a shilling – a modest gift which pleased them so mightily that they broke into a wild piercing shrilling of appreciation as they went their merry way. Hours later we saw them again, still dancing and drumming, outside the bride's home.

The Emir received us in the domed audience hall soon to be redecorated with an English steeplechase frieze. He was attended by three Councillors, but there was no interpreter and little of the old-fashioned formality of the Kano Palace. Basha was there in a grey gown with blue kohl painted round his brilliant eyes. On a large table were interesting replicas of the past – suits of mail captured from the Crusaders, a long double-edged executioner's sword so flexible that it could be bent into the shape of a croquet-hoop, huge wardrums and an enormous copper bowl.

'I cannot beat the drums now,' said the Emir, 'or my servants would bring my car. It is the signal. But in time of war they are beaten through the city to call my warriors, as they were centuries ago.'

The copper bowl was mercifully no longer used for its ancient purpose. In the days of tribal warfare it had been filled with soup made from the bodies of lepers. The leper, in those days, was doomed, a man who welcomed death. The warriors believed that by imbibing the soup they would

307

become imbued with the spirit which cares for nothing and does not even fear death.

The Emir clapped his hands three times, and we went out into the sun-dazzle of the courtyard, where a man stood with the first 'richly caparisoned steed' I have ever seen. It was a white Arab charger, padded with scarlet silk and draped with chain mail. A visor covered its aristocratic nose, silver stirrups dangled from the stamped leather saddle, and on its mettlesome head bobbed curling coloured feathers.

By way of anti-climax, an ageless tortoise hobbled forward. It was part of the Palace scene. Like a pretty woman or the school-boy, Hamsa, no one could be exact about its age. But it was, without question, the oldest inhabitant.

After admiring these things, we passed through a massive iron door, taken, lost and retaken in many wars, down a cool dim winding passage into another palm court attached to the women's quarters.

Mrs. Stephenson murmured to me, 'Your husband and the Flag Lieutenant are being brought here too! That *is* an honour!'

Woven rugs, a few chairs and a garden swing on a dais furnished the room into which the Emir led us. Basha pranced ahead, very much on his own ground here.

The four wives were presented to us, and spoke shyly to the Acting Resident Commissioner and Mrs. Stephenson in Hausa. All wore the traditional draperies and turbans. The senior lady was the mother of the boy at school, a mature matron of a 'sensible age', two younger wives wore gold brocade and cyclamen, but most glamorous was the youngest and favourite wife, Leila, whose voluptuous and obviously productive curves were swathed in gold-striped ruby velvet and on whose dainty head was poised a splendid emerald green turban. Her teeth and features were small and her eyes full of laughter and allure. Azure kohl enhanced the eyes of the women, and their palms were painted with henna. A chaperone lurked in the background, and out in the courtyard two elderly concubines crouched in pleasant

308

idleness – the relicts of the late Emir enjoying their declining years like honest retired horses put out to grass.

'Would you like to see Leila's bedroom?' suggested the Emir.

What a charming fantasy! A great four-poster covered by nine different coloured coverlets, and on the shadowy walls of this inner room was the rainbow gleam of hundreds of patterned and coloured china plates. And, here and there among the plates was the sombre glow of some copper or pewter kitchen utensil or frying pan.

We bade the ladies farewell and followed the Emir to his private study. A few good hunting prints, and a cabinet filled with cups won by his horses and those of his father before him, were the only personal touches. Basha skipped, pranced and postured ahead of us like an impish projection of his grandparent's alert and curiously happy personality. Every now and again the little boy paused to fling his arms round my legs and hug me, and at some time in our meanderings he acquired a toy revolver and lurked round corners saying 'Bang-bang!' as he shot us. His high spirits bubbled over incessantly, yet he never became a nuisance.

As we took our leave of the Emir, he suggested that the Mayor accompany us to the Court of Justice which we were about to visit. As he did so he shook Basha out of his robes like a stink-bug, and the child, almost on wings, flung himself into the car with the Mayor and away we went.

We arrived outside the pink mud building just as the *alkali* (the judge) galloped up on a white Arab steed, which was tethered by a waiting minion as the young judge bowed to us in the modern fashion and bade us welcome.

The Court of Justice was cool and rather dark. Chairs had been placed for us near the dais on which the *alkali* sat on the woven multi-coloured rug. At a table to one side of the dais sat the *muhutai* (assessors and scribes). Accused, accusers and witnesses grovelled at the judge's feet and gave their evidence in that position, while a Nigerian policeman stood over them. Interested people squatted in the background. Any woman giving evidence did so off-stage through a slit in the wall behind the dais, so that the judgment of the *alkali* should not be influenced by her charms.

In many ways it seemed to me that the Moslem law was less of 'an ass' than ours. For one thing the *alkali* was given the fullest possible data about the parties concerned in a case, and for another the oath was not taken as a formula, but as a solemn religious rite, and only if necessary. It retained thus the power of a curse. Judgments were given on a basis of plain good sense and knowledge of human nature, and did not rest upon legal quibbles.

We heard several cases and Mr. Stephenson made them most interesting for us by his quick lucid translations of the Hausa.

There was nothing very complex about them. A woman wanted a divorce because she said her husband did not give her sufficient housekeeping money. The husband, a surly-looking fellow, denied the charge.

The *alkali* had removed his plimsolls, which stood, laceless at the foot of his dais. His face, under the high white turban, was bland and calm, almost expressionless, but I observed that his eyes never lost a look of intense concentration. It was as if every word uttered fell not upon his outer ear but upon his inner consciousness. This was wise young man who saw deeper than the pock-marked skin of the man at his feet. While he asked questions, he picked at his bare toes with long supple fingers. Basha, who never doubted his welcome anywhere, sat for a while in the *alkali's* lap a small grey figure lost in the folds of white material. I do not think that the judge was aware of the child's presence between his knees. When he was bored Basha climbed off the dais and put his four-year-old feet into the empty plimsolls and walked around in them. No one paid any more attention than if he had been a sparrow picking about in the sunny dust outside the courtroom. And although he was more entertaining than a sparrow, he was also more silent. Not a chirp. Only his brilliant painted eyes laughed and flashed under the dense curling lashes, and made a mock of the solemn procedure of the Law.

310

At length the wise judge said to the husband.

'You will pay me three shillings, and this money will be given to your wife. If you do not continue to pay her a reasonable sum with which to buy food I shall know. I shall be kept informed of what happens in your house, for you have many neighbours.'

To the wife, invisible to him behind the aperture at his back, the judge spoke with his head half turned so that she should hear and weigh his words.

'This is the first time you have come here to ask for a divorce. You must go home again for a fornight. After that, if you are still dissatisfied, you may return to this court. Take the three shillings which your husband has paid, and buy food.'

As the case was dismissed he said to us, 'Her brother died recently. She was very fond of him, and since then she has been unbalanced.'

Last came a theft accusation. Many words of wisdom were spoken as evidence was sifted, and many penetrating questions were asked. At last the *alkali* said to the accused:

'Will you swear upon the Koran that you have not taken your neighbour's corn?'

'I will swear,' said the man.

Two policemen led him outside to wash and purify himself before taking the oath, and one of the *muftai* rose and brought the Sacred Book out of a carved chest. It was carried into the sun. And there, in the presence of many who gathered to hear him, the accused swore three times that he had not taken his neighbour's corn – and, if he had, might Allah slit him from top to toe and strike down his favourite child, and more beside.

'That oath really means something,' Bertie said to me. 'I wonder if ours does any more.'

After lunch with our kind host and hostess we returned to Kano. Lunch was curry.

'Mommie,' said Caroline, 'Why are you eating dog?'

311

'Pay no attention,' said Mrs. Stephenson to me. 'We are not eating dog. *Kare* is the Hausa word for dog, and it is pronounced in the same way as curry!'

The children's first words had been Hausa. Rather nice first words.

'*To*—' Caroline had said. It was pronounced 'toe', but it had nothing to do with the 'little piggies that go to market,' it meant 'All right'.

Later, as we left the city, we saw the camel-train plodding out once more on the long road to the north. The camels walked in single file, roped one behind the other like Alpine climbers. They were heavily laden with saltpetre, and attended by the fierce Touareg nomads of the Sahara, dressed all in indigo, with long Turkish trousers, stamped leather aprons, sharp scimitars tucked into their sashes, and yashmaks to cover the lower half of their faces.

'If you pull down a Touareg's veil it is like you pull down his trousers,' the Mayor of Katsina had told us. 'He will kill you.'

Tony got out of the car to take photographs, and a Touareg obligingly posed for him, his eyes smouldering above the indigo veil, the curved steel knife gleaming at his waist.

I smiled as the Flag Lieutenant returned reluctantly to the car wondering if the red-haired young man would ever cast a girl a look so full of yearning and so sad at parting as the look he had given the moth-eaten camels setting off on their long journey across the ever-shifting sands where no tree casts its blessed shade. Girl-proof he might be, but desert-proof he was not.

CHAPTER TWENTY-FOUR

LAGOS – 'YE! YE!!'

IT is three hours' flight from Moslem Kano and the savan-
nahs of the north to the lush tropical oil-growing south and
the teeming tumultuous African life of Lagos, a real Nigerian Cosmopolis and the capital of the Territories. From
the air we looked down upon Lagos Island, attached to the
mainland by the Carter bridge.

In the early days of British colonization Lagos, which in
Portuguese means 'lake', was a cluster of mud huts round
one of the greatest slave marts of the coast. Now it is a city
of magnificent buildings and cathedrals with beautiful residential areas growing hourly. Much of it has been built on
land reclaimed from the sea. It never seems to occur to the
African clamouring for the British to 'get out and let us run
our own show!' that he owes his 'own show' so prosperous
and rapidly developing – entirely to White capital and en-
deavour and the security which comes from a sound administration. If all these should be withdrawn there would be an
inevitable reversion to tribal warfare and the possible se-
cession of the North from the South.* Not a tempting
prospect for the foreign investor whose money would be
required for the further development of the country.

'There she is!' said Bertie, as the aircraft banked and
circled preparatory to landing.

And there lay the *Bermuda* – a slender sun-silvered silhouette, small as a minnow out on the lake beyond the
fringe of palms and gardens. And up the creek, moored
alongside the Marina, just across the road from

* *e.g. The tragic Biafran war.*

Government House, was the frigate, *Nereide*. From above, she looked like a gondola in a Venetian waterway at the steps of the Doge's Palace.

The 'Doge' – in this case the Governor, Sir John Macpherson – was away on leave, and his palace was being repainted in his absence, so we were to stay next door with his Deputy, the Government Secretary, Mr. Arthur Benson, and his Rhodesian wife, Daphne, a member of the well-known Fynn family.

The Captain of the *Bermuda* was being put up ashore by Major-General Fairbanks, the General Officer Commanding West African Forces; and a number of officers stayed with friends, for the heat onboard was intense, and the local hospitality most generous. If it were really possible to be killed by kindness I believe the officers of H.M.S. *Bermuda* would have passed away during our week in Lagos! In fact, they nearly did.

As far as the sailors were concerned, life was a little more complicated. Various African Societies very kindly entertained them – the hosts usually arriving some time after the guests, for punctuality is not an African characteristic, and naturally young African ladies were produced as dancing partners. In Simon's Town it had been explained to them that if they associated with Coloured girls they ran the risk of being arrested under the Immorality Law of the Union. Now, in West Africa, it was equally carefully explained to them that there was no colour bar and that Africans must be treated upon a basis of equality. For boys of seventeen and eighteen, the distinction between two such different attitudes must have seemed puzzling. I heard one Colonial Official say to the Captain:

'I hope your ship's company realize that they are not in Dr. Malan's country here.'

Philip Currey answered drily:

'The trouble will be to make them realize that they are not in West Africa when they get back!'

The Bensons made us feel at home immediately, for they both possessed great charm and warmth. Arthur was tall

314

and always immaculately dressed in spite of the collar-wilting climate; he had tea-coloured eyes (no milk or sugar), fine hands and a great capacity for hard work and for enjoying life. Daphne's elegant simplicity of dress was astringent against the flamboyant background of the Tropics, and her shining brown hair was done in a neat coil round her small well-shaped head. She had a delightful gift of observation and picked the core of drama or humour from any situation.

Our airy white bedroom, which was almost entirely composed of windows, looked over the garden and the lake, and we shared it with a large coal-black Yoruba named Moses. Moses was our personal attendant, and, like the poor, he was ever with us. I believe he slept on the mat outside our door.

At night we could hear the fruit-bats go *ping*! one after the other in the mango-trees.

'We must do something about those bats,' said Daphne. 'It's an infuriating noise.'

I didn't find it infuriating. That resonant repetitive *ping* was much less irritating than the drip-drip of a water-tap. In Lagos, however, the dripping was done less by taps than by humans. The humid heat lay in a damp curtain over everything and exploded from time to time in a tropical rainstorm.

I said to Daphne in despair. 'It's no good, I can't keep the slightest curl in my hair in this humidity. Where can I get a perm?'

She rang up Kingsway Stores and made an appointment for me.

Kingsway Stores is the local Harrods where you may buy anything within reason. (Things not 'within reason' people buy in the Native Market, but more of that anon.) The assistants are all African and their clients every colour under the equatorial sun. The costumes of the shoppers were infinitely varied. The women in their bright cotton prints were cleaner and more decorative than the men, for the coast Natives combine anything they please in their dress, with some curious results. There was none of the white-robed dignity of the north. The ladies and gentlemen behind the counters performed their duties with African languor and sublime indifference. Perhaps the cosmetic department was the most interesting, for it catered for complexions ranging from ebony to ivory. Not even in the South of France at the height of the sun-tan summer, have I seen such a range of face powders, from 'purple plum' to 'angel pink'.

The hairdresser was English and he gave me an excellent permanent wave. In the cubicle next door an African lady of fashion was having a 'stretch'. The coarse frizz of her hair was drawn to its utmost length and oiled. Before being submitted to a de-crimping machine. Poor old Mother Nature! None of us is ever satisfied with her intentions.

Most of the trade in West Africa is in Syrian hands. And while I was sitting peacefully in Kingsway Stores, only a few doors away fecund Africa was causing a diversion in a Syrian shop. Reporting in African papers is lively and exuberant, and Daphne showed me the front page story next day. It was written in expressive English, for Lagos, like a South African mine, is a Tower of Babel, and those who cannot understand other African dialects can often understand English, which is therefore the language of a great proportion of the local press.

'LADY GIVES BIRTH TO CHILD IN MID-STREET
CHILD BORN IN A SHOP SETS PEOPLE AMAZED'

These somewhat contradictory headlines led into the very human story with its unconscious little touches of African and Syrian character.

' "Ye! Ye! shouted an expectant mother in the shop of a Syrian, Mr. Alli Jammal. In the next two minutes a female child screamed 'Mueh Mueh, mueh!'

'It was an unexpected birth of a baby by an African woman later known to be Mrs. Bolaji Awodolapo Latifu.

'Syrians in the shop also were surprised.

' "How did it happen?" asked one of them.

'The woman was there to buy a cloth for herself in preparation against the coming baby.

'She asked the price of the brocade, and when she was told, she replied with "Ye! Ye!!" and held fast to her waist.

She ran to a corner of the shop just by the entrance. 'The seller was still looking on, thinking that the price which he had quoted caused the woman a surprise as too high.

' "Women are noted for that type of shout when they are astonished," he said later.

'That was not.

'It was the coming of a baby girl.

'Within three minutes after her "Ye! Ye!!" shout, a child cried out and an N.A. Police Constable (John Oradugba) ran to the scene. He fetched some water and cleansed the baby's eyes and nose before everybody knew what set the Street agog.

'The baby was hale while the mother appeared as if she did not labour at all.'

If, as the Syrian merchant remarked, 'Ye! Ye!!' is the 'type of shout' for which women are noted when they are astonished, there were many times on the coast of West Africa when I, too, might have 'set people amazed' with loud cries of 'Ye Ye!!'

For instance there was Lagos Market. Major Allen, the Commissioner of the Colony, was my escort, and I found, in our tour, an element of purest fantasy. He drove me in a glittering black vintage Rolls-Royce, and in the back seat, as translator, came a highly intelligent and fine-looking Yoruba Boy Scout called Alatya, whose aim in life was to became a 'crime investigator', a profession bursting with opportunity in Lagos.

The Commissioner's Rolls was evidently well-known, for everything gave way before us. Burnished new export cars, owner-driven by reckless Africans in striped pyjamas and fezzes, skidded madly out of our path, wobbly cyclists took to the side-walk at our approach, mowing down a few pedestrians as they did so, women with burdens on their heads side-stepped our juggernaut, groups of corner-boys dressed in anything or near nothing stopped their heated political arguments in mid-speech to avoid us, and naked children, pigs, poultry and goats scattered at our approach. It had been raining and the Native town was a morass.

'To educate these coastal people to an appreciation of beauty or cleanliness is no easy task,' said the Commissioner. He showed me a clearing littered with rubbish. 'We made that into a garden playground only a few months ago. Look at it now! The children preferred the gutters, and at night everybody dumped their muck there.'

Ye! Ye!!

The waterfront was like a Chinese creek jammed with sampans amid a miasma of unspeakable smells. Rude shelters were embedded in sewer filth and the clean rain of heaven was kept out by palm thatch.

'Illicit squatters,' said Major Allen. 'As fast as we turn them out and pull down their huts they come back. They like their squalor. Yet here is the meat-market. See how clean, and hardly a fly! *We* are responsible for the cleanliness of *this* market. The Native Market is another matter.'

The Native Market was like something out of a Necromancer's Dream.

We plunged into an airless twilight inhabited by a pungent community of buyers and sellers. Old half-naked mammies with breasts like worn razor-strops crouched over weird concoctions on little braziers, sinister as Shakespeare's witches.

'Fillet of a fenny snake,
 In the cauldron boil and bake;
 Eye of newt, and toe of frog,
 Wool of bat, and tongue of dog,
 Adder's fork, and blind-worm's sting,

318

Lizard's leg, and owlet's wing,
For a charm of powerful trouble,
Like a hell-broth boil and bubble.'

Others, fat as peach-fed pigs, squatted amid their wares and
their prodigious families; men slouched and jostled, children swarmed and squealed, the roar of many tongues
spoken at once surged and broke about us in the dark covered
alleys between the close-crammed booths, and wherever we
looked there were the sleepers. Strange, these sleepers! They
sprawled anywhere in any attitude, in ones and twos, in
heaps like discarded gollywogs; infants, lolling in slings on
their mothers' backs, seemed about to be overlaid by the hot
recumbent body overwhelmed with the need for sleep. Children, suddenly tired, curled up kitten-wise anywhere. The
hubbub around them, the turmoil and the shouting did not
wake them or even disturb them, for the sleepers of Africa
sleep deep.

Throughout this mêlée strode a tall fine mammie with a
basin on her head piled high with Blue bell and talcum tins,
chipped platters, old saucepan and tea-pot lids, and a motley
collection of other odds and ends.

'Must weigh a ton!' I said.

'The tins are empty,' said Major Allen. 'Whatever is
thrown away in any household finds its way to this market to
be sold for money. A cigarette?'

'I'd like one. It's necessary!'

We were passing the fowl coops.

'Here is the pharmaceutical section,' said the Commissioner.

As my eyes grew accustomed to the gloom of this particular part of the market I discerned such ingredients as
would entrance the witches. Their Scotch Broth would seem
a poor thing compared with the mighty possibilities of
Africa.

Skull of horse; dead bat – maggots crawling in its belly –
snarling jaws of rats in scores; dried chameleon, pickled
lizard; beak of vulture, claw of cock; tail of civet, fang of

319

snake; frogs, leeches, praying mantis; spiders of gigantic size, ape's ears and croc's eyes, and things I couldn't recognize.

'Whatever's this? I indicated a large flat leathery affair hanging up beside what looked like a flying-fox.

The Alatya said: 'That is the ear of an elephant.'

'What is its use?'

'I cannot say. The herbalist tells someone what they must bring him, and how to use it.'

'Are his brews supposed to be cures for the sick?'

'They are for many purposes,' said Alatya darkly.

The Commissioner added. 'You'd be surprised.'

'I am.'

'Many of these things are used as charms against disease – smallpox, barrenness, impotence, or they may be bought to make *ju-ju* against an enemy. Or, if you suspect that your enemy is making *ju-ju* against you, you must find a doctor who will give you a still better magic with which to defend yourself.'

'They really believe that an enemy's *ju-ju* can harm them?'

'If they think a spell has been put on them, they lie down and die with no trouble at all.'

An old unsavoury hag, straight from the witch's cave, dragged at my skirt and thrust a basin of live fish at me.

'What are they?'

'Electric fish,' explained Alatya.'If you touch one you will get a shock. See, like this!' He touched a fish and sprang high into the air, and the fish, for its part, seemed to suffer an equally severe shock.

'Would you like to try?' I declined.

As we made our way out of the market past the booths of the cloth-merchants selling narrow stencilled lengths of Native cotton woven on primitive looms, the crowds seemed to press more closely about us and children tugged at my dress and peered up at me curiously. Would-be vendors yelled after us imperiously and incomprehensibly.

'Would it be all right to come to this market alone?' I asked.

The Commissioner hesitated. 'You might find the people noisy and tiresome – because they'd be interested and inquisitive. But they are all right. The only trouble they give is down by the waterfront. A sailor comes ashore with his pay-packet, and maybe he gets drunk. Then he is likely to be robbed.'

Sailors – the 'lost tribe' especially merchant sailors. I could imagine the heat on board a ship in harbour, and the men feeling that they would give anything to get away from the steel box that is a furnace at the end of the day. Where to go? What to do? And, waiting for them, skulking round the wharfs, those who prey upon them . . .

Yet, when I think back of Lagos, the hours that come most readily to mind were the pleasant evenings we spent at Government Secretary's House.

After dinner chairs would be placed in a horseshoe on the wide lawn under the tall palm tree. The moon shone on the lake and cast its mysterious shadows on the grass; and across the massive tropical hedge loomed the white palace of the Governor, empty and majestic. On the Marina sailors waited to take the liberty boat back to the *Bermuda,* and sometimes the Captain of the *Nereide* stepped across the road from his frigate and joined our circle. Curiously enough, Commander Dudley Norman, D.S.O., had served in submarines during the war with Paul Thirsk, the Governor's Secretary, an R.N.V.R. officer who had been awarded a D.S.C.

Those evenings I received glimpses of the gipsy life of the Colonial Service and of the pack-and-follow spirit of the wives who bushwhack for months on end with their husbands and live cheerfully under what are often extremely difficult conditions.

For instance, Arthur and Daphne Benson had married very young when Arthur was stationed in Rhodesia. Before she was twenty-one Daphne was the mother of two little

321

girls, and six weeks after the birth of her first baby she had toured the wilds with her husband.

'We went by bicycle and on foot, and the baby was strapped to a cycle and kept in a meat-safe so that the mosquitoes should not harm her. We loved it, but what would have happened if the infant had got ill I can't imagine! I knew nothing about sickness – or babies!'

'Daphne and I were in the bush once for three months without seeing another European,' said Arthur. 'And then, one day, as we were playing tennis, we heard a car in the distance. We rushed to the net and stared at each other. Who – *who* – could it be?'

'Weren't you wildly delighted?' I asked – thinking meanwhile that it was characteristic of a British outpost to have a tennis court!

'No. Horrified. You get into a state of mind where you cannot endure anyone, or anything, interfering with your routine. But afterwards, when the travellers have appeared and been made welcome, you begin to talk. And then it seems as if you can never stop!'

'Nigeria is new to us, but so interesting,' said Daphne. 'On our first tour of the Northern Region we happened to visit a Fulani village at the very moment when the Whipping Ritual was taking place. It is unbelievable. The young men regard this ordeal as the gateway to manhood. They are a handsome people, as you know, and the young men, naked but for a loin-cloth, stands in the centre of a circle of girls. He holds a mirror in one hand and a comb in the other, and, with arms upraised and head gracefully lifted, he smiles at his own image and combs his hair while his comrades beat him about the body with heavy sticks. Each time the stick strikes it lays the skin wide open. He doesn't even wince, but continues smiling at his reflection, like Narcissus, and combing his hair. When the girls think he has had enough they call a halt. He wears his scars like decorations for bravery.'

'Why isn't this stopped? It sounds so cruel.'

'It is – cruel and shocking – yet somehow magnificent. In

any case, it is tribal custom, and it is not wise to interfere with tribal custom unless absolutely necessary, as with tribes who practise cannibalism.'

I noticed during these talks in the semi-circle under the tropical moon that everybody showed a particular loyalty to the province of which they had the greatest experience. And I was struck anew at the peculiar affection the British administrator always seems to feel for the backward people under his care, no matter how tiresome they may be. Certain Lagos journals attacked the Government daily in the most immoderate terms, yet, whatever his feelings on the subject may have been, the Government Secretary displayed the greatest forbearance.

'One has to remember that the wide mouths and corner-boys of Lagos are only a symptom of African emancipation,' he said, gently and insistently. 'They are by no means typical of the feeling of the country in general.'

'You are a Northerner,' Arthur would say, turning to one of his District Officers, who might be in Lagos for a few days, 'What do you think?' Or he might draw out someone with special knowledge of the West or South. The 'Northerner' invariably thought the Hausas the salt of earth, while a 'southerner' would defend the trouble-making Ibos of his region.

'They may be difficult and quarrelsome – too intelligent and politically conscious – but, *if you understand them*, they are the best of the lot.'

The same applied to the Fulanis, the yorubas or any other tribe. Each had their champions. Like earwigs or stink-bugs, I thought, your own particular pest is the best pest.

I said as much to Bertie afterwards, and he laughed.

'It's plain and simple old school tie, that's all. You may *loathe* them, but they are your loyalty. You may have four dog-toothed men in your charge who murder their wives, beat their children and fry the cat's brains over the fire. But, however much you hate them, they are yours. Let anyone criticize them and you are up in arms extolling their few virtues. It's not peculiar to West Africa. It's just old-fashioned British public school stuff – the sort of thing that makes foreigners believe we are mad.'

One night we dined with Major-General Fairbanks and his wife in their rather fantastic house on the shores of the lake. The African boys waiting at table were very exotic in white gowns and vermilion sashes and boleros.

'They are all Northerners,' explained the General. 'It is best not to mix one's staff. The Head Boy is a Fulani, and sometimes on moonlight nights he goes crazy and leaps and dances across the lawns like a vision out of the Sadler's Wells.'

It occurred to me that it did not take a Fulani to do that. Our Second Cook at Admiralty House had put up a very spectacular impromptu performance the night he had done a fire-dance over the burning logs at Piet and Glen's *braaivleis*.

But at least our cooks – bizarre or not – had never been reported to the Commander-in-Chief by the Chief Steward for putting *ju-ju* in the staff meals! Whereas Major-General Fairbanks' boys had come to him with troubled faces to say that they had found paper and string in their meat and this was undoubtedly part of some *ju-ju*. The cook, when taxed, had been indignant. It was not *bad ju-ju*, he protested, but *good ju-ju!* Nevertheless he was sacked, and the word *ju-ju* was, from then on, forbidden in the house.

'But forbidding mention of it doesn't stop the boys from believing in it. *Ju-ju* is as much part of Africa as the African. All the same, there's no need to encourage it!' said the General.

The social life of Lagos, made gayer by a regular garrison, revolved round Ikoyi Club with its golf, tennis and dancing, and a wonderful dance was given there in honour of the naval visit.

Next day we all had to shake ourselves awake, for it was November 11th and there was an Armistice Service at the Cathedral. It was suffocatingly hot, and the great church was packed with officials White and Black. Everybody wore full regalia, and the African judges in their long wigs must have

324

boiled. Several of them used the locks as an elephant uses his ears, flapping them to and fro to fan their dewy faces. Afterwards there was a ceremony at the cenotaph at which the Deputy Governor and my husband laid wreaths and inspected a parade of African troops and a Royal Naval guard from the British ships. The whole city had turned out for the occasion, and the Navy received an ovation. The 'get out and leave us to run our own show' element was clearly off duty that day.

Our last afternoon we spent quietly with the Bensons at Tarqui Bay in the Government House bungalow on Lighthouse Beach. It was only a short lake crossing, but the air was lighter and cooler. The surf beat upon the long shore fringed by coco-palms, and some sort of pink convolvulus covered the sands. I wondered if such a lovely plant could not be persuaded to grow over our own ever-shifting wind-driven South African sands and help to bind them. Had the 'Cape Doctor' begun to pile up the dunes yet? Surely it was too early still. It would be the lovely intermediate month between spring and summer in the Peninsula, with sunny days and cool nights. Children like Ronnie with bright eyes and rosy cheeks would be playing under the oaks and paddling in safe rock-pools. No need for mosquito-nets over their cots, no constant fear of dysentery, fever, bilharzia or guinea-worm to disturb anxious mothers. No need for long vacations in a healthy climate – the birthplace and homeland of Europeans who belonged there and loved it with all their hearts.

Back in Lagos the heat came down like a pall. Every slightest effort took its toll of sweat.

We closed the last suitcase and rewarded Moses for his fidelity. The Head Boy called out, with the bossiness of any West African in a position of authority:

'Get five boys help with this luggage! Quick! Governah's ordahs!'

The *Bermuda*'s motor-boat waited at the little jetty at the bottom of the Marina steps, and the Bensons strolled down with us and we tried to thank them for all their kindness.

'We'll miss you,' they said. 'The Navy means a great deal to all of us!'

Once again Their Lordships had given permission for the Commander-in-Chief's wife to take passage in the Flag-Ship for the official visits to the Gold Coast, Sierra Leone and French Senegal. The scene in West Africa had changed greatly since the war, and the White Man's Grave was now the temporary home of many British women and children. The warship, showing the Flag, would be entertaining the wives of British officers in the Army and Colonial Service and of business men, as well as African officials and their wives. Even so, my air passage from the Union to West Africa and back again was at my own personal expense.

And, to me, it was well worth it. In our crowded happy two years on the South Atlantic Station, the West Coast stands out very clearly as an experience of great interest and strange glamour. It was the sharp contrast to the far south.

The tremendous impetus of African Nationalism was the absolute antithesis of Afrikaner Nationalism. In the Union the Nationalists were, in certain respects, putting the clock back. In West Africa they were moving the hands violently forward. There was a touch of lunacy in both extremes, in the stubborn defensive retrogression of a great percentage of South Africans, and in the aggressive tempestuous frothing of the politically conscious minority of West Africa, for ever on the verge of running amok. In White Africa the European intended to *remain* boss, in West Africa the African intended to *become* boss. Would a Capricorn Africa Federation one day be a compromise buffer between these two forms of Nationalism? The changing pattern of Africa was easy to see, but to prophesy its shape and form a century hence was another matter.

Anything can happen in Africa. Death has a thousand faces, and pity is as blind as her sister, Justice. Birth is swift and easy. 'Ye! Ye!!' and the baby is there – millions and millions of little Negro babies born into a new Africa, made safe for their survival by Western medical science, millions

326

of bonny piccaninnies who will grow up and throw the European out of their country when he is of no more use to them. Meanwhile they are learning from him – and fast. For he is spoon-feeding them with his own all-powerful *ju-ju* – education.

CHAPTER TWENTY-FIVE

GOLD COAST*

OUT at sea it was silken and calm and I was able to have a chair under the awning on the quarterdeck, except when a sudden squall blew up and sheets of tropical rain obliterated sea and sky and drove me below.

Everybody was exhaused after the heat and gaieties of Lagos, and the thirty-six hours of sea-routine before we reached Takoradi must have been a relief and refreshment to the jaded spirits on board.

Bertie took me up on the bridge, and together we examined the chart of the great bulge of Africa between the Bight of Benin and Dakar. I had studied it before in my School Atlas and been thrilled by the names written across the blue of the Atlantic along the stretches of coast. From south to north – the Slave Coast, the Gold Coast, the Ivory Coast, the Grain Coast (so named, I was told, for the pepper grains of Liberia and Sierra Leone), and the Guinea Coast.

Somewhere about the fifth century B.C. Hanno, the Carthaginian mariner, had sailed down this coast of wealth, sorrow, spice and mystery. it was an adventurous expedition, and the mixed cargo with which he returned to North Africa included 'three hairy men' from the West African jungle. Unfortunately he did not bring them back alive, for they proved impervious to persuasion or discipline and were so dangerous that they had to be killed. But Hanno hung their pelts in his temple as an offering to his gods in thanksgiving for a safe return from an odyssey fraught with peril.

* Now Ghana.

Perhaps the giant apes were lucky that death and not slavery was their fate.

Even in those distant days gold and precious stones, ivory, apes and bright parakeets were imported from West Africa to the Mediterranean by the bold Carthaginians. And, even then, African slaves were the best value of all. It is probable that the Carthaginians made the desert crossing to Kano too in search of salt and 'black ivory'.

We could see the flat coastline with the long frills of surf and the sand-bars muzzling the river mouths. Down those rivers had been washed the gold-dust that had tempted the early sailor-explorers, and on the rocky promontories, backed by fever-stricken marshes, the Portuguese had built their castles that were fortresses, treasure-houses and trading bases all combined, and later – in the grievous era of the slave-trade – prisons too. Other nations had been lured, and the strongholds of the Dutch, the Danes, the French and the British had risen to proclaim their interest in so rich a region. And many of those castles are still used.

We reached the Gold Coast port of Takoradi in the early morning. Here there is no longer any need for Native surf-boats to meet the ships, for there is a fine breakwater with safe anchorage for many vessels. Takoradi is a busy port. Timber from the great forests of Ashanti lay roped in the water awaiting transportation. Gold, diamonds, palm kernels cocoa and spices were among the cargoes which merchant ships would carry back to Europe and America. The hill behind the harbour was lush green velvet, shimmering in the heat and blazing with bursts of scarlet blossom. New houses and buildings were going up, and new plans were being made for the extension of the docks. There was no stagnation here. Takoradi was typical of the coast from Lagos to Dakar. It was expanding to meet the ever-growing oversea need for minerals and raw material. No wonder the Africans were in a combustible state. Fortunes were being made in West Africa once again, and they wanted those fortunes for themselves. But fortunes are not wrung from the earth without experience or the touch of Rhodes, or of

329

Taubman Goldie of the Royal Niger Company. Moreover stability is essential to trade, and the Africans have a long way to go before they will learn the art of stable administration.

We lunched ashore with Mr. Salkield, the Director of Railways. His fine modern house on the hill was cool and airy.

'It's only been built four years,' said Mrs. Salkield, 'and I planted practically every shrub in the garden myself. Yet look at it now! Anything grows here. It's a natural hothouse.'

'It's glorious,' I agreed. 'All that tropical colour! A garden of Eden.'

During lunch Eden yielded up its serpent.

As the sweet came in we heard a din on the terrace outside the open French doors. Several gardeners with sticks were beating at something which was evidently heading straight for us.

'Snake-hunt,' announced Mrs. Salkied, who had the brisk north-country personality of Gracie Fields. 'Like a look?'

The kill was made on the mat, and we watched the gardener land the final blow on the narrow head of a long writhing snake.

'Bad one,' he said. 'This very bad one.'

'I should say so,' said Mr. Salkield. 'That's a green mamba. One bite and you'd have less than seven minutes to say your prayers.'

The 'bad one' was more beautiful than impressive. We measured it. It was five feet long and three and a half inches thick, with clear lovely colours, olive-green shading to a yellow belly.

'Don't leave it near here,' I said. 'The mate will come.'

The gardeners laughed. But next morning the night-watchman reported to Mrs. Salkied "Madam was right. Mate came last night but no could catch.'

'They'll get it,' said Mrs. Salkied serenely. 'More Africans get snakes here than snakes get Africans.'

The *Bermuda* remained four days at Takoradi, where Bertie, Tony and I left her to fly to Accra and spend three days with General L. G. Whistler, the Commander-in-Chief, West Africa.

Accra is the capital of the Gold Coast* and ships still call there, but they have to lie out in the bay and their only communication with the shore is by Native surf-boat – a long slender dug-out canoe manned by experienced paddlers who know exactly how to ride the tumbling rollers.

It is less than an hour's flight along the coast from Takoradi to Accra – a coast as golden as its name. The gently scalloped palm-fringed beaches are broken by rocky headlands and patterned with surf-boats drawn up neatly in the shade while fishing-nets are spread to dry in the hot sun. On every headland there is a fishing village, or one of those grim old fortress-castles that bear witness to the hey-day of the Atlantic slave-trade. Beyond lies the interior – the Northern Provinces and Ashanti, the home of fetish and tribal war, where so many British soldiers died unspeakable deaths. Yet in World War Two some of the Allies' best warriors were West African troops.

Our military plane circled low over the historic castles – fifteenth century Elmina of the early Portuguese (now used as a Police Post), British Cape Coast Castle, and Danish Christiansborg, which is today Government House at Accra.

The Governor, Sir Charles Arden-Clarke, was away on tour, but we were to spend forty-eight hours at Government House on our return journey to the Union, so I will write of Christiansborg, and also of the new Gold Coast Parliament, in a later chapter.

The General's official residence was large and modern and cooled by the breeze which blows all day at that season and only drops for a few hours during the night. Mrs. Whistler was one of those admirable hostesses who believe in letting their guests do as they like.

'People cannot have every moment of their day planned for

* *Accra is now the capital of Ghana.*

331

them in this climate,' she said sensibly. 'You must just wait
and see what you feel up to.'

Her little dachshund, Hansel, sat panting at her feet.
There was only one thing *he* always felt up to, and that was
teasing Jennifer Whistler's bushy-tailed cat. Jennifer and
Penelope Whistler, the daughters of the house, both worked
in Government offices. In the late afternoon they played
tennis or swam off Labadi Beach, where there was reasonably
safe surfing, 'so long as you don't go out too far because of
the backwash and the sharks'. On days when the bathing
was dangerous the coastguard ran up a red flag. But, as the
red flag gave no warnings while we were there, we swam
every afternoon and enjoyed our picnic tea in the General's
bungalow under the palms. Tall Black Beatrice came round
with a basket of plantains (giant bananas) and enormous
pineapples on her head, and we bought the juicy pines to
help quench our thirst.

Afterwards, on our way home in the cool of the evening,
we passed the swarming Native villages, where everybody seemed to be busy queueing for a wash under the
pump.

'They are very clean,' said the General, 'really fastidious.'

One notices the women most. There seem to be unusual
quantities of them, and their printed cottons and flounced
bodices are very decorative. West Africa has matriarchal
tendencies. The women are the merchants and financiers,
even the money-lenders, and their somewhat raucous voices
are heard loud and long in the 'Palaver Square', where most
of the trouble starts when trouble is brewing. The ram-
shackle Native buses are called 'mammy-wagons', the toga
slung over a man's or woman's shoulder is known as a
'Mammy-cloth', the word 'mammy-palaver' covers a multi-
tude of sins and wickednesses, and the rows and rows of huts,
in which the families of African troops live, are 'mammy-
lines'.

The men are swamped by all this mammy business, but,
even so, they can make plenty of noise in the Palaver Square

above the harbour where surf-boats put to sea, for noise is a feature of their lives. Noise and excitement.

One morning Mrs. Grant, the wife of Brigadier Grant, the General's chief of Staff, took me to see the Native and European Army Schools.

The African children learned in sheds near the communal laundry of the mammy-lines, and it was clear that lessons were not labour to them but fun.

'The children bluff their ages,' said the officer showing us round. 'They are supposed to be between five and fifteen. But take this boy here, he has an *old* face, he is clearly over fifteen and getting away with it.' He said to the boy, 'How old are you?'

'Old Face' sat in sulky silence, and, when pressed, declared he did not know.

Three classes were going on. The little ones were learning in their own Twi dialect, the next class in Hausa, and the seniors in English. The teachers were African. The seniors gazed attentively at a blackboard on which was drawn a fly.

'Heah is the house-fly,' said the teacher in his quick jerky English. 'He is very detty, he likes detty things, he sits on them, then he sits on food and food becomes detty. When you go to latrine—'

'This isn't quite what I expected,' murmured our guide. We will go and ask the children to sing.'

Never have I heard such singing! The African master gave them the note – first for tenor, then for alto. Then, at a given signal, they opened the superb cavities of their mouths and raised the roof with a Hausa hymn. Enormous white teeth and the glint of rolling eyes illumined small chocolate faces.

'What is their favourite song?' I asked.

'You'll hear.'

Off they went again – tenor and alto beautifully attuned – and the song they had chosen was 'Auld Lang Syne' in Hausa.

The Coloured children of the Cape have this same passion for song. All over the countryside the little coons sing and dance, and young wandering minstrels stroll among the vineyard paths with mandoline or guitar. In the Homes for Crippled Children I had heard boys and girls sing their hearts out as they lay helpless with wasted tubercular limbs in splints or stretchers, and I had seen the crippled lads whittling away at home-made bamboo pipes which would presently sound sweet and haunting as the pipes of Pan.

Yet here song burst forth even more irrepressibly – in a great shout of triumph. And then, as I looked at the healthy happy children, the ghosts of Elmina and Cape Coast stood at their shoulders. These piccaninnies were singing *our* hymns and songs with such joyous gusto, but the music those less fortunate Africans had taken to the New World had been the mother and father of the wailing blues – melancholy and monotonous, all in a minor key, sometimes mad, always sad, the music of forgotten Africa, of a dark long-ago heartbreak – the songs of slaves.

Mrs. Grant said, 'We'll go to the European School now. It's very crowded. Families are swarming out to the coast and we can't get teachers or quarters fast enough. After they reach the age of sixteen it really isn't possible to educate them here.'

The European Kindergarten sang for us too. 'Three blind mice – see how they run!' But this time no heads were flung spontaneously back with mouths open to their utmost capacity. It was a timorous performance – almost as if the three blind mice were the singers.

The children – some hundred and eighty – were being well taught, and they were obviously as contented in their work as any sophisticated European child could be. It is only the little African who regards the classroom as the ante-chamber to paradise. The Headmistress had a brisk way with her and good-tempered control of her ever-growing flock.

We went back to lunch at the Chief of Staff's house, where Brigadier Grant and my husband met us.

'You come back at two o'clock, Poem,' said Mrs. Grant

to our African driver. She turned to me. 'While he waited for us this morning he was studying his school books. They are all mad on learning. To be literate is to be somebody.'

'To be Poem is also to be somebody,' I laughed. 'What a wonderful name! And the General's boy who looks after us is Azuri and the Head Boy is Adrissa.'

She said, smiling: 'Their names are not all so romantic. For instance, our cook has just become the father of twins, and he has named them Brigadier Grant and Missus Grant. Of course he expects us to dash him something for the compliment. The schools here are full of Colonels and Majors and Captains aged six or seven. No one finds it absurd.'

At luncheon we met a very pleasant and feminine army nursing-sister. She was a Colonel. I found it absurd.

When we left Accra Mrs. Whistler lent me a book. 'You can return it on your way through in a fortnight's time,' she said. It was a beautiful and very special volume, and it had something in common with the hat I had borrowed in Salisbury – the hat with a touch of magic – for this book, as I discovered later, had also been borrowed three deep, and it too had magic. It was Mary H. Kingsley's 'Travels in West Africa' first published in 1897.

This remarkable Victorian explorer had made several African expeditions. She was a niece of Charles Kingsley, and her pen was as lively as that famous writer's, if not as literary. She was one of those individuals who do not really belong to the era to which they are born. She belonged not to her time but to ours – to the mid-twentieth century when adventurous women are no rarity. In her day the West Coast was an unheard of place for a White woman, but Mary Kingsley didn't care. She took the dangers of fevers, fetish, cannibals and 'old Coasters' all in her stride, and on her return she never stopped fighting to interest the British Government in the potentialities of West Africa. She was on her way to West Africa once again when the Boer War broke out, and she died in Simon's Town, where she had been nursing wounded soldiers – Boer soldiers.

335

Mary Kingsley was afraid of nothing. Not even of speaking her mind. In her brief contemporary history of West Africa she pointed out that in the middle of the nineteenth century France was actively expanding her African interests, having realized the unlimited potentialities of this great new raw material market, while '. . . England's home Government was suffering from "healthy colony" on the brain which blinded her, for the time being, to the importance of markets; so great regions of feeding grounds for our home-staying population, both away in the Far East and in West Africa, today belong to other people'.

One of these 'great feeding grounds' belonging to other people is French Senegal, and, when we rejoined the *Bermuda* at Takoradi, we set course northwards for Dakar and a week's official visit to our French neighbours on the outside edge of the West African bulge.

CHAPTER TWENTY-SIX

SLAVE COAST. 'AFRICA FOR THE APE!'

WE were a week at Dakar resuming the ties of the Anglo-French *vieux ménage* as we had done in Madagascar in the Indian Ocean.

We stayed with the Consul General and his wife, Mr. and Mrs. Donald Cameron, in their cool Spanish-style house looking out to sea. Donald Cameron was an accomplished linguist and could conduct a conversation in French, German, Italian, Spanish, Roumanian and Chinese. And Lily, his wife, could speak at least three of these fluently, for she had been brought up in the cosmopolitan atmosphere of Shanghai. They had recently come from Madrid, where they had fallen in love with Spain, and they had bought a Spanish farm. Their fifteen-year-old son was at school in England.

In Dakar we remarked, as Mary Kingsley had done seventy years ago, that France attached considerable importance to her West African trade. The beautiful and sophisticated modern city of Dakar is the capital of French West Africa* and the chief port of Senegal. Strategically it is well placed on the direct air and sea route between Africa and America, and being fairly far north of the Equator, it is much cooler than Britain's West African possessions. Some thirty-thousand so-called Europeans lived in Dakar alone, as compared with seven thousand in the whole of the Gold Coast. And most of the thirty-thousand were restive in face of Britain's example in granting self-government to the people of the Gold Coast, who are still more than ninety per cent illiterate. After all, African Nationalism was a catching

* *French West Africa now independent Senegal.*

disease and might well spread to the vast 'feeding grounds and markets' which, in French opinion, were not destined to be more than French provinces. In her own way France was as irritated by Britain's liberal policy in Africa as Dr. Malan was in his. The *vieux ménage* on this point did not see eye to eye.

Dakar's western skyscrapers rise above exotic features. The Natives are Negroid or of Moorish origin, and tall Moslem Senegalese stride about the streets in a variety of picturesque garments, while the women wear flimsy saris or printed flounced cottons. Many of the married women flaunt two little black wool plaits under their head-gear, curving out and up like a pair of dainty black horns, which lends them an air at once bovine and diabolical. Everybody rides about in decorative little horse-drawn sledges, and overhead the vultures and sea-hawks circle, thick as flies, drawn by the magnetism of the abattoir near the big Native Market.

Dakar is an important naval base, and we were able to renew our war-time friendship with Admiral Georges Gayral, who was in command, and his English wife, Sylvia. Georges had been with the Fighting French Forces at Portsmouth in 1942 when my husband had been Captain of Whale Island, the Naval Gunnery School. Sylvia's spiritual home was Paris, and she had recently arrived in Dakar from that lovely city, bringing with her Mustapha her Afghan Hound. 'I cried all the way here from Le Bourget,' she said, 'because poor Mustapha was forced to travel in a basket much too small for him. When they took him out here – so cramped! – Georges cried too.'

Mustapha cast her a tender glance. His narrow biscuit-coloured head was crested with a soft feather top-knot to match the upswept plume of his tail, and his bearing was so evidently regal that it was no wonder his mistress believed him to be a reincarnated Sultan.

The official entertaining, both ashore and on board the *Bermuda,* was intense, and I was struck by the fashionable elegance of the French women, and also by the fact that those Africans we met socially were always cultured and well-mannered. This is not necessarily the case in a British Dependency. For example, at a cocktail reception in the *Bermuda* at a certain West African port the behaviour of some of our African visitors was astonishing. The list of guests is compiled by the local authorities, and in this instance, it was swelled by the presence of a number of uninvited small children, who accompanied their parents, and the large retinues of one or two Chiefs. It was customary for the stewards to offer trays of glasses containing a tot of whisky or gin, with soda and water served separately. Various gentlemen ignored the soda and water and simply poured all the tots into one glass which they tossed off neat, much to the confusion of the steward. Ye! Ye!! The Captain, always on the alert, issued an immediate order that drinks be offered ready diluted. But he had no quick solution for the monkey-tricks of some of the ladies, who were happily popping sausages down their bodices as well as their necks, and tucking their empty cocktail glasses into handbags already bursting with what food they could find. The wardroom mess 'lost' ninety glasses in that one evening. The French believe that there should be no colour-bar, but their conviction is a perfectly genuine attitude of mind, realistic and not sentimental. They demand the same reasonable social conduct from a Black guest as from a European. In either case, if the person in question does not measure up to the conventional standard required in polite society, he will not be invited to social functions where his ignorance will place him at a disadvantage and embarrass his hosts.

Across the harbour is the rose-coloured Isle of Goreé, once a most desirable slaving-base, which in the bad old cut-throat days changed hands time and again as one European nation and then another gained ascendancy in that lucrative trade. For Goreé had the great advantage of being in a healthy zone with the shortest and coolest sea-passage to America. Moreover, the islet made an impregnable prison for slaves awaiting transport.

We went across to the island with Georges and Sylvia in Bertie's barge. The dazzling sea beating upon its high cliffs formed a magic circle encompassing the past. The twin forts of Orange and Nassau dominated the small landing stage where several fishermen were examining an astonishing fish whose head was bigger than its belly.

'Nassau is a prison now,' said Sylvia. 'Come along Mustapha, hurry up, there's a sweet boy.'

The reincarnated Sultan scrambled out of the barge and strolled with us through the streets of this ancient and exquisite setting for drama and bloodshed. The ruined houses were faded cobalt or rose, with weathered tiles, little Moorish balconies, and storm lamps on wrought-iron brackets leaned from crumbling walls over narrow winding alleys. In the shady rustic Square an ancient tailor in a white robe and turban hemmed flounces for the stately women who dwelt in this atmosphere of bygone days. The gnarled, bleached baobab trees were in young leaf, wearing their tiny green shoots like monstrous dowagers in bikinis. Swallows darted in and out of the eaves of a nineteenth century Cathedral, and, in the open space in front of it, brown barefoot boys kicked a football without much enthusiasm.

Georges took us over the house on the cliffs where he soon hoped to be installed. It was next door to *la Maison des Esclaves*, where once the slaves awaiting transportation had been incarcerated.

'You'll be haunted,' I said.

'I daresay,' agreed Sylvia equably. 'Ghosts love me. I'm psychic.'

She did not seem to care. She was in love with Gorée – with its island spell distilled from sun, sea and solitude. 'Here I will get away from the chit-chat of Dakar,' she said. 'I'll have my piano, my singing and my painting for company. And on weekends Georges can fish.'

We went into the palm court of the cloistered naval convalescent hospital and sat for a while in the cool green silence. The French naval doctor lived on the island, and it was only recently that a telephone system had been arranged. Before that, a gun on the mainland had been fired to summon him. If it was for a confinement of the 'Ye! Ye!!' variety, his patient no doubt beat the gun.

There were no vehicles in Gorée, so it seemed hushed, as in a dream, and I thought of the Chinese island of Wei-Hai-Wei opposite the blue Shantung Mountains. There too no traffic was permitted, save the rickshaw; and the long summer days were full of this same dream-silence broken only by the soft pad-pad of the rickshaw coolies' feet and the fall of acacia petals or a pomegranate flower. On the eaves of the little temples sacred animals and gargoyles had gazed down at the grey-robed Chinamen and naval officers in tropical whites – and out in the bay had been the warships. They are there no longer. For in the Far East Britain's influence has dwindled sadly. In Malaya she still struggles on, as the other partner in the *vieux ménage* struggles on in Indo-China. Far and wide new world forces are rising and the scene is changing, as it had changed so often here in the Isle of Gorée – as it might change again.

Georges said: 'When there was an English occupation here, the Governor was a hasty and hot-blooded fellow. One day, in a fit of rage, he killed a soldier. Twelve years later he returned to England. All that time his conscience had troubled him greatly, till at last he voluntarily confessed his crime. He must have been profoundly shocked when he was hanged for it. In France it would have been considered a *crime passionnel*, and the years of remorse and the act of confession would all have weighed in his favour. But your British justice is a cold affair!'

His cherubic features widened into laughter.

Sylvia smiled. 'Which only goes to show. Confession – outside the confessional – is a dangerous form of self-indulgence!'

'How much the stones of this island could tell us – if they had the power of speech!' I said. 'So much history and tragedy has been compressed into this little island. And now it is so at peace – all passion spent. . . .'

'Aren't you crazy about it?' said Sylvia. 'Anyone would

fall for Gorée. *No*, Mustapha! Leave that cat alone! Come here angel.'

The cat was small, but it was spitting and quite ready for a boxing match. The Sultan returned obediently to his mistress.

I agreed that Gorée was a gem. 'It induces thought and stimulates the imagination.'

Yet, for all its strange forgotten-of-the-world enchantment, I found my heart turning towards our own sea-garden with the Simon's Berg towering behind Admiralty House, and Flora gazing out across False Bay, and the baboons careering down the kloof to steal our potatoes, and all the little birds setting the trees aquiver.

'One gets so fond of places,' I said a little sadly. 'It's silly.'

'Yes,' said Sylvia. 'I could get very fond of Gorée. But I couldn't be happy very long away from Paris.'

One day we made an excursion with the Gayrals to Bathurst in the Gambia, where we were to lunch with the Governor, Mr. P. Wyn-Harris. We flew in a French naval aircraft, a Junkers 52, and Tony, and Colonel R. Houghton of the Royal Marines, my husband's intelligence officer, made up our party.

The Gambia* is a narrow British wedge up the river of that name between French Senegal and the Portuguese and French Guinea Coast. It was also the scene of the Colonial Development Corporation's ill-fated Gambia Egg Scheme. We flew over the grandiose deserted hen-coops, the empty, air-conditioned houses and shops, and thousands of acres of expensively cleared ground on which the necessary amount of chicken feed had refused to grow. The American

* *The Gambia and French Guinea now independent. Portuguese Guinea, now called Guinea-Bissau, is considered by Portugal to be part of Portugal itself, a 'multiracial unitary state made up of territories which, although geographically separated from one another, enjoy full judicial equality in terms of the Portuguese political constitution.' (Quoted from the Portuguese Ambassador's note to the U.N. chief in February, 1973.)*

Manager called in to launch the scheme had evidently regarded a pilot-plan as not worth while, so, like the disastrous ground-nut plan for East Africa, Gambia Eggs had left a rotten taste in the mouth of the British tax-payer.

Bathurst is a modest little town set in tropical gardens at the mouth of the great river. Unfortunately miles of beautiful foreshore cannot be enjoyed by the living because they are already occupied by the dead. The Moslem cemeteries straggle along the grassy cliffs between the sea and the palm plantations. The humid heat, after the fresh breezes of Dakar, was most oppressive. Government House, set in a superb park, was old, rambling and full of character. On the verandah, outside the main reception room, was an aviary of vivid birds of the parrot family.

Mr. Wyn-Harris is a famous mountaineer who has already conquered many of the snow-capped peaks of Everest. Yet, there he was, in the hot flat tropics without so much as a *koppie* in sight! However, if he regarded his Gambia appointment as a mountaineer's pennance, he gave no sign of it. In fact he clearly enjoyed it, and, if for the time being, the challenge of the heights was for others, the steamy Gambia River yielded him a rich harvest of interest and pleasure. His favourite recreation was to travel up-river in his launch with his family and a few friends. Unfortunately we did not have time to accompany him on such an expedition, and we did not meet Mrs. Wyn-Harris as she was in England with the children.

The Governor was stocky, grizzled and immensely energetic. One felt that neither heat nor cold could knock him out. With the failure of the Egg Scheme – which had been initiated before his time – he had determined to find some second crop in addition to Gambia's main export of ground-nuts, and he was trying to persuade the Natives to clear the mangrove swamps and plant rice.

'But one of our greatest pests is the dog-faced baboon,' he said. 'They are dangerous and destructive and ruin the crops. We are waging total war on them, and are offering two shillings a tail to the Natives. Not long ago I went up river with

343

my wife and children, and when we wanted to go ashore it was impossible. The baboons were lined up along the bank like soldiers, and very ugly and threatening they looked!'

I could well imagine it. Even our civilized Simon's Town baboon troop, dwelling in the kloof above the port, have been known to turn nasty, and their country cousins might easily be even more offensive. Yet, to be fair, one must look at the situation from the ape's angle. The Gambia baboons were, after all, the indigenous population of the area, and they saw no good reason why White men should come chugging up their river to develop their country. 'Africa for the Ape' was their slogan, and if they had cleared no mangrove swamps, and planted no crops, but had, on the contrary, stolen the eggs from under the fat foolish hens whose clucking had resounded all the way from the Gambia to the Thames at Westminister, that was their business. The Gambia was their country, and all they asked was that the European should get out and leave them to run it for themselves in their own way. They particularly resented the fact that he was up to his old tricks again – fomenting internecine strife for his own profit. In past centuries the White trader had come with gin and guns to induce the Native chiefs and headmen to sell their little brothers and sisters down the river – and the chiefs and headmen had needed small persuasion. Now, once again, they were at it, but this time they were not bartering for living 'black ivory', they were paying the fabulous sum of two shillings for a poor dead baboon's tail! No wonder the warriors of the hairy tribe awaited Wyn-Harris on the banks with menace in their deep-set eyes and murder in their hearts!

But the Governor was not interested in the ape-angle.

'Already over thirty-thousand tails – some very decomposed – have been handed into District Officers,' he said, and about twelve thousand monkey tails. If we are to preserve the crops we must get rid of the baboons. Of course, it's a continuous war.' His eyes twinkled. 'We share a very long border with the French, and French baboons come crashing in – but, on the other hand, I'm told that British baboons are taking out French papers.'

This brisk lively man told us many amusing stories of his predecessors in the Gambia.

'They were always sent here with considerable pomp and splendour. In fact, the tradition still exists. But one early Governor, rather overwhelmed at the wonderful suite he was given on his outward-bound passage, said to someone at the Colonial Office, "This is all very magnificent, but will I be treated equally well on the return trip?" The official looked nonplussed. "The return trip?" he said. "Ah well, my dear Governor, let us consider that when the time comes." It wasn't often that the time came. With yellow fever, malaria, blackwater and a few other things, a Governor was expected to last about nine months.'

Of course a few stalwarts put up records, like Governor MacCarthy, who was for many years Governor of Sierra Leone and the Gold Coast Colony. He was killed in the Ashanti War of 1824 at the Battle of Assamako, and legend has it that the Ashanti made powerful *ju-ju* out of his head and used his skull as a drinking cup. But, the Golden Stool (or throne) of Ashanti still owes its strongest magic to this gruesome relic of a brave Irish warrior, no European eyes have ever beheld it. The whereabouts of the skull of Mac-Carthy is as much a mystery as it was a century ago.

On our last night in Dakar we dined with the *Haut Commissaire*, Monsieur Cornut-Gentille, in his Palace, which was like a Greek temple on the edge of a flowering cliff. He was a serious handsome man, surprisingly young for so important a post, to which he had recently come from French Equatorial Africa. He worked himself and his staff extremely hard, devoted as little time as possible to social occasions, and observed a strict *régime*. I noticed that he neither ate nor drank at the excellent banquet offered to his guests. Like the Governor of the Gambia, he too was enduring a plague. Not baboons but cats. His vast palace was infested with cats, and he hated cats.

345

'I will have to shoot them,' he said with distaste.

'Then you may be infested with rats,' I suggested.

He looked at me wearily. 'At present there are three cats to every rat.'

The life and soul of the party was the African Aide-de-Camp, a tall young dandy in uniform with gold-rimmed spectacles and a passion for Paris, French art and the theatre. On my left at dinner was the African Mayor of Dakar, a man of culture, well-known in Paris as a politician, for he had served some years in the Legislative Assembly. His wife was dressed by a famous Paris *couturière*, and could talk well on any subject. She was much in favour of the emancipation and education of African women.

'But one must begin in a practical way,' she said. 'There are courses at Dakar University which include lectures on domestic science, child welfare, physical culture, social etiquette and civic responsibility. These things are of more value to them than mathematics and Latin. The *evolué* must be able to marry a woman who will be a companion to him. In Africa the women are still very backward. If they are to take their place in the new scheme of things they must be educated. But, at this stage, emphasis must be laid on the social side. The academic education will come with the next generation.'

I was in complete agreement with her.

We left Dakar in the early afternoon. The Consul-General and Mrs. Cameron, who had lunched on board, seemed tiny and forlorn on the quay as we drew away. The Marine band played under the long barrels of the guns, and sailors and Marines manned the quarterdeck, and, as we passed the breakwater, a French Naval band played the *Bermuda* out of the harbour.

'We do that in Malta,' said Bertie. 'How like Georges Gayral to remember and think of doing it for us here!'

Out in their launch, near the rosy Isle of Gorée, Georges and Sylvia tossed on the sapphire sea and waved us good-

346

bye. I saw the blonde top-knot of Mustapha wind-blown in the sun.

I felt very sad. The day after tomorrow we would be in Sierra Leone, and that, for me, would be the end of sailing in the *Bermuda*. Yet how lucky I had been to enter the little world of a warship at sea and learn from it something of the kindliness and tolerance peculiar to the Royal Navy!

As if to stamp itself forever upon my memory, that last day on board was a day apart. The sea was a strange apricot pink, more like stretched silk than water, losing itself in the shell pink haze of the horizon. In the 'dog watches', between four and six o'clock, officers in white shorts, many of them with bare sunburned torsos, came up on to the quarter-deck, where they strolled about, or sat on the wooden gratings, reading, or talking idly.

My volume of Mary Kingsley lay open on my lap, but I was not inclined to read. So haunting was the beauty of this last evening that I wanted only to absorb it.

Sometimes a thread was drawn in the taut fabric of the sea by little birds swooping, landing, skimming and taking off again, leaving, as they did so, a thin Jacob's ladder in their wake. Once Bertie pointed out the dark dorsal fin of a hunting shark and the sinister submerged silhouette. 'He's after that shoal over there!' Not far off, the water boiled suddenly with racing fish, and above them hovered a white canopy of gulls. From time to time a gleaming school of porpoises tore the smooth silken sea with their leaping and diving, and we heard the slapping sound of their belly-flops, and the kittenish inoffensive mewing of our host of following birds.

A Lieutenant-Commander, who had been stitching at a gros-point fire-screen, rose and carefully folded his canvas with the many-coloured wools. A companion asked him how it was getting on, and he smiled and replied that it was nearly done. Nobody seemed to think it odd that he should sit on the capstan grating and work at his embroidery. They leave each other alone, I thought, they respect each other's hobbies and relaxations. Tony Harris, oblivious of all about him, was deep in his tome on Army Law. He would leave us after the Sierra Leone visit and sail in the *Bermuda* to St. Helena and back to Simon's Town. His examination papers had already arrived and he was to write his promotion exam on board while we flew back to the Cape, breaking our journey at Abidjan and Accra. The long grey barrels of the guns were trained aft, their aggressive mouths muzzled by the ship's crest – a rather absurd nautical lion who looked more like an owl or a koala-bear.

I wanted to remember these things, and many others. Divisions in the mornings, the sound of footsteps at the double – sailors' sandals, flapping like schoolboys', the noisy clopping of Royal Marine boots, the quick shuffle of men taking position and distance from one another, and strong voices raised in a hymn to the accompaniment of the Band. The Band. I could not help smiling. At every West African port we had entered, it had struck up vigorously with the martial strains of 'Rule Britannia' – *Rule Britannia! Britannia rules the waves! Britons never, never, never shall be slaves* . . . The irony of it, all up and down the Slave Coast! Receptions on board the quarterdeck gay with bunting and fairy lights, the white uniforms of the hosts among the guests – such odd guests sometimes, and always such good hosts. Yet few of these young officers had been brought up to the social side of 'showing the flag', most of them had been trained in the bitter days of war when the decks had been stripped for action and no quaint lion had decorated the roaring mouths of the guns. My husband had said, in one of his many addresses, that a warship was the only vehicle of war open to attack from the air, the surface of the sea, and under the sea, and that it was also unique in being the living quarters of its fighting personnel. There was no 'behind the lines' in a fighting ship, no safe place. In action every man shared the same danger, from the Captain to the cook. On this coast alone the Navy had hunted pirates and engaged the enemy for hundreds of years. What of the future. . . .

'There's been a casualty.' The Captain, spruce and

brusque as usual, was speaking to me. His eyes were laughing in spite of his words.

'A casualty?'

'One of the civet-cats.'

'Good.'

I did not like the civets. They had joined the *Bermuda* at Takoradi. An 'old coaster' had brought them on board and left them with the sailor in charge of hats. 'For the Captain,' he had announced, putting a cardboard hat-box on the trestle-table. Inside it were two crawling baby civet-cats and one half-chewed banana.

'They'll devour every rat in the ship,' he promised the Captain. 'Just you wait!'

They began by almost devouring Blackie, the legitimate ship's cat. She had just produced kittens outside the Captain's quarters, and the two young civets were put with the family. They immediately abandoned their bruised banana in favour of the milk-bar so unexpectedly placed at their disposal, and poor Blackie found herself being brutally suckled by the savage baby civets who elbowed her own kittens rudely out of the way. They were dun-coloured, with rat tails and beady selfish eyes, and the silky little black mother with the big surprised agate orbs grew thinner and thinner under the perpetual greedy attacks of the two African cuckoos in her nest. Yet she never protested. She took the insufferable wretches to her bosom in every sense of the word.

'Didn't your steward move Blackie and her family – civets included – to the capstan engine flat yesterday?' I asked.

'Hence the casualty,' said the Captain. 'Blackie preferred her luxury apartment in my quarters and decided to move straight back. She made five journeys to carry her three kittens and the two civets back again. Evidently the second civet was too heavy for her, and she dropped it and broke its neck.'

That evening we saw the film, Miranda, in the hangar. We teased the Captain, an inveterate fisherman, and warned him that if he wasn't careful the lovely mermaid, Miranda, would get him and take him to her ocean cave.

'I needn't worry, like some of you,' he said crisply, with a glance at the tall handsome Surgeon Commander. 'I'm one of the little ones she'd throw back.'

After the film, Bertie and I remained a while on deck in the calm tropical night. We were reluctant to go below where the heat would enfold us in its moist embrace.

'The West Coast – all West Africa – has been a great experience so far,' I said, 'just as you told me it would be.'

Bertie agreed. 'It has something the Congo and many other parts of Africa lack – a very old, adventurous and dramatic history.'

'I'll never forget any of it,' I said rashly. 'And I'll never forget *this* either. I'll be grateful for *this* part of it always.'

The wake of the *Bermuda* was shot with phosphorus and moonlight, the thin strands of wire between us and the sea were almost invisible, the white mess jackets of those few officers still on deck were light patches in the heavy shadow of the gun turret, their low voices carried to us companionably.

An old sad memory stirred in me.

'The last time I saw Freetown was in the war – on my way home to South Africa in 1943. It must have been somewhere not very far from here that our ships passed in the night. Do you remember? You were in the *Warspite* on your way to so much danger, and I was in that little merchantman torpedoed on her next voyage ... We missed each other in Freetown by hours—'

He said, 'It was one of those heart-breaking things. I had thought – hoped – that we might have seen each other there.'

The peace of the night was so perfect that it almost seemed as if Fate wanted to wipe the slate clear of even this small aching recollection of the anxious years when Fear was my familiar.

CHAPTER TWENTY-SEVEN

CARGOES OF CHIMPS AND PARAKEETS

WE saw the jungle-clad mountains of Sierra Leone in the dawn. The rising sun was a veiled red disc, half hidden in the sultry *harmattan* haze – early this year – while the steamy clouds above the lion peaks were lined with unearthly gold. Dark figures in dug-out canoes paddled towards the ship; and the port, meandering between the folded hills, borrowed enchantment from the width of silken pink water between it and the *Bermuda*.

Freetown was originally founded as a home for freed slaves, and it is the descendants of these freed Africans, re-imported from Britain and the New World, or rescued from slave-ships captured by the Royal Navy, who regard themselves as the *élite*. Their White blood is evident in their lighter skins and their educated outlook, and most of the professional classes are drawn from his Creole minority. They look down upon the pure-bred Africans, and the Africans resent this attitude. Only the British love everybody. The word Creole, as applied in Africa and certain islands off her coast, must not be confused with the Creole of the American deep south, where no Colour stigma is attached and family tradition still holds dominion.

Many things have altered in West Africa since the days of that adventurous Victorian, Mary Kingsley, but I could not help being amused to find that her description of the populace of Freetown was as apt today as it had been when she stepped ashore from S.S. *Batanga*'s boat in January 1895, nearly sixty years earlier. She wrote:

351

'It is the costume of the people in Freetown and its harbour that will first attract the attention of the new-comer, notwithstanding that the noise, the smell, and the heat are simultaneously making desperate bids for that favour! The ordinary man in the street wears anything he may have been able to acquire ... such as an umbrella with the stick and the ribs removed, or a shirt. This last-mentioned treasure, which usually becomes the property of the ordinary man from a female relative or admirer taking in White men's washing, is always worn flowing free, and has such a charm in itself that the happy pos-sessor cares little what he continues his costume with – trousers, loin cloth, red flannel petticoat, or rice bag drawers, being, as he would put it, "all same for one" to him ...

'The ladies are almost as varied in their costume as the gentlemen, but always neater and cleaner; and mighty pic-turesque they are too, and occasionally very pretty. A market-woman with her jolly brown face and laughing brown eyes – eyes all the softer for a touch of antimony – her ample form clothed in a lively print overall, made with a yoke at the shoulders and a full long flounce which is gathered on to the yoke under the arms and falls fully to the feet; with her head done up in a yellow and red handkerchief, and her snowy white teeth gleaming through her vast smile, is a mighty pleasant thing to see, and to talk to. But Allah! the circumference of them!'

Agreed, Mary Kingsley! But I must add that the children are also worthy of attention for their white teeth and vast smiles. But their costume is less striking, for it seldom exists. A fortunate few possessors of that shirt which has 'so much charm in itself' do not bother to 'continue their costume' at all, not even with 'rice bag drawers'.

We were to spend a week with the Governor and Lady Beresford-Stooke in their delightful Government House two thousand feet above the town, and, as the car sent to fetch us sped through cobbled streets and alleys and wound up into

352

the hills, we caught intriguing suggestions of the pattern of life in Freetown. On a wall was white-washed in enormous letters 'BUY VIMTO. VIMTO KEEPS EXPECTANT MOTHERS FAT ALWAYS.' From what Mary Kingsley and I had observed, nature could be relied upon for that. But perhaps in a land where a man evidently buys his woman by the ton a little Vimto to keep her fat and fit is all to the good. Then there was a delightful hoarding covered with a picture of a gay Negro riding a glittering Raleigh bicycle with a raging lion in hot pursuit. Inset is a smaller picture of the lion falling back exhausted while the Raleigh rider continues triumphant on his way. Many innocuous British home remedies are endowed with curiously potent qualities by African advertisers, and it is quite common for an African servant to come and ask his mistress to give him a dose of Sloan's Liniment to take internally!

Bertie pointed to a tumble-down gate. 'There's a notice to interest you.'

'MANSARY. DEALER IN WILD ANIMALS AND SNAKES', it read.

Road signs carried fascinating names, such as 'King Jimmy Pier', 'King Tom Pier', 'Pirate Bay', 'Kru Bay', or 'Kissy Harbour'. Each name held its bit of history, as did the names of the Creole mountain villages, of Waterloo, Wellington, Regent or Wilberforce.

Government House was an attractive rather old-fashioned house set in a lovely garden, and from our bedroom window we could see down through the trees to the bay where the *Bermuda* lay. We discovered that Sir George Beresford-Stooke and his wife both knew the Union well, and that, in 1939, they had cycled from Cape Town to Port Elizabeth along the Garden Route.

'It took us about three weeks,' said Lady Beresford-Stooke. 'We carried a satchel each with a change of clothes, and for the rest we bought food and found lodgings as we went along. Often we stayed a night at a Boer farmhouse, and we met only kindness and hospitality.'

They were both enthusiastic walkers and cyclists, and

they seemed impervious to the heat. There was hardly a jungle track or cove in Sierra Leone unknown to them. Lady Beresford-Stooke wore her fair hair short as a boy's, and she was never happier than when she was in the open. Their children, Peter and Cara, were flying out to West Africa for the holidays, and the whole family planned to spend Christmas camping out. Sir George's ability and sincerity had endeared him to the very mixed population of the Colony and Protectorate. But he admitted frankly that the authority of a Colonial Governor in Africa has been whittled down to the minimum. Today a Governor in West Africa needs to be a diplomat who can persuade his Legislative council to give *him* the advice *he* would like to give to *them*. Perhaps this is not surprising when one considers the proportion of Black to White. In Sierra Leone there are over nineteen hundred Blacks to one White, in the Gold Coast a thousand to one, in Nigeria about two thousand to one. Whereas, in the Union of South Africa, that proportion is only four to one.* A very different matter.

In Sierra Leone the effect of education is being felt, and a race of clerks is growing up instead of the much-needed agricultural workers.

'What is the answer?' I asked the Governor.

He adjusted the eye-glass which he always wears. We were sitting on the verandah after playing tennis, sipping iced lemon and barley.

'Agriculture must be mechanized. Make it easier and better paid, and evolve a class of technicians and mechanics.'

He was very enthusiastic about developing the economic resources of the interior, and training the various headmen of the Districts to establish their councils and think for themselves. He encouraged a spirit of healthy competition. Like Nigeria, Sierra Leone was growing gradually from local and provincial government towards central government. The Gold Coast had jumped this intermediate stage – with what results remain to be seen. When the Colonial Sec-

* *Now six to one, an ever-increasing gap.*

retary, Mr. Lyttleton, said that 'the surest way of putting the clock back is to put it forward too quickly,' he knew what he was talking about.

In the evening there was a Cocktail reception at Government House at which we met many distinguished Creoles and Africans. I was introduced to a Creole doctor, who was also an historian, and he offered to take me round Freetown next morning. I accepted eagerly.

What an interesting tour it was!

We visited the hospital; and the cathedral, crowned with birds of prey; the shopping centre with its inevitable Kingsway Store; the harbour and the new deep-water dock in process of construction, and the residential areas. In some parts of the town we saw the mansions of Freetown's *nouveaux riches* side by side with the mud huts of Yorubas from Nigeria.

'There are people who live in some of those houses who have money but no manners,' said the Doctor. 'The house is a whited sepulchre. Inside they eat and sleep on the floor as though they still lived in a mud hut. It takes three generations to make a gentleman.'

Splendid new storehouses were being built by the Syrian traders who, in West Africa, are as great a commercial force as the Indians on the east Coast.

The Doctor took me to the historic fortress-castle that was being converted into a new Government House. It was well placed upon its promontory above the sea, but surely the spirit of old battles would still clash here, and the echo of old debaucheries linger among the grey phantoms of degradation and despair.

'Now we will go and see the archivist,' said the Doctor.

In the cool office-library in the prefabricated Government buildings we were shown old documents relating to the growth of the settlement. What a grim story it was!

Like so many idealistic schemes it was badly put into operation.

The unlucky forbears of the oldest Creole families had

355

sailed from Portsmouth, England, in 1787. Out of three hundred and fifty Negroes and sixty White women, eighty-four had died of sickness on the voyage and two hundred had arrived more dead than alive. It was the rainy season and no preparations had been made for the reception of these hapless settlers. Nevertheless, they set to and built huts in this pitiless 'land of freedom', so much worse than anything they had yet endured. The ships of the expedition sailed home leaving two hundred and seventy-six settlers to their fate. In time, the Sierra Leone Company was formed to develop this wretched colony and an Agent General, Alexander Falconbridge, was appointed in charge. Falconbridge, who had been a surgeon on board slave ships must have been a robust and determined character moreover he was blessed with a brave wife who accompanied him into what must have been hell on earth at that time. She wrote many letters describing her voyages and adventures and the new colony. In one of these she says:

'It was surely a premature, hair-brained and ill-digested scheme to think of sending such a number of people all at once to a rude, barbarous, and unhealthy country before they were certain of possessing one acre of land, and I very much fear will terminate in disappointment, if not disgrace to the authors, though at the same time I am persuaded the motives sprung from minds unsullied with evil meaning.'

But, with that super-human capacity for survival which seems to characterize the most improbable settlements, the colony grew. The settlers were augmented by shiploads of Africans from Nova Scotia who had fought in the American War of Independence, by Maroons – slaves who had fled from Jamaica – and liberated Africans from slave ships captured in hundreds by the indefatigable Royal Navy. Then a new plan was introduced for absorbing still more settlers. The newcomers were 'apprenticed' to the inhabitants and received their keep in return for their work.

And there you were – back where you started from in the good old African way! The masters of the new 'apprentices' understood this sort of thing perfectly, and immediately and frankly called their assistants 'slaves'. So the beautiful notions derived from 'minds unsullied with evil meaning' degenerated into time-honoured custom, and one slavery was exchanged for another, even less desirable.

It was not till the time of Governor MacCarthy – that interesting Irishman who left his head for *ju-ju* in Ashanti – that 'apprenticeship' was stopped.

'Is there anything else you want to see?' asked the Doctor.

'Well, yes,' I admitted. 'But it's an anti-climax.'

He mopped his brow. Outside the archivist's office the heat waited to devour us. I drew a Freetown newspaper cutting from my handbag.

'I'd like to know more about this.'

The Doctor read the advertisement without enthusiasm. It was clear that the subject did not appeal to him. It was taken from that morning's *Sierra Leone's Daily Mail,* and was dated December 1st, 1951.

> ### SONGO WILD ANIMAL FARM
> ### THE LARGEST IN WEST AFRICA
> is now ready to purchase Every
> Living Thing that crawls, flies
> or swims
> Highest prices are paid for
> Chimpanzees, Rare Birds, Parrots
> and Reptiles.
> For particulars please call . . . etc.

'Well', he said, pondering a while. 'I can take you to a place of the same sort where I know a merchant. Do you want to buy a rare bird, or a monkey – or perhaps a snake?'

'I'd like to see them.'

We drove to a narrow street with an Alice Through the Looking Glass flavour to it. Outside an ironmonger's shop we drew up. The window was full of children's roller skates. On the door was a notice.

'WANTED. Wild Animals, Birds, Reptiles and Venomous Snakes.'

We found a cross-looking Creole merchant behind a counter piled with old tennis shoes waiting to be vulcanized. The inside of the store was a conglomeration of every known and unknown form of ironmongery, old and new.

In response to the Doctor's inquiry, the merchant scratched his thick black thatch. He pouted.

'I thought you were a seller. I have very little at present. Some birds, a few monkeys and iguanas. Now, if you come last week, you seen something, but I just sent a big consignment to America, including two chimpanzees – male and female.'

Alas, poor Cheeta-Cheeta! My heart bled for those chimpanzees!

'Does all your stuff go to America?'

'Yes, they want monkeys for experiments – like monkeys best and chimps better.'

He told us to follow him. We waded through a back room stacked with old inner tubes, motor tyres, shoes and vulcanizing apparatus. We crossed a yard, where some exotic washing hung limply on a clothes line, climbed a winding wooden staircase and emerged on to a roof-top menagerie, where rows of empty cages stood in the sun while the full ones were placed against a low parapet which gave a little shade.

He waved at the new cages. 'I make ready for plenty creatures.'

An appalling stench came from those already occupied. One was bursting with little finches twittering madly as if imploring their liberty. It was the incarnation of imprisoned feathered panic, all flutter and tiny palpitating hearts. Next to it were seedy parrots and parakeets that must once have jewelled the forest like emeralds and rubies embroidered on

358

a royal robe. In a third, a huddle of little grey monkeys too cramped to play, too sad to chatter, stared at us with round soft eyes reflecting a world of hopeless despair. Poor little prisoners awaiting transportation to the New World as once men and women had waited on this cruel coast! Poor little victims destined for the laboratories of men – each one of them a small grey sacrifice to the great God of Science, a tiny Simian drop in the ocean of human knowledge. I turned away from those haunted eyes to a long narrow hutch. Two iguanas gave us a baleful glare. The huge lizards – perhaps four feet long – were not at all resigned to their fate, and, as the merchant tapped on the wooden struts of their front door, they lashed their tails like angry cats, swelled up their throats and let out a long powerful hissing noise.

'He sounds like a punctured tyre!' I said.

'He is not at all punctured,' said the merchant crossly. 'He is angry. He don't like being disturbed.'

As we made our way back to the shop I said: 'That must be quite a dangerous job for you – I mean, when you have a full consignment up there.'

'I am glad you see it that way,' he said in a gratified voice. 'It is dangerous, and hard work too. Taking them water three times a day, and cleaning out the cages – not even a monkey can clean his own cage – and not long ago one bit me. By afternoon my hand was very sore. I went to the hospital and the doctor said I was smart. Infection had begun. I might have died.'

'A King of Greece once died of a monkey bite.'

The Merchant didn't care. He was as cross as his iguanas, and presently I discovered the reason for his annoyance. He had failed to get on board the *Bermuda* the previous afternoon when she had been open to the public. He was indignant with the Navy.

'All afternoon I hang about King Tom Pier in the heat. I have my ticket but I get no chance to show it. And for why? The first people to go on board go round the ship, come off, go straight back. Some go seven times on the same tickets. Tickets should be collected by officers on gangway.'

It did not occur to our merchant that those to blame for his disappointment were, in fact, his own people who had seen fit to abuse the privilege of visiting the flagship.

As we left the shop we heard a loud cry behind us – '*One escapes!*'

Leaping over the yard wall on to the narrow pavement, almost under our feet, came a grey monkey. He looked neither to the right nor to the left, and on his small face was an expression of extreme concern. Unfortunately for others – if not for himself – he landed right under the broad bare soles of a portly dame with a basin of plantains on her head. She lost her balance and screamed, and as her outsize seat struck the pavement, the outsize bananas shot from the basin and bombarded a very lively stark naked boy, who ran so fast that he ran straight into a gentleman wearing a pea-green mammy-cloth and a red tarboosh. The monkey never looked back. Regardless of the havoc he had caused, he continued his headlong flight over the road, up a narrow lane and sideways up a garden wall and into a mango-tree. He was happy in Africa. He had no wish to cross the Atlantic in a slave-ship and contribute to 'experiment'.

I held thumbs for him. Good luck go with you, little chap!

A few weeks later I read in the *Cape Times* about four chimpanzees who were put into a V2 rocket and shot eighty-five miles into space. One died of heat prostration at the time, and the other three survived the experience – for a while.

'The chimpanzees, which were given the code names of Albert 1, 2, 3, and 4, were placed in a pressurized cabin in the rocket, and were the first earthly creatures to leave the earth's atmosphere.'

But chimpanzees love the earth's atmosphere, and the strange importance men attach to record-breaking, is, to a chimpanzee, only heart-breaking. He does not cry for the moon or seek to string the stars round the hairy throat of his mate, for he is indeed a very 'earthly creature' and prefers to remain so.

I thanked the kind Doctor for the interesting tour he had given me and said: 'Then we will see you next on board the *Bermuda* at the reception this evening?'

'I hope so,' he said. But my patients are the trouble. Somehow I must finish them off in time to be there.'

And on this somewhat cryptic note we parted.

On Sunday – our last day in Sierra Leone – five carloads of us went for a picnic. The road led through the mountains covered with lush tropical bush, and past the pink laterite churches and wooden houses of Creole villages among the banana groves and the dark foliage of breadfruit, mango and indigo trees. Naked children danced and waved at us, but many adults were already absorbing the Sunday spirit in palm wine, and by the afternoon they were spread about the roadside in attitudes of deep repose from which nothing would rouse them till Monday's painful dawn.

The Governor was driving his own car. He slowed down at a lovely spot between the mountain and the shore. 'Here we are!' he said. His Native boys, who had gone ahead in a lorry – for this was a well-organized picnic – were waiting to carry our bathing things and books, rugs and cushions. They seized them from us and led us down a bush-track to a beach curved like a golden scimitar. At its hilt was a rocky outcrop, shaded by magnificent trees, and at its distant point was a fishing village among the coco-palms. Under the trees trestle-tables were spread with a cold buffet, soft drinks and beer. Dividing our picnic spot from the fishing village flowed a dark mysterious river. Its crumbling sand-banks were punched with the neat small holes of colonies of land-crabs. The seashore was deserted save for ourselves and what I called 'the shadow picnic'.

This shadow picnic was composed of naked African lads who squatted on some boulders on the river bank. They laughed and joked, and suddenly did handsprings on the sands and chased each other and played leap-frog. They ate the meat of coconuts, drank the milk and flung away the hairy gourds. It was understood that they should remain at a distance till we moved to go home, when they would rush forward, carry the 'chop-boxes' to the lorry, and anything else they could grab, and, for reward, would receive everything left over from our lunch and tea.

After a swim and lunch, the Governor said, 'Everybody does exactly as they like'. He settled himself for slumber, and we all followed suit.

Bertie and I found a corner by the water's edge in the shade of great trees. While he dozed I used the siesta hour to scribble in my diary. That day tropical Africa was as near Paradise as mortal man could wish. The beauty of the scene was wondrous to behold, despite the recumbent forms of weary naval officers surfeited with the hospitality of Freetown and exhausted by the merciless heat on board their ship. The dark shadow picnic, with its curious blend of immobility and erratic activity was an integral part of the picture, and the echo of its gay communal voice was complementary to the outbreaks of monkey-chatter from a little green island not far from the shore. I would have liked to swim to that islet but we had been warned that, as it was beyond the surf-line, there might be danger from sharks or barracouta. The sea in our deeply curved bay was gentle and contented, that lovely afternoon. It purred like a great cat, and its voice was a drowsy accompaniment to small individual notes – the dry crackle of a falling leaf, the whisper of a vagrant breeze in the grasses, the scuttle of a lizard, fluted bird-calls and the occasional fat *plop* of a wedge of sandy bank collapsing into the river. Now and again members of our party plunged into the luke-warm waves, or broke away and strolled along the beach. Everyone enjoyed himself in his own way. It was a day to remember and re-live, for it was indeed a day of peace – as Sunday should be.

There was a most unlikely room in Government House. It was light and airy and furnished only with necessities. There was a cupboard in it, a table and a large, very fine hand-loom. On this loom was a partly finished length of herringbone tweed intended for an overcoat – as fine a quality as ever came out of Bonnie Scotland.

I could not believe my eyes when I was shown this cloth.

'*You* made it!'

The Governor laughed, and Lady Beresford-Stooke said, with a smile:

'He only took it up a year ago.'

'Can you weave too?' I asked her.

She shook her head.

'I am allowed to pass the threads when my husband is setting up the loom.'

'Setting it up must be an intricate business.'

'It's highly mathematical,' said Sir George. 'As exact as a Bach study.'

In fact the pattern for setting up a loom reads like a piece of music. The Governor had many books of patterns which he varied according to his fancy. On the table lay samples of his work – brocades of mercerized cotton, tweed for his wife's country suits, light woollen scarves, and local cotton woven with a design of indigo, clean, primitive and attractive.

'Please do a row or two,' I begged.

He took his place at the loom, rather like a pianist about to perform. And then he began to weave, smoothly and dexterously, feet and hands in perfect co-ordination. I was fascinated to watch the movements – catching the threads in the tenterhooks, drawing them tight, but not too tight, and passing the shuttle swiftly. Gradually the pattern evolved and grew.

For the first time I realized what a tenterhook was – the length of wood holding the threads at tension. To be 'on tenterhooks' – what an apt description for the feeling one has when every nerve of the system is held taut and expectant, but not yet at breaking-point!

Well, one man's relaxation is another man's headache. The very notion of setting up a loom with every knot and

363

thread exactly right would horrify me. Yet it was easy to see that the Governor derived genuine mental refreshment from the rhythm and monotony of this work. His fine hands accomplished their craftsman's task in time to some inner musical sequence, exact and emotionless. After the turbulent and often senseless emotionalism of African politics and reactions, this quiet occupation must form an ideal outlet for almost daily exasperation. It was even soothing to watch – hypnotic. Perhaps the unequal tension of the human nervous system passed, by the very act of weaving, into the balanced pattern on the loom, perhaps bursts of red and orange anger could fade and level into the neutral colours of a fawn herringbone tweed. I thought of Lieutenant-Commander in the *Bermuda* stitching at his gros-point fire-screen on the quarter-deck and of Bertie, patiently and restfully disbudding carnations in the kloof garden on a summer's evening. To work with the hands rests the mind. The active brain seeks respite in the craftsman's daily task – to saw wood, to lay bricks, to weave.

In the early morning, as the mists dispersed, we saw from our window, the *Bermuda* steaming out to sea on her way to St. Helena. We would see her again in Simon's Town in a fortnight's time. Tony sailed with her.

CHAPTER TWENTY-EIGHT

SPICE AND IVORY COAST

A FEW hours later we left Freetown by Air France. Our destination was Accra, where we were to spend two days with the Governor, Sir Charles Aden-Clarke, but Air France breaks its journey twice – once for lunch at Roberts Field in the Black Republic of Liberia, and then for the night at Abidjan on the French Ivory Coast.*

Colonel Robert Houghton, Royal Marines, accompanied us, while Tony, somewhere out at sea, was immersed in the last minute cramming for the promotion exam he was to write within the next few days.

On the plane was General Missonier and his *métis* (half-caste) Aide. We had already met the General in Dakar, a dashing and vivacious personality.

Below us spread the densely wooded forests of Liberia, which owes its modern progress and prosperity to the activities of an American rubber company. The harbour of Monrovia was built during World War Two by the United States Navy for the export of Liberia's valuable products. A fellow passenger with considerable experience of this African Republic told me that when last he had visited Monrovia he had been accosted in the street by a policeman who demanded to be 'dashed' a small sum. 'Why?' asked the European. 'Because I say so,' replied the Black custodian of the law. The European refused. He was taken to the magistrate's court and fined for obstructing the police. Magistrate and Constable split the fine. 'That's the form in Liberia,' said my informant with a grin.

* *Now independent Ivory Coast.*

365

Once this had been called the Grain Coast, because the pepper grain grew in Liberia. Now rubber is the main export, and iron-ore is being mined.

At Roberts Field we were met by the American Manager of the airport, a young officer lent by the United States Air Force. He was as immaculate as any human being could be in heat that turned a clean shirt into a damp clinging rag, he had beautiful manners and assured us naively that he and his wife felt certain that they would be 'very very happy' in Liberia. They had recently arrived and the 'tour' would not be a long one.

'We have a good house', he said. 'And only a few miles away is the Rubber Plantation with two social clubs, swimming pools, tennis courts and a golf club in the making. They have a hospital and a school with American doctors and teachers. Why, they have seven very, very fine American doctors there! About five hundred Europeans are employed there, and they've made us welcome. If there's time I'd like to take you to my house for a rest after lunch.'

Unfortunately there was no time. We lunched at a table with the French General and his Aide and Robert Houghton, and, since we were on our way to the Ivory Coast, the conversation naturally turned to ivory in the raw.

'*L'éléphant? Mais oui, il y a des éléphants.* If you wish, you shall see some. They are in the marshes where no man may follow them. They rest in the water up to their bellies with troops of *buffles*. If a man walked there he would sink, but it is possible to fly over them. I will ask the pilot.'

As the gallant General went over to the pilot's table, my husband gave me one of his long resigned looks.

'Do you always have to be so *interested*?'

'But I am!'

'You've seen so many elephants – elephants galore all over Africa.'

'But darling, this is different. They are longing to *show* elephants.'

'Show off, you mean. I know French pilots. You've stuck your neck out.'

366

'All our necks,' murmured Robert, with a wry grin. 'I've been shown elephants on this run. It's hair-raising.' On such occasions it was clear that he regarded Air France as Air Chance. And he was a family man with a charming wife and three small children.

The dashing General came back to us, beaming broadly.

'The pilot says, but naturally. *Eléphant* he will show you, *buffles*, and also the *hippopotame.*'

As we got back into the plane Bertie was wearing his look of sullen courage.

At a given moment in the peach-coloured evening light the second officer came into the cabin and invited me to go forward with him. I was to take his place beside the senior pilot.

Between sea and forest lay a stretch of mangrove swamp, intersected by creeks and lakes wherein wallowed the great beasts we sought. As we swooped down giant trees soared up to meet us and waved furious green hands in the fierce wind of our rushing wing-tips; monstrous birds flew in fright from our headlong approach; the paddling herds of buffalo plunged, panic-stricken, through the swamp and the vast nostrils of *l'hippopotame* were trained upon us from the water. I could almost see the love-birds in the branches and the leeches in the mud, and with very little effort I could have counted the ticks on *Buffle's* back.

'*Voyez!*' cried the pilot at last. '*Voyez-vous les quartres bêtes?*'

And there they were, *l'éléphant* and family, moving ponderously through the mire attended by a white cloud of egrets. The pilot had opened his window the better to show me this noble sight, and now he banked so steeply that I nearly fell over him and out on to *l'éléphant's* ears. Again and again we circled and dived and at last headed out to sea. The pilot nodded and smiled, I shouted my thanks and tottered feebly back to my place.

'Did you see them?' I asked Bertie.

'Some buffaloes and a wretched hippopotamus.'

'And those last four elephants?'

'At that speed anything could be an elephant.'

He mopped his streaming brow. We were still flying low and the heat was unbearable.

'Sir!' said Robert Houghton, as we banked before landing at Abidjan. 'There's a guard on the aerodrome. Evidently an official welcome.'

We did not hear my husband's reply as he tried to straighten his crumpled white uniform.

Never in all our African travels had we seen such a dramatic Guard. Le Garde Rouge is the West African version of the Spahis, and each man seemed at least ten feet high in his long full white Turkish trousers, his tall red Moroccan head-dress and long flowing scarlet cloak. A fine fanfare of trumpets greeted us as my husband stepped on to the airstrip and saluted.

The Governor was in Dakar in hospital and his Deputy had come to meet us. The Port Captain and his wife were also there, and a number of officers. The Acting Governor, who was most kind and charming, took it for granted that we would spend the night at the *Résidence*, and he told us that, in the absence of his senior, he was giving a dinner party in our honour.

'How would you wish the ladies to dress?' he asked me.

'How would they wish to dress? What is customary?'

The Port Captain's wife shrugged her shoulders and smiled. It was as I pleased.

The evening dress I had worn the night before lay on top of my suit-case.

'Shall we say evening dress?'

'*Entendue*,' she said. '*Tenue de soirée*. I will tell them.'

We sped through the dusk to an impressive new town growing like a beanstalk above the busy port, here a great French liner lay, illuminated and symbolic of the West against the landward background of dark jungle forests.

The Acting Governor pointed to the building sites.

'Abidjan will soon be as important as Dakar. All this is a true indication of her growth.'

'Is your main export still ivory?' I asked.

'Not any more. There is some, of course, but today our main products are timber, coffee, cocoa and ylang-ylang – but mostly timber.'

Somehow the Garde Rouge, hastily bundled into a lorry at the airport, had succeeded in arriving at the Governor's *Résidence* before us, and there they were, lining the wide stone steps of a modern palace with a splash of exotic splendour.

Within the great open doors of the palace was an impressive arrangement of elephants' tusks. The monster fangs seemed bared at the White intruder, or perhaps at the ageless God of Trade, for down the centuries the elephant people of this land had been sacrificed on the altar of Commerce. This was the Ivory Coast – the birthplace of white ivory, and 'black ivory' too . . .

The vast lofty pillared hall into which we followed our host was decorated with panels of Native life – Native fishermen in dug-out canoes, Natives hunting the elephant, or felling ebony trees (the 'almug' tree of the bible), or following other pursuits of their daily lives. General Missonier and his Aide and Robert Houghton had arrived, but by now even the dashing General's sparkle had swooned a little. The Governor's African Aide was addressing me. His strong white teeth flashed in the midnight of his face.

'You will take a glass of champagne before you retire to your room?'

His uniform scarcely held his powerful frame. He seemed immense, the dominant figure in that palatial salon. He clapped his hands to summon a servant in a white tunic and scarlet sash.

'Champagne!'

He turned to me once more. Had we flown low and seen the elephants? – Indeed, yes. We had almost brushed the egrets from their backs. He said, *'Mais oui, les pilots français sont magnifiques!'*

I wondered if he really regarded himself as a Frenchman.

A waiter poured the champagne with a soft festive hiss. His narrow dark hand with the livid square nails tipped the gold-necked bottle with trained familiarity. So much – a pause for the bubbles to subside – and now a head on it . . .

Up and down, up and down in the high ceiling shadows, between dim lights and whirring electric fans, flew a trapped bat.

When one is very tired the mind is curiously receptive to fanciful impressions, it is easily invaded. Just for a moment that evening, as we stood in the great white palace of a European Governor in the steamy heat of tropical Africa, I had the illusion that past, present and future were all one – that this era of African prosperity and education, this talk of democracy in a land where Chiefs and Sorcerers had held dominion down the centuries, was but a flash between the dark and the dark.

For the swift space of a dream – even as my lips formed the conventional phrases to the tall African sipping his French champagne – I was aware of the remote past when Solomon's ships had sailed south down the East Coast in search of 'almug trees and precious stones' and 'gold, and silver, ivory and apes and peacocks' – and of the fleets of Carthage adventuring down this West Coast and returning home with treasure-trove and gold dust, with Black slaves and 'hairy men and women' whose skins were hung in the Temple of Juno. And that distant time seemed to leap the narrow beam of present light and merge with some dim future wherein the old cruel mysteries would once again prevail and the White man be swept into the sea whence he had come.

The ancient primeval force which ruled in Africa before the days of White infiltration is very close in West Africa. It presses upon the narrow coastal fringe of civilization and surrounds the outposts of the hinterland. It wears the fearsome mask of *ju-ju* and drinks human blood from the skull of a brave White leader. And the eyes behind that mask are the pitiless eyes of a killer.

When one is tired one is fanciful.

I heard Bertie say, 'I think my wife would like a bath and change. Perhaps we should go to our room.'

We went up the great marble staircase between the huge salon and banqueting hall, and the bat-wings brushed nearer as we mounted.

Our bedroom had no fan and no windows, for a bathroom flanked it on one side and a passage on the other. The passage had windows, and from them we could see the liner looking strangely unreal at the bottom of the garden. The bathroom had windows too, and they looked into a park, and beyond it to the forests.

The heat occupied the bedroom like a damp living presence. Opposite a large bed, draped in mosquito curtains, was a macabre modern picture. A voluptuous black nude in an attitude inviting love lay with her head turned away and her face hidden by an ebony arm from the glowing diabolical gaze of a horned lustful satyr leaning over her shoulder out of the shadowed background.

Bertie called out, 'The bath is already filled. That is a sinister sign.'

'Why?' I asked.

'Come and see.' He had turned on the basin tap and from it flowed a mixture of mud, oil and water. 'And I noticed a candle on your dressing-table,' he added. That's another bad sign. I don't trust this whited sepulchre!'

As if to justify his words the lights dimmed three times and went out.

I was hunting in my suitcase for an evening bag, shoes and other necessities, and time was growing short. With every movement one dripped.

An African came in bearing a lamp.

'*Lumière finit,*' he remarked rather obviously.

Was there anything he could do? He could press my dress. But, alas, he could not, for there was no electricity for his iron. The lamp, one of those you pump up, gave a small

371

localized white glare, and a fierce heat. By it I attempted to do my hopelessly damp face.

Down in the marble halls the soft whirring of the fans had ceased, and there was only the winged rush of the tireless bat. A few of the harsh white lamps stood here and there.

Two by two came the guests. '*Enchanté, Madame, bon soir*—' over and over again. Following them were officers and officials whose wives were in France, or who had no wives. On all the women the tropics seemed to have left their mark, either in duskiness or in pallor. In the French colonies the *métisse* is more usual than in the British. In these mixed marriages I have noticed that the man usually marries his dark-skinned wife in Africa where little else is offered him, whereas the woman more often marries a man of Colour in Europe where he evidently exercised the attraction of the exotic.

The dinner was superb, and everybody most charming to us. The lights returned gradually and shakily and the hot lamps were taken away. Somehow the bat found his way into the night once more. The heat, when at length we went to bed, was too great for the mosquito-net to be bearable. It was better to be bitten than to shut out one faint breath of air.

At four in the morning we were wakened with coffee and rolls. We must get ready to go to the aerodrome.

The Acting Governor was waiting for us in the garden when we went downstairs.

'But you must not think of coming to see us off,' we said.

'Of course I will come,' he smiled. 'This is the most beautiful time of the day.'

He was right. It was cool and tender, a pearly light upon water and tree-tops, and, as we drove to the airport, the forests seemed to be standing in pale phantom marshes, the ground-mists of night not yet dispersed.

We bade goodbye to a group of French officers who had obeyed a rigid protocol to do my husband the honour of seeing him off, and once again he saluted the Guard as we

372

stepped on board the plane for Accra in company with a magnificently arrayed crowd of passengers, including a Chief in a gold hat and a small child with a black baby doll so realistic that I took it for a piccaninny till the child dragged it in the dust by the heel, and it uttered no complaint.

The sense of the fantastic and perilous was still with me as we looked our last at the Ivory Coast swathed in its white low-lying mists with the copper and green foilage of its wealth of raw timber touched to gold by the sunrise. To me this was the Ghost Coast – shrouded and mysterious, awaiting the new period of White exploitation. Grim, enticing and incalculable, dark Africa mocked the march of progress. You may hew down my trees, she seemed to say, you may mine my earth, destroy my elephant people, cure my black humans of their fevers, educate their children, erect your buildings and institutions and construct your harbours – but there are things I can do to you that would pass your poor imagination! You have armed your bodies against me with drugs and hypodermics, with hygiene and research, but how will you arm your inmost selves? It is a strong spirit that is able to resist Black Africa!

The phantom swathes writhed and melted below us as the sun rose. At nightfall they would gather again upon the breast of Africa – the souls of the alien dead, chill and formless, clinging forever to that which had destroyed them.

The Gold Coast came clean and bright after the dark forests. There was the white lace of surf frothing up the beaches that themselves seemed fashioned of gold dust, there were the ant-like naked Black men launching their surf-boats to go fishing, there were the fortress-castles – Elmina; Cape Coast upon its green hills; and at last, in time for breakfast, Christiansborg.

CHAPTER TWENTY-NINE

CASTLE IN ACCRA

MUCH of my life has been set in strange and lovely places. But when Fate offered me my glimpse of Christiansborg, it was as if she intended to add one last gem to a wealth of memories which already included such jewels as Peking's Forbidden City, the Golden Horn, walled Katsina and the mediaeval maritime city of Ragusa on the Adriatic.

Christiansborg juts out to sea on the towering cliffs of one of the headlands dividing the long scooped strands. It is as much a part of them as a limpet is part of a rock. It was built in the seventeenth century by the Danes, and was conquered and reconquered many times. It was a fortress, a castle, a storehouse for gold, precious stones, ammunition, liquor and slaves. Once it was captured by an African Chieftain, Asameni, who came to buy flint-lock guns. He had eighty followers with him all secretly armed with bullets, and, in pretending to test the guns, they loaded them and massacred the garrison already decimated by fever. When this wily warrior was at last ejected from the fortress he fled to his home village, taking the great keys of Christiansborg with him – and there they still remain, the symbol of a brief victory, and, like the head of Governor MacCarthy, they form part of some powerful *ju-ju*.

After the Napoleonic Wars, the Danes, who had long since abolished slavery, could no longer afford to keep their West African possessions, so they sold out to Britain for ten thousand pounds, and Christiansborg became a British base against piracy and the now discredited slave-trade. Eighty-five Danish Governors had served the ends of commerce in that castle, and thirty-five of them had died there. They had been 'recruited unto death' when they had entered the service which required them to leave their cold northern homeland for the cruellest corner of the Tropics. It is interesting that now – after exactly a hundred years – the Danes are returning to the Coast where they have bought an important timber concern from a British firm.

A few years after the British had taken over Christiansborg a terrible earthquake shook Accra and the castle was badly damaged. After that it was used as a lunatic asylum, and, where once the slaves had been crowded in hopeless misery, there were now confined those other outcasts, the demented possessed not of man but of the devil.

It was only in 1900 that the castle was made the official Government House of the Gold Coast, which had been moved from Cape Coast to Accra some twenty-five years earlier.

As we drove up to the arched gateway in the dazzling light of nine o'clock in the morning, Christiansborg gave no sign of its long and gruesome history. Here was none of the other-world dilapidation of Gorée, or the sombre grey of Elmina; here was a white and shining citadel with turreted walls and battlements clear cut against the pure blue sky. To landward flowered gardens and parks, on either flank stretched the golden sands and coco-palms, and the long narrow fishing boats lifted over the rollers, as they headed for deeper waters.

As we went with Mr. Hamilton, the Governor's Aide-de-Camp, through the great arched gateway, we stepped over a burnished bronze plate which commemorated one of those thirty-five ill-fated Danish Governors who had perished on the coast. After his death a cannon had been melted over his body to form a warrior's tomb, thus one's first step into Christiansborg is taken literally over the White man's grave.

In the courtyard was a wild fig-tree by an ancient well, and round it were storerooms over the dungeons that had once housed the slaves.

Sir Charles and Lady Arden-Clarke came onto the terrace to meet us.

They both knew South Africa well, for Sir Charles had been in Bechuanaland and Basutoland before his appointment to Accra, and their three children had received part of their education in the Union. Their two daughters were both student nurses at St Thomas's Hospital, London, and their son was in the Tanganyika Police Force.

The task of this Governor was probably the most delicate and difficult in West Africa, for the Gold Coast had recently taken one great leap from government 'by persuasion' through the chiefs, to government by an elected parliament. Only a strong and tactful man could hope to handle this precocious and impetuous territory. Sir Charles was both. He had introduced fearless political reforms while he was Resident Commissioner in Basutoland (with some unhappy repercussions discussed in a previous chapter) and here he was once more in charge at a moment of transition, a dangerous and inflammable period. Although his manner was easy and unhurried, this tall attractive man could take instant decisions, and there was a determined set to his mouth and chin. His eyes, sea-green and piercing, were mesmeric. If this experiment in the Gold Coast could be made to succeed, here was the man to put it into effect.

Lady Arden-Clarke was small with a clear cameo profile and upswept steel grey hair.

'You must be exhausted,' she said. 'We will send breakfast to your rooms, and then you can bath and rest.'

After a few words of greeting the Governor excused himself.

'We are in the middle of a crisis,' he said. 'I must go and deal with it.'

His smile suggested that he rather enjoyed dealing with a crisis.

'There is practically never *not* a crisis,' said Lady Arden-Clarke, as we followed her to our rooms on the ramparts overlooking the sea. 'Everybody would be dreadfully bored if we went any length of time without one.'

Later, during the morning, we saw a dusky gentleman with a brief-case step over the melted cannon into the courtyard on his way to the flying buttress that was now converted into the chamber where the Cabinet met next door to the Governor's study.

He was quite a small man with a high domed forehead, an agreeable smile and a manner both volatile and voluble. His name was Kwame Nkrumah, and he was the Prime Minister of the new Constitution, and the Leader of the Convention People's Party, which was frankly clamouring for total independence within the Commonwealth. This party had been voted into power earlier in 1951 by an electorate over ninety per cent illiterate.

The elections had been a farce. Nobody, except a few up and coming politicians, had had the faintest idea what was happening, in spite of the noble efforts of British Government officials who strove to teach the primitive populace the meaning of a central parliament and a general election.

Douglas Brown, the special correspondent of the *Daily Telegraph*, writing at the time, put the situation realistically.

'Next week the people of the Gold Coast will be the first in Colonial Africa to elect a popular Parliament. The Colonial Government, observing strict neutrality, exercised considerable skill in explaining to them what holding an election implies. Meanwhile the Convention People's Party is urging the voters to use the election as a step towards destroying Colonial Government. It is rather as though a British official were handing a Native a pistol and carefully explaining its mechanism while the Native's only other counsellor was showing him how to level it at the donor.'

Vote-catching, in the circumstances, was open to all the chicanery which comes so easily to the African with political ambitions. There was never a dull moment. One candidate who ventured into the interior to press his claims was never seen again, and it was generally supposed that his constituents, finding themselves unable to swallow his policy, had swallowed the candidate instead. And, while all this was going on, Dr. Nkrumah, the Leader of the Convention People's Party, was serving a sentence for sedition. In the process he was rapidly acquiring the status of a modern saint, and his name was substituted for that of Christ in well-known hymns that were sung loud and long to glorify him, for that is an old African twist to mission teaching. After his party had swept the polls the Governor announced that Dr. Nkrumah and six other Natives would be released from Fort St. James Prison 'as an Act of Grace'.*

A contemporary newspaper account describes the scenes in Accra on that auspicious occasion.

Preceded by a large figure in white – one of his colleagues who had shared his cell – Dr. Nkrumah was driven straight to the Western Arena where he gave a public address.

'On the platform a black lamb was slaughtered on Dr. Nkrumah's bare feet to purge and cleanse him after the imprisonment and to propitiate the "old gods". While the priest who had cut the lamb's throat held a bloody knife up for the crowd to see, blood was allowed to run over Nkrumah's feet. Blood was also smeared on the foreheads of the men released with him.

'Through the loudspeaker Dr. Nkrumah thanked the crowd for its wonderful reception. "The struggle continues," he said.'

On our second morning in Accra, when the 'crisis' had been resolved, we went to see the new Parliament in session. Unfortunately Prime Minister Nkrumah was continuing the struggle elsewhere and we did not see him or hear him speak. But a British official from his office took charge of us and was most helpful in explaining what was going on. We were relieved to learn that vital Departments were still under

* *Dr. Nkrumah now in exile and Ghana a dictatorship.*

378

British control – Defence and External Affairs, Finance, and Justice.

'And the Governor has the right of veto,' he added.

There were also six European representatives of industry and commerce, though only two of these could vote.

'Then they still have a long way to go towards real self-rule?' I said.

'To a certain extent – yes' he answered cautiously.

It is illuminating that in 1953, after two years in office, Nkrumah publicly expressed the wish that the British administration would not withdraw from the Gold Coast too fast. Already experience had taught him that Colonial Administration cannot be learned in a day, and the value of an administration free from the taint of corruption.

The building in which Parliament assembled was a makeshift, but we saw plans of domed halls and offices on a grandoise scale. Presently, from our seats in the visitors' gallery, we looked down upon a pantomime which might well have been set to music.

The Bill in progress dealt, inevitably, with Education. The Gold Coast was as usual, giving a strong lead to the other West African Territories. Its fine University College of Achimota – generously subsidized by Colonial Development and Welfare funds – is as important to West African higher education as the much older College of Fourah Bay in Freetown.

The object of the Bill was to establish a 'corporate body, the purpose of which will be the holding of such examinations in the British West African Territories as may serve the public interest and assist the development of sound education'. It was contended that examinations in West Africa were too 'closely tied to examinations in the United Kingdom'.

The Bill would obviously receive little opposition and I was more interested in the performers on the parliamentary stage than in the debate. Comparatively few wore European suits, and those who did looked hot. Many members wore loose short-sleeved tunics like artists' smocks, or gay 'mammy-cloths', or long garments like old-fashioned night-dresses. Owing to lack of accommodation, a number of Government supporters were compelled to sit in the Opposition benches, while, in the raised back row behind the Government seats, were the Chiefs of the Northern Territories, all very imposing in togas with gold embroidered hats, richly brocaded turbans and fanciful varieties of fez or tarboosh.

The Gold Coast dialects are many, and English was the medium used, but some of it was so original that, for all I could make of it, it might just as well have been Twi, Ewe, Ga or Dagomba. I doubt if the decorative tribal chiefs understood it either, for they reclined with a drugged look upon their faces, as if in a mental *harmattan* haze, their wits obscured with the winy eloquence of the front benchers. Under their voluminous robes they flapped their legs gently together and apart as an elephant flaps his ears to fan himself.

Sometimes, when a member failed entirely to make himself understood in English, the Speaker, from his throne, demanded that he sit down. Other orators – mainly those in European suits – were remarkably fluent and highly excitable, firing their staccato harangues directly at the somnolent Speaker – 'I would heah like to stet, Mistah Spikkah ...' – and out would come some dramatically delivered statement. One, at least, of these gentlemen had received his training tub-thumping in Hyde Park, while another was the barrister who had defended a number of his compatriots in a notorious and ghastly case of ritual murder. The Minister of Education, on the contrary, expressed himself quietly and lucidly, his points carried conviction and it was a pleasure to listen to his measured and well-informed speech.

One of the most enthusiastic actors in this parliamentary play was an enormously stout policeman, dressed in a thick serge skin-tight navy blue uniform patterned exactly on the British model. He must have been stewed alive. His large hands were encased in snow-white gloves, and his sole task seemed to be to raise and lower the mace in accordance with the correct procedure. This he did with incomparable dignity, the wide black moon of his countenance shining with sweat and pride at playing a part which so constantly offered him the centre of the stage.

'He makes a big thing of moving the mace,' murmured Bertie. 'Like a weight-lifter.'

Afterwards, as we stood in the entrance hall waiting for our car, we glanced at some of the literature set out on a small bookstall. 'GOOD ENGLISH', 'EVERYTHING HAS A HISTORY', and, given pride of place, 'GUNPOWDER PLOT'.

'You can learn it all here,' said Bertie. 'Even how to blow up Parliament!'

In the afternoon we went swimming with our friends, General and Mrs. Whistler, and returned to Christiansborg just before sunset.

'Let's watch the surf-boats come in,' I said.

So we stood on the beach in the shadow of the castle on its towering cliffs. The long canoes were surfing in on the waves, paddled by the naked fishermen wielding short three-pronged oars with the dexterity of long practice. As the boats neared the shore a dozen or more lads plunged into the sea to help drag them up the beach. They were very jolly, laughing and joking, and spreading the empty nets to dry. Evidently all the fish had already been sold further along the coast.

Up on the battlements the flags were lowered as the bugler sounded 'Sunset'; the evening breeze stirred in the coco-palms; the fierce heat of the day subsided; and the white castle walls, the grim rocks, and the long seashore were painted with a glowing flamingo pink.

There was a formal dinner party that night at which we met the three British *ex officio* Ministers and the Judge President of the West African Appeal Court and their wives. Our fellow house-guest was Lord Hemingford, Director of Teacher Training at the Regional College at Kumasi. He was serious and self-effacing, but blessed with an original sense of humour which must have stood him in good stead in the course of his work.

It was our last night in West Africa, and something of its glamour lingers with me as I write.

As the guests mounted the wide stone steps from the courtyard to the terrace they passed between a guard in scarlet and gold standing to attention. The night breeze fluttered the light skirts of the ladies, and the raised pennants of the Guard, the air was heavy with the cloying sweet scent of frangipani. After dinner we sat out on the terrace and listened to the Band playing on the 'haunted buttress' between the beach and the gardens.

'Is it really haunted?' I asked the Governor.

'Who knows?' he said. 'There is enough history in this place to account for anything! Some people declare that they *feel* unseen presences on the ramparts, or that they wake as something brushes against the mosquito net – something that might be human yet has no substance—'

The Governor's A.D.C. had his own theory.

'There is in the night a moment of extraordinary stillness,' he said. 'It comes at the turn of the tide – or when the wind drops – and sometimes people wake in that pause, when nature seems to hold her breath. It's a strange moment – ghostly, if you like to put it that way.'

Before we went to bed I stood on the battlements above the sea. The surf thundered against the cliffs, against the dungeons where once so many doomed human beings had been chained in the foul dank heat. Could the despair of centuries substantiate into some dark presence that might make itself felt, or be heard to moan in that 'strange moment of pause'? Much despair had run its tragic course in this place – White as well as Black. Men and women had come to Christiansborg never to return home. They had stood, as I was standing now, and listened to the ceaseless crash of the waves. Perhaps they had watched the dwindling sails of some schooner homeward-bound and had felt themselves abandoned on this stricken coast far from the fields and woods of Europe, far from winter snows and the meadow flowers of spring, far from the cities and hamlets of home, from men and women with fair skins and voices speaking their own tongue. Many had stood here and watched the long white combers swell and break, swell and break, like a sick heart of a lonely human being . . .

The Coast does not easily relinquish its victims. Even those who escaped were often lured back. Victorian Mary Kingsley had felt the draw of its magnetism, irresistible as death. And that night, under the stars, I too, was caught in the spell of the Coast. Much had changed in sixty years, but the pen of Mary Kingsley had revealed those things that are changeless when it committed to paper her poignant memories of the 'painful charm of West Africa'.

'It give you pleasure when you are out there, but when you are back it gives you pain by calling you. It sends up before your eyes a vision of a wall of dancing white, rainbow-gemmed surf playing on a shore of yellow sand before an audience of stately coco palms; or of a great mangrove-watered bronze river; or of a vast aisle in some forest cathedral; and you hear, nearer to you than the voices of the people around, nearer than the roar of city traffic, the sound of the wind talking on the hard palm leaves and the thump of the Natives' tom-toms; or the cry of the parrots passing over the mangrove swamps in the evening time; or the sweet, long mellow whistle of the plantain warblers calling up the dawn; and everything that is round you grows poor and thin in the face of the vision, and you want to go back to the Coast that is calling you, saying, as the African says to the departing soul of his dying friend, "Come back, come back, this is your home".'

Mary Kingsley had set out once more in search of the vision that made everything around her seem 'poor and thin'. She had answered the call of the Coast, but the Dark

Angel had met her halfway, and if, at the end, that last African entreaty sounded in her ears, *'Come back, come back, this is your home!'* its echo found her in the shadow of the Simon's Berg under the Southern Cross. It found her at the turn of the tide – in the moment of strange stillness.

CHAPTER THIRTY

SCENES FROM THE GREAT BALLET

WE were back at Simon's Town in time for Christmas, and, to our great delight, Bertie's sister, Dorothy, and her husband, Professor Norman Capon of Liverpool University, came to stay with us for a few weeks. Norman was a child specialist of renown, and his holiday was combined with a series of lectures and medical conferences. Piet was as thrilled to see his aunt and uncle as we were, because not only had they been his guardians when he was at an English preparatory school and we were abroad, but he too was now well on the way to entering the medical profession.

We settled in at Admiralty House for the rest of the summer, and those few lovely months are engraved on my mind against the background of the Van Riebeeck Tercentenary and many national happenings both grave and gay.

Once, long ago, a young Frenchman in Peking, the Chinese City of Emperors, told me that no place could ever mean anything to a woman unless she had had a love-affair in it. A very Latin point of view. But its application could well be widened to include other emotional experiences. In my many years of travel I have discovered that at certain times one is living intellectually and at others emotionally – living 'with one's head' or 'with one's heart' is how I think of assessing places, people and experiences. On our African journeys I lived that way – detached and invulnerable, tremendously interested in my new surroundings and all they had to offer. But in Simon's Town I lived mostly with my heart. There was my family, there was the beautiful Cape Peninsula, there was the Royal Navy with all it stood for in our lives – the Navy which had given me, in full measure, the joy and anguish of a close personal relationship, and which was, to my husband, the force and devotion which had shaped his life from the age of twelve.

The little clear snapshots, and the great tableaux of those months stand out clearly in my mind.

Ronnie was, at that time, embarking on the big adventure of moving about on two legs instead of four, and his collapsible progress resulted in many a crash-bang. I had never before seen my brother-in-law exercise his particular charm for children, and to watch our grandson's response to his wiles was, as Nannie put it, 'every bit as good as a play'.

One day, when Norman was relaxing on the sunny lawn near the little gold-fish pond, a light straw hat tipped over his kind blue eyes and a book in his thin hand, Ronnie came staggering off the stoep on to the terrace, his fists full of the ash-trays he had collected from here and there with the express purpose of throwing them into the pool. We heard a loud thump as Ronnie lost his footing and landed on the stone paving, ash-trays scattered to right and left. As the dazed child lifted his injured face to bawl his woe aloud, he suddenly saw his great uncle's head tip forward and the light straw hat sail off it and land on the grass. To Ronnie this was evidently an enchanting and convulsing sight. Ash-trays and tears forgotten, and with a purple pigeon's egg rising on his forehead, he scrambled after the hat and offered it to the smiling Professor. The clown's trick was performed again, and yet again, and each time it was funnier than the time before, so that finally Ronnie was rolling on the grass helpless with baby laughter.

'How on earth do you do it?' I asked. 'You don't even work for it. You just toss your hat off your head, or say "Boo, boo, boo", and he's yours – laughing his head off in the best of humours.'

Norman said, 'It's simple. If you want to be good with children, you mustn't mind making a fool of yourself, and you mustn't get bored with repetition. Children and backward

386

people – if you make them laugh they'll trust you, and if you
repeat yourself endlessly they'll understand you. With
animals you only have to bother with repetition, but it's the
same principle.'

The *Bermuda* arrived on 20th December, and all the Port
was happy and excited at getting their men-folk home in
time for Christmas.

Tony came ashore with a new gleam in his eye and sparks
coming out of his red hair. I decided that he was relieved at
having written his examination, for better or for worse. He
immediately got on excellently with our quiet Professor, for
he discovered that in World War One Norman had been in
the Camel Corps and shared his own strong sentiment about
the peculiar charm of the desert.

Dorothy said to me, 'Never mind about the fascination of
the desert! Which of the girls does Tony take out?'

'He doesn't get much time,' I said, 'and anyway he's girl-
proof.'

She laughed, and raised her eyebrows.

Norman and Dorothy were easy peaceful people who enjoyed the Cape in their own way. They often just lazed in the
sun on our little beach and watched the Sherwin children at
play; or David Barrow with his misleading child-angel look;
and the little Norton brother and sister who darted about
like birds, for, since they were the children of an artist and a
a ballerina, they possessed a special rhythm of their own –
and often seemed to perform some wild irresponsible ballet
set to the brief rhapsody of childhood.

Norman and Dorothy observed life. It was their study and
their recreation. Little things pleased my sister-in-law
greatly. When they came up across the lawn from the beach,
she often brought back Venus-ear shells that were both
practical and ornamental. 'This one is big enough to use as
an ash-tray,' she say. 'Isn't it lovely! All that blue pearl
colouring!'

But when Ronnie came on Sunday with his parents, he
flung the Venus-ears into the gold-fish pool. Life was never

387

dull for our goldfish. And they needed a few ash-trays, because, at our larger parties, people frequently threw their cigarette ends into the pool.

It was strange to our guests to enjoy Christmas in midsummer, and a naval Christmas too.

The Dockyard Padre's wife, Joan Rea, had trained her Sunday School for their yearly Nativity Play. We went to see it in the little church in the old Sail Loft. It was a very unpretentious performance, and altogether charming. No child was left out. Even the smallest of them toddled up the aisle to lay their cuddly toys at the feet of the Holy Babe asleep in his little wooden manger – and clutched them back almost immediately, lest there be any mistake about their final ownership. Colonel Houghton's ten-year-old daughter spoke her part as the Virgin Mary in a clear childish treble, and gave humble Joseph his instructions with such unconsciously feminine self-assurance that it was the very quintessence of sublime innocence. The three Kings had borrowed some gaudy finery, but most of the cast wore mother's dish-cloths round their heads and coloured bathing towels as skirts. The angels had lovely silver-paper haloes, and the shepherds had taken their baby relatives' woolly lambs for the occasion.

Yet, as their combined voices were raised in the sweet carol 'Away in a manger . . .' I found my thoughts drifting to West Africa – to the Gold Coast school-children with their heads thrown back and their white teeth and the whites of their intelligent eyes so striking in their dark faces as they sang their Hausa hymn with uninhibited abandon. Our Simon's Town children sang of the 'Little Lord Jesus' very touchingly, but the small Africans sang with all their ardent hearts because song made them happy. Song was self-expression.

On Christmas Eve the wives and children of our house staff and Admiralty House Compound came to receive presents stacked under the tall Christmas tree in the corner of the big inner hall. The children were beautifully dressed and behaved, but before long, the gold-fish were gazing astonished at a small leather sandal. The Chief Cook's young son always lost a shoe in the pond when he had occasion to visit Admiralty House garden. It had become a habit. The Chief Steward's little girl was as dainty as the doll she carried, and the boy's shirt and neat bow-tie proved that Prince Charles was already a leader of male fashion. The South African wives of our two young seamen came with their families, one of them holding a fine new baby in her arms with happy pride. Ronnie – who, with his parents, was staying with us – tottered in and out of the hall with a glorious wooden pulling-toy he had been given by his Great-Aunt. Little Judy Sherwin, who could both walk and talk very nicely, embraced him fervently every time she saw him, but he received her advances with loud cries of alarm, frankly suspicious that she intended to deprive him of his precious toy.

David Barrow and the little Nortons discovered Sammy on the stoep, and strove to put a paper-cap on the Great Dane's head. He glared at them and they ran away. The glare of Sammy's one gold and one diamond eye would strike terror into the boldest soul. Then, all in a moment, the children cast away restraint, and, waving streamers and paper windmills, they raced for the swing at the end of the lawn. They moved like a cloud of birds, on one impulse, with a high shrilling note. Then we knew they were really enjoying themselves.

On Christmas morning we went on board the *Bermuda* to church in the quarter-deck, and afterwards round the messes and finally to the wardroom for a glass of champagne.

The Service was short but satisfying. There were carols instead of a sermon and the ship's company sang as if they meant it. The sun shone and a light breeze ruffled the surface of the sea. But suddenly a cold little thought crept into my heart. Was this, perhaps, our last Christmas on board a warship – my husband's ship? I shook it away quickly. Sally the Seal frisked through the bright water, playful as a porpoise, and the gulls cried aloud to the glory of this lovely day.

When Norman and Dorothy sailed for England we were all sorry to say good-bye to them.

Mother said, 'I wish they weren't going. I've fallen for both of them.'

They had fitted easily and happily into the life of our little port, and there were many in Simon's Town who missed them when they left. Something kindly and safe went with them, and, a few days after their departure, the month of February took upon itself all the grim portent of the Ides of March.

Pet and Glen and Ronnie left us too to spend the rest of the Christmas vacation with Glen's mother and stepfather, Mr. and Mrs. K. G. Macleod, at Balgarthen, St. James.

Grant Macleod had in his day been a triple blue at Cambridge, the idol of every young sportsman in Scotland and England, but he was now compelled to concentrate on golf and racing. His golf handicap was low and the quality of his horses was high. One Saturday afternoon, when we were all at the Races, we met our old friends, Lord and Lady McGowan, who had just arrived in the Union on a short holiday. Harry McGowan, whose remarkable initiative and industry had done much to build up the important Imperial Chemical Industries, was in his most sparkling form, full of little jokes and stories, and dear motherly Jean, with her dry Scottish wit and the twinkle in her shrewd blue eyes, was, as usual, playing up to him perfectly. Everything seemed to go just right that day – even the horses – and the McGowans rejoiced to be in sunny South Africa during the cold English winter. Before we parted Dorthy Macleod insisted that we all dine with them at Balgarthen on the following Wednesday – 'and we'll celebrate today's win!'

But the following Wednesday was 6th February.

That day Jean McGowan was taken ill, and Harry no longer had any heart for his little jokes. A few weeks later their many friends were saying of Jean McGowan – 'She was so lovable – so full of fun – and always so kind.'

390

It was her motherly kindness we remembered most.

Wednesday, 6th February, 1952.

I was sitting in my sun-trap on the window-sill when Bertie came upstairs. I did not look round at the sound of his step.

'Look, down there, in the sunk garden,' I said. 'Veronica is widening that little grass path along the bank. Don't you think it's a good idea? It was always so topply.'

He didn't answer. Just put his hand on my shoulder. I looked up then, and saw the sorrow in his face and heard it in his voice.

'The King is dead.'

What a sad day that was – how very sad!

The little port of Simon's Town mourned a Sovereign and a fellow Naval Officer. It grieved as for a personal friend. The King was dead – our sailor King . . .

South Africa mourned him too. Many arrangements had been made for his convalescence in Natal, and a sincere and affectionate welcome had awaited him from every section of the community. Hope for his complete recovery had transcended foolish strife, for he was a good King and a good man, and he and all his family were well loved.

In Kenya the young Elizabeth and Prince Philip heard the sad news, and the long-planned tour of the great loyal dominions of Australia and New Zealand crumbled away like a child's sand-castle caught by a full tide.

As in a vision, I saw this young Elizabeth – twenty-six years old, the same age as the first Elizabeth when she too had ascended the throne and assumed the burden of a crown – and I saw a grey Presence enter her life, never again to leave it. Since her childhood that Presence had waited in the shadows, exerting his power, but now, with the passing of George VI, he stepped into the open. He lifted the proud chin of the new Queen with his icy touch. '*Look into my eyes,*' he said. '*Obey my dictates! No Queen is free. From now until the end you belong to me.*' Her steady gaze met his, and I seemed to hear her clear voice. 'I know you well

391

and I accept your dominion.' And the fair head that bowed to no man bent in all humility before that stern grey Presence whose name is Duty.

Towards evening, Bertie and I strolled in the sea-garden, sad and silent. He had been at Dartmouth with the King, and had many times met and talked with him in the course of his naval career. His heart was heavy. And in our garden too, there were memories of that good King who had 'walked with death and did not fear him'. There was the yellow-wood tree he had planted during the Royal Tour of South Africa in 1947, there were the paving stones that had widened the porch so that it should easily receive the long royal Daimlers. Even upstairs, in Admiralty House, a bathroom had been added and a guest-room re-furnished before the visit. That year all the children of the Peninsula had come to Simon's Town in a joyous pilgrimage to welcome the King and Queen and the two Princesses. The little Europeans had sung 'God Save the King' in greeting, the little Coloureds had lifted up their voices in the beautiful 'Stem van Suid Afrika' – Voices of South Africa – and the Native children had chanted the haunting 'Nkosi, Sikelel' i Africa' – God Bless Africa.

The sun went down behind the hill and again my thoughts turned towards the great hinterland of Africa and a young Queen whose father had once said from the wisdom and understanding of his heart, 'Poor girl, she will always be lonely'. And I was glad to know that this loneliness would be lessened by the love of a husband and children and the devotion of her people. Waiting at Westminster to receive her upon her return would be her Prime Minister, Winston Churchill, a venerable and mighty figure whose actions and oratory had saved the sceptred isle in her darkest hour. In those hard-pressed days, when the air armadas of Hitler had blackened the sky above England's fields and cities, we had known Winston Churchill for what he truly was, and men and women had said to one another: 'He's an Elizabethan – you only have to hear him speak to know that he's really an Elizabethan!'

392

For, in fact, he seemed to belong to that brave century of wars and threats of invasion, of bold sea-farers and great discoveries, of bombast and chivalry and the golden poets – the days of the first Elizabeth. And now in our own troubled era, it was he who would guide the Ship of State into the reign of Elizabeth II.

But tragic events often bring a trail of lesser woes in their wake. During the war when my husband – somewhere in the cold Atlantic – was mourning the terrible loss of H.M.S. *Hood*, with her complement of more than fifteen hundred souls – many of them his friends and former shipmates – a little black kitten had died in his quarters and was committed to the deep with a tiny Union Jack as a shroud.

So now, one day, he came from his carnations and said, 'They're nearly all drooping. My carnations have got red spider into them.'

And under the bamboo shelter, by the rocky bed of a dry summer stream, the straight stems and stiff rust-stained leaves wilted, and the pretty heads of purple, scarlet and sulphur-yellow withered till only a few remained to smile at the sun.

And now misfortune cast her net wider. This time she aimed to trawl the children. Some slipped through like little fish, but those in our Admiralty Compound were held fast. They were caught with Sally the Seal. And their fears and their sufferings were great.

It was evening and they were playing on the grass between Veronica's 'NO ADMITTANCE' cabin and Commander Norton's timber cottage. There were the two small Nortons, three little Sherwins and David Barrow. Baby Barrow's mother was putting him to bed. Suddenly Martin Sherwin cried, in his curiously deep four-year-old voice:

'There's Sally!'

Sally the Seal was coming up out of the sea on to the beach. This she had done many times to bask in the sun. But now the sun had gone down, and Sally was doing a new thing. She was dragging herself up – past 'NO ADMITTANCE', on to the turf – and on – and on . . .

The children stopped their play, and suddenly Sarah Norton put her hands over her face and gulped, and one of them said, very loud and frightened:

'She's *crying*! Sally is *crying*.'

The seal, writhing in unaccountable agony, lifted her round black head to the darkening sky and groaned like a human being in the last extremity, while the tears poured down her cheeks. And presently she died on the soft turf between the stream and sea, and she died weeping. The children wept too, so long and bitterly that it seemed as if they could never be consoled. Especially the little Nortons, for only last week their dog too had gone to heaven, but not in the dreadful manner of Sally. It took her mother, that graceful ballerina with wide-set eyes and ballets forever flying and floating in their grey depths, to find a way to ease the children's grief. She told them a story.

The King, she said, was lonely in his heaven. The King had begged for earthly friends. So the dog and the seal had gone to keep him company. The children listened and believed and were comforted. For them a nightmare was transformed into a dream. A Good King, wearing his crown, sat upon a golden cloud, with a little brown dog and a shiny black seal at his feet. Sometimes the little brown dog licked his hand, for that is the way dogs show their love to human beings, and at others the Monarch's fingers gently stroked Sally's round black head, so that she looked up at him and smiled – for of course seals can smile as well as weep.

Perhaps it was a scene from a ballet – happier than the ballet of Hans Andersen's 'Little Mermaid'. For what, after all, are life and death and the hereafter but one great Ballet performed against the dark star-studded curtain of Eternity.

CHAPTER THIRTY-ONE

FIRE AND FESTIVAL

FEBRUARY is a bad month for fires at the Cape. The south-easter blows hard to fan the flames, and at Simon's Town it blows hardest of all.

But in this February of 1952 – this cruel month – a new and shocking element entered into the normal fire menace. More fires blazed than ever before, there was a pattern to them, and the Simon's Town end of the Peninsula was clearly Target Number One.

In 1953 the Minister of Justice, Mr. Swart, announced in Parliament that he had received definite evidence that European Communists were teaching Native and Coloured people to become 'fire-bugs'. They were learning fast enough in 1952!

A windy night was chosen, about sunset a bush conflagration was started, and a couple of hours later another was set alight somewhere else, and then yet another. For weeks the fire-fighters of Simon's Town and many other areas had no rest.

In Simon's Town the Municipality, the Union Defence Force and the Navy worked together, and, since a tragedy some years earlier when two young sailors were burned to death on the Simon's Berg, co-ordination had reached a very high pitch of efficiency. Even so, that February and most of March tested it to the uttermost. At times I found it horribly reminiscent of the blitz.

One evening, when my mother was staying with us, the Dockyard sirens sounded the Alarm to which we had become well-accustomed. For the past three nights men had been

395

fighting flames in our area. In Tony's office the telephone shrilled. He went to answer it.

'A new one, Sir – near Froggy Pond,' he said, as he came back.

Bertie glanced at his watch.

'It's ten o'clock, Joy. I suggest you and Mum get to bed. A fire near Froggy Pond isn't going to endanger the port. I'll go along with Tony and see what's happening.'

Mother's room overlooked the sea. The clanging of fire-engines and rushing of cars and lorries in the road did not disturb her, and she was soon asleep. But I drew my curtains and opened my windows to the night with its tumult of sound and wind. I looked out over the lovely and familiar scene – the garden, the sea, and westwards the kloof and the hill. As my eyes sought the hill I saw a snake of flame crawling towards Simon's Town civilian hospital and the Palace Barracks of the U.D.F. This was the real danger – Froggy Pond was only the diversion! I ran down through the Compound to 'NO ADMITTANCE' to call Veronica. Our kloof-garden was threatened. As we hurried back across the lawn together we saw Corney mustering our young stewards for fire-fighting. Bertie and Tony were already on the spot, and the civilian authorities were evacuating the hospital. An army of Coloured men and boys were beating methodically at the wall of flame. From childhood they had fought bush and mountain fires. The girls and children not actively engaged were shrieking in shrill excitement, occasionally giggling wildly. The Berg wore a terrible helmet of fire and the relentless south-easter filled the air with flying sparks. Outside the hospital stood Ron Stewart, the Magistrate, his face ashen in the glare of a street lamp – a patient face as a rule, now angry and bitter.

'This is devils' work,' he said. 'Three fires, three nights running, always at sunset, always when the wind blows, and always a new one beginning before the old one is out.' His eyes turned sorrowfully to the burning hill. 'Our berg was so beautiful with its trees and proteas! All the colours in the world. It will be ten years before it can be beautiful again.'

Bertie came to where I stood, and said, 'I'm going down to headquarters in Jubilee Square. Do you want to come?'

Veronica had picked up a green branch and was helping to beat the flames that were now blowing away from the hospital and licking at the flowering gums and young oaks over our garden wall.

Fire fighting headquarters was a Nissen hut in Jubilee Square. There we found a great deal going on in an atmosphere of cheerful and disciplined calm. No one on duty had had any sleep for nights and eyes were red-rimmed as I remembered the eyes of men and women during the blitz.

The Municipal Authorities are responsible for ordinary fires, but whenever a conflagration gets out of hand they call in the Navy and the Union Defences Forces to lend a hand.

Mr. Llewellyn Gay, the Municipal Engineer, was in the nature of 'Supreme Allied Commander' on this occasion, ably supported by Joe Selby, the Captain in Charge of the Dockyard, and Major Klootwyk, in charge of the Simon's Town Garrison. With them were Mr. Laubser, the Town Clerk, and Lieutenant Commander Barrow, the Signal Officer. Mr. Preston, who had left Simon's Town and handed over the mayoral duties to his Deputy, Mr. Van Breda, had driven to the port on hearing the grave news of this fire, and they were both there. So was Mr. Lewis Gay, yet another ex-Mayor, who was now our local Member of Parliament.

We heard Arthur Barrow speaking slowly and clearly into the walkie-talkie. 'Lieutenant Waller will collect his Bantus and wait for his relief . . . Lieutenant Waller will collect his Bantus and wait . . .'

Lieutenant Lambert from the *Bermuda* came in to get his iron-rations. He was dressed in fire-fighting rig – blue shirt, dark trousers stuffed into gum-boots and a helmet. Lorries came and went, packed with sailors or the Dockyard Bantus. We heard the walkie-talkie reports as they came in.

'It's easing up – it's blowing away from the hospital . . . it is under control . . .'

It was near midnight when we returned to Admiralty House. The Chief Steward brought a whisky decanter and soda on to the stoep.

'The Coxswain has sent back the stewards, Sir,' he reported. 'He doesn't need them any more. I have informed them that they may turn in.'

'Thank goodness Mum's room faces away from all this,' I said. 'I've just been upstairs to peep at her. She's sound asleep.'

A few minutes later Tony came on to the stoep, still in fire-fighting clothes, grimed and rather wild-looking.

'Sir, there's a new one. In Waterfall Kloof. It's blowing straight for the magazine. I've called out all hands.'

We saw the tall figure of Commander Peter Norton coming across the lawn towards us. This new development might be very serious. The magazine at the top of our kloof-garden was near the big Coloured tenements.

Bertie said to me: 'You stay here, Joy-Joy. You *must* in case Mum wakes. There will be nobody else in the house. We need everybody'.

I went alone to the White bedroom overlooking the road and the kloof-garden and the waterfall. Old remembered fears prickled in the palms of my hands, and, as I had done so many times while London burned, I made an entry in my diary.

'*February. Midnight.* For three days and nights huge bush fires have burned in our area. Tonight the whole berg is ablaze. It is like the blitz. How I hate and fear fire! Clouds of dust are whirling in the half made road outside Admiralty House as the south easter blows, and along the ridges of leaping flame, are silhouetted the little figures of the beaters. A long red dragon is making its fiery way to the magazine. If it gets there and the ammunition blows up what will happen to the Coloured Waterfall Flats – and will this old house stand? It may – it may not.

'1 *a.m.* Bertie has just come in. The fire was terribly near the magazine, but everybody helped load the ammunition and they got it all away in time. He says Mr. Bethel and his Armament Supply people were wonderful.

'My darling Mum slept through it all. I longed to wake her and say "Come and look! All Hell is burning on our doorstep." But was it fair to wake eighty from tranquil slumber to give her a glimpse of the inferno?'

Next afternoon I added a postscript.

'My darling Mum is furious. "And you let me go on sleeping!" She says. Words fail her. She hates missing a good show. My maid, Gadys, was ten minutes late this morning – the first time she hasn't been punctual to the second. She was on duty at the First Aid Post till 4 a.m. Many burn injuries among the Coloured beaters. Jubilee Square to-day looks like the aftermath of Palm Sunday. It is littered with Palm branches abandoned by the beaters. The wind still blows – and, as I write, the Dockyard sirens wail. Another fire!'

At last the wind ceased to blow with daily and demoniac fury. Fate had done with her Technicolor backgrounds in orange and gold, and she turned once more to her puppets. Perhaps she smiled as she rounded off yet another fragment of a naval story.

That summer, while were were at Simon's Town, we were in the happy position of being able to have people to stay. We had the rooms and the staff, and we hoped some of our friends would be able to make the journey.

So now Captain Philip Glover, R.N. (Rtd.) with his wife, Nancy, arrived from England on a three weeks holiday. It was almost like an epilogue to my girlhood memories of Admiralty House, for Phil Glover had then been Flag Lieutenant to Admiral Bentinck, and it was he who had removed the outrageous meer-kat, Riki, from the drawing-room the day I had upset my tea and Bertie had rescued me from the animal's unwelcome attentions.

Phil was a fine tennis player, who had won the Naval

Singles Championship for many years, and he and my husband had often partnered each other successfully in Inter-Services matches. Now they had graduated – or perhaps declined – into the veterans' class where they were still a formidable pair.

Nancy, who before her marriage, was Nancy Lyle, had represented her country at tennis in many parts of the world, including South Africa, so they both had many friends at the Cape and were in much demand. The sunny days of their visit passed all too soon, and when they sailed we were swept straight into a vortex of official functions connected with the Van Riebeeck Tercentenary in Cape Town.

In 1652 Jan Van Riebeeck, the first Dutch Governor, landed at the Cape of Storms, changed its name to the Cape of Good Hope, and established the first civilized settlement in South Africa. It was only a small victualling station for the ships of the Dutch East India Company trading to and from the Far East, but an important beginning had been made. The contemporary diary of Van Riebeeck's period of Governorship had been translated into English and was published in 1952 by the Van Riebeeck Society, and what delightful reading it is!

Van Riebeeck had his Native problems with the Hottentots, the Strandloopers and the Bushmen, although the Bushmen had already been driven into the hills by the Hottentots. But, there they were, in the kranzes of Table Mountain, and killing and devouring cattle was their favourite pastime. Van Riebeeck was long-suffering with them, for his instructions from the Dutch East Company were explicit. He was to build a fort, plant market gardens, see that there was always plenty of fresh water for the ships, and keep on good terms with the Natives for the sake of the cattle trade. He described the Hottentots frankly as 'faithless rabble', but many of them professed Christianity and inter-married with the garrison who were thus the original progenitors of the Cape Coloured.

This aspect of life in the first settlement was glossed over during the Tercentenary, except by the sly Indians. When the Natives and Coloureds, smarting under the application of new *apartheid* laws, threatened to boycott the Festival, the President of the Natal Indian Organization publicly stated that 'to the non-Europeans the celebrations should have great historic significance because Van Riebeeck broke all rules of *apartheid* and arranged the first mixed marriages in South Africa'. The Malays, who were among the earliest imported slaves and craftsmen from Java, took an active part in the pageantry. This exotic self-sufficient Moslem community, with the pilgrimage to Mecca as the goal of one and all, has always been a real asset to the Cape.

Since Van Riebeeck's day South Africa has travelled a long way, and the Tercentenary celebrated three centuries of growth and progress. Every phase in the country's development, every aspect of its life, art, culture and industry was represented. And other countries sent exhibits too. The whole wide foreshore, recently reclaimed from the sea, blossomed with temporary villages, pavilions, halls and funfairs round an immense stadium. You could visit the ruins of Great Zimbabwe, have lunch in Van Riebeeck's birthplace, the Dutch town of Culemborg, and tea at Much-Binding-in-the-Marsh, or you could go to the Gold and Diamond pavilions and study the working models of mines. You could also stroll round the elaborate British exhibit – sent on from the Festival of Britain – which showed the growth of Parliament. And there baffled Afrikaners 'came out by the same door wherein they went'; they said in Afrikaans to Martlie Malherbe, who was in charge, 'But what, then, *is* the British Constitution?' And Martlie replied with irony in her brown eyes, 'There is none'.

Or some English-speaking visitor asked the sailor at the entrance:

'What do *you* make of the British Constitution?' And he replied with simple candour, 'No more than you do, M'm.' All he knew was that there wouldn't be any British *anything* if it weren't for the Royal Navy, and that was good enough for him. But I heard one cynical individual state that the

British Constitution existed solely as a test for drunkenness.

'If you're had up in England for driving under the influence, they make you walk along a straight line and they ask you to say "The British Constitution". That shakes you!'

The wives of the Ministers had gone back three hundred years, and cast away the cares of the present. So had attractive Mrs. Strauss, the wife of the Leader of the United Party, and the wives of the Provincial Administrators who were in the mother-city for the celebrations. They all went into the voluminous skirts and great puffed sleeves of the mid-seventeenth century for every official, diplomatic or stadium event, and this made them easily distinguishable and lent the whole Festival an added importance and intimacy.

Every town and city in the Union played its part, and the horse-drawn coaches of the old days rumbled once more down the length of South Africa from the great cities of the Union to Cape Town, the oldest of them all. When the coaches arrived in the stadium they carried, as passengers, their respective mayors and mayoresses who were greeted by the seventeenth century ladies of the Cabinet and 'entertained to tea' in an enchanting pageant, while Dr. Dönges, the Minister of the Interior, addressed the drivers who had travelled hundreds of miles on their long journey.

Charles te Water was sitting beside me on the stand. He was one of the 'hosts' to the official guests.

'Look at that!' he said, as the ladies played their parts with ease and grace. 'It's superb – the poise and dignity of those women! We Afrikaners are a matriarchal people. The women rule the roost.'

The Afrikaner women are very conscious of the history of their country. They enjoyed this old Dutch play-acting. But the Voortrekker Centenary of 1938 had meant even more to them. Then, in the *kappies* and gowns of their grandmothers, they had re-lived the finest hour of the Boers –

402

when the women too had been pioneers, urging the men to trek on into the unknown, facing danger and death in the search for freedom and a land of their own.

The most attractive scene of the Festival was the climax, when the *Drommedaris* sailed again with Van Riebeeck, his wife and child and their party. The Royal Cape Yacht Club manned the replica of the ship, one-third of her original size, and handled her beautifully.

Watching from Green point strand we saw her coming across the bay with her sails filled in a light wind. The sea was a-dazzle with sun-diamonds, the air was keen and bright. The boats put out from the little sailing-ship, and the first landing party planted a wooden cross on the turf above the foreshore. Then came Van Riebeeck (played by the South African actor, André Huguenet) and his wife and child and their attendants. Under the Cross Van Riebeeck gave thanks for a safe arrival and prayed for the success of his enterprise. The oration was delivered in seventeenth-century Dutch, but, as he spoke, the hazards of the voyage and those of the future of this tiny outpost in a savage land moved us deeply and we, too, were caught in the spell of the brave past.

Somewhere behind us, on Signal's Hill, hundreds of homing pigeons were released. They had been brought here from every town and city in the Union, and they carried home a message of hope. Now they whirled and circled against the great mauve mountain and the blue sky, all together for a few confused minutes before instinct took possession, and the little messengers scattered, each finding its solitary way many hundreds of miles across the heavens, irresistibly guided to some roof or garden that called with the voice of home.

And, as the pigeons flew north, east and west, Commander Van Riebeeck's party began to walk slowly up the hillside away from the sea towards the future of a new land and a new nation.

But the Festival itself was only a small part of a year of grace. Art and culture from Europe flowed into the Union

403

in honour of the Tercentenary. Holland sent a wonderful collection of old Dutch Masters, and Great Britain and France sent contributions of art and sculpture, both traditional and modern. The Old Vic Company toured Southern Africa, and the Viennese Boys' Choir held crowded houses enthralled. There was ballet and opera. And, in the old Castle, there were superb displays of Africana.

My mother, who was determined to miss nothing this golden year could offer her, walked down the Avenue under Simon Van der Stel's oaks to the National Gallery, where the works of Henry Moore were surprising the more conservative Capetonians. From there she continued her artistic education by going to the exhibition of French Impressionists.

She rang me up to give me her opinion. She was indignant.

'The whole thing is a hoax!'

'Oh, no, darling,' I assured her hastily. 'Some of it is abstract art—'

My mother is a factual person who likes to know what she is looking at.

'Abstract! Don't make me laugh! I walked round one of those Henry Moore things *three* times trying to make head and tail of it. It was impossible. It looked like—'

'Shh!' I said hastily. 'The Dockyard operator might be shocked.'

'Well—' She restrained herself. But she gave me her views on the French Impressionists, and finally summed the whole thing up. 'It's no use saying I react in this way because I'm eighty and completely out of date. Believe me, my child, those so-called artists are putting it over on you. *They are making fools of the lot of you!*'

The official visitors returned to their respective countries – except the British representative, Admiral of the Fleet Lord Fraser of North Cape, who continued his tour of South Africa, with his Flag Lieutenant and a car and driver put at his disposal by the hospitable Union Government.

On his way back to England he spent a few days with us at Admiralty House, much to the joy of the Navy at Simon's Town, for this ex-First Sea Lord, with his chubby face, boundless vitality and great war record was much loved in the Service. At the Festival he had 'stolen the picture' on countless occasions, putting the other guests in the shade with his glamorous uniform of an Admiral of the fleet and his easy breezy manner.

Just before he left, Philip and Elspeth Rhodes arrived from England to spend a month with us. Philip, who had recently retired from the Stock Exchange, was Bertie's oldest friend, and we had been delighted when, earlier in the year, they had written to say that they intended shipping themselves and a car to Mombasa and then driving by easy stages down Africa. Philip and Elspeth were excellent drivers and the car they had chosen was a good English make, but even so it was a long journey, and we were thrilled when they really arrived safely at Simon's Town.

Philip had been brought up in the Navy; he had been in Bertie's term at Dartmouth, and had served in both wars, so the naval atmosphere was to him like the 'voice of the trumpet' to the war horse in the Book of Job.

'He goeth on to meet the armed men . . . he saith among the trumpets, Ha, Ha; and he smelleth the battle afar off, the thunder of the captains and the shouting.'

I can well believe that my husband's Captains – Captain Selby, in-charge-of-the-Dockyard; Captain Currey, his Chief-of-Staff and Flag-Captain; Captain Jameson of the Frigate *Actaeon*, and Captain Brooke of the Frigate *Nereide* – might be thunderous men upon occasion, even shouting to great effect if necessary, but we saw them only in their milder moments when they came to meet Lord Fraser.

'I must say,' said Philip to Bertie. 'Your Captains are a fine-looking lot!'

'And they picked very creditable wives,' agreed my husband.

I thought their grown-up daughters were an asset to us too. Susan and Carol Selby and Elizabeth Currey were the naval nucleus of our young people's parties. Susan, particularly, seemed prettier every time we saw her – a slim straight wand of a girl with clear-cut features and a soft voice.

Philip Rhodes, big, warm-hearted and persuasive, is always doing astonishing things. This time he had borrowed a West African chauffeur from a friend in Kenya and brought him to the Cape 'to give him a lift on his way to Lagos'. Never had I heard of such a round-about lift! The West African, of course, was never allowed to drive, he merely changed the wheels when the inevitable punctures occurred cleaned the car and made himself useful in a thousand ways

'Dear old Sosah,' said Philip. 'I don't know what we'd have done without him! But I hope he won't upset the household, what with *apartheid* and all that. He is a bit *nie blanke*!'

'Dear old Sosah' was as *nie blanke* (not white) as they come, except for a frill of ivory teeth sticking straight out of his face in a most alarming fashion, but he could, as Philip explained, 'get on with anybody anywhere', and Corney soon fixed him up in a disused outhouse, which he regarded as the height of luxury, and he was soon on the best of terms with the household, which was not one to be easily upset.

This remarkable West African had been batman to an Army officer in World War Two, and some years later had heard by 'jungle telegraph' that his master was farming in East Africa. He had therefore trekked from Lagos to Nairobi – a journey of several months – and eventually presented himself at his master's door where he was received with open arms. He was now on his way back to his own people for a holiday. That the way was extremely devious did not trouble him. An African has no sense of time, and little of distance, so to travel to Lagos 'via the Cape' seemed very reasonable to Sosah, especially in such good company.

Philip loved 'dear old Sosah' for his loyalty, and Elspeth loved him for making her laugh.

Perhaps those are the two most lovable qualities in life – loyalty and the gift of making others laugh. Philip himself possessed both in full measure.

Those weeks of early autumn were bright and crisp, and often, when I looked out of my window, I saw Elspeth, dark-eyed and delicate, with her startled Bambi-look, picking her way daintily through the sea-garden seeking a sprig here or a spray there for some charming flower-decoration she was creating. Elspeth did not 'arrange' flowers – much less 'do' them – she created a thing of beauty, ephemeral as youth, and when it became tattered and faded she was sad, as if a butterfly had folded its lovely wings and died while she watched it, helpless to prolong so frail a life.

Admiral Fraser and his Flag Lieutenant sailed for England with many souvenirs of their visit, including supple ostrich-skin shoes and a photograph of the Admiral riding a wild-eyed ostrich in Outshoorn. And a little later the Rhodes went north by car to catch the 'Comet' somewhere in Equatorial Africa, while 'dear old Sosah' packed his new shirts and ties and two bottles of gin in his little tin trunk and boarded a small cargo boat bound for Lagos and the coast where the dancing rainbow-gemmed surf plays 'on a shore of yellow sand before an audience of stately coco palms.'

The winter rains began to fall and only Veronica rejoiced and lifted her face to the heavens and said 'This lovely rain – just what the garden needs!'

CHAPTER THIRTY-TWO

THE CRUEL COUNTRY

EARLY in June we paid a flying visit to South West Africa,* accompanied by the Flag Lieutenant.

And here let me make one thing quite clear. Whatever may be said at U.N.O., or by the Reverend Michael Scott, who claims to represent the Hereros (a proportion of 70,000 Natives out of a total of 300,000), every sensible being in Southern Africa, no matter what their political or physical complexion, recognizes South West as part of the Union – geographically, economically and ethnologically.

It was captured from the Germans by Generals Botha and Smuts in World War One in the campaign of 1915, and after that war was mandated to the Union by the League of Nations, since when it has been admirably administered by successive Union Governments, and will no doubt continue to flourish as an important part of the Union, though possibly with certain distinctive laws and features of its own.

We were to be the guests of the Administrator and his wife, Dr. and Mrs. Van Rijn, whom we had already met at the Cape during the Festival. We had also met Mr. and Mrs. Neser, whose kindness and thoughtfulness added so much to the pleasure and interest of our week in South West. Mr. Neser was the Secretary for Native Affairs, and his knowledge and experience of the people under his care was as wide as his work on their behalf was indefatigable.

South West is a strange country. The people there say 'It

* *South West Africa is a prosperous part of the Republic of South Africa fully represented in the Republic's Parliament. But it remains a perennial bone of contention at U.N.O.*

gets you!' That can be taken two ways, but in either sense, it makes you *feel* as well as think. You may fear it, hate it or love it – and those three are more akin than they might seem – but you cannot remain indifferent to its particular character.

Our aircraft took off in the cold misty dawn of a winter's morning, and a few hours later we were in the sun, flying over the diamond diggings at the mouth of the Orange River.

Atlantic rollers crashed upon this desolate shore – ice cold rollers, for here the Antarctic current makes the waters ideal for fish and lobsters. Whale and seals follow the fish, while men follow everything. Along the coast lies the Namib Desert, rich in minerals and precious stones. Many prospectors venture into that waste never to return. They call this stretch 'the Skeleton Coast', and fog and thirst are the killers. Ships and men find their graves in the cold sea, and fortune hunters lie buried beneath the shifting desert sands.

As we headed inland I stared down at this pitiless Namib waste. It was a painted desert – sulphur yellow, red-core, and all the pastel shades of pink and blue – flat and empty till it rose in ridged escarpments and crumpled suddenly into high volcanic peaks, like a smooth papier mâché mask thrust aside to reveal the cruel ravages of time.

I glanced across at Tony. Here was a sight to rejoice his desert-loving eyes. But he was writing a letter.

The air-hostess, a Windhoek girl, leaned over my shoulder. Would I like a magazine? No ... The desert *was* weird, wasn't it? You'd think no living thing could exist down there. But sheep did.

It seldom rains, but they lick some desert-plant that holds the dew.'

'If there are sheep there is a farmer and a house,' I said. 'One never sees a house.'

'Farms are big in South West,' she said. 'Many thousand hectares – thirty square miles on an average. The house is always near a water-course, or a damn, or a well.'

'If there is a farm there is probably a farmer's wife ...'

She made a wry face and tossed her short fair curls as if to say, 'Wouldn't suit *me!*'

I think that was when a sense of intense loneliness first gripped me. So much land, and all of it thirst-land!

In the South West Section of the Festival we had visited the Bushmen's Enclosure. A troupe of little Stone Age families had come to see the great city, and the great city had flocked to see those who, according to the Bantu, 'were in the world with the other animals before the Great One brought man out of the rock'. If any Native in Southern Africa had the right to say 'Africa for the African!' it was only this dwarf, less than five foot high, with the protuberant belly and rump supported by spindly legs. The little sallow wedge-shaped faces of these pygmy people were wild as jackals'. Their habits were those of fauna rather than of human beings, and in their own environment they eat their game raw, hide, entrails and all. They are nomad hunters, the natural enemy of the herdsman. In their enclosure they carved their ostrich-shell beads, and fashioned their bows and arrows, but the arrows were not tipped with snake venom, for at the Festival they were sold to children. They made their friction-fires by whirling a stick in a hole in a log, and they spoke their primitive clicking tongue as they exclaimed in horror at the 'hideous white faces' of those who stared at them. Yet, though they lived in their own land like the coelocanth in the Indian Ocean – survivals from the remote past – they were accustomed to aeroplanes, 'the White Man's Bird', but the train which had brought them south had been a novelty, 'a big long centipede, swallowing black stones and belching smoke'. They had feared the sight of the sea, and welcomed the return to their waterless Kalahari where only one law prevailed – the right of a clan to its own water-hole. Like the fat-tailed sheep and the humped cattle, they could live on the minimum of moisture and trek many miles to quench their thirst.

'MAK FAS U GORDEL!' 'FASTEN YOUR BELT!' flashed the electric sign, and the plane hiccoughed over the thorn-covered mountains that hold Windhoek like a basket of flowers.

It was 1.30, the sun was hot and high in the heavens, and the air was keen, for Windhoek is 5,500 feet above sea-level. When I combed my hair it crackled and sprang up like a gollywog's – dry as hay.

The Administrator and Mrs. Van Rijn, the Nesers, and the Administrator's Secretary – a charming young man everybody called Japie – met us on the aerodrome, and somewhere in the background I was aware of the anxious scrutiny of a nimble wiry man. This wiry man was misnamed Round, and he had come secretly to estimate our size and weight. For he was the pilot of the tiny Post Office Piper plane which was presently to take us into the interior of South West *if* we could be squeezed into the interior of the Piper. But we were then oblivious of these plans and of the apprehensions of Mr. Round.

From the high stoep of the Administrator's residence the town spread beneath us – a prosperous, pretty town set in colourful gardens alive with the twittering of birds in the plane-trees, palms and cypresses. Windhoek's water supply comes from hot springs gushing out of the earth at just the right temperature for a nice hot bath. For other purposes it has to be cooled. Most of the houses are single-storeyed, but modern blocks of flats and housing estates are going up rapidly. The streets and avenues have the charm of Continental boulevards, where the citizens may enjoy a cup of coffee on the terrace of a café, or in the shade of the trees, while they watch the world go by. Of course there used to be a Beer Garden, but it has been demoted to a Koffie Huis. German, English and Afrikaans are all spoken in this trilingual town.

Dr. Van Rijn could speak the three languages with equal facility. He had been educated at Stellenbosch and Heidelberg University, and was well known as a writer and one-time editor of an important Afrikaans paper. He was tall and spectacled, a personality both kindly and forceful. Mrs.

411

Van Rijn was small and maternal, and although she was deeply interested in South West, I think she was often homesick for her children and grandchildren in the Free State.

'Is it true that Goering was born in this house?' I asked.

'No', said the Administrator. 'This used to be the old German Government House, but when Hermann Goering was born in South West, Windhoek was not the capital. His father was German Commissioner and was trying to persuade the Hereros to accept German rule.'

'The Germans lived well when they were here,' said Mrs. Van Rijn. 'You can see the castles they built on the ridges above the town.'

These old castles still dominate the arid African scene with the same assurance that the *Schloss* of the *Vaterland* looks down from its wooden height upon the River Rhine and the rock of the Lorelei.

But Windhoek's real pride is its Cemetery, and when you arrive, you are immediately told that you must go to the Cemetery – a suggestion which carries no sinister significance. The Cemetery, with its well-kept graves behind tall box-hedges, its plane-trees and bowers of roses, is as pleasant a place for an hour's reflection as you could wish to find. Many of the German tombstones have little seats attached to them so that the descendants of the honoured dead may contemplate the resting-place of the departed at their leisure.

Behind the Cemetery is the Herero location, and there recollections of the German departed are less agreeable.

From the Cemetery boundary, thin-leafed and wintry in June, you may see the tall Natives in their dusty paths, the women in their Victorian gowns and high head-dresses and the men shabby and sullen, and only the children carefree and near-naked in the sun.

When South West Africa was colonized by the Germans towards the end of last century, the Hereros became a subject race. Till then they had been the overlords, owning their slaves, and, like many slave-owners, intermarrying with

412

them. With the arrival of the Germans the Hereros found their land being appropriated and their stately women consorting with colonists and soldiery.

In 1904 they rebelled, and after that the Germans gave their merciless 'extermination order'. Many fled to Bechuanaland where old Chief Khama gave them sanctuary. From that time on it is said that the women refused to have children and that no Herero voluntarily spoke to a White person. Today, under the Union administration, their numbers are increasing once more, and the majority of them are satisfied in their Reserves, breeding cattle, but there are many malcontents among them who would like to set the clock back to the days when the 'klip-kaffirs' (rock natives) were their slaves, and the whole land, unsullied by a White foot, their grazing ground.

Work is anathema to the Hereros – 'although the women are wonderful laundresses,' said Mrs. Van Rijn at lunch, 'but then look at their own dresses – never less than twelve yards to a skirt, and they are always neat and clean.'

'I wonder where they got the fashion from?' I said.

'From the first missionaries – but somehow it alters its character!'

With their flounced skirts, high wasp waists and tight bodices, the women might be some strange gaudy reflection of the Victorian era, but there was nothing Mission-school about their appearance, which was both enticing and forbidding. If you were to pull a Herero girl's tall turban from her head it would be as bad as pulling down a desert Toureg's veil. She might not kill you for the insult, but she would clutch her bare head in shame. Worse still, you might find stolen jewels or silver in the edifice she had worn with such arrogance.

There were times when the Administration's patience was sorely tried by these proud people.

'They will not do a thing for themselves,' said Dr. Van Rijn. 'Some while ago they complained that their cattle were straying. We told them to fence them in. They said "Give us the fencing". We agreed, and the Government sent them all

413

the fencing they needed. Some months later they again complained about straying. We said. "What about those fences? Don't they keep your cattle in?" They said, "We are waiting for the White men to come and put up our fences".'

'You must have a rest after lunch,' said Mrs. Van Rijn to us. 'I know you got up very early this morning. And later we will take you for a drive.'

The Administrator bowed his head, and said grace. I was touched to observe that he had said it before lunch in Afrikaans – his own home-language – and after lunch in English, which was ours. Afrikaner hospitality is seldom at fault, even in small matters.

On the evening of our first day at Windhoek Mr. and Mrs. Neser gave a party for us. It was a real South West party, which means it was a very good one. About twenty people came in to an informal supper with hot curry and rice, venison and vegetables, salads, sweets and the light ale and delicious white wine of the country.

'We all sit where we like and change places after every course, if we feel inclined,' smiled Mrs. Neser. 'But we like to eat in comfort, so there are plenty of tables. In South West people take their food seriously!'

She led me to a table where I was introduced to Dr. Marais, who had been some twenty-five years in the country and knew it well.

Although my mother's maiden name had been Marais, we decided that we were not related, which, if we were right, made us almost as rare as white rhinos, for practically all the old families of South Africa are related in some way or another. My companion was excellent and amusing company, especially when he talked about the little Bushmen who were his special study. He had lived in their part of the north-west and knew them well.

'If you want to shock a Bushman to death – quite literally – give him a bath!' said the Doctor. 'He is a creature of the thirst-land and he has never used water except for drinking. He stores it in blown ostrich-eggs, and it is more precious

414

than any other possession. One of our little fellows who went to the Cape for the Festival got sick and they sent him to hospital. The nurse washed him. It nearly killed him – in fact it was kill or cure, and in this case it was cure. He escaped before she could do it again! You can't keep a Bushman in a room. He has to feel the sun and see the stars.'

Mrs. Marais came and joined us. Like all the women I met in Windhoek, she was well dressed, charming and gay. They wore the lovely precious and semi-precious stones of South West in their dresses, and Karakul or seal-skin capes over their shoulders. They laughed and said, 'If you stay here five years you'll never go! It gets you . . . this is a fascinating country, people don't understand. . . .' They said, 'It's a pity you won't have time to go to Ovamboland, and the Itosha Pans. That's the beautiful part, you can see all the wild animals in creation there – elephant, lion, rhinos – and Bushmen too . . .' And they said, 'We are taking a holiday next summer and fetching our children from school at the Cape . . .' or 'We hope to go overseas next year . . .' And when they spoke of the Cape or 'Overseas' their eyes were more brilliant than the aquamarines or tourmalines flashing at their throats – a hungry sort of brilliance as if they felt an unacknowledged need to escape from this land which 'gets you' – a similar need perhaps to that of the little Bushmen at the Cape who had returned so gladly to their own sandy waste.

'We want to give a little party for you before you go', said Mrs. Marais. 'Do you think you can fit it in?'

I said I was sure we could if the Administrator had made no other arrangements. They were so kind. In all three languages 'hospitality' was the key-word in South West.

When we said good-night, a slim Herero girl brought my coat – Helga, the daughter of a Native mother and a German father, light-skinned, small-featured, and in her own way, beautiful.

Next day we made a journey to the Herero and Damara

Reserves with Mr. Neser and Mr. Round in the little Post Office plane.

Mr. Round's job was to service the remote radio stations that kept the interior in touch with Windhoek, and he loved his little Piper as a huntsman loves his horse – in a highly personal way. As Bertie and I were successfully stowed into the back seat (with no room to spare) he looked pleased. He had judged the bulk of his passengers to a nicety at the aerodrome the day before. Mr. Neser squeezed into the front seat beside him, Mr. Round sprang in and seized the controls, someone slammed the doors, and off we set with a fine roar of our single engine.

Toony had gone on by car the evening before, driving through the veld all night with the advance party.

Mr. Round did not bother with charts. He knew South West from end to end, and we simply soared away over the arid mountain ranges into the blue beyond while the semi-desert of the karakul spread its fawn carpet far beneath us.

The Magistrate of the District, the Welfare Officer and the Assistant Native Commissioner were there to meet us when the Piper landed with a few expert gyrations to counteract a strong cross-wind.

The Native Reserves of South West are not eroded desert-lands. They are good cattle and sheep country, and wells have been sunk by the Government. If they were not set aside for the Native they would soon be snapped up by European farmers. The Native's security, tribal and economic, is the certainty that his territory is inviolate.

At first glance the administration of these areas seems a casual affair. Unlike the High Commission Territories, there is no elaborate colonial administration, and no permanent Police Force on the spot. It is not necessary. The sole European authorities are the Magistrate and the Welfare Officer, and the Police are not allowed to enter the Reserves except in cases of serious crime. Here and there a mission station – usually German or Finnish – has its church, school and clinic, and, according to its needs and the good it does, it receives a subsidy from the Government. It is reckoned in South West that at least £50,000 a year is spent on the Natives by the Government, roughly £1 a head from every White inhabitant of the country.

'We encourage the headmen to manage their own affairs', said Mr. Neser. 'We want them to keep their own customs and traditions intact, within reason. We teach them how to improve their land and their stock and their health and education, but they must continue to develop their own culture. We have to go carefully here among the Hereros because their history is full of tragedy and bitterness. With the Ovambos, further north, it is easy. They are a happy people. Ovamboland is rich and beautiful and it is from there that most of our domestic and mine labour is recruited. An Ovambo contracts to work for six months in a European settlement, and then returns to his tribe. He is not allowed to be more than two years at a stretch away from his own people, or he would become detribalized. He must keep in touch with them.'

It was only a short drive to Omajette, the Herero cattle country among the thorn-trees and softly waving grass, and there, near the Native *stat*, was the house of the Welfare Officer, Mr. Adams.

Mrs. Adams greeted us with cheerful warmth and gave us a delicious morning tea with scones and cakes. She introduced us to the only other European woman in her neighbourhood – the widow of the store-keeper, who was carrying on her late husband's business – and to the wife of the Magistrate, who had driven over with her husband from Omaruru.

'You must find it terribly lonely here,' I said.

She laughed and said, 'Oh, I have plenty to do!'

Both she and her husband had learned the elements of a medical training, and the Natives brought their sick and injured to the Welfare Officer's dispensary from all over the Reserve.

'Often we are awakened at dead of night,' said Mrs. Adams. 'Usually some emergency like a case of snake-bite or somebody gored, or some other veld casualty. We have no electric light and no telephone, so we just have to do the best we can by lamp-light, and, if necessary, by what our medical books tell us.'

Their only entertainment was a battery wireless set. And books – to be read slowly, word by word, since there was no library where they could be changed. No wonder the old Voortrekkers knew their Bible by heart. It was not only the the Good Book, but their only reading matter.

Across the sandy track from this old German Colonial bungalow was the school and not far from that the Native *stat* (village) and the trader's store, where the Herero women could buy their twelve yard dress lengths of flowered cotton, and the men their corduroy trousers and fancy shirts.

We strolled across after our lavish 'elevenses' and found the children marshalled in the sun outside the little white school-house.

Mr. Neser addressed them in Afrikaans, which was interpreted into their own tongue by a Native gentleman who could speak at least six Native languages in addition to English, German and Afrikaans.

Mr. Neser told the goggling children that we were personages of the utmost account. The Admiral was the man who protected the shores of Africa from all enemies. If he had his cannons with him he would be able to shoot over yonder hill and strike whatever man or beast he wished, invisible though they might believe themselves to be! He could, with one shot, demolish whole *stadts.* But he had come in friendship, and with his great powers he would protect these people. His wife was a daughter of South Africa, who had written famous books, and who would write of the Native peoples of South West Africa, and who would describe the fine singing of these particular children so that the world might know of them.

After such an address I cannot let Mr. Neser down, so I hasten to discharge my responsibility to that score or more of Herero children and the world which waits so anxiously to know how they sing. Hear then, that these small brown

418

boys and girls in their neat European school-suits sang their woolly heads off, after which they were given a holiday and handfuls of shiny rainbow-coloured sweets shared out by their Herero teacher. This fortunate teacher had recently married the sewing mistress, a girl of rare beauty, who wore her high head-dress like a coronet, and who clearly did not endorse the barren intentions of an older and sadder generation

In the school kitchen the cook-girl was making a stew, 'But the children need more meat,' she said.

'We will get it for you at once,' said Mr. Adams. 'The Admiral will shoot it for you himself.'

So the Admiral was hurried into a jeep with the Flag Lieutenant, who had rejoined us, and most of the men of the party, and off they rushed in a cloud of dust to get meat for the children.

Within an hour a dozen springbok were hanging in the shelter behind the Welfare Officer's house. Bertie, I was told, had brought down seven, each shot through the heart. He had refused to shoot them on the run for fear of wounding them. He had used sixteen cartridges, and the Native boys said with respect, '*Die oubaas skiet goed!*' (The old master shoots well.)

The Natives in the cattle Reserves are doing well with their creameries. They have their own separators, and the cream from their cows is sent to the nearest butter-making centre. Much of the Union's butter comes from South West Africa. The profits go to improving the quality of the herds.

The advance party had arranged a wonderful *braaivleis* for us under the camel-thorn trees, and we ate the grilled liver and ribs of the newly shot springbok, as well as many other delicacies cooked over the wood fires.

'This is rhino country,' said Mr. Adams. 'Two were seen here not long ago.'

'Don't be alarmed,' smiled the Magistrate. 'Rhinos don't hunt people, people hunt rhinos.'

All the same I kept an eye on the thorn scrub in case some

419

well-meaning rhino should blunder into our midst. The *oubaas* might *skiet goed* and Mrs. Adams might be able to cobble up a gore-wound quite neatly, but I was content to take both assumptions on trust. However, no rhino passed that way that day, and presently, weighing a good deal more than we had done, we once more clambered into the back seat of the Piper and took to the air with Mr. Round and Mr. Neser.

At Okombayé, the Damara Reserve air-strip, we were met by Mr. Hemming, the Welfare Officer for the territory, who drove us to his house some miles away. The face of the country had changed and we were among rocky mountain ranges where lived the 'Klip' (rock) Damaras who had once been Herero slaves. Vultures wheeled in the sky and the long grasses stirred as some wild creature went about its business. There was a savage lonely beauty about the scene.

The courtroom of the Elders was attached to the house of the Welfare officer, but that afternoon a Council Meeting was held outside it under the palms and trees with the blue ranges in the distance.

The Damara Elders came through a little wooden gate like a primitive chorus, each mahogany ancient carrying an empty milk-pail, which he up-ended and used as a seat. We took our places behind a table facing them, and the wise dark patient faces examined ours. These old men of the tribe wore European clothes, and their grizzled heads were bare. In the morning we had met the Herero Headmen – impassive and polite – expressing themselves satisfied with the progress of their Reserve. The Damaras were more responsive. The old eyes, intent and grave, were yet ready to crinkle into merriment, as they did when Mr. Neser said, 'Your milk-pails are empty. I hope that is not also the case with your cows!' He then introduced us in the flattering formula to which we were growing accustomed, and added:

'I have come to you in friendship to hear how you are and what you need. The Admiral and the Admiral's wife also wish to see how you live and know if you are content. You may speak freely and say what is in your hearts.'

Salatiel Seibib, a weathered ancient, rose from his milk-pail and spoke in deep slow tones.

'You come to us as a father, and it is good when a father comes often to see his children. We welcome you, and we welcome this great General of the sea and his wife.'

He went on to say that the creameries were doing well, and that the water was sufficient, except in one place. The people were troubled that the vultures were changing their habits and no longer waited for dead creatures but took young lambs. There were lion on the air-strip. It was a pastoral news report.

'And the new people who have come here? How are they fairing?'

A representative of the 'new people' said that they were settling down well.

Mr. Neser turned to us. 'The Reserve near Windhoek was too overcrowded, and we had to persuade a proportion to move here. Such a thing can only be done if they wish it and realize that it is to their interest. Even so, they must send their representatives to the Cape Parliament, and, only if that Parliament agrees, can we shift part of a population We may never deprive them of land.'

I noticed that whoever he spoke to, wherever it might be, his first query was always, 'How is the water?'

Somehow that question – *'How is the water?'* – has dripped into my memory and left there a small indentation, the imprint of South West Africa, the light sound of a drop of precious water fallen upon the dry sandy earth and instantly absorbed.

It was the same next day when we went to the Government Research Farm near Windhoek. How was the water? The Manager shook his head. It was getting low, the cattle might soon have to trek to the next borehole.

The Administrator and Mrs. Van Rijn were with us, and Mrs. Neser had come too. Before we were shown the treated karakul skins, a grand march past of the animals took place. The wind blew cold across the veld and raised clouds of dust from the hoofs of sheep and cattle. I was fascinated by the baby karakul lambs, and was glad to know that they were already too old to be slaughtered, for the lamb whose fleece keeps women warm and smart is killed a few hours after birth.

'No wonder it's so profitable,' said one of the Agricultural Officers. 'The lamb doesn't have to be fed or looked after, and the ewe breeds again all the sooner for losing the lamb.'

'But isn't it cruel to *her* to kill her baby?'

'A sheep has very little maternal instinct,' he said.

He showed us the fine little pelts – fleeces like moiré velvet, in black, brown, grey, fawn and white, and the coarser inferior quality.

'We are breeding up our sheep to produce the skin most like that of the unborn lamb – but we do *not* use unborn lambs, as some people think. We don't want to ruin valuable ewes, for one thing, and it is not allowed in any case.'

'It seems sad all the same,' I said to Mrs. Naser.

Her expressive short-sighted eyes filled with pity.

She said, 'To me the seal industry seems sadder. At six months old the young seals, basking on the rocks with their mothers, are clubbed to death. Hundreds of them.'

'Don't the mothers fight for them?'

She shook her head. 'When the men come the mothers abandon their young. But as they slither into the sea they utter terrible cries!' She sighed. 'A famous writer came here not long ago. I asked him to tell me his impressions of South West. He said, "I can sum them up in one word". For a moment it crossed my mind that the word might be – hospitality . . . but it was *cruelty*. "Your karakul industry – your seal industry," he said, "cruelty!" '

Cruelty? Is it really more cruel to kill a new-born lamb than a sheep for meat? Crueller to club a seal than to hook a fish or slaughter a calf? It may be so.

On the following day we went with the Administrator and Mrs. Van Rijn to Rehoboth.

Dr. Van Rijn had not long been Administrator, and this

was his first visit to the people of the *Baster Gebied* (Half-Caste Territory). He was going to meet their *Raad* (Council) and address them and hear what they had to say about the progress of their land.

Rehoboth is some sixty miles from Windhoek.

'The finest grazing in the country,' said Dr. Van Rijn, as we drove through the waving golden grasslands. 'There are Europeans who would give anything to get their hands on this area.'

'Can they?'

'They cannot *buy* one hectare. They can only lease it, and even then the *Baster Raad* has to give permission. Many men here are rich, others dreadfully poor. The man who works makes his fortune, and the idler or the drunkard goes under.'

The Afrikaans dictionary meaning of the word *Baster* is 'bastard or hybrid'. It is in the latter – the half-caste – sense that it is applied to the people of Rehoboth. Their language is a mixture of Afrikaans and High Dutch, and their names are Dutch, English, Scottish and German. They originally came to South West to form a *Baster* Republic in a new empty land. Many were descendants of the *Voortrekkers* and their chief pride was in their White blood. But their opportunities in the White man's territory were slight, and so they followed the example of their White progenitors and trekked to seek a national home. They found it in the wilderness of South West Africa where they settled on the best land. They called their town Rehoboth, for hot springs gushed from the rosy granite rocks and no man disputed their ownership. Like the *Voortrekkers*, the *Basters* identified themselves closely with the wandering folk of Genesis and Exodus, folk who also dwelt in the lands where water was precious.

'Genisis. Chapter 26, verse 19.

'And Isaac's servants digged in the valley, and found there a well of springing water.

'And the herdmen of Ge-rär did strive with Isaac's

herdmen, saying the water is ours: and he called the name of the wall E-sĕki, because they strove with him.

'And they digged another well, and strove for that also; and he called the name of it Sit-nah.

'And he removed from thence, and digged another well; and for that they strove not; and he called the name of it Rĕ-hŏ-bôth; and he said, For now the Lord hath made room for us, and we shall be fruitful in the land.'

When the Germans came the Rehoboth people welcomed the arrival of the foreign settlers with its promise of a new infusion of the longed-for White blood. And, in the Herero Rebellion of 1904, they fought with the Germans. Right or wrong, the half-caste follows the call of his White blood against the Native. As a reward for their help the German Governor endorsed their ownership of the valuable land near Windhoek so that 'in terms of their expressed wishes, we should place them as near as possible to the Whites', and gave them many other privileges. During the South African-German campaign of 1915 in the First World War most of them transferred their allegiance go General Botha's forces. The rights they received from the Germans have been increased.

The small town of Rehoboth, with its stores, hotel, pretty church and little white houses was in gala to receive the Administrator and his guests. A platform had been erected in the sunny Square under the old camel-thorn tree beneath which the original *Baster* leader, Kaptein Hermanus van Wyk, had dispensed the law. A great banner with WELKOM written across it fluttered over an arch of palms. The burghers from the country round had assembled there, and the school-children stood in their different age-groups. I felt a sharp pang of pity as I looked at those children of mixed blood, some fair-skinned and blue-eyed, some with blonde hair and the heavy features of a darker race, and others with little trace of their White blood in their faces. '*The Lord hath made room for us . . .*'

424

First the little ones sang in Afrikaans, and then the older
girls and boys sang beautiful old English songs – 'I walk
beside you' and 'Drink to me only with thine eyes' –
specially in our honour. The mournful sweetness and purity
their voices in the dry dusty sunshine was deeply moving.

The Secretary of the Raad made an impassioned address
of welcome in Afrikaans and pleaded for more teachers for
his people.

This gave Dr. Van Rijn an opportunity he desired, for it
troubled him greatly that the people of the *Gebied* did not
send their children to school regularly, but how and when
it suited them, and many took them away after the first
year.

He was an experienced and convincing orator, and he impressed upon the listening people the meaning and value of
education. A year was no use – nor were a few lessons here
and there – the children must go to school consistently. He
spoke in pastoral terms, which evoked vivid images for these
people, and he promised that if the *Raad* would make
proper use of the schools they already had they would be
given more by the Government.

Afterwards, in the *Raadsaal* (Council Room) the Elders
met and talked to Dr. Van Rijn as to a friend, and many
problems were considered and discussed. About a hundred
men were in the *Raadsaal*, and, as I observed their faces and
features – some so pale and some so dark – it passed through
my mind that *physically*, in this small community of about
eighty thousand people, one could see the result of a 'pilot
plan' for South Africa as the Communists would like it, with
no social barriers and inter-marriage between Black and
White the order of the day.

When we returned to Windhoek that evening someone
asked me where we had toured that day.

'To the "Baster Gebied",' I said.

'Ah, yes,' said this man. 'The best grazing land in the area,
as well watered as anywhere in South West, not far from
Windhoek – but, for all that, the land of the lost . . .'

In the plane on the way back to Cape Town I made an entry in my diary.

'*June 5th* 1952. We have had a wonderful time. The Administrator and Mrs. Van Rijn were hospitality itself. So was everyone else. The pretty town of Windhoek has an air of prosperity. South West has so much wealth – diamonds, semi-precious stones, tin and other minerals, cattle, sheep, the seal and karakul industry, abundant game and fine fisheries. But every drop of fresh water is life-blood for that plateau wedged between the cruel deserts of the Namib and the Kalahari.

'First and last I have been impressed with a sense of desolation.

'When we were with other people this feeling was in abeyance, a loneliness forgotten. But after the party, when we were back in our room in the old German Government House and the lights were out for the night, it began to gnaw.

'Strange, for this was no melancholy that came from within. It came from the dusty land, from the silent Hereros, from the Basters who live out their lives "on the wrong side of the fence" – no matter how good the grazing may be on their side of it – and from the east wind that sighs in the cypresses.

'The near, resonant bell of the new Dutch Reformed Church strikes the hours, and towards midnight there is a little train that is always very busy, shunting, puffing and being important in the silent city under the brilliant stars. It has come a long way across the waste and no doubt it has a long way to go to the Skeleton Coast where the wives of the pilchard trawlers wait at Walvis Bay or Luderitz. .... At length it blows its whistle and the sound of its wheels fades, and I am haunted by something indefinable in the eyes of the women – a nostalgia that creeps up on them when they are off guard. The company in South West is the best – warm and friendly – but when the talk and the laughter are silent, one is aware of something else. *It is then that the deserts draw near*. It is in that lonely hour that the garden city and all the wide plateau in the waterless vice holds its breath, listening for the dry march of the Namib and the Kalahari. Will those inexorable foes of man meet in the centuries to come and clasp burning fleshless hands over the buried treasure of yesterday's prosperity? . . .'

CHAPTER THIRTY-THREE

THE KOWIE, AND THE VALLEY
OF KUMALO

IT was near the end of June and the time had come for the East Coast cruise once more – Port Elizabeth, East London and Durban. With it we combined the breaking of new ground – Pietermaritzburg, the capital of Natal, where my husband was to open the Agricultural Show; the Game Reserve of Hluhluwe; the Union Native Territories of the Transkei, and finally the Native college of Lovedale and the University of Fort Hare, where Tshekedi Khama had been the best student of his time.

Port Elizabeth entertained the *Bermuda* and ourselves with her usual generosity, and, on our way to Pietermaritzburg by car, we spent a much needed quiet weekend at the lovely little seaside resort of Port Alfred on the Kowie River.

Tony had gone on ahead to Durban in the *Bermuda* and was to meet us at Pietermaritzburg for Show Week.

From Port Elizabeth to the Kowie is about three hours by car, and we arrived at lunch-time a few minutes before the *Bermuda* sailed across the bay on her northward passage. Everybody in our small hotel on the hill was on the stoep, eager to see her, and the children were all dancing up and down with excitement. We felt very proud of my husband's Flag-ship steaming so serenely up the coast with the sun shining on her armaments – a brave little bit of the distant island so dear to the Eastern Province. She evoked a sense of security. If the Navy is at hand all is well!

Opposite the hotel was a white turreted house with an

aeroplane lying in the corner of the garden like a huge butterfly.

'Did it crash there?' I asked the Proprietor.

'No,' he said. 'It's the children's playroom. There was an Air Force training station near here in the war, and afterwards the Anson trainers were dismembered and disembowelled and sold. You could buy a frame for a song. Lots of the Natives bought wings to use for making huts.

The Proprietor turned out to be the son of Doctor Barrow-Dowling, the late organist of St. George's Cathedral in Cape Town, who had taught St. Cyprian's girls singing in my school-days, and who had also coached my mother. To a child the lame singing-master had been a formidable figure as he stumped into the school hall with his stick and his music-case. He was a tiger at spotting those whose lips moved in silent song. Out would fly that stick.

'You there, Miss! Sing up!'

How he would have loved the little West Africans! Yet, in our drawing-room at Tees Lodge, accompanying my mother in the ballads she sang with such charm and sentiment, he was no longer fierce at all.

For myself, I had liked the Doctor best when he was the invisible power behind the swirling waves of sacred music that filled the shadowed Gothic nave of the Cathedral when my mother was the soloist at some friend's wedding, and her voice floated down from the heights of the organ-box, warm and true, in the haunting beauty of an Ave Maria.

'There's a friend of yours staying here,' said Mr. Barrow-Dowling to my husband. 'Sir Lionel Fletcher. He's a mad keen shot and knew you at Bisley when you were in charge of the Naval rifle and revolver teams.'

This valiant marksman, who had now settled in East Africa, had driven down the continent from Tanganyika with his friend, Major Russell. Between them, their ages totalled over a hundred and fifty years.

Sir Lionel was tall and distinguished with keen brown eyes for ever narrowed down a real or imaginary gun-barrel, while his companion had merry blue eyes and a fine fog-horn of a voice. One evening, when we were all dining together, Major Russell suddenly pulled four horn articles out of his pocket and flicked them on to the white cloth like dice.

'Lion's claws,' he said to me: 'They're lucky. Take your pick.'

I chose a large unblemished claw.

'That's a good one,' he said. And, with a dashing gesture, slapped down a furry affair next to it. 'The paw. They come out of this.'

I shuddered, preferring claws to paws.

People were very nice to me at that little hotel. They gave me things.

It was an unpretentious hotel with a long narrow passage running straight from front to back with the bedrooms on either side and the bathrooms at the far end. One morning I passed by the open door of a little boy's room. He was sorting his sea-shells, and Jacqueline Barrow-Dowling was perched on the end of his bed watching him with a critical bird-like glance.

'Come in and look!' she called to me. 'Basil has some nice shells. Mine are nice too.'

Laid out on the bed were panther-speckled cowries. Venus-ears, rainbow-hued fans, frilled Dolly Vardens, and ridged cornucopias. I took up a conch and put it against my ear.

'Can you hear the sea?' asked the little boy breathlessly. 'Some people can.'

'Ssh . . . I'm listening.'

They watched me intently. There could be no bluffing them. If the deep ocean-murmur failed me, they would know by my eyes. I closed them. I too had sought sea-treasures as a child along the beaches of Onrust, Hermanus and Mossel River with my friend, Marjorie.

Hush! Here, indeed, is the summer whisper of that other shore and the eager voices of the past – children's voices – 'See, Marj, a purple fan – and perfect!' And her cry, 'There's

430

a golden Venus-ear – baby one! When the wave goes back we'll get it!' The brittle suck of shingle with the retreating line of foam, and there, among Neptune's broken crockery – tiny and delicate as the ear of a new-born babe – little golden shell whirls and gleams as Marjorie's nine-year-old hand catches it in the ebb – 'Oh, Joy! It's the loveliest we've ever found—'

'You *are* hearing something!' said Jacqueline.

I gave the conch back to Basil and he laid it carefully with the others – a singing shell still echoing with the past.

'You may choose one of my collection,' he said impetuously. 'For your very own – whichever you like!'

It was a generous offer. I glanced at his flushed face, the flax-blue eyes resting anxiously on a certain freckled cowrie, and the silky hair, pale as cellophane, ruffled by the small hand he ran through it.

I touched the freckled cowrie and saw his teeth grip his under-lip.

'This is a real beauty, Basil. But I like this fan even better if you can really spare it.'

Through a heartfelt sigh of relief, he said, 'Take it! And these too. You can use these mussels as ash-trays. Daddy does.'

It was too cold to swim at that season, so we spent a good deal of our time on the Kowie Golf Course, which is excellent but strenuous.

The President, Secretary and Committee treated us with great friendliness and made us honorary members, and we were shown the tee from which Edward, Prince of Wales, had attempted to drive a ball over the bush into the sea. As the sea was more than a mile away, the drive failed in its object and the ball was later recovered by the Secretary's dog, and its chewed remains repose in a glass case in the Club House as a souvenir of one of royalty's lesser frustrations.

As we were about to leave the pretty little port among the sand-dunes and bushy hills Jacqueline ran to the car and pressed a carboard box into my hand.

'Shells,' she said. 'Some of mine – a present for you!'

We had decided to make our night-stop between the Kowie and Pietermaritzburg at Ixopo, the base from which the film of Alan Paton's book, *Cry the Beloved Country*, had been made. The Flag Lieutenant's brother, John Harris, had been one of Zoltan Korda's photographers on the spot and had spent a few days with us at Admiralty House on his way home, so we had become very interested in this picture which was later awarded an Oscar for its outstanding quality.

The Eastern Province is rough masculine country, and we travelled through bush ablaze with flaming aloes, up the spectacular Kei Cuttings on to the high plateau of the Transkei and Griqualand, and then down into the tumbled hills and vales of fertile Natal. Beautiful Natal is a woman – Aphrodite with her swelling seductive curves caught in the ruthless embrace of the towering Drakensberg Range – Mars, her lover and protector.

At Ixopo we stayed at a pseudo-Tudor Hotel, which seemed curiously out of place in the veld. Mr. Zoltan Kirda had stayed there too with his film company, and I do not suppose it seemed at all odd to him, because place and period are constantly lifted out of their context for the benefit of the camera. The Proprietor and his assistant were called Aulsebrooke and Benningfield, names which had for me a fascinating ring of long ago English battles – *Glad tidings ring through wood and weald of Aulsebrooke and Benningfield* . . .

The story of Alan Paton's fine book is well known. Briefly it is the tale of the old Zulu Pastor, Kumalo, who leaves his home valley to seek his son and his sister in the wicked city of Johannesburg and bring them back. It is a sad quest. His son has been led astray by bad companions and is in prison for the murder of a White man who happens to be a true champion of the Native people, and his sister has become a prostitute. But although he fails to bring these two lost ones back to the fold, with him instead comes the girl

432

who is to bear his son's baby, and his sister's little boy. Despite its melancholy theme, the story has a message of hope and humanity and is written with rare beauty and no bitterness. And Kumalo's valley is as alive as any of the characters – one comes to understand its needs and to know and love its moods.

Major Aulsebrooke drove us there in his car after lunch. He had seen most of the film in the making and could tell us many interesting things about it. We followed the winding road that 'runs from Ixopo into the hills. These hills are grass-covered and rolling and they are lovely beyond any singing of it. The road runs seven miles into them to Carisbrooke: and from there, if there is no mist, you look down on one of the fairest valleys of Africa.'

There was no mist, and it was as Alan Paton had described it. Standing on the ridge by the tiny siding of Carisbrooke, we looked down into the great fair valley on one side, and into the smaller valley of Kumalo on the other. It was the dry season and the undulating grassy landscape seemed covered by an old threadbare lion-skin kaross. Here and there were the red wounds of erosion, but patches of blue-gum and acacia and the curved tracks of contour ploughing proved that men strove to save the soil of this place from washing away into the distant sea. Little kraals and houses were dotted about the slopes.

We stolled down the valley to the little school-house of Kumalo, for the Pastor is also the teacher. It was holiday time and everything was deserted.

For a few moments I went off by myself and sat on the sun-warmed grass to look at the valley, and listen to it, and feel it.

The air was dry and very clear. Near the battered tin-roofed shanty of the old school a new one was going up, more solid and dignified, but very simple, for the people of the place were building it themselves although the materials had been given to them by the Film Company. Over the roof of the original shanty a wintering syringa cast a thin tracery of shadow, and a grove of blue-gums sheltered the spot. The quiet was broken from time to time by some sound which served to intensify it – the crowing of a cock, the barking of a dog, far away the shrill sound of children at play, and near at hand the *bzz-bzz* of a fly.

Major Aulsebrooke said, 'Sounds carry a long distance in this atmosphere. That was one of the difficulties when Zolly was making 'Cry'. Of course sometimes it was an advantage – perhaps a bird sang or cattle lowed at the very moment when it heightened the effect. But there were notices all over here, DO NOT COUGH, SILENCE, and so on. Then one wretched man sneezes! Zolly stops everything. 'Cut!' he yells. And turns to the sneezer and asks, "Do you know two hundred and fifty yards?" "Yessir", says the man. "Then see how goddam quick you can use it!" says Korda.'

We went into the little school-house with the leaky tin roof, where old Kumalo had taught and prayed.

'There have always been Kumalos in this valley,' said Major Aulsebrooke. 'The character of the old Native parson was drawn from life, and Canada Lee made him live again. Of course the story itself was fiction, but it could so easily be fact. Paton used to teach at Ixopo, and then he was Head of the Johannesburg Reformatory. He knows these people—'

The late afternoon sun slanted through the broken windows in long fingers of gold that striped and warmed the low wooden benches polished for many years by much use. A lectern for a teacher, or a preacher, faced them.

'It has the look of a chapel,' I said.

We heard a shrill giggle. A sophisticated Native school ma'am had joined us. She wore a mauve dress, black beret and gold-rimmed spectacles.

'Schoolhouse all week, church on Sundays,' she said.

'Do you teach here?' asked Bertie.

She drew herself up. 'No, I teach in Durban. I am only back here for the holidays.'

'Do you like this valley?' I asked.

She looked across the softly swelling folds of her birth-place, and, in clear clipped accents, spoke her mind.

434

'This valley is no good. It is all up and down. In the town we have tram-car and trolley-bus. Here the people must foot it everywhere. It would be better if it was flat. For farming a plain is best. I am going to Carisbrooke to meet a friend on the train. We will have to foot it back up there – and with luggage!' Her tone was half indignant, half contemptuous. She saw no abiding beauty here, only inconvenience. A boy passed by on a mule, riding bare-back in a leisurely fashion – not 'footing it'. He gave a us a grave salute.

Beside the old school-house, the new one was going up. On the foundation stone was inscribed:

This Building is the
Remembrance
of the taking of the Film
Cry the Beloved Country
by

Zoltan Korda $\left.\begin{array}{l} \\ \end{array}\right\}$ Aug.
Alan Paton $\hphantom{Zoltan Korda}$ 1950
$\hphantom{Zoltan Korda}$ A.D.

Zoltan Korda and Alan Paton – an odd pair to be bracketed.

'Everybody is building it,' said the sophisticated school ma'am. 'Even the children.'

'I am sorry the children are not here,' I said, 'I would like to have seen them – perhaps heard them sing.'

'You have come at the wrong season,' she said. 'If it was not holidays they would sing to you. They sing very nicely.'

Very nicely. When Korda had heard them sing he was moved to tears.

'Well', said the school ma'am, looking enviously after the departing tail of the mule. 'I must foot it up to Carisbrooke. Good-bye.'

'Good-bye,' we said.

We drove on towards a patch of tall trees shading the homestead of the farm where Canada Lee and Charles Macrae – the two American Negro actors who had played

Kumalo and his friend – had stayed on location with Mr. and Mrs. Francis, close relatives of Alan Paton.

Mrs. Francis gave us tea out on the stoep. We could see the red Ayrshire cattle coming slowly over the rise – the High Place of the book – and we could hear the reed music of a little Zulu herd-boy, a thin high piping, sweet and monotonous as the call of a bird to its mate.

We spoke of Alan Paton.

'He holds a science degree but he loves literature,' said Mrs. Francis. 'He never lets up in work to improve race relations. He is shy and retiring – moody. He is a good man.'

'His wife – Mrs. Francis's sister – helps him indefatigably,' said Major Aulsebrooke.

They told us about Canada Lee, the rich successful American film star, who had returned to the continent of his origin to play the part of the humble faithful Kumalo. Perhaps, though he knew it not, this last film was some sort of spiritual fulfilment.

'There was that scene when Kumalo comes back,' said Mrs. Francis. 'Will you ever forget it? The day all the trippers came from Maritzburg and Durban to watch the filming – the scene when old Kumalo returns from Johannesburg, bringing the girl and his sister's little boy with him. His wife and his friend have met him at Carisbrooke to tell him that the people of his valley know everything – and now he must face them. How will they receive him?'

'I'll never forget it,' said Major Aulsebrooke. 'The rise round the school-house was covered with trippers . . . none of us will forget Canada Lee in that scene . . .'

He described it – and we saw it too. We saw Canada become Kumalo as Korda spoke to him.

'Remember, Canada, your sister is a prostitute and her child of sin holds your hand. Your son is a convicted murderer and your daughter-in-law will bear the child of a condemned man. How will your people welcome you? They know these things! *All that must be written on your face when you come round that bend—*'

436

The little party – the old Native Pastor, his wife and his friend, the pregnant girl and the little boy come down the dusty path to the school-house that is also their church. Humility, hesitation, all the suffering of a deep heartbreak are written upon the face of the old man ... the audience feels a tightening at the throat and the prick of tears ... What now? How will those who wait for him receive Kumalo?

'There is a lamp outside the church, the lamp they light for the services. There are women of the church sitting on the red earth under the lamp ... they rise when the party approaches and one breaks into a hymn, with a high note that cannot be sustained; but others come in underneath it, and support and sustain it, and some men come in too, with the deep notes and the true. Kumalo takes off his hat and he and his wife and his friend join in also ... it is sung in love and humility and gratitude, and the humble simple people pour their lives into the song.

'And Kumalo must pray. He prays, Tixo, we give thanks to Thee for Thy unending mercy. We give thanks to Thee for this safe return. We give thanks to Thee for the love of our friends and our families. We give thanks to Thee for all Thy mercies.

'Tixo, give us rain, we beseech Thee ...'

The cameras and Company, and all the paraphernalia of film-making have gone from the valley long since; the new Tudor Inn where King Korda slept has changed hands; the third-class wooden railway coach he bought has gone from Carisbrooke siding, and the people of the valley – thrown off their balance for a space by being fabulously paid to do as they always do, plough and sing and herd cattle – have settled down once more, and their willing dark hands set the stones for the new church one upon the other. The name of Canada Lee is not anywhere inscribed upon those stones, and Canada Lee is dead. But he played his last great part in that valley among the hills 'lovely beyond any singing of it', and something of himself must linger there in the strangely

437

clear air where every sound carries for miles – an echo
perhaps of Kumalo's prayer – 'Tixo, give us rain, we beseech
Thee' – for, when the story of a man is done, be it Kumalo
or Canada Lee, there is still the Beloved Country.

CHAPTER THIRTY-FOUR

TOWN AND COUNTRY – PIETERMARITZBURG AND HLUHLUWE

NEXT morning we went on to Pietermaritzburg, the historic capital of Natal, where we were to stay with the Administrator, Mr. Denis Shepstone and his wife, and where Bertie was to open the Agricultural Show.

Pietermaritzburg, or Maritzburg as it is always called, is a city both beautiful and kind. Its old fashioned colonial houses, set in radiant gardens, lie among the rolling hills and breathe an air of peace. But it was not at all peaceful when we were there. For one thing, the country was coming to town for Show Week, and for another Lourenço Marques radio had described the capital as 'Sleepy Hollow', which had drawn immediate protest from the inhabitants who were feeling very wide awake. But so charming and disarming was the Portuguese apology that Maritzburg responded by sending the offending commentator a great bouquet of the lovely exotic flowers that grace this dreaming corner. (There, I've done it too! *Dreaming corner* indeed!)

The shadow of the past rests upon Maritzburg with the enchantment of evening shade after the heat and burden of the day. Once it was a British Garrison Town with all the glamour of the red-coats, and that is the time most nostalgically remembered. But, as its name implies the first settlers in the hollow of the hills were Voortrekkers under the leadership of Pieter Retief and Gerrit Maritz. That same Pieter Retief and his band of fifty men going to treat with Dingaan were massacred by the treacherous Zulu King; and their families were murdered in their *laagers* by Dingaan's

439

impis. The Boers called the place of their death Weenen, which means weeping. Vengeance came from Maritzburg when Andries Pretorius and his commandos, including many English settlers, went forth and met the Zulu hordes on the banks of the Tugela. And the name of the place where the few with the guns defeated the many with the assegais was called Blood River.

The early history of Natal, like the early history of the Eastern Province, was one of co-operation and goodwill between the Boer and British settlers. They needed one another. They still do, but they keep forgetting it.

Parkside, the Administrator's home, is an old colonial house cleverly modernized and made into a suitable official residence with stately reception rooms. It had originally been built by a great-uncle of the Administrator. Shepstone is a famous name in Natal and is immortalized in its history and place-names. In the garden at Parkside is the great spreading tree under which Pretorius and his *Volksraad* accepted British rule, which pursued the trekking Boers into the interior like Nemesis. A brass plate tells the short tale in English and Afrikaans.

Monuments Commission.
Around this tree
Commandant General A. W. J. Pretorius
Members of the Volksraad
And the Burgers of the Republic of Natalia
decided by a majority on 5 July 1842
to accept British rule.

At a reception given for us by the Administrator, an old gentleman, Mr. Gert Maritz Botha, confided in me that his great aunt and many other Boers had protested bitterly against this acceptance of the inevitable.

'We have trekked all this way from the Cape to get away from British rule,' they said to Pretorius. 'And you would put our heads back into that same noose! We will have none of it! We will trek again!' And they did.

440

The Administrator was as distinguished as his name – a tall thin man with a crest of white hair, fine bird-like features and shrewd kind eyes. He was much loved in Natal, where the Natives called him *'Jiba'*, which means 'the corn the birds don't eat', in other words, as his daughter, Louise, put it, 'no flies on him'.

Our hostess was one of those people who seem to have strayed out of another century. In face and figure she was Edwardian – a George du Maurier picture. She had been a professional concert singer, and she had the charm and poise of an attractive woman accustomed to captivating her audience. The two Shepstone girls, Louise and Denise, were as decorative as they were well-mannered. Louise was auburn like her mother, serene and demure, and the servants called her *'Thulete'* (the quiet young girl), whereas her sixteen-year-old sister, Denise, was just beginning to emerge from the chrysalis, and her friendly ways had earned her the name of *'Ntombenhle'* (the kind girl).

A magnificent young Zulu, called Samuel, took charge of our material needs, aided by Ida, a stout dame like a mild hippo, who waddled in to fetch those of my dresses that needed pressing. When I gave her a gown and said, 'for tonight', she answered in her sonorous Zulu voice, 'Yehz, Nkosikasi, too-*naart.*'

Samuel had a fluff of woolly whiskers disposed here and there about his chocolate countenance, a rumbling voice and a flashing smile. His English was uncertain and all important orders were given to him in Zulu by the Administrator, who spoke the Native language perfectly.

There were many orders and much pressing of dresses for various occasions, for not only was it Show Week, but the Governor-General and Mrs. Jansen had honoured Maritzburg with their presence for a few days, which lent to most events an added importance.

Bertie opened the Show with a new version of his 'Food from the Sea' theme, which had even greater success than it had had in Port Elizabeth in the previous year.

This time I paid less attention to prize cattle and con-

441

centrated on the homely charm of pigs. Among these solid animals I was delighted to find Gustav Fichardt and another friend of the Brandkop days of my youth, who was winning innumerable prizes with his vast lily-white ladies and their porcine litters. Gustav, who was President of the Bloemfontein Agricultural Society, had come to Maritzburg to borrow a few bright ideas.

'You'll like the bird section,' he said. 'That is something few Shows can produce as well as this.'

It was a trilling hall of song and dazzling plumage, for the birds of Natal are exquisite, but it was a short-lived Section, for the birds were only allowed to be caged for two days. Then they returned to their aviaries to enjoy the illusion of freedom.

That night was the County Ball. I gave old Ida my most glamorous dress, and it was only afterwards I found that *Ntombenhle* (Denise), 'the kind girl', had ironed it for me because the cook had fallen ill and Ida had taken over her duties. Mrs. Shepstone was gorgeous in gold, and only Denise came in to dinner in her school-girl grey skirt and a blouse.

'Why aren't you dressed yet?' I asked, surprised.

Her pretty face was crestfallen. 'I haven't been asked to the ball. I'd *love* to be going!'

Bertie cast me a 'you've put your foot in it' look, and Mrs. Shepstone put in quickly, 'She too young for these functions.'

Eighteen-year-old Louise, in her charming flame-coloured tulle dress, looked down at her plate, sorry for her younger sister, and I would willingly have bitten out my thoughtless tongue.

Denise saw us off, her heart in her eyes, while her knitting, lying on the fender, invited her to spend an old maid's evening.

'It's awful,' I said to Bertie in the car, as we drove to the City Hall. 'We go to the Ball and pretty Cinderella sits by the fire and spins.'

He agreed. 'No fairy godmother. It's too bad.'

The Ball was wonderful and all the decorations had a naval flavour in honour of the guests from the *Bermuda*, and the Royal Marine Band had come from Durban to play the dance music. They had already endeared themselves to Maritzburg in the afternoon at the Show by their Beating of the Retreat.

The Governor-General and Her Excellency arrived presently with their party, and a little while later I said to Bertie as we were dancing: 'Look! It's Cinderella!'

And there, light as a feather in a mist-blue gown, was Denise waltzing with the Governor-General's young Air Force Aide de Camp, newly returned from the war in Korea.

The Government House party had been a girl short and someone had been inspired to ring up Parkside and tell Denise to put on her best dress, borrow a spare pair of her mother's gloves, and come to the Ball.

So perhaps, after all, there are fairy godmothers keeping an eye on any Cinderella whose second name is *Ntombenhle*.

Maritzburg is blessed with remarkable Elders. At eighty they are still spring-chickens there. They are not ignored and thrown aside by their juniors, they are venerated as they deserve, and what strong and original personalities they develop! The 'old soldiers' of this not so Sleepy Hollow do not fade away, they go from strength to strength, and eventually one can only suppose that they are swept up to heaven in fiery chariots. It would not have astonished me in the least if we had seen a sheet of flame shoot upwards into the star-studded sky and been told that old Mr. So-and-So or old Mrs. Such-and-Such had just taken their last journey.

This kind city has its sanctuaries. Two of them are very beautiful – the Queen Mary Place Homes for the aged, and the bird sanctuary. In both nature goes her way undisturbed and protected. The tiny cottages in lovely gardens, where old couples or single people may live out the twilight of their days, are the Memorial to the 1849–51 settlers of Natal, and how satisfying these 'living' memorials are! Several of the ladies of Queen Mary Place and their friends knitted comforts for the men of the *Bermuda* to show their affection for the Navy in peace as well as in war – a very kind thought.

The bird sanctuary is sheer enchantment, especially in the evening when the boughs are white with egrets, and flamingoes spread their rosy wings while swans float in regal majesty upon the sunset waters of the lake.

One morning I was entertained to tea by the Members of the Federated Women's Institutes of Natal, Zululand, East Griqualand and Pondoland.

Among those who greeted me outside the hotel was a childhood friend, Molly Smith, who had once been 'the little girl next door'.

As she greeted me, she murmured, 'There are about four hundred females waiting for you in there, from all over the countryside – but don't worry. We are all friendly!'

She was quite right. They had asked me to address them, and they received my impressions of West Africa with enthusiasm. Afterwards I realized once again the importance of women's influence in South Africa. They interest themselves not only in domestic science, but in culture and progress in all its forms. They set the standard, and, even in the remotest outposts, refuse to vegetate.

Before we left Maritzburg for a few days rest in Hluhluwe Game Reserve, the Shepstone girls told us with amusement that they had discovered that we had been given Native names by their servants. Bertie was '*Thanda Bantu*' ('he likes the Bantu people'), and I was '*Hleka Njalo*', which means 'full of laughter'.

When Samuel took leave of us very politely, he said to Bertie, 'God bless you wherever you go,' and to me, with smiling naïveté, 'Don't forget to laugh! I like you laughing.'

Hluhluwe is north of Durban, about six hours journey from Maritzburg.

444

We drove our own car down through the Valley of a Thousand Hills to the port so popular with the Navy, left most of our luggage at the hotel on the Esplanade where we had stayed the year before, and continued our journey in one of the Administrator's official cars with a government driver who knew the road. Tony, who had a great deal to arrange about the Durban programme, left us to go back on board the *Bermuda*.

The coast road north follows the soft green sugar country into the blue mountains of Zululand.

We entered the Reserve at dusk, and, as we passed through the gates, the grass-lands and thorn bush changed. The tapestry had come alive, and wherever we looked we saw game, the gentle buck who had laid up under the trees in the heat of the day, wildebeest and zebra grazing in company, and the ugly likeable wart-hogs with their families. But no Rhinos!

'Do you think we will really see rhinos?' I asked.

'That is largely what we've come for,' said Bertie.

Hluhluwe is a tiny Reserve compared with the great area of the Kruger Park, or even with Wankie, but it is the natural home of the rhinoceros. In its hundred square miles you may see both the fierce black rhino and the rare white, or square-lipped, variety running wild.

The Camp, high on a grassy ridge, was dotted with little thatched white cottages and *rondawels*, and behind them were the open communal kitchens where the camp-boys cooked the visitors' food. This charming Camp was run by Captain Potter Senior, who used to be Chief Conservator of Game before his son, Peter, took over that exacting task.

Our three days at Hluhluwe, between the heavy social and official programmes of Maritzburg and Durban, is a sylvan idyll in my memory.

The best time for seeing wild life is in the early morning and the evening, and during the day both humans and animals rested.

There was a miraculous peace about the Camp. In the bright glory of the mornings I set a little table in the shade of

445

a wild fig tree and brought my diaries up to date while Bertie sun-bathed and read the historical books and biographies that are his favourite reading matter. On either side of the ridge the hills and vales of Zululand rose and fell, grassy green with denser patches of thorn bush and wooded knolls. With the naked eye we could see buffalo and buck grazing on the slopes. At dawn rivers of silver mist filled the valleys and the knolls pierced those phantom waters like green islets. In the evenings the periwinkle blue of the distant mountains turned gauzy rose, and, as night fell, we became aware of the life of the wilds stirring – of the stealthy hunter stalking his prey.

The sounds of the Camp had their regular rhythm. At dawn and in the late afternoons cars started up and parties set out with the Zulu game-guards, whose quick eyes could penetrate nature's camouflage, and knew by instinct and experience where the rhino might best be found. In the mornings two Zulu camp-boys working in the washroom behind our cottage sang a sonorous duet. They made up the words as they went along, but the monotonous melody was pure Africa, sad without knowing the reason for its sorrow. The leaves of the wild fig tree were quick with bird-life and bubbling trills, and over the trumpets of sweet-scented flowers there was a constant whirring – the glittering vibration of sun-birds' hovering wings as their long beaks robbed some delicate goblet of its honey-dew.

We were unpacking a few clothes on the evening of our arrival – slacks and clean shirts – when a pretty girl with dimples and a mane of tawny hair came in to see if there was anything we needed. She was Mrs. Peter Potter, the wife of the Chief Conservator.

There are families in South Africa with a peculiar love and understanding of wild life born in them and developed by their surroundings to a most uncanny extent – like the countryman in England, although his interest in nature will seldom lead him into violent physical danger. Such a family were the Potters, father and son, and their wives.

446

'Peter and I suggest that you have your meals over at the house with us', said Valerie Potter, 'except breakfast, of course. The boy will bring you that when you shout for it. Captain and Mrs. Brooke are here too, and we would be so pleased to have you all.'

We thanked her, and asked her the way to the house.

'It's not far. Just up at the end of the road through the camp. Captain Brooke knows the way. He'll drive you over.'

'Do let's walk,' I said. 'I'm dying to stretch my legs.'

'Please not. There are rhino very near.'

'We'll take a torch.'

She shook her head and her dimples deepened. 'That would be a bad idea. Rhinos charge a light – any light.'

'Don't argue,' said Bertie to me, and to Valerie, 'What time would you like us to come?'

'About half-past six. We go to bed early here, because most people are up at dawn. I'll tell Captain Brooke.'

When she had gone I said to Bertie, 'Rhinos near the camp! Those words were music in my ears.'

'I don't know about music,' he answered, 'but it was first class showmanship.'

Next day we were not among those who rose at dawn. We slept until well into the morning. And later, when I saw Val Potter, I told her what Bertie had said.

'Showmanship!' she exclaimed. 'Just come and look in our garden. After you left last night we had a visitor.'

And there, among the quince and guava trees and azalea shrubs, were the huge footprints of the rhinoceros.

'Black or white?' I asked.

'Black,' she said. 'Black is a leaf-eater and white is a grazer. Black likes our guava trees.'

The young Potters had a delightful house and garden, a flaxen-haired two-year-old daughter and a rather new and very lovely baby boy. Little Cherril was as used to wild beasts as most children are to cats and dogs; she feared nothing, and it was with difficulty that her parents prevented her from straying off into the much-too-near rhino haunts.

447

The garden where the infant Denis slept his mornings away was a bird sanctuary of great enchantment.

Peter Potter had qualified as a surveyor at University and had served in the South African Air Force during the war, and then the call of the wilds had been too strong for him. But a splendidly polished propeller on his dining-room wall served to remind him of the days when men were more dangerous to one another than wild beasts.

Just down the path was the cottage of Captain Potter Senior and his wife.

Captain Potter, now nearing seventy, was very tall and sinewy with the light blue eyes one associates with the physically fearless. His Native name meant 'monkey rope', and was apt enough, for he was in fact like one of the strong flexible lianas the monkeys use as trapezes. Mrs. Potter had been a trained nurse, and when accidents occurred, as they must do in the wilds, she was the one to whom everybody turned. In the living-room of Captain Potter's cottage were many strange ornaments – each with its own story. There were bead girdles and necklaces, primitive carvings, snake-skins, karosses, floor-rugs of zebra, giraffe or antelope skin and a cruel-looking Zulu axe, which had been the main exhibit in a murder case.

'Have you ever used the axe?' I asked Mrs. Potter.

'Once,' she said. 'I came in here and found a nine foot black mamba coiled up in that corner where you are sitting. I reached for the axe instinctively, but as I hooked it down I heard a shot behind me. My husband had got in first.'

'And just in time,' smiled the Captain.

Captain Potter is one of those remarkable people who has the best and most exciting wild life stories to tell and absolutely no desire to see them in print. Neither journalists nor friends can persuade him otherwise.

'Far too much is written about wild life as it is,' he declares. 'And most of it nonsense.'

He is a particular authority on the rare white rhino, which he refuses to call white.

'It is no more white than a Xosa boy covered in white clay

448

during his initiation period. Someone saw the square-lipped rhino when he had been wallowing in white clay and he was dubbed white. He is different from the black rhino in that he is much heavier and has a big square lip for grazing. He weighs about four tons to the black rhino's three. Both have the double horn, but the black animal is fiercer. The so-called white rhino is timid, and makes a good mother. She guides her calf in front of her with her horn, while the black rhino has a very poor maternal instinct.'

It was clear that the Captain had a soft spot for the square-lipped variety. He told us about the white mother rhino who fell over a kranz, and the baby was found trying to fight the vultures off her dead body. That baby is now one of the very few white rhinos in captivity. He is in the Pretoria Zoo, and his name is 'Folozi, after the still unopened Reserve of Umfolozi from which Captain Potter had enticed his mother to Hluhluwe with a trail of molasses. He now has a young female called Zuluana to keep him company.

'It remains to be seen if they will mate under artificial conditions,' said the Captain. 'They have to have a tiled bath in the Zoo to conform to the regulations of hygiene. A tiled bath for a rhino who wants a mud wallow! If the money spent on Zoos could be used to bring parties of school children to places like this, and for developing natural Reserves how much better it would be!'

Early on our second morning Peter Potter took us out through the Reserve. Zeta a little old Zulu game-guard came with us.

As the lion is the chief show-piece of the Kruger National Park and the elephant is the King of Wankie, so the rhino is the star turn of Hluhluwe, and I must confess that anyone who has once looked into that prehistoric face will never forget it!

We discovered at once that the black and white rhinos of Hluhluwe observe strict laws of *apartheid*. They tolerate one another, but they keep to their own residential localities: they require a different diet, and they do not inter-marry;

each branch of the rhino race develops along his own lines according to his lights – which are not very bright, for all rhinos are nearly blind. The blacks are rude, ferocious and polygamous, while the more massive whites are modest and retiring and are imbued with a strong sense of responsibility towards family obligations.

In Wankie and the Kruger Park it is forbidden to leave the cars, but in Hluhluwe parties with game-guards may actually stalk rhinos. The game-guard knows just what can be risked, as we presently saw for ourselves.

Suddenly Zeta said something in Zulu.

Peter slowed down. As he stopped the car he pointed to a patch of thorn bush on the slope of the valley beneath us.

'There! Two black rhino in the shade of those trees.'

The sun had dispersed the ground mists, and we could see vaguely the two huge square shapes.

'Zeta will go down and chase them out for us,' said Peter.

The little Zulu, in his uniform khaki shirt and tunic, ran down the slope towards the clump of thorn bushes, and we stood on the rise looking down at him.

Bertie gave me his binoculars. 'Look at that face!' He was not referring to Zeta.

I gazed aghast. The powerful glasses brought the animal so near that I was looking it straight in the eye and could hardly believe that it was quite unaware of our existence. The long heavy head, weighed down by the two horns on the nose, the tiny eyes set so low that one felt the creature should have a face-lift, the expression of obstinate armoured ferocity terrified me. Meanwhile, Zeta had drawn near enough to the great beasts to pelt them with stones.

'Zeta isn't being as foolhardy as he looks,' said Peter. 'You will notice that he is keeping up hill and down wind from them. They won't get his scent and they won't charge uphill. Remember that they are very nearly blind.'

Suddenly the two big animals, with snorts and plumes of dust, broke cover and burst into a trot – away from the game-guard.

'Now we'll cut them off,' said Peter.

As soon as Zeta rejoined us Peter drove rapidly round the hill towards the thorn-veld on the other side, and presently we found ourselves driving parallel with the two monsters who were trotting along in the veld at an easy twenty miles an hour. One had big open sores on the shoulders.

'It's not an injury,' said Peter. 'It's a sort of musk gland. They are really very dumb animals, and, instead of a mating call, that sore opens up in the mating season and puts out some alluring odour.'

'How often do they mate?'

'About once in three years, and the period of gestation is about thirteen months – so it's a slow process to increase their numbers.'

'They've kept this pace for five minutes,' I said, glancing at the speedometer, still showing twenty. Occasionally the trotting pair half swerved towards the road, and then, frankly to my relief, they turned away into the thorn bush.

'If they charge they can go much faster,' said Peter, 'but they can't maintain it.'

In the grazing lands we found a little family group of four white, or rather, square-lipped rhinos, even more tank-like than their black tribal brothers, and their vast heads hung much lower, for they were not accustomed to seeking their snacks from the foliage of young trees. Bertie gave me his glasses. 'Mouth like a dredger,' he said.

We walked down the grassy bank to within six feet of them, and, as they became aware of us, they moved slowly away, father, mother, and two younger relations.

On a sandy bank we found a big crocodile basking, for already the sun was strong.

A big notice informed all concerned that this was no place for laundering or swimming, and the Natives know that a notice is usually a warning, even if they cannot read the words. 'But they come here just the same – although we forbid it. Last week a woman was taken by a croc. Now they will pay attention for a few days, and then they'll be back, scrubbing and beating their washing on those rocks.'

451

Of the many animals which inhabit the reserve, the only ones Peter hates are the dog-faced baboons. They are his enemies.

'There is a belief that they only eat roots. I know better. They take our young nyala and impala buck. I came across one old man baboon with a disemboweled nyala lamb in his lap, and another was devouring a duiker doe. In your little Nature Reserve at Cape Point you should get rid of your baboons, then you'd have plenty of buck.'

There are few leopards and no lion in Hluhluwe, so baboons prosper till wardens thin them out.

'Once I was unlucky enough to wound the sentinel,' said Peter. 'He put out his S O S, and in a few seconds I was surrounded and had to shoot my way out.'

Mr. Wyn-Harris, the Governor of the Gambia, would have found much in common with the views of Peter Potter on baboons. Yet, in spite of their malicious habits and destructive ways, the ugly baboons have a strange fascination for visitors, who see in them the burlesque of the human race – and although Simon's Town may regularly condemn its sub-human population, both in the port and in the Nature Reserve at the Point, I would willingly wager that the sentence will never be carried out *in toto*.

We returned to the Camp with an enormous appetite and very pleased with our morning's sight-seeing.

Peter had been brought up in Hluhluwe. Like little Cherril and baby Denis, he had opened his eyes to the world of wild things and all-pervading peace. To him, and to all the Potter family, Hluhluwe was the most satisfying place on earth.

'And would you believe it,' said Val, all dimples. 'When we take a holiday we go to the Kruger Park! Crazy, isn't it?'

In the Third Report of the Natal Parks, Game and Fish Preservation Board 1950–51 we read a report of two cars going out with our little Zulu game-guard Zeta in charge.

452

'One black rhino, a battle-scarred old female, approached the stationary leading car, and, apparently without malice, placed its head under the rear mudguard and commenced to rock the vehicle. The Game-Guard, with commendable courage and presence of mind, got out of the car and dealt the rhino a blow on the head with his belt, to which latter his handcuffs are always attached.

'Surprised at the attack the rhino moved off and was encouraged in its retreat by the Game-Guard who threw his belt at the animal which carried the handcuffs round its horns for some 100 yards before freeing itself and disappearing into dense bush. (This may perhaps be regarded as the first occasion upon which a rhino has been placed under arrest.)

'The car was not damaged and the occupants, having recovered from their fright, regarded the episode as a unique experience.'

As we drove back to Durban, I said to Bertie, 'And now for the world of people again!' and sighed a little, thinking with absurd pleasure of the frankly hostile, fearfully hideous countenance of the honest rhinoceros. Never would he smile a sycophantic smile. He was as Nature had designed him in the primaeval days of great beasts. He had the perfect integrity of a child – an integrity, which so soon, and so properly, fades as the child is taught that 'Manners maketh man'.

'With a rhinoceros at least you always know where you are,' I added.

'Up a tree if you have any sense,' said Bertie.

CHAPTER THIRTY-FIVE

NATIVES – RED, WHITE AND BLUE

OUR crowded delightful three weeks in warm sunny winter Durban flashed by as quickly as they had done a year ago, but this time the gaiety – as far as we personally were concerned – was tinged with regret, for already those who had welcomed the new Commander-in-Chief so warmly were officially bidding him God-speed and good luck. It was a farewell visit.

Before meeting the *Bermuda* at East London we had arranged to spend a few days quietly at the beautiful little seaside village of Port St. John's on the Transkei 'wild coast'. So we set off again in our own car, breaking our journey at Umtata, the capital of the Transkei – the biggest Native Reserve in the Union of South Africa. We stayed at an excellent hotel, and Mr. Yates, the Chief Magistrate, very kindly sketched out a plan which would enable us to get a glimpse of the territory through the eyes of those who understood it best. In the Transkei the magistrates are automatically Native Commissioners and the Chief Magistrate is Chief Native Commissioner and Chairman of the Native Parliament known as the *Bunga*.

Umtata is a pretty white town in the middle of the rolling grasslands which are inhabited by about a million and a half Natives. It was once a British Garrison Town and many of its citizens are descendants of early British settlers and soldiers. The European members of the Administration of this important tribal Reserve are largely drawn from families who have been in the Transkei for generations. Governments may change, but the Administration is outside politics and has continuity, so the Natives trust in it and do not worry their heads about what brand of Government happens to be in power. To them the Government is known as 'Father', and they approach it through the *Bunga*.

The *Bunga* building is a fine white edifice dominating Umtata, and is the Administrative Centre and House of Assembly for the Chiefs and Representatives of all the tribes of the various districts. At the annual meeting every grievance is aired and discussed and every advancement is noted.

'And they learn from one another,' explained Mr. Yates. 'As the backward districts see the results of soil conservation and limiting of stock, they begin to withdraw their objections and gradually realize the wisdom of following a progressive example.'

The main language of the country is the clicking melodious Xosa tongue as familiar to every European brought up in the Transkei as it is to the Natives themselves.

Some of the people are more sophisticated than others and wear European attire. They are known as the 'dressed' Natives, but for the most part they cover themselves with ochre paint and wear ochre blankets and are called 'red' Natives. The 'dressed' Natives prefer the hospital to the herbalist, and do not observe the old initiation ritual. But they are all cheerful law-abiding folk, and the proportion of police in the Territory is one member of the Police Force to over two thousand people. Of course there are faction fights from time to time, or someone is knifed or has his skull cracked by a knobkerrie, but the traditional crime is stock-theft. For the Native loves his cattle, his women and his beer, in that order. And he likes plenty of all three commodities. So he will part with his cattle to pay *lobola* – bride price – to his prospective father-in-law, and what better excuse for a beer-drink than a wedding – anybody's wedding! Thus the three main interests of his life are delightfully and sentimentally linked.

The real danger in the Transkei does not come from Native criminals, or even ancient witchcraft. It comes from the glib tongues of Communist agitators, who would dearly like to see the 'red' Native still redder.

The climate of the Transkei is bright and healthy, but the morning we drove from Umtata to Libodi to see a Chief's Native Court, it was cold and windy, with a suggestion of snow.

The waves and troughs of the undulating veld were in parts as threadbare as worn plush, and *dongas* showed the ravages of erosion. On the hills and in the vales, surrounded by seisal hedges, stood the round Xosa, Tembu, Pondo or Fingo huts – bold little white blisters, neatly thatched, with none of the secretive charm of Swazi or Basuto kraals melting into the shadowed *kranzes*.

At Libodi, the Magistrate, Mr. Grant, met us. His house adjoined his court-room where he tried criminal cases, but cases concerned with Native custom were dealt with directly by the Chief.

'We don't interfere with Native custom,' said Mr. Grant. 'We govern by persuasion through the Chiefs – on the British pattern.'

Chief Poto's court was a shed on a wind-swept height. It contained a few plain benches, a witness box, and a dais on which bland grizzled Poto sat with his clerk behind a table stacked with documents and ledgers. Against the wall, to the right of him, were his Councillors. It was the object of the Chief and his Councillors to dig truth out of her well and arbitrate between the parties in the case.

The headmen were 'dressed' and muffled up in old army coats and scarves, but most of those present were wrapped to their ears in their blankets like ochre cocoons. There were a few women in their blanket-skirts and shoulder-cloths and turbans.

Mr. Grant translated the proceedings for us in an undertone, and how he sorted out the case I cannot imagine. A strange tale emerged during the expert interrogation of a Councillor who was obviously an artist at extracting salient facts from endless irrelevant rigmaroles. What a superb actor he was! He cajoled, compelled and intimidated by turns, he rocked gently from one foot to the other till the witness was hypnotized, when he suddenly shot forth an accusing hand narrowed like the striking head of a venomous snake. He was vehement one moment, purring the next, clicking like castanets or shaking his head with a patient 'tsk, tsk, tsk ...'

'He brings them back to the point,' murmured Mr. Grant. 'A difficult thing to do without upsetting them. If you put a Native off when he is embarked on one of his long tales, he will start all over again at the beginning. He is quite incapable of answering a simple question with a simple answer.'

The case in point was characteristic.

The dispute seemed plain enough at first glance. It was about the number of cattle paid in *lobola* for a certain woman.

The plaintiff said ten head of cattle had been promised and only seven had been delivered to the bride's father. The defendant contended that all ten beasts had been sent as arranged. So far, so good. But when Mr. Grant explained that the bride in question was the great-great-aunt of the plaintiff and dead these many years, and that the defendant was the youngest great-grandson of the bridegroom, and that all evidence was therefore likely to be hearsay only, it did not seem quite so straightforward.

'They inherit these debts and quarrels,' he explained. 'But here *is* a witness who says he remembers the case. He was a small boy at the time ...'

A nonagenarian now staggered into the box, leaning heavily on his knobkerrie and clutching his blanket tightly round his scrawny throat with a gnarled hand. His rheumy eyes looked blindly into those of the interrogating Councillor, who treated him gently and with the deference due to his years.

Bit by bit we learned new facts about this long-ago business.

The bridegroom, it appeared, had found soon after his

457

marriage that his bride was bewitching him – not in the
entrancing sense of the word one normally associates with
honeymoons – but quite otherwise. She was giving him, not
the glad eye, but the evil eye. So he had chased her from his
home and sent her back to her father, demanding, at the
same time, the return of his seven beasts. Her father had not
given them back.

'So now,' groaned Mr. Grant, 'we have the makings of a
counter claim! Shall we go?'

'Aren't you glad these cases don't come to you?'

He laughed bitterly. 'They *do*. If anyone is dissatisfied
with Chief Poto's judgment they can come to my court, *and*
take the case on and up from there.'

Bertie changed the subject slightly, and with less than his
usual chivalry.

'Ten beasts for a woman – seems rather much doesn't
it?'

'The price has gone up since great-great-aunt's day,' said
Mr. Grant. 'It's more like fourteen now. But for a beautiful
Tembu girl a man gives far more than that!'

After lunch at Umtata the Chief Agricultural Officer, Mr.
Welsh, drove us out to a high ridge from which we could
look out over the veld for miles. The remains of deserted
and demolished huts stood round us on ground seamed with
dongas and skinned by over-grazing. It was a place sick unto
death.

'In time we hope to rehabilitate this area, said Mr. Welsh.
'To do so we have had to persuade the people to move from
here. Over on that brow across the valley they have put up
their huts in a planned residential area. We are trying to get
the Natives to build in villages instead of how and where
they please. Then we can give them a well, a school, a church
and a store, certain grazing grounds while we rest others,
and arable land for their crops. But naturally they hate
moving, and we never force them. Our greatest ally is a wise
and progressive Chief.'

Mr. Welsh's work was sometimes rewarding, but very

often it was disheartening. Thousands of tribesmen go yearly to the mines, and leave the old men and the women and children to care for the crops and herds, and, in spite of constant instruction from Government-trained Native agriculturalists, they slip back into the old easy ways, and, with every rainy season, more red soil is washed away to the sea, draining the country of its life-blood.

When the present Governor-General, Dr. E. G. Jansen, who has twice been Minister for Native Affairs in a Nationalist Cabinet, visited the Transkei Territories twenty-two years ago he warned the people of these grave matters.

'Europeans look with envy at your fine country,' he told them. 'They say, "This land is too good for the Natives, who are only spoiling it." To such Europeans we say that this land has been set aside for the Natives and it will remain so. We point out to them what you are doing to help yourselves through your Councils and Schools of Agriculture. ... You need not fear that the White man will ever take this land from you, *but I am very much afraid that if you do not greatly improve your methods of agriculture Nature herself will take it away.*'

Nature is taking it fast, and the White man is struggling to prevent her, but only with infinite patience and perseverance can he make an ally of the tribesman whose battle he fights so unremittingly. For the Native wants to put his hut where it suits him – and never mind the Government's well and its school, and a church and a store; he likes to plough the easiest way – up and down; and to ask him to reduce his stock is to place a weapon in the ready hand of the Communist.

'Government wants your land and your cattle for the White man! Defy this Government you call "Father"!' says the agitator.

'But we are getting results,' said Mr. Welsh. 'And people talk about them. To see is to believe. There are many old Chiefs who at first set their faces most stubbornly against our agricultural reforms and who now come and beg us to put our plans into operation in their district as soon as we can.'

He had a gaunt tired face, and his task was unending. Such requests must have gladdened his heart – but sometimes they came too late.

Next morning was cold and bright and we went for a drive with Mr. Kenyon who had been for many years in the Transkei Administration. He was very proud of his son, Basil, the playing Captain of the magnificent Springbok Rugger Team which had recently returned from an outstandingly successful overseas tour.

With us was Pakati, a large happy-go-lucky interpreter with a flashing smile. He spoke English with a delicate accent, and Xosa with gusto, as we heard when he recited a verse from the Xosa poet, Rune Mgayi, that was all clicks from beginning to end, no two of them alike.

'The poem describes the moods of man,' said Pakati. 'One day a man is wise and solemn as a secretary bird; he paces through the grass, thoughtful and observant, seeking the snake. Another day he is stupid as a water-logged melon. It is a long poem, for man has many aspects. . . . Here, Sir, this is where we turn off the road. We must follow the track up the rise.'

At the top of the rise we found the Chief waiting for us. Like most Chiefs he wore a European suit and was educated.

The intention of Mr. Kenyon was to show us an *abakweta* dance – the dance performed by the young men when they have passed through the initiation period – but this was not to be, as the candidates were not yet fully initiated.

'However,' said the Chief. 'There are always people dancing. So if you will walk down to my village we will find something going on.'

Something was going on. In the dusty clearing between the huts a group of red-hot mommas in their hot red blankets were stamping round and round in a happy circle, chanting shrilly as they went. Naked piccaninnies cavorted happily round their revolving relations, and only stopped to stare when we arrived. The mommas went right on with their performance until Bertie presented them with half-a-crown through the medium of the Chief. They then sang his praises and danced with even more enthusiasm.

'They are very happy,' said the Chief. 'They will buy snuff with the money.'

Down in the valley was one of the *kweta* huts where the lads, aged between eighteen and twenty, lived together during their period of isolation after circumcision. It was out of bounds to all females, even mothers. But an exception was made in my case.

The Chief called to them, and four lads emerged from the hut. They were swathed in the old blankets they would presently burn, and every visible portion of them was covered in dead-white clay. They looked like weird and rather terrifying clowns. At a word from the Chief, they greeted us with an extraordinary lion-bark produced straight from the stomach – '*Bayete!*'

'When the initiation period is over,' said Pakati, 'they burn this hut and their blankets and rush to the river to wash off the clay. They must not look back, or even turn their heads. Behind them everything of childhood is burned and gone, and they must run forward into manhood! They are changed! They are men! Then they dance . . .'

As I looked at the white masked figures, my thoughts flew back to Hluhluwe. So this was how the square-lipped rhino had come to be called white. Some astounded hunter had seen the great beast rise from his white clay wallow – a monstrous initiate, who was surely more than welcome to his splendid isolation!

After lunch, when we were ready to go on to Port St. John's we found Pakati outside our hotel carefully dusting our car. Squatting on the kerb beside it was a handsome Tembu woman who must have fetched a bride-price of many cattle in her day.

'This is my relative by marriage,' explained Pakati, with

461

his dazzling display of teeth. 'She is the cousin of the husband of the sister of my wife. We hoped perhaps we might have a lift in your car. She lives near Lodi and I a little further. It is on the way to St. John's.'

'Get in the back,' said Bertie. 'If there is room for your relative's bundle as well as yourselves.'

Room was made, and Pakati and his relative sat stiffly in the back and cracked their heads smartly on the roof as Bertie took a bump in the road too fast. They both roared with laughter and relaxed. Nothing evidently could have pleased them better.

'Do you come into Umtata every day?' I asked.

'Yes,' said Pakati, still overcome with amusement at the playfulness of the man at the wheel. 'Every day I take a lift in the station wagon of my kind friend, Mr. Eric Dash, who has a farm near Libodi. He is a good man. He says to me, "They may fight and quarrel in parliament down in Cape Town about Black and White, but we do not fight and quarrel here, Pakati. We are all on good terms here in the Transkei. You and I are on good terms." And I say to Mr. Eric Dash, "Yes, we are on good terms." Once he took me into his beautiful house, and showed me all the rooms, and then he sat me down in his fine kitchen and gave me a round square meal. The quarrelling is between the politicians, says Mr. Eric Dash, it is not between the people.'

We liked the sound of Mr. Eric Dash – and the 'round square meal'.

'Please stop,' said Pakati. 'That very nice house with the blue door belongs to my relative. Just up this hill.'

The Tembu lady got out, placed her large bundle on her head, thanked us politely for the ride, and walked away across the veld to the hut with the blue door.

'My house is right on top of the hill,' said Pakati. 'From it I can see far and wide. I have a wife and six children. Two will go to Lovedale College soon. They will be teachers.'

Indeed one could see far and wide from the thatched square house of Pakati. The vast threadbare lands rolled away on either side of the hill and were lost in the glow of the setting sun. The smoke of cooking fires rose in the pure air and on the horizon we saw the Bantu frieze of a woman bearing a water calabash upon her head, slow and queenly, with sure bare feet treading the well-worn path from the stream to the hut.

Presently we came into the land of the blue Pondos. Here the blankets were clear ice-blue, dyed with a solution of a well-known rinse. White is the colour of mourning, and there had been many deaths among the Chiefs of this tribe, so gradually the 'white' blanket had become customary. There seems to be something strangely elusive about the correct definition of the word 'white'. Just as we call the square-lipped rhino 'white' for the most fictitious of reasons, so these people of Pondoland speak of their blue blankets as 'white'. But red, white or blue, the Bantus of the Transkei are high-spirited and good-humoured. They salute the stranger who leaves them in the red dust of his motor-car's wake, the women smile their slow shy smiles at him, and the children wave and caper out of sheer *joie de vivre*. It is the land of greetings and fluttering fingers.

Near Port St. John's the scene changes and becomes tropical, with citrus and banana farms, and banks of giant ferns and bracken leading up into the wooded hills. They call this the 'wild coast' because so much of it is still unspoilt, the paradise of the camper. St. John's is a little place of rare beauty. A river runs into the Indian Ocean there, snaking down to the sea between high jungle-clad cliffs inhabited by the baboon, the leopard, the dassie and innumerable birds.

The name of the river is Umzimvubu – the Hippopotamus River – but today it is no more a hippo-haunt than a rhino is white. Yet some time ago an innocent young hippo was taken in by the lovely promise of that name. This hippo was called Hubert, and the legend of Hubert's great trek from St. Lucia on the Natal coast to the Umzimvubu will never be forgotten. The animal's progress into the Eastern Province was followed with interest by naturalists and the Press till the sad day when a farmer near King William's Town shot Hubert, much to everybody's indignation. It was then discovered that Herbert was really Huberta, a lone girl on a vain quest, seeking her Prince Charming in the pools abandoned by his ancestors for more than a century.

We rested for three days in the quiet of St. John's and then continued our journey to East London to meet the *Bermuda*.

CHAPTER THIRTY-SIX

'NKOSI, SIKOLEL' i AFRICA'

EAST London treated the *Bermuda* and us with its usual kindness and generosity, but once again we realized only too well that this was a good-bye visit and that the sands of two wonderful years were running out fast.

On our way back to the Cape by car we made a detour to visit the two most important Bantu educational centres in Southern Africa – Lovedale College and the University of Fort Hare.

Lovedale and Fort Hare are in the heart of the bush country of the Ciskei which was once a constant battle-ground between the early settlers and the Kaffirs. In fact the University is built on the site of one of the old forts garrisoned by the 'red-coats' and frontier patrols of the first part of the nineteenth century. Yet today it is the spearhead of Native advancement; it is affiliated with Rhodes University at Grahamstown and is handsomely subsidized by the Union Government and the *Bunga*. It is endowed with a great many bursaries and scholarships, and students come to Fort Hare from all over Africa. They can live and work there for £60 a year. The hostels for residents have been established by various missions but the University is inter-denominational.

Professor Dent, the Rector, showed us round the fine dignified buildings, but 1952 was a difficult year, and the temper of the students reflected its frustrations and uncertainties.

'Their moods blow up suddenly out of nowhere,' said the Rector. 'We try to keep them non-political, but they read of bad examples – like the Egyptian students who are always in the forefront of every political demonstration. And the Gold Coast example has its repercussions too.'

There can be no doubt but that Fort Hare, like every other University, breeds its Communists, but, as one rather cynical professor said, 'It may be better to train your agitators in your own country – *and know them* – than have them go abroad and learn their lessons!'

The great majority of the students are Bantu, but there are Indians and Coloureds too, and many from Rhodesia and even East Africa.

In the library I noticed a young Bantu translating Ovid from Latin into English, and I wondered how much the exercise would really help him or his people. In the natural history laboratory we saw many strange creatures in and out of bottles, and on a wide shelf I thought I had spotted a piece of typical modern sculpture of the Henry Moore School which had so baffled my mother. But it turned out to be an elephant's skull.

In the museum, which showed the primitive Bantu way of life, hung a royal leopard-skin kaross presented by one of Fort Hare's best students – Tshekedi Khama.

In the previous year of 1951 – thirty-five years after its inception – Fort Hare had advanced another notable step. Then, for the first time, the graduation address was given by a Bantu Professor, whose portrait, painted by a Tembu artist, shows a face filled with wisdom, kindliness and humour – and fire too.

Professor Jabavu knew his people well. The last thought he left in the minds of the graduates was to forget their own achievements and remember their fellow Bantus.

'Strive constantly to live in touch with your people in as many ways as you can devise. Avoid living in an abstract world of your imagination, working out geometrical calculations and ethical possibilities about your people, detached from them. *Get among them!* Contrive to be genuinely happy as a "good mixer" with the less privileged groups, learning from first hand how to use your higher education for their uplift. That is the quintessence of goodwill in action.'

After our tour we had morning tea with Professor and Mrs. Dent on the sunny stoep of the Rector's residence, and met two of the European Professors and their wives, and Miss Darke, who was in charge of the Women's Hostels and who had, for a time, been Headmistress of my old school, St. Cyprian's.

Mr. Brink, the Chief Native Commissioner of the Ciskei, who had met us at King William's Town and given us a lead to Fort Hare, said:

'I don't want to appear in a hurry, but I am responsible for getting Admiral and Lady Packer to Lovedale by eleven forty-five on the dot—'

Professor Dent laughed. 'And Mr. Shepherd has a great deal to show them. We'll all be in trouble if you are late!'

I went with Mr. and Mrs. Brink, and Bertie followed in our car. It was only a few minutes drive to Lovedale on the height opposite Fort Hare. Lovedale has been in existence for over a hundred and ten years, and in all that time there have only been four Rectors. This Scottish Missionary Institution carried on its work throughout the successive Kaffir Wars of the turbulent nineteenth century. The Reverend Shepherd had been there twenty-five years and was due to retire very soon. The rambling buildings of the College stood among the blue-gums and willows. They had grown from small beginnings like the early British settlements, and with the same phoenix-spirit that rises indestructible from the flames: Lovedale had been burned by those it served, and rebuilt that it might serve them again.

As we drove up to the old fashioned double-storeyed house of the Rector, Mrs. Brink smiled and said: 'Mr. Shepherd has his watch in his hand.'

He was standing on his high narrow stoep – a wiry elderly man, taut as a well-coiled spring.

'Here we are, in good time,' said the Chief Native Commissioner. The Rector smiled and answered briskly, 'Exactly five minutes late.'

We were introduced to Mrs. Shepherd, and then her husband said to us, 'I'm going to whisk you round in my car – to give you the atmosphere. That's all we'll have time for, if you really must leave directly after lunch.'

'Unfortunately we must,' explained Bertie. 'We have to be in Port Elizabeth this afternoon.'

Although we were not able to dawdle, the Rector really did 'give us the atmosphere' – and it was a sound and wholesome one, with that particular quality of good fellowship which is so often evident in vocational work.

'We teach our pupils lessons, and we also teach them trades,' said Mr. Shepherd. 'They are all ages, from twelve upwards. We teach them building, carpentry, printing, dairy-farming, and we train teachers and parsons. We do everything for ourselves here. We put up our own buildings, make our own furniture, print and bind our own school-books and churn our own butter.'

We saw the classrooms, canteens, dormitories, carpentry-shops, forges, printing presses and book-binding machines, and we observed the contentment on the faces of those engaged in their various tasks.

Within recent years three splendid Native hospitals have been built at Lovedale – general, orthopaedic and tuberculosis. Their presence is a tribute to the wonderful work of the College, for all are fully endowed, both privately and by the Government, and they are staffed by students and ex-students of the College.

At the T.B. Hospital we met the European doctor in charge, who took us to the children's huge sunny wards and nurseries. A young Bantu sister was looking after them.

'Sister is on light work,' said the Doctor. 'She has come back to us after an operation for the removal of a lung. Poor girl, she knows about the disease she is nursing from experience as well as training.'

Fighting the battle against T.B. among the Natives is one

of the Government's gravest responsibilities. Tremendous preventive campaigns have been launched and immense sums subscribed, but there can be no slackening, for the White death attacks the Black man with even greater ferocity than it attacks the European.

'Everything in this hospital is found by the Government,' said Mr. Shepherd. 'But it is our responsibility to staff it. Our student nurses are trained in these hospitals.'

He took us presently to the chapel which is the core of Lovedale. In fine weather church is held out of doors under the trees. We stood there for a moment in the bright sparkling mid-day sunshine, and it seemed to me that the vivid personality of the Rector had impregnated every corner and cranny of this Institution – infusing life, co-ordinating effort, and dispensing good fellowship.

Odd how well some people were named, I thought. Mr. Shepherd was one.

Once more he glanced at that watch, for he had been forced to compress a great deal into a very short time.

'Before we have lunch there will be an assembly, and the choir will sing for you,' he said. 'Two songs.'

He was, in all things, exact.

The College hall, in which meetings, debates and concerts were held, was crowded with students – about six hundred of them – boys and girls, men and women. Mr. Shepherd led us on to the platform, where the choir had already taken their places to the right of us. There were about thirty of them, mostly male voices.

The Rector introduced us briefly, and made a sign to the choirmaster. Every dark face in the packed hall turned towards the singers.

The song they sang was an epic of history – the story of the Xosa prophetess, Nongquawuse, who led her people to destruction. She told them that, if they would kill their cattle and burn their crops, on a certain day their ancestors would rise up, fully armed, and drive the White man into the sea. Fine cattle and crops would spring from the earth, and the sun would stand still in the heavens while these great events transpired. The Amaxosa did as she had told them, but their ancestors remained beneath the blackened grass of a land laid waste, the sun moved on its appointed course, and at last the starving remnants of a broken nation crawled to the farms of the White frontiersmen and begged for food and work. Thus here, in the Eastern Province, a people had perished – and the Kaffir Wars had ended. . . .

The grief in that song was almost unbearable. There was no accompaniment, and none was needed. Threading the magnificent sombre voices of the male choir were the pure high tones of the women – true and silver-sweet as the boy voices of Westminster Cathedral. And, as they sang in their own Xosa language, of warriors bewitched, and slaughtered herds, of burning corn, disillusion and defeat, the tragedy of their nation lived again, and the high sad notes of the women sought out some corresponding pain in the listener and melted his heart to tears.

Yet the second song was gay with mimicry. It was about a party of parsons walking down a country path, and, although we could not understand the words, the humour was infectious.

Afterwards Bertie spoke a few words of thanks and wished the pupils good fortune. Then everybody rose, and with one great voice they sang the Bantu hymn that has become accepted as their national anthem.

The first and the last two verses of 'Sikolel' i Africa' – Lord Bless Africa – embody the Bantu essence of old and new blending and clashing in this country that is theirs – and ours.

> 1. Lord, bless Africa
>   May her horn rise up;
>   Hear Thou our prayers
>   And bless us.
>
> 2. Bless our chiefs;
>   May they remember their Creator,

Fear Him and revere Him,
That He may bless them.

7. Bless our efforts
Of union and self uplift,
Of education and mutual understanding
And bless them.

8. Lord bless Africa;
Blot out all its wickedness
And its transgressions and sins,
And bless it.

Afterwards, when we had driven through the attractive
town of Alice which serves this district, and Mr. Brink had
set us on the right road for Port Elizabeth, I said to
Bertie:

'That singing made me want to cry. In fact, it made me
cry.'

After a pause, he said, 'Are you sure it was the singing?'

'What else?'

'The singers, perhaps.'

Then I remembered the dark faces, born and destined to
shadow, and wondered why they should have moved me so
deeply.

The Red, White and Blue Natives of the Transkei had not
made me feel sad. They were happy by nature, and discon-
tent with them was a passing state. The tribesman evokes no
pity. He lives, within reasonable modern limits, according to
his ancient traditions.

But the man who stands on the threshold of the world he
may not enter – the prisoner of his dark skin – is spiritually
alone. It is seldom that he wishes to do as Professor Jabavu
has urged him – '*Strive constantly to live in touch with your
people . . . Get among them! . . .*' He wants to go on – and
leave them behind. He wants to escape the bondage of his
heritage. From the pinnacles of higher education he sees the

471

golden gates of the White man's Valhalla, and climbs on and up, armed with the passport of his hard-won diplomas. Yet, beyond the golden gates, many doors remain barred – social, economic and political – and he learns at last that if he would find fulfilment, he must turn again to his own people and his own world.

Two of Lovedale's most remarkable pupils came to my mind. Sobhuza II, Paramount Chief of the Swazis, and Seretse Khama, one-time Chief of the Bamangwato.

Sobhuza had gone back to his country and his people, and was using his knowledge and enlightenment to help the European Administration solve the problems of Swaziland.

Seretse Khama had tried to live in both worlds. And had failed. His was the fate of the exile.

Lovedale had gone a long way in one century, and a hundred years hence many barred doors must and will open to the Bantu. Canute could not hold back the tide with his word of command, but tides can be guided and used for the welfare of humanity. The Union of South Africa – under changing Governments – has done more for its Native populations than any other trustee nation has been able to do for its Black dependents. And I believe the Union will continue to follow the principle of *Give and Take* in all practical respects – although she will never give away her idea of a White civilization.

Only time will show whether this unique experiment of a White civilization in the southernmost portion of a dark Continent can survive. But fear on one side, and frustration on the other, are poor allies for goodwill. If the White races are to survive in South Africa they must unite, and if the 'beloved country' herself is to survive, White and Black must both help to save her.

It seems simple enough on the face of it – but, in fact, I suppose, it is another problem for the TOO DIFFICULT basket.

Simon's Town was in a blustering winter mood when we

returned. The kloof-garden stream was in full spate, and the Coloured children of the Waterfall Tenements ski-ed down the open water-filled culverts on wattle wands and sections of old walking-sticks.

Change was the order of the day.

A new Chief Cook and his assistant had taken charge of our big airy kitchen. They had been shipmates before and were a first-rate team who could produce a fluffy rum-omelette to perfection, even if neither of them was likely to perform a fire-dance in the garden on a summer's night – an exotic accomplishment not usually associated with naval cookery. The potato-peeling, carrot-scraping Bantu had ploughed through the Book of Genesis in his Xosa Bible, and was now – too significantly, I thought – wading through the Book of Exodus.

In his shop, over by the garages, the Chief Joiner was hammering at fine strong dove-tailed packing-cases. Bertie, on his way to his carnations, stopped to look at them, and said, a little sadly:

'There's an end-of-commission bite to this lot, Chief Joiner. I wonder whether the Chief Coxswain has started making the paying-off pennant yet?'

Kathie Sherwin wandered up to Admiralty House with little Martin and Judy. She was looking less exuberant than usual. Philip had sailed for England the week before with the Major of Marines and his wife and family.

'He's nearly nine,' said Kathie. 'Time goes so fast! And he has to go to his Prep School. Tim's mother will see him through all that. I expect old Philip will settle down all right.'

Does any mother really expect as much?

'Poor old Philip,' I said. And thought, 'Poor Kathie too—'

The Barrows left that month, and the children of the Compound were reduced by two more – David and baby Peter, but they were augmented again by the very small son of the new Signal Officer and his pretty Scottish wife.

Then one day men came with crates to take away and

store the pictures Charles te Water had lent us, and that was when Veronica's pets began to wonder what was happening. How animals hate it when humans begin packing! The pictures lay on the stoep, waiting to go into the straw-filled cases, and Sammy came and examined them sadly, sighed deeply, and leaned against me with his full weight. And when a great Dane, filled with heavy misgivings, leans against you, it is as much as you can do to remain upright.

'It's all right, Sammy,' I said. 'Not everyone can take Maggie Laubser's art, but I'm going to miss her absurd ducks and the little Bantu goat-herd playing his pipe under the greenest tree in creation.'

Meanwhile our social and official engagements continued with unabated vigour, but the one that stands out most clearly for various reasons was the première of the film, 'The Sound Barrier'.

David Lean, the director, and his wife, Ann Todd, the star, had flown out to South Africa for the first showing of this important British picture in Johannesburg and Cape Town.

We had last met David Lean during the war when he was making Noel Coward's naval epic 'In Which We Serve'. The two films have much in common. Both are records of courage and achievement. Both are part of Britain's story – in war and in peace, at sea and in the air.

David and Ann came to lunch with us at Admiralty House – David rangy and dark, the human receptacle of compressed nervous energy, and Ann, lovely and intense, with deep-set dark blue eyes and pale urchin-cut hair.

'I cut it myself with my nail-scissors in Johannesburg. David was furious!' said Ann.

She gets desperately nervous when she has to appear in person on the stage.

'It isn't like acting,' she said. 'It's quite different. It terrifies me. I dither. In Johannesburg I dried up completely and David had to come to the rescue.'

They talked a great deal about the test pilots who had given them so much help – so much background – 'Cat's

474

Eyes' Cunningham, John Derry, and other human pioneers of the great element which still guards its grim secrets of life and death, its invisible barriers of sight and sound, and pitfalls undreamed of, even now.

As we sat beside David and Ann at the première I was aware not only of the film, but of their feeling for it and excitement in it. To each of them it was a projection of themselves, of something cerebral or spiritual, given, transmuted and recorded. David's use of supersonic sound was so brilliant and so sinister that one felt it to possess a shocking and dangerous life of its own, an infernal impulse to kill and destroy. After certain sequences I was surprised to find the screen intact. It should have been ripped to tatters, buffeted to the point of disintegration in common with most of the audience.

David and Ann were back in England just in time for the great Air Display at Farnborough, where British test-pilots crashed the sound barrier repeatedly with a noise of gunfire. Two days before the Show, David and Ann were photographed with John Derry, de Havilland's ace test pilot, and his wife and two children, and the stars of the film which had been based on the lives of just such families.

Forty-eight hours later, at Farnborough, in the presence of 120,000 people, John Derry took up de Havilland's newest jet-fighter 110. The B.B.C. commentator was saying that he had never seen or heard such a fine example of an aircraft going through the sound barrier, when he broke off with a cry of horror.

'Oh, my God! Look out!'

Another life was gone – lost, alone in space – lost that man might conquer speed.

CHAPTER THIRTY-SEVEN

LAST JOURNEY

BERTIE was to open the Agricultural Show in Salisbury at the end of August. And as he was to be relieved by Vice-Admiral P. B. R. W. William-Powlett in September our flying visit to Southern Rhodesia had to be a very short one. Three days.

It was spring in Salisbury. The avenues of pale pink beauhinias were in full bloom, lovely as almond blossom in an English meadow. The days were hot. Government House stands in a hundred acres of park and gardens, and the core of this fine house was brought out from England by Cecil Rhodes, but the guest wings were added later.

Our guest wing gave on to a green lawn bordered by night-scented stocks, and, on the other side, our windows faced a green bamboo thicket alive with weaver-birds. When the Sunset bugle sounded they seemed to regard it as some sort of assembly signal, and they darted into the heart of the thicket from everywhere and nowhere like winged assegais hurled by the dusky hand of approaching night.

The Governor, Sir John Kennedy, had been in the Navy and had later transferred to the Gunners. He was very tall and imperturbable, although at that time Government House was like an exclusive hotel with official visitors arriving and departing daily, and the general atmosphere of the country was charged with the controversial Federation issue. Should Southern Rhodesia, Northern Rhodesia and Nyasaland form a Central African Federation or not? There were many opinions on the subject and everybody everywhere, White, Black and eloquent Red, was saying their say at the top of their voices.

Lady Kennedy was slim, attractive and amusing, and, in the midst of endless obligations found time to play tennis with her eighteen-year-old step-daughter, Susan, and Susan's brother, Hugh, home from Eton for the holidays.

When we arrived we found that Henry Hopkinson, the Minister of State for the Colonies, was staying at Government House. Henry was an old friend of ours. He had been First Secretary of the British Legation in Athens when Bertie had been Naval Attaché there in 1938, and during the war he and his American wife, Alice, had lent us their lovely home in Devonshire for a very happy fortnight's leave and rest.

Henry had been touring the Rhodesias and Nyasaland, to put before them the full implications of the Government's plan for a Central African Federation. In the north he had tried to make the African extremists see that their interests would not suffer by the inclusion of Southern Rhodesia, and in Southern Rhodesia he had explained that 'Europeans who have made their homes here and are here to stay will not find themselves swamped by a "Gold Coast Government" in Northern Rhodesia and Nyasaland.'

He left for London by air next morning, and a few hours later Mr. and Mrs. Clement Attlee arrived.

Mr. Attlee had been the guest of that ardent protagonist of Federation, Mr. Roy Welensky, the Leader of the Unofficial Members of the Northern Rhodesian Legislative Council. Mr. Attlee too had been touring the three territories in question, and, in an article quoted from the *Daily Herald*, he had also mentioned the Gold Coast.

'The African his his feet on the road to progress, though he has still far to go. But this progress has raised a very hard problem.

'In other colonies, such as the Gold Coast, the European has come as a trader or official into countries where he has no desire to settle. In the Rhodesias he has come to stay.

'The problem is: How are these two communities at such different stages of civilization to live together? . . .

'The majority of Africans are opposed to federation. No doubt many do not understand the question and are influenced partly by their dislike of change.

'Some of the leaders have personal ambitions and unrealistic dreams of African domination in a short time, but there is a genuine fear that federation will be dominated by the Southern Rhodesians and that the African will cease to advance. . . .

'On the other hand I met influential sections of European opinion in Southern Rhodesia who opposed federation for precisely the opposite reasons. They feared that in a short time the federation would be dominated by Africans. Some Northern Rhodesians agree with this view.

'Between these two extremes are the advocates of federation. They are liberal-minded and look ahead, seeing the solution of the problem in a partnership between the two communities, though obviously for some time the European will be the senior partner.'

Both statesmen had seen the essential difficulties of the problem – the fundamental conflict between White Africa and Black Africa. And both had shown, by their references to the Gold Coast – where 'the European has come as a trader or official into countries where he has no desire to settle', and the Rhodesias, where 'he has come to stay' – their recognition of an absolute and clear-cut distinction between the two.

At the time of writing, the outcome of the federation proposal is still obscure.*

That evening there was a dinner party for fifty guests at Government House.

* *The Central African Federation came into being but was short-lived and the three components (Northern Rhodesia, Nyasaland and Southern Rhodesia) split into the three states now known as Zambia, Malawi and Rhodesia.*

Mr. and Mrs. Attlee and Bertie and I met the Governor and Lady Kennedy in the study at five to eight, and soon after eight o'clock, an A.D.C. told us that the guests were assembled. We went into an ante-room where, waiting for us, were the Comptroller, the Flag Lieutenant, Susan Kennedy – looking very charming in a white tulle dress – sixteen-year-old Hugh, and two cheerful young A.D.C.s. It was evident that they had some surprise in store for us, for they looked as if they had been hatching a plot.

In the next reception room the guests had already 'made the cricle' so that Their Excellencies and their party could go round and bid them good-evening, each in turn.

The Comptroller explained that an A.D.C. would take Mr. Attlee round, Hugh would introduce Mrs. Attlee, and Susan was to take me. Then came the surprise. He turned to my husband.

'Your Flag Lieutenant will introduce you, Sir.'

Even Bertie looked astonished.

'But how *can* he?' I asked Bertie in a quick undertone. 'Fifty people – and Tony doesn't know any of them!'

'The Comptroller knows what he's about – and so does Tony,' Bertie murmured back. 'Relax!'

The double doors were flung open and we entered the large room and went slowly from one person to the next in the wide circle which had been formed strictly according to protocol. The Prime Minister and Mrs. Huggins were there, the Chief Justice and the Cabinet Ministers and their wives, the President of the Agricultural Show, and, in fact, anyone holding an official position. Young Susan took me in charge and introduced everybody by name without a moment's hesitation or confusion. *What good training!* I thought.

The Flag Lieutenant was doing the same for his Commander-in-Chief.

Afterwards I asked him. 'How could you do it? Fifty people you didn't know.'

'Our party was counted in the fifty,' Tony said. 'I knew *them.* And then many of the others had their wives with them. That halved the number of names to be memorized.'

479

He laughed. 'It *would* have been funny, though, if anyone had got out of place in the circle. Then I should have been completely had!'

Sir Godfrey Huggins was on my right at dinner. 'It's his deaf side,' Lady Kennedy had warned me. 'But don't let that worry you. He's wonderful. He hears what he wants to.'

Sir Godfrey, who has for years striven to bring about the Central African Federation, is a fascinating personality. We met him again next day when Bertie and I lunched alone with him and his wife in their simple, rather old-fashioned home overlooking the veld.

He is small and slight with thick iron-grey hair and a pair of mischievous eyes. They are remarkable eyes. Sir Godfrey is stone deaf in his left ear and does not hear too well with the other one. So his eyes have taken over extra duties; they are amazingly observant and quick – two vigilant sentries in his narrow clean-cut face – nothing gets past them. When he talks to someone, he pulls his right ear forward. It is characteristic that he does not merely cup it, but gives it a good tug, and, after twenty years of this stern treatment, it has responded by remaining out, while its mate nestles peacefully against his head, sleeping a deep aural sleep from which, alas, nothing can wake it.

The Rhodesians love their Prime Minister. They say, 'What would we do without our "Huggie"?'

Their 'Huggie' is full of devilment. Politically he loves to be outrageous, to shock people into attention and watch their reactions. Even his own people are submitted to the shock treatment. 'Rhodesia looks like being the nut in the nut-cracker between an Afrikaner Republic and a Black State – *if* federation doesn't go through!' As he says it, you can almost hear him thinking – *That'll scare 'em into voting the way they should!*

He likes shocking the Union too, but the Union knows his tactics. And 'Huggie' admits, 'We are on much better terms than you'd suppose. On the whole we understand each other very well.'

Over a quarter of a century ago General Smuts tried to

480

persuade Southern Rhodesia to join the Union, and young Dr. Huggins – not yet a politician – was all in favour of it. But his wife was dead against it. On the day the referendum was taken, their son was born, and sentiment triumphed. Neither parent voted.

Before emigrating to Rhodesia in 1911, Huggins, who had high surgical degrees, had been House Physician, and later, Medical Superintendent, at the Great Ormonde Street Hospital for Sick Children. During most of his long and successful political career he has continued to practise his first profession, though mainly as a consultant.

The day of the Show dawned bright and beautiful, and Bertie opened it with yet another variant on his Sea-Theme. It was developing the infinite possibilities of a Bach Etude. Having established his *motif* the composer continues to use it in an endless number of ways.

After the Grand Parade of prize cattle I was requested to hang their diplomas on the winning bulls. This was a new and alarming experience. The lesser beasts *mooed* their way out of the arena, and three magnificent creatures remained facing the audience. Each was attached to its owner by a sort of boat-hook through its nose.

I stepped down among them inwardly quaking, but outwardly – I hoped – gay and unconcerned, head in air.

'Now,' said the Ring Master, handing me streamers of baby-blue ribbon strung through the awards. 'You simply take this ribbon and tie it round their horns.'

So, for the first time in my life, I literally took the bull by the horns. And a few minutes later the splendid animals, with their prize cards dangling on their massive chests, and blue ribbon knotted round their curly heads, plodded away amidst enthusiastic applause.

As I returned to the stand I noticed my husband's eyes on my white shoes and a look of horror on his face. Mrs. Attlee turned to him with her gentle smile, and said quietly:

'I'm afraid Lady Packer didn't look where she was going!'

Our three days in Salisbury were too few. We only just had time to greet friends and acquaintances, and to dine at June Hill with Ellis Robins and meet Lady Robins, and then we were on the wing again.

Tony, who had not seen the Falls, took a later plane than ours to make the detour; and we broke our journey in Johannesburg to stay with the Cameron McClures.

They were two quiet and delightful days. Mac and Cicely's charming home, Klein Schuur (Little Barn), stands on a ridge outside Johannesburg and commands a view of the whole wide veld. We lazed in the sun, and we both regretted that the Commander-in-Chief South Atlantic has so little excuse for visiting the City of God, since Pretoria, only an hour away, is the winter capital.

One evening we dined with Noel and Marjorie Gilfillan at their farm on the far side of the great spreading city with its skyscrapers and mansions, its parks and gardens and its slums and shanty-towns. The next we spent at Klein Schuur where Nicholas Monsarrat and Philippa Crosby made up our six.

We had already met the author of *The Cruel Sea* several times, for Nicholas was Public relations Officer to the High Commissioner. At a dinner given recently by the Port Elizabeth Branch of the Naval Officers' Association he had been the speaker, to follow the Commander-in-Chief. Whether he is speaking in public or in private Nicholas is as brief and incisive as the dialogue of his book. Nobody 'rambles on' in *The Cruel Sea* and nor does Nicholas.

'It is a great privilege for me to speak after an Admiral,' he told the Naval Officers' Association. 'It is the first time I have done so. Although I have heard an Admiral speak before. When I was bringing my corvette into Harwich during the war I fouled the boom. The Admiral ashore sent for me and I heard him speak for a long time. But he did not invite me to speak after him.'

Nicholas Monsarrat wears his success like armour over a hypersensitive personality. If his expression were less sardonic it might be unhappy. At a small party he shines, but

482

when many people are present he has a curious gift for suddenly making himself invisible – as an animal in a thicket freezes and becomes part of the background – watchful, listening, sensing every slightest sound, alert for the unfamiliar, for the dangerous. At those moments he has become the analyst of human nature – and more. For it is not enough for a novelist of distinction to observe and examine his characters from outside. He must think and feel as they think and feel – however wicked or stupid they may be. For just long enough to sustain a character, he must understand and live its depraved or foolish life. Then he is free of it – able to forget it – as Tony was free to forget the thirty or forty names he had memorized when that particular effort of Pelmanism was no longer required.

A few weeks later Nicholas Monsarrat married Philippa Crosby, the attractive South African journalist to whom he had dedicated his successful book.

At noon next day Corney met us for the last time at Wingfield aerodrome.

'Did your wife and the boy get off all right?' I asked.

'Yes, thank you, your Ladyship. And there were one or two people the wife knew on board.'

Mrs. Corney and Melvin had gone back to the Isle of Wight to prepare the home once again. This was Chief Petty Officer Corney's last Commission in the Navy. In spite of the lovely spring day a cold current of sadness ran through me. Only three weeks to go . . .

The flag of the Commander-in-Chief fluttered bravely on the bonnet of the official car as we drove down to the sea. The breeze was soft and sweet with the fragrance of mimosa on the flats and water hyacinths in the *vleis*.

'There'll be a lot to do when we get back,' said Bertie. 'The next weeks aren't going to be easy.'

Tony arrived by the afternoon plane, and that evening the three of us went to Belmont House, where Captain and Mrs. Selby had something they wanted to tell us.

There was champagne in an ice-bucket in the corner of the

lofty drawing-room, and there was such a sparkle in pretty Susan Selby's eyes that it hardly needed her father to say:

'Tony and Susan want to get married. Shall we wish them luck?'

We wished them happiness and good luck with all our hearts.

'Did you guess?' Susan asked me.

'Yes, Susan, I certainly did.'

She laughed and blushed – she had a charming way of blushing.

'When?'

'When we were flying to Windhoek across the Namib Desert – the most beautiful painted desert you ever saw – and our desert-loving Flags didn't so much as glance at it because he was writing a letter. That day I knew he wasn't girl-proof after all.'

CHAPTER THIRTY-EIGHT

AND NOW WE SAY GOOD-BYE

VERY soon packing cases appeared on the upstairs land-ing, and the seamen mustered our odds and ends from all over the house and put them in the white room from which I had watched the berg burn and thought of the London blitz. A plump moon-faced Malay packer arrived from the Dock-yard and began to wrap things up very tidily with the deft craftsman's hands of his race.

My maid, Gladys, carried armfuls of dresses to the blue room, and the stewards brought our trunks and suitcases from the box-room and dusted them and set them ready for packing. As Gladys cleared the landing cupboards she came upon the box where 'Bones' lived.

'What shall we do with the skeleton, Milady?'

'We'll give him back to his rightful owner – Mr. Peter.'

At this suggestion all her superstitious dark blood rose in revolt.

'We *can't*, Milady! Not now – not with Mrs. Packer having a new baby any day!'

I sighed. 'But Gladys, that baby is due the day we leave this house.'

However, I rang up Mother, as her children and grand-children always have done when help is needed.

'Mum, Gladys says we can't give Piet's skeleton back till Glen's had the new baby.'

'Gladys is perfectly right!' said my mother firmly. 'I never heard of such an idea – a skeleton in the house at such a time! Send Bones here and I'll put him in the cellar.'

So Corney took him to Tees Lodge, which is an old home

and no doubt he found there other skeletons to bear him company. But, with his departure, Admiralty House became just a little bit less personal.

Baby Christopher was born the week before we left Admiralty House, and Ronnie's round blue eyes grew rounder and more astonished than ever. But he was delighted with the new occupant of the family treasure-cot which had cradled all my mother's children and grandchildren, and now her great-grandchildren. When little Chris cried, Ronnie comforted him by throwing some offering into the cradle – anything from a half-chewed rusk to one of the dogs' bones. Love may take many forms.

Farewell engagements crowded in upon us – all of them naval, and all of them building up inside us something that ached and made it difficult to laugh, and dangerous not to laugh. We went to the Chief Petty Officers' dance at the Blue Moon – as good and gay a dance as the Chief Petty Officers always gave – and at midnight the band stopped playing and we were asked to step on to the platform, where the Chief Petty Officer Master of Ceremonies made a little speech, and presented us with a water-colour of the South Atlantic Squadron painted by the Chief Diver who had always designed the scenery for the *Bermuda*'s Concert Parties.

'We have thought of the Commander-in-Chief and Lady Packer as our good friends,' he said, 'and we wish the Commander-in-Chief success and happiness in the future—'

The days flew by, and each was lovelier than the last. Never had the garden been so breath-taking in its spring cloak, the lawns so emerald, the rockeries so rampant with colour, or the bougainvillaea so heavy with its red and purple flowers. Never had the boughs been so vibrant with bird-song, the doves so tender in their cooing, or Flora, our figurehead, so splendid between the tarnished gleam of her ancient cannons. The dazzle of the sea was brighter than the dreams of youth, and, over against the dockyard wall, the *Bermuda* was slim and grey, flying the flag of a full Admiral, the Commander-in-Chief South Atlantic. Next week there would be a new Commander-in-Chief and a new flag. Next week my husband would bid farewell to his last – his least demanding – grey mistress.

When I saw the Flag-ship from my sun-trap, Madagascar and the boisterous days of beating into the South East trades came back to me and the silken calm of the Gulf of Guinea, with the golden palm-fringed shores of West Africa in sight, and the sea smooth-stretched and rosy. So often the *Bermuda* had received and made me welcome as she went about her peacetime business of 'showing the flag'. For two years she had been my friend, and never my rival – years to be cherished and remembered.

Sunday came and we went for the last time to the little Dockyard Church and climbed the narrow stairs into the old Sail Loft. How bright it was! How polished! The familiar prayers moved me as never before – '... preserve us from the dangers of the sea and the violence of the enemy ... that we may return in safety to enjoy the blessings of the land and the fruits of our labours ...' There was Edgar Rae, our trusted, well-liked Padre, telling us from the pulpit about 'minus people' and 'plus people'.

'Minus people are not sufficiently grateful for their blessings; they grumble and ask for more; they feel themselves to be ill-treated; they are the *takers* ... If you would be a plus person, you must be a *giver*. Bear your burdens with courage and share your good fortune. Learn the meaning of giving, and of gratitude. ...'

Of gratitude.

Thank You for these two happy years, and all the happy years that have gone before them ... thank You for all that the Navy has given me – so much more than it has taken ...

The choir was leading the last humn – one verse sung kneeling –

> O Trinity of love and power,
> Our brethren shield in danger's hour;
> From rock and tempest, fire and foe.

Protect them whereso'er they go;
Thus evermore shall rise to Thee
Glad hymns of praise from land and sea.

How often I had heard those words sung – on the quarter-deck of a warship, in a naval church or chapel – the hymn of the Navy and of seamen the world over – *'Protect them whereso'er they go . . .'*

The choir walked sedately out, first the black-gowned seniors, followed by the girls and boys, and I noticed – as I had always done – the high-heeled shoes of the big girls, and the white socks and sandals of the little ones showing under their purple gowns, and the small boys' square-toed shoes, beneath their long scarlet skirts and crisp white surplices, itching to break into a run or kick a football.

Then it was our turn to walk down the aisle, to smile at Joan Rae's Sunday School children gathered in the recess at the back of the church just above the stairs. Next Sunday someone else would be doing this.

Monday – only three days to go. The packing of our effects was nearly finished.

The Malay with the bland round face was dealing with the last cases. In twenty-five years employment at Simon's Town Dockyard he had stowed away the possessions of a dozen Commanders-in-Chief in similar circumstances to ours.

He said, 'In that room, Milady. Those are the last things.'

I went into the white room. On the bed lay the 'last things'.

A carved ebony head of a Malagasy girl kept strange company with a coconut gargoyle from Fiji, whose history I had never really learned, for he was before my time. There was the opium pipe from Chungking that we had never smoked, the green porcelain dragon from Hong Kong, the little ivory man from the Congo, and the Copenhagen china dog dear Hillie Longstaff had given us four years ago in

Denmark. A sewing basket I seldom used sat on a copy of Beverley Baxter's autobiography, *Strange Street*.

Fragments of past and present lay there awaiting interment.

Bertie's letters in a wooden box lay next to some of my old diaries; and near them was an album called 'PETER' full of snapshots of a baby in Malta, a toddler in South Africa, a little boy in England and Greece – then the war had come and the album had been set aside. There was a photograph of me in my wedding dress that Bertie had taken with him whenever he joined a new ship, and on it lay an enlargement of the cruiser, *Manchester*, to remind him of campaigns in Norway and the Mediterranean. I picked up a tattered copy of a magazine produced by the ship's company of the 'Lucky *Calcutta*' in the midst of a bitter war at sea, and dark days in Grimsby came back to me – icy winds and blizzards and a little old cruiser getting no rest, guarding the coastal convoys day in, day out.

'People collect a lot of stuff,' said the Malay. 'This thing here is heavy. It must go with the books.'

He found a place for the 'heavy thing' – a paper-weight made from a scrap of metal taken from the *Warspite* when she was damaged at Jutland – my husband's first battle – and another for the log he had kept on board that same ship after his last battle thirty years later when he had commanded the 'Old Lady' and brought her safely back to port with the wound of Salerno gaping in her side and her dead committed to the deep. I touched a lamp-stand carved out of *Warspite*'s heart of oak, taken from her when the Navy had no more need of her and she was consigned to the shipbreaker's yard – and suddenly my heart was full of tears.

'It'll only take half an hour now,' said the Malay. 'But there's this sword. Can it go in that case of unwanted things, or will somebody need it?'

He held up Bertie's midshipman's dirk, the proud little sword of a very young officer.

'Put it with the unwanted things,' I said. 'No one will need it.'

'And this box?'

'Put that in the unwanted case too.'

Medals were in it – and among them was the King's Medal for the best cadet of his term in the year 1911. It was solid gold and stamped with the bearded profile of George V. From the age of twelve my husband had served the Royal Navy – forty-five years – well-nigh all his life. Four Kings and a Queen he had served . . .

I heard his step on the stair – weary.

The Malay said:

'These cases will be finished this afternoon. Can we nail them down?'

They were the strong cases made by our Chief Joiner – with rope handles at either end, lined, and painted black, like coffins.

Bertie came on to the landing, and looked round at them, and at the things still lying on the floor – nothing of any real value.

'Nail them down,' he said.

He put his hand on my shoulder.

'Shall we take a breather? Stroll round the garden—'

He was smiling, but his hand was heavy. I nodded.

'Yes, let's stroll round the garden.'

On Tuesday night the wardroom dined him.

On Wednesday morning he went on board the Flag-ship and was piped over the side for the last time. He addressed the men of the South Atlantic Squadron, and said his final good-byes to the Heads of Dockyard Departments.

In the evening – our last at Admiralty House – the officers of his personal staff and their wives came in to sundowners with us very informally. Tim and Kathie stayed on a little longer when the others had left, for this was the end of a twelve year partnership in peace and war.

For Chief Petty Officer Corney, the Coxswain too, it was the end of many commissions together – the end of life in the Royal Navy. When Bertie presented him with a memento of the fourteen years in which they had been shipmates,

490

the big man from the Isle of Wight did not smile his usual ready smile. He began to say something, but the words remained unspoken as he saluted and turned quickly away.

On Thursday we went into Cape Town to meet the mail boat and our successors.

At the head of the stairs I stopped with a queer little shock. There was a new photograph in a severe black frame at the top of the stairs. 'All those Admirals!' I had said when we arrived two years ago – and now another . . .

Downstairs, in the big inner hall, the seamen moved their polishers to and fro over the oak boards as usual, and the Chief Steward waited at the double doors. In the inner hall, above a new visitors' book, the eighty-first name had been inscribed in gilt lettering on the polished board that had recorded the first Commander-in-Chief in 1795.

The day was as glorious as the day of our arrival had been. We lingered for one last walk alone together in the sea-garden. At Flora's parapet we paused to look across False Bay to the blue mountains beyond, and then to the Naval Dockyard sheltered by the high shoulder of Simon's Bay.

The sun caught the *Bermuda* still flying the flag she had flown so proudly round the African coast for the past two years. Some time tonight that flag would be lowered for the last time and tomorrow the flag of a new Commander-in-Chief would flutter in the morning breeze.

As we turned silently away we knew that this was our real farewell to the Royal Navy.

THE END

1950–1952
Admiralty House, Simon's Town.
'Tees Lodge', Cape Town.
'Cape Town Castle', Atlantic Ocean.

NOR THE MOON BY NIGHT BY JOY PACKER

For two years they had written letters to each other – Alice Lang, the English nurse, and Andrew Miller, the Game Warden of Velaba. And now Alice stood in a Pretoria garden listening to Andrew's sister . . .

'You'll hate me for this,' said Meg. 'But Alice, don't marry my brother! You don't know Andrew . . . what can you possibly know about a man with the wilderness in his blood. I know the men of my family, and what they expect of their women . . . they've broken the hearts and the health of their wives for generations . . .'

It was sound advice – but Alice was a young woman keen for life, longing to love and be loved, wanting desperately to meet and marry the man whose letters had sustained her for so long . . .

0 552 09305 X   40p

THE HIGH ROOF BY JOY PACKER

When she was fourteen she had been shattered by the news that her mother, who was beautiful, soignée – and thirty-eight years old – was to marry again. The marriage, to a man twelve years her junior, completely destroyed any relationship between Kirsten and her mother.

Four years later, returning to the lush Cape Peninsular from school in Europe, a compromise was effected – a compromise helped in some degree by Kirsten's own marriage to a young and gentle man who adored her.

The two marriages, one so young and confident, the other based on the nervous love of an ageing woman for her young husband, moved side by side in a mounting crescendo of tension. The 'High Roof' of marriage was steep and slippery indeed for the two couples who were moving irrevocably towards a dramatic crisis . . .

0 552 09306 8   40p

PACK AND FOLLOW by Joy Packer

To 'pack and follow' is the proverbial lot of the naval man's wife, and its truth was fully experienced by Joy Packer, when as wife of the late Admiral Sir Herbert Packer, K.C.B., C.B.E., she accompanied him on his assignments. These took her East to China and Japan, and then, with the shadow of war approaching, to Turkey, Greece and Yugoslavia.

In this, the first of her autobiographical books, Joy Packer tells of the experiences and people she encountered on these travels in a way that is at all times lively, fascinating and amusing.

'Vivid as good fiction and holds you as good fiction ought.' – *Cape Argus*

552 09448 X   50p

GREY MISTRESS by Joy Packer

Joy Packer writes:
'In peace-time it is possible for a woman to share her man with his ship. But in time of war the Grey Mistress takes full possession. Her needs are inexorable. Women yield their men – not readily or easily but with the courage of understanding . . .'

And in *Grey Mistress*, the second volume of her autobiography begun in *Pack and Follow*, Joy Packer relates her life as a naval wife during the war years when she needed a great deal of that understanding. 'It is,' said the *Scotsman*, 'an exciting story, full of human interest, all infused with the kind of courage and good humour under trying conditions that the Navy likes to associate with its wives.'

0 552 09449 8   50p

THE GLASS BARRIER BY JOY PACKER

The four of them grew up together, sometimes in Cape Town, sometimes in the lush countryside of the Paarl Valley. They were days of sunshine, and shared confidences and future hopes.

And then the two girls discovered that they wanted the same man. Maxie Lamotte, sensitive and vulnerable was too shy – or proud – to fight for Simon. Rima, who was vital and determined, had no such scruples. She wanted Simon, her adopted brother, and would do anything to get him. Maxie's brother Claude wanted a girl too, but here the barrier was tougher than merely defeating a rival suitor. For Claude was white, and Fara, the girl he loved, was coloured . . .

552 09316 5   40p

DINNER AT ANTOINE'S BY FRANCES PARKINSON KEYES

Antoine's was New Orleans' most exclusive and gracious restaurant. The men who dined there were rich and successful, the women beautiful, vivacious, and talented. Orson Foxworth's party on 2nd January, 1949, was as glittering a company as any the restaurant had seen.

But the evening, on the surface so gay, was fraught with tensions and jealousies . . . all centering around Odile St. Amant, the young bride with the handsome but inattentive husband . . . the bride in the white dress. And when the dress was suddenly stained with the mark of red wine, it seemed a foreboding of the passion and death and drama that was to follow . . .

0 552 08834 X   40p

A GEORGIAN LOVE STORY BY ERNEST RAYMOND

Set in London during the Edwardian and Georgian years, Ernest Raymond's novel relates the simple and moving story of a young boy and girl separated by background and birth but joined by a deep love.

Stewart O'Murry, whose family lives in respectable Hollen Hill, longs to know what goes on in the disreputable Hollen Dene area a few streets away. In his search for the unknown, he follows a seductive girl into a tobacconist's shop, and there the first of many great surprises awaits him . . .

0 552 09125 1   40p

THE INVITATION BY CATHERINE COOKSON

When the Gallachers received an invitation from the Duke of Moorshire to attend his musical evening, Maggie was overwhelmed. Naturally, she did not see the invitation as the rock on which she was to perish; nor was she prepared for the reactions of her family. Her son Paul, daughter Elizabeth and daughter-in-law Arlette were as delighted as she was but the effect on Sam, Arlette's husband, was to bring his smouldering hate of his mother to flashpoint. Maggie herself, however, was to be prime mover of the downfall of the family she loved too dearly . . .

0 552 09035 2   35p

A SELECTED LIST OF FINE FICTION FOR YOUR READING PLEASURE